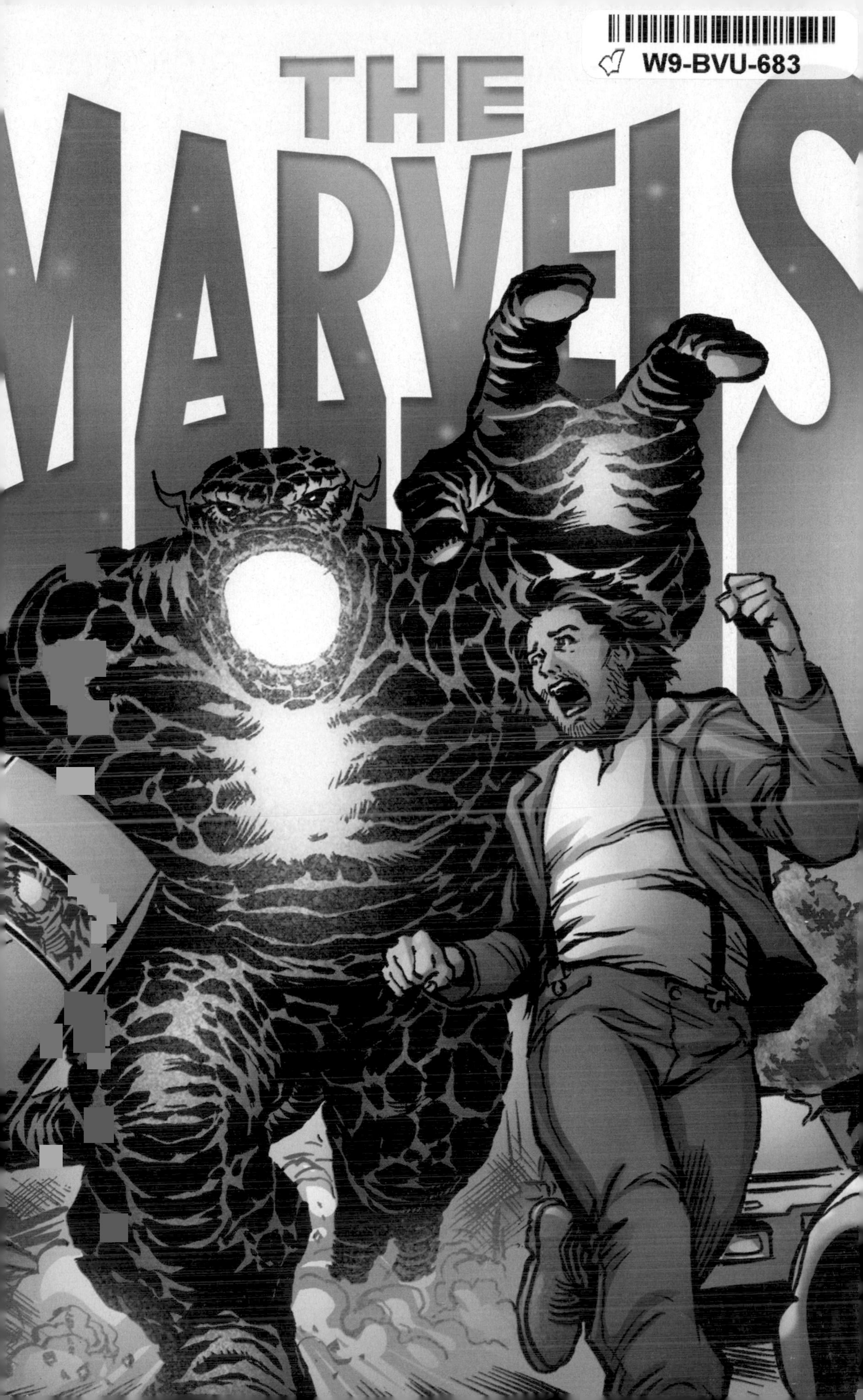
THE
MARVELS

Anyone. Anywhere. Any Time.

The Marvel Universe. From before the Big Bang to beyond the End of Time. From the Avengers to the X-Men, from Aarkus to Zzzax, from the Kree Empire to the Dark Dimensions and into the unknown it ranges, vast and deep. And there have been adventures too big for any one series. Until now.

MAR

The War in

Kurt Busiek
WRITER

Yildiray Cinar
ARTIST

Richard Isanove (#1-5) & **Guru-eFX** (#6)
COLOR ARTISTS

THE MARVELS VOL. 1: THE WAR IN SIANCONG. Contains material originally published in magazine form as THE MARVELS (2021) #1-6. First printing 2021. ISBN 978-1-302-92152-1. Published by MARVEL WORLDWIDE, INC., a subsidiary of MARVEL ENTERTAINMENT, LLC. OFFICE OF PUBLICATION: 1290 Avenue of the Americas, New York, NY 10104. © 2021 MARVEL No similarity between any of the names, characters, persons, and/or institutions in this book with those of any living or dead person or institution is intended, and any such similarity which may exist is purely coincidental. **Printed in Canada.** KEVIN FEIGE, Chief Creative Officer; DAN BUCKLEY, President, Marvel Entertainment; JOE QUESADA, EVP & Creative Director; DAVID BOGART, Associate Publisher & SVP of Talent Affairs; TOM BREVOORT, VP, Executive Editor; NICK LOWE, Executive Editor, VP of Content, Digital Publishing; DAVID GABRIEL, VP of Print & Digital Publishing; JEFF YOUNGQUIST, VP of Production & Special Projects; ALEX MORALES, Director of Publishing Operations; DAN EDINGTON, Managing Editor; RICKEY PURDIN, Director of Talent Relations; JENNIFER GRÜNWALD, Senior Editor, Special Projects; SUSAN CRESPI, Production Manager; STAN LEE, Chairman Emeritus. For information regarding advertising in Marvel Comics or on Marvel.com, please contact Vit DeBellis, Custom Solutions & Integrated Advertising Manager, at vdebellis@marvel.com. For Marvel subscription inquiries, please call 888-511-5480. **Manufactured between 11/12/2021 and 12/14/2021 by SOLISCO PRINTERS, SCOTT, QC, CANADA.**

10 9 8 7 6 5 4 3 2 1

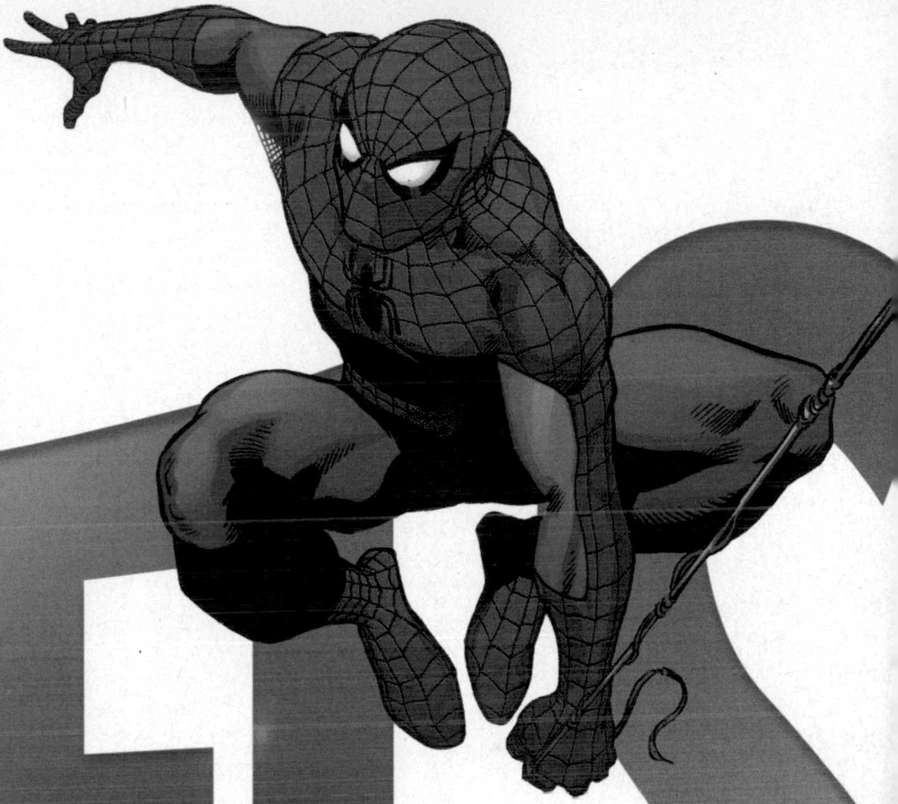

Siancong

Simon Bowland
LETTERER

Alex Ross
COVER ART

Martin Biro
ASSISTANT EDITOR

Alanna Smith & **Annalise Bissa**
ASSOCIATE EDITORS

Tom Brevoort
EDITOR

Jennifer Grünwald COLLECTION EDITOR · Daniel Kirchhoffer ASSISTANT EDITOR
Maia Loy ASSISTANT MANAGING EDITOR · Lisa Montalbano ASSISTANT MANAGING EDITOR
Jeff Youngquist VP PRODUCTION & SPECIAL PROJECTS · Jay Bowen WITH Carlos Lao BOOK DESIGNERS
David Gabriel SVP PRINT, SALES & MARKETING · C.B. Cebulski EDITOR IN CHIEF

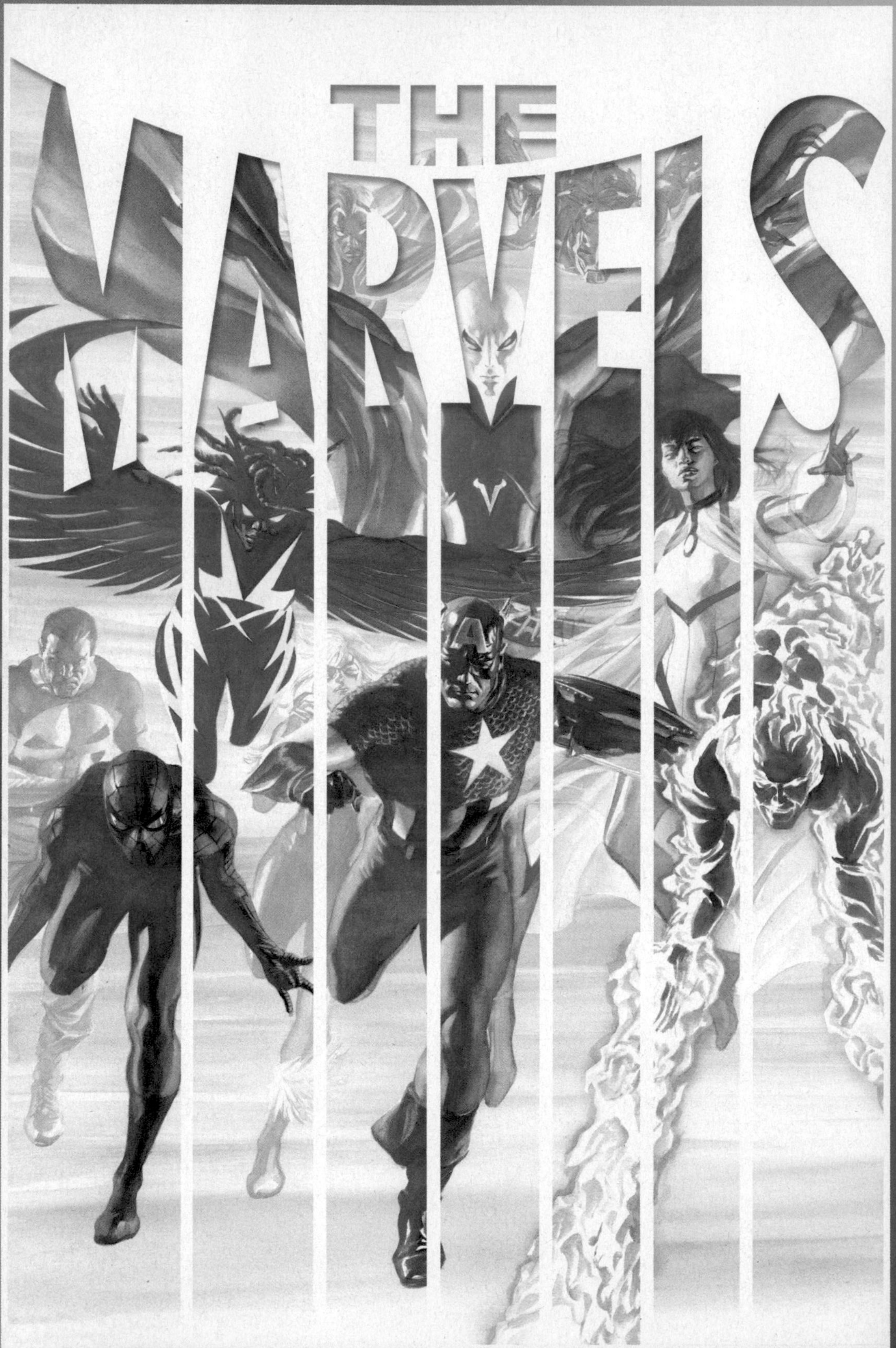
THE MARVELS

PART ONE: **"...the Birth of Madness"**

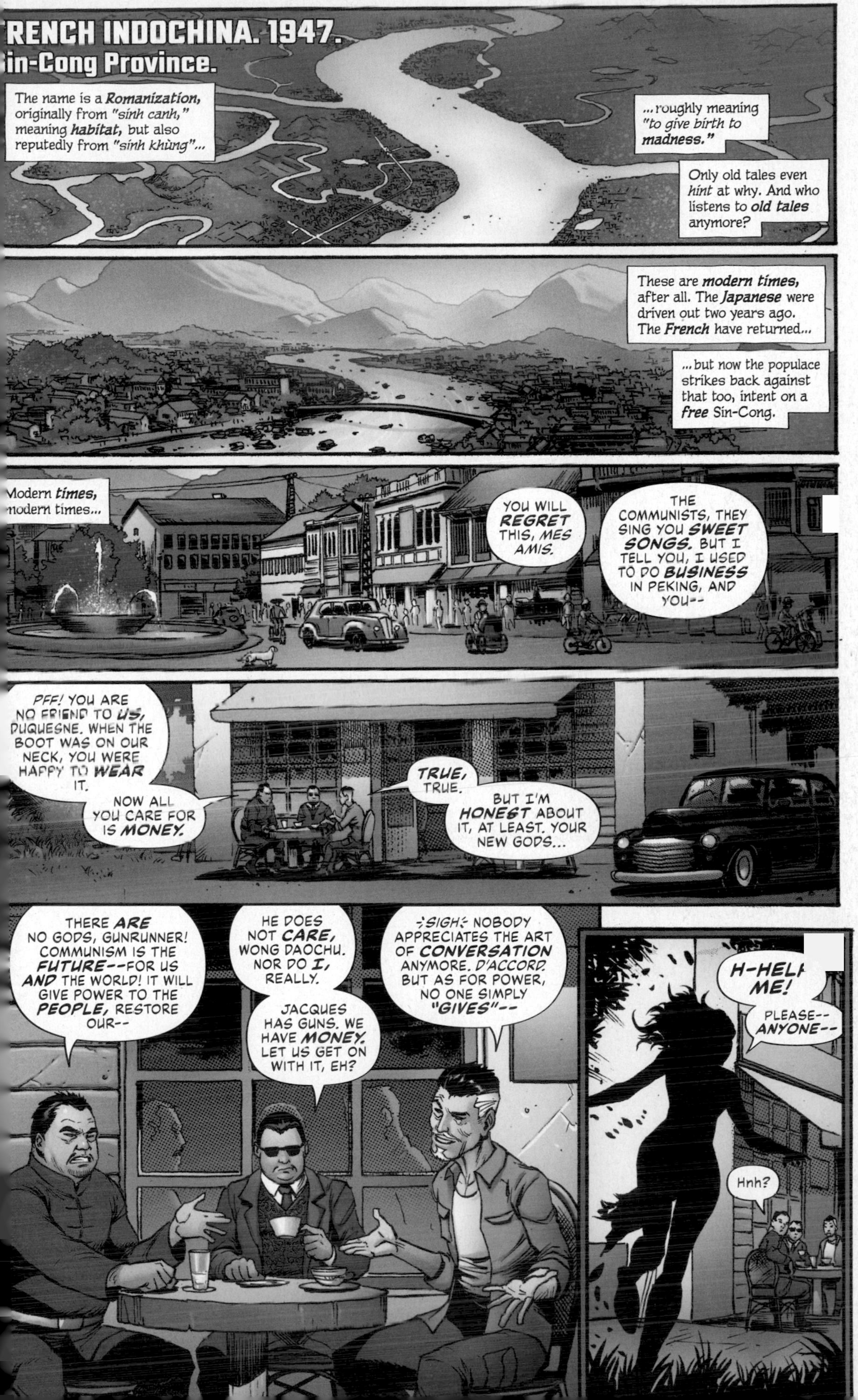
RENCH INDOCHINA. 1947.
in-Cong Province.
The name is a Romanization, originally from "sinh canh," meaning habitat, but also reputedly from "sinh khùng"...
...roughly meaning "to give birth to madness."
Only old tales even hint at why. And who listens to old tales anymore?
These are modern times, after all. The Japanese were driven out two years ago. The French have returned...
...but now the populace strikes back against that too, intent on a free Sin-Cong.
Modern times, modern times...
YOU WILL REGRET THIS, MES AMIS.
THE COMMUNISTS, THEY SING YOU SWEET SONGS. BUT I TELL YOU, I USED TO DO BUSINESS IN PEKING, AND YOU--
PFF! YOU ARE NO FRIEND TO US, DUQUESNE. WHEN THE BOOT WAS ON OUR NECK, YOU WERE HAPPY TO WEAR IT.
NOW ALL YOU CARE FOR IS MONEY.
TRUE, TRUE.
BUT I'M HONEST ABOUT IT, AT LEAST. YOUR NEW GODS...
THERE ARE NO GODS, GUNRUNNER! COMMUNISM IS THE FUTURE--FOR US AND THE WORLD! IT WILL GIVE POWER TO THE PEOPLE, RESTORE OUR--
HE DOES NOT CARE, WONG DAOCHU. NOR DO I, REALLY.
JACQUES HAS GUNS. WE HAVE MONEY. LET US GET ON WITH IT, EH?
SIGH NOBODY APPRECIATES THE ART OF CONVERSATION ANYMORE. D'ACCORD. BUT AS FOR POWER, NO ONE SIMPLY "GIVES"--
H-HELP ME!
PLEASE--ANYONE--
Hnh?

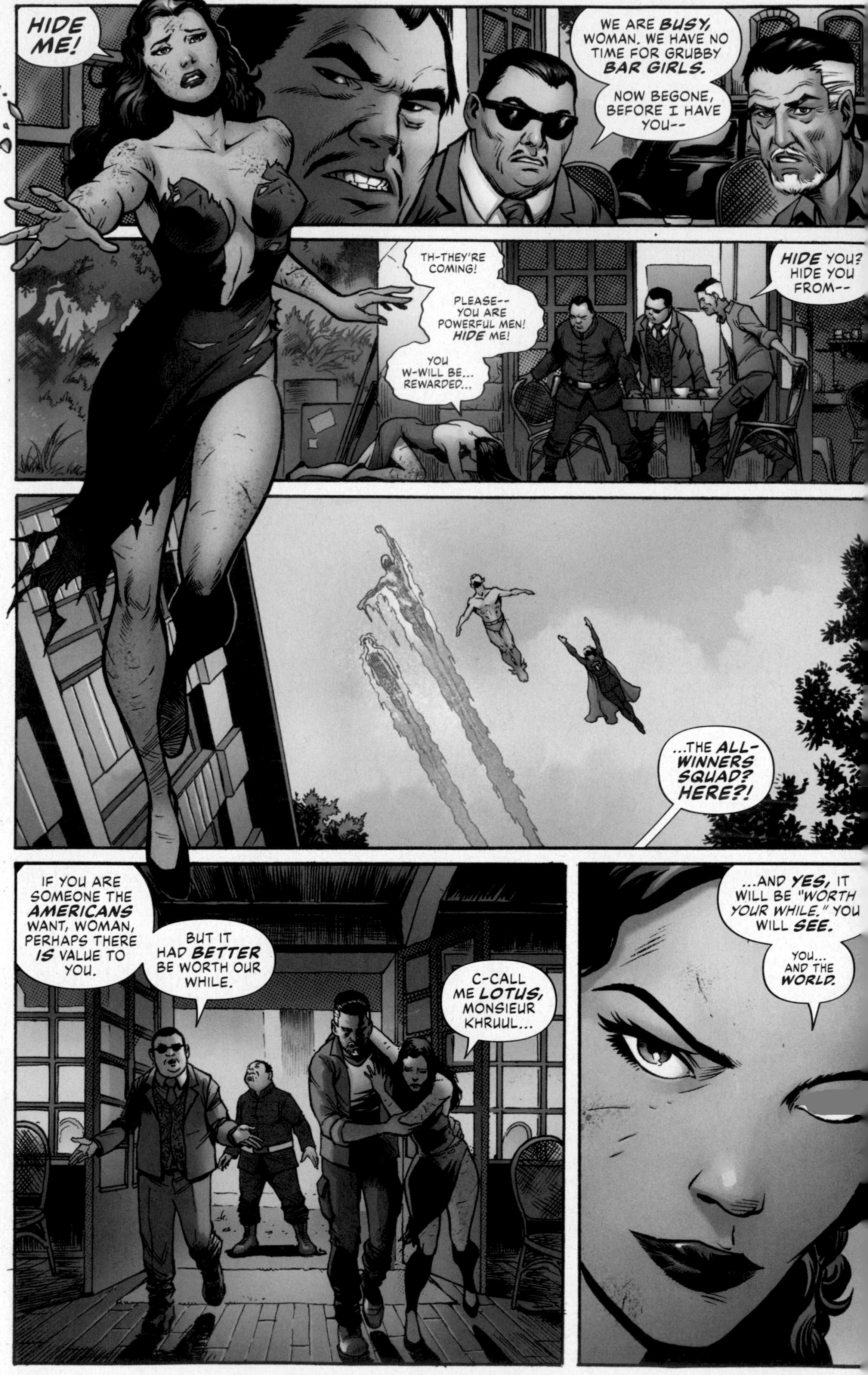
HIDE ME!
WE ARE BUSY, WOMAN. WE HAVE NO TIME FOR GRUBBY BAR GIRLS.
NOW BEGONE, BEFORE I HAVE YOU--
TH-THEY'RE COMING!
PLEASE-- YOU ARE POWERFUL MEN! HIDE ME!
YOU W-WILL BE... REWARDED...
HIDE YOU? HIDE YOU FROM--
...THE ALL-WINNERS SQUAD? HERE?!
IF YOU ARE SOMEONE THE AMERICANS WANT, WOMAN, PERHAPS THERE IS VALUE TO YOU.
BUT IT HAD BETTER BE WORTH OUR WHILE.
C-CALL ME LOTUS, MONSIEUR KHRUUL...
...AND YES, IT WILL BE "WORTH YOUR WHILE." YOU WILL SEE.
YOU... AND THE WORLD.

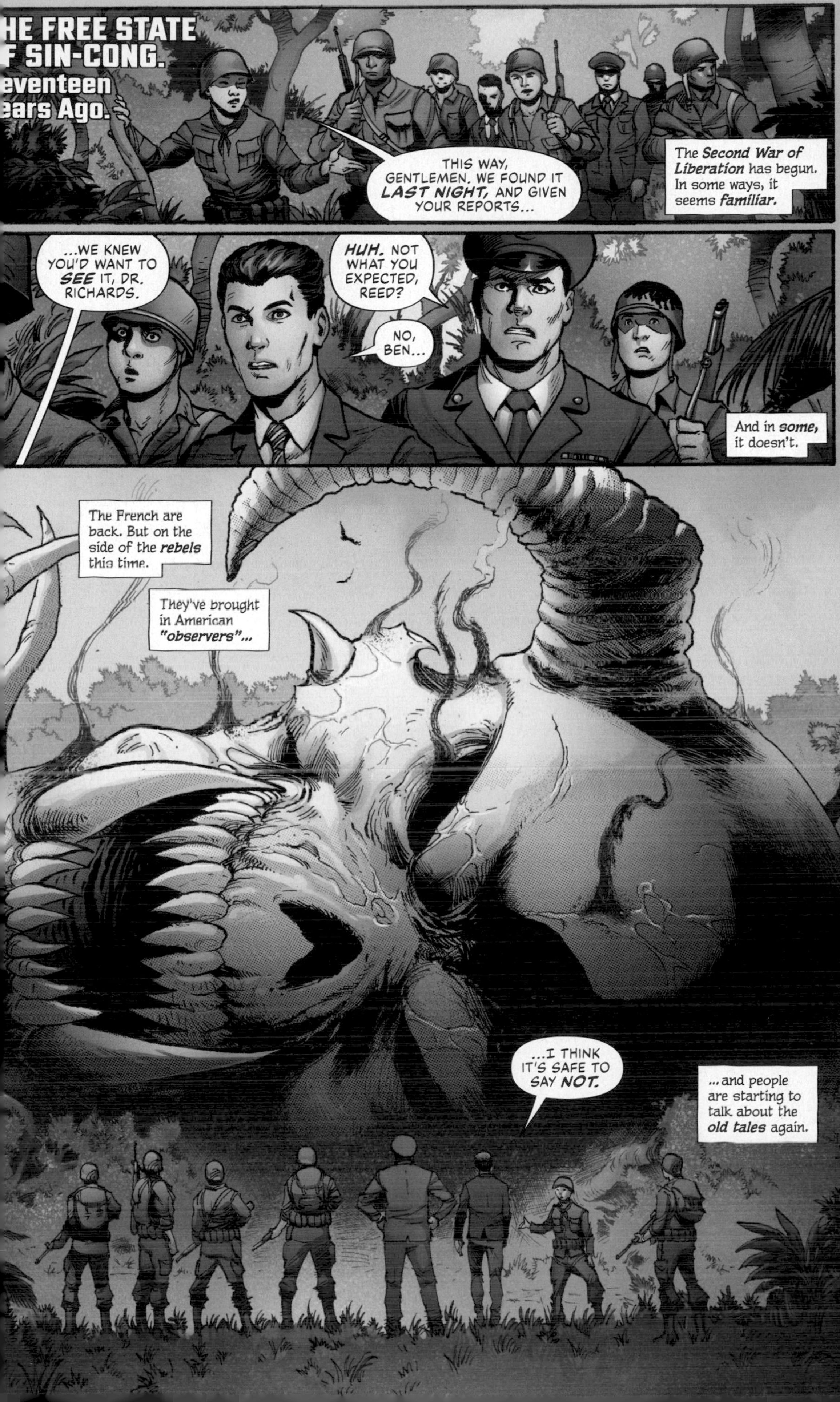
HE FREE STATE F SIN-CONG. eventeen ears Ago.
THIS WAY, GENTLEMEN. WE FOUND IT LAST NIGHT, AND GIVEN YOUR REPORTS...
The Second War of Liberation has begun. In some ways, it seems familiar.
...WE KNEW YOU'D WANT TO SEE IT, DR. RICHARDS.
HUH. NOT WHAT YOU EXPECTED, REED?
NO, BEN...
And in some, it doesn't.
The French are back. But on the side of the rebels this time.
They've brought in American "observers"...
...I THINK IT'S SAFE TO SAY NOT.
...and people are starting to talk about the old tales again.

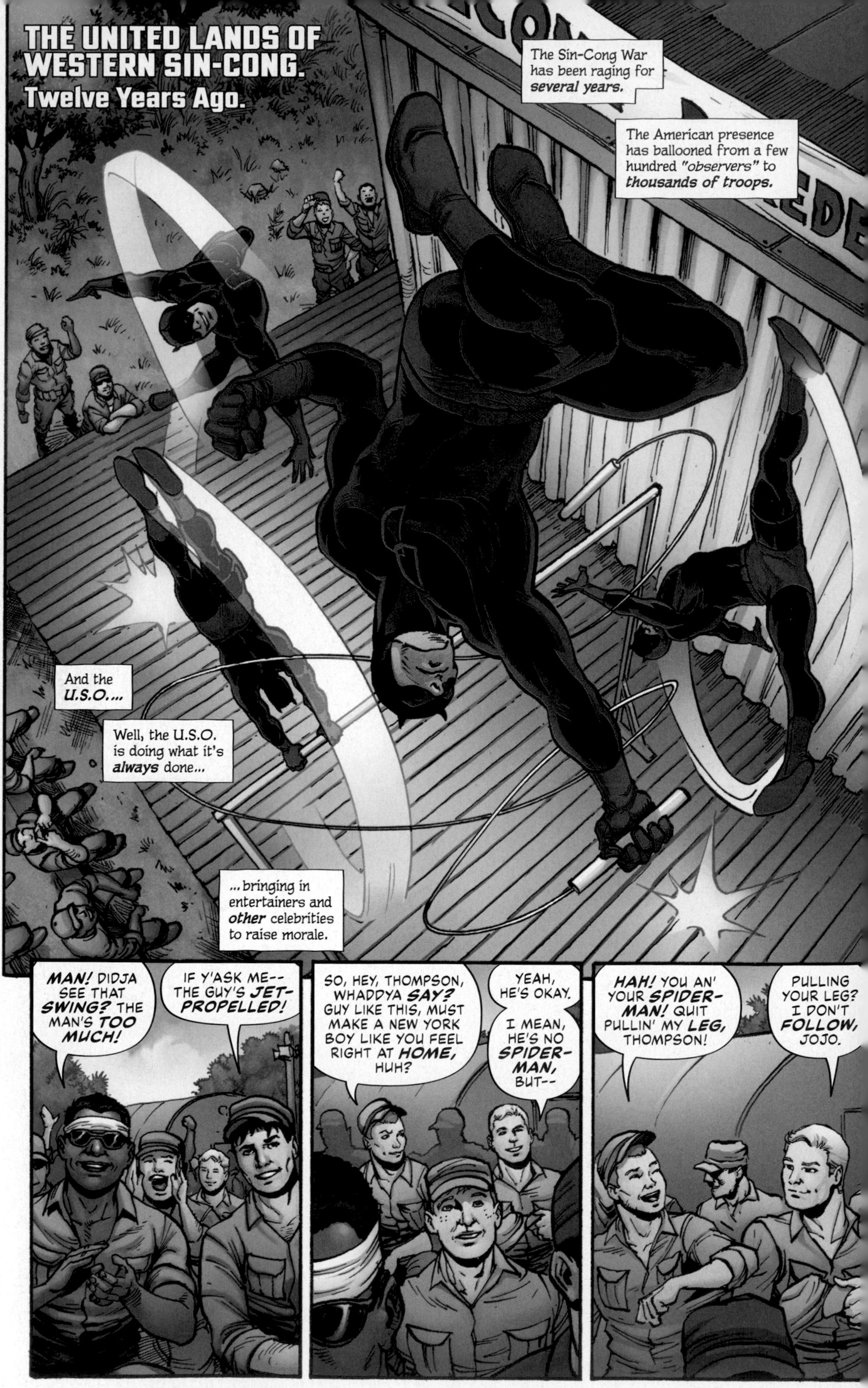
THE UNITED LANDS OF WESTERN SIN-CONG.
Twelve Years Ago.
The Sin-Cong War has been raging for several years.
The American presence has ballooned from a few hundred "observers" to thousands of troops.
And the U.S.O....
Well, the U.S.O. is doing what it's always done...
...bringing in entertainers and other celebrities to raise morale.
MAN! DIDJA SEE THAT SWING? THE MAN'S TOO MUCH!
IF Y'ASK ME-- THE GUY'S JET-PROPELLED!
SO, HEY, THOMPSON, WHADDYA SAY? GUY LIKE THIS, MUST MAKE A NEW YORK BOY LIKE YOU FEEL RIGHT AT HOME, HUH?
YEAH, HE'S OKAY.
I MEAN, HE'S NO SPIDER-MAN, BUT--
HAH! YOU AN' YOUR SPIDER-MAN! QUIT PULLIN' MY LEG, THOMPSON!
PULLING YOUR LEG? I DON'T FOLLOW, JOJO.

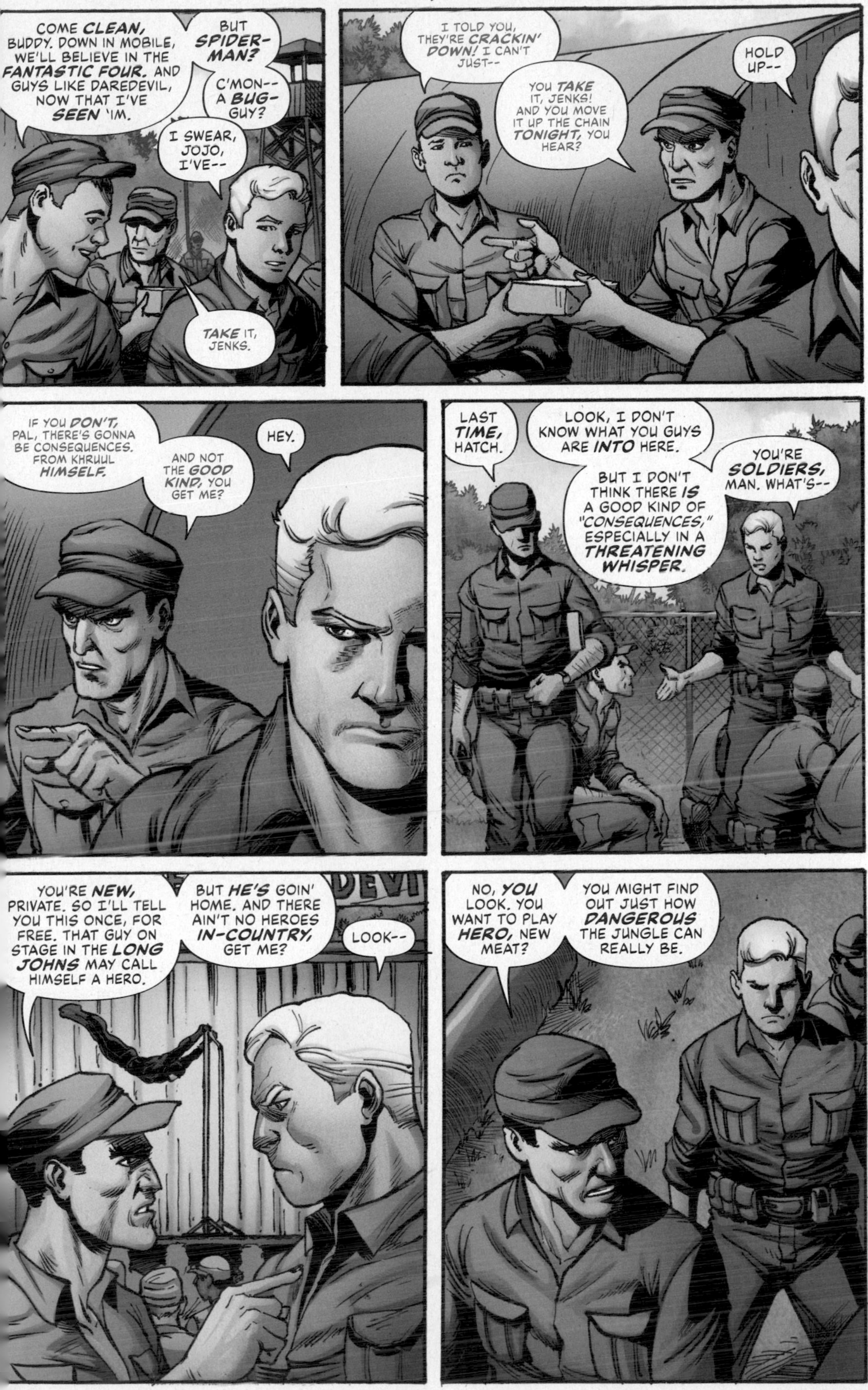
COME CLEAN, BUDDY. DOWN IN MOBILE, WE'LL BELIEVE IN THE FANTASTIC FOUR. AND GUYS LIKE DAREDEVIL, NOW THAT I'VE SEEN 'IM.
BUT SPIDER-MAN?
C'MON-- A BUG-GUY?
I SWEAR, JOJO, I'VE--
TAKE IT, JENKS.
I TOLD YOU, THEY'RE CRACKIN' DOWN! I CAN'T JUST--
YOU TAKE IT, JENKS! AND YOU MOVE IT UP THE CHAIN TONIGHT, YOU HEAR?
HOLD UP--
IF YOU DON'T, PAL, THERE'S GONNA BE CONSEQUENCES. FROM KHRUUL HIMSELF.
AND NOT THE GOOD KIND, YOU GET ME?
HEY.
LAST TIME, HATCH.
LOOK, I DON'T KNOW WHAT YOU GUYS ARE INTO HERE.
BUT I DON'T THINK THERE IS A GOOD KIND OF "CONSEQUENCES," ESPECIALLY IN A THREATENING WHISPER.
YOU'RE SOLDIERS, MAN. WHAT'S--
YOU'RE NEW, PRIVATE. SO I'LL TELL YOU THIS ONCE, FOR FREE. THAT GUY ON STAGE IN THE LONG JOHNS MAY CALL HIMSELF A HERO.
BUT HE'S GOIN' HOME. AND THERE AIN'T NO HEROES IN-COUNTRY, GET ME?
LOOK--
NO, YOU LOOK. YOU WANT TO PLAY HERO, NEW MEAT?
YOU MIGHT FIND OUT JUST HOW DANGEROUS THE JUNGLE CAN REALLY BE.

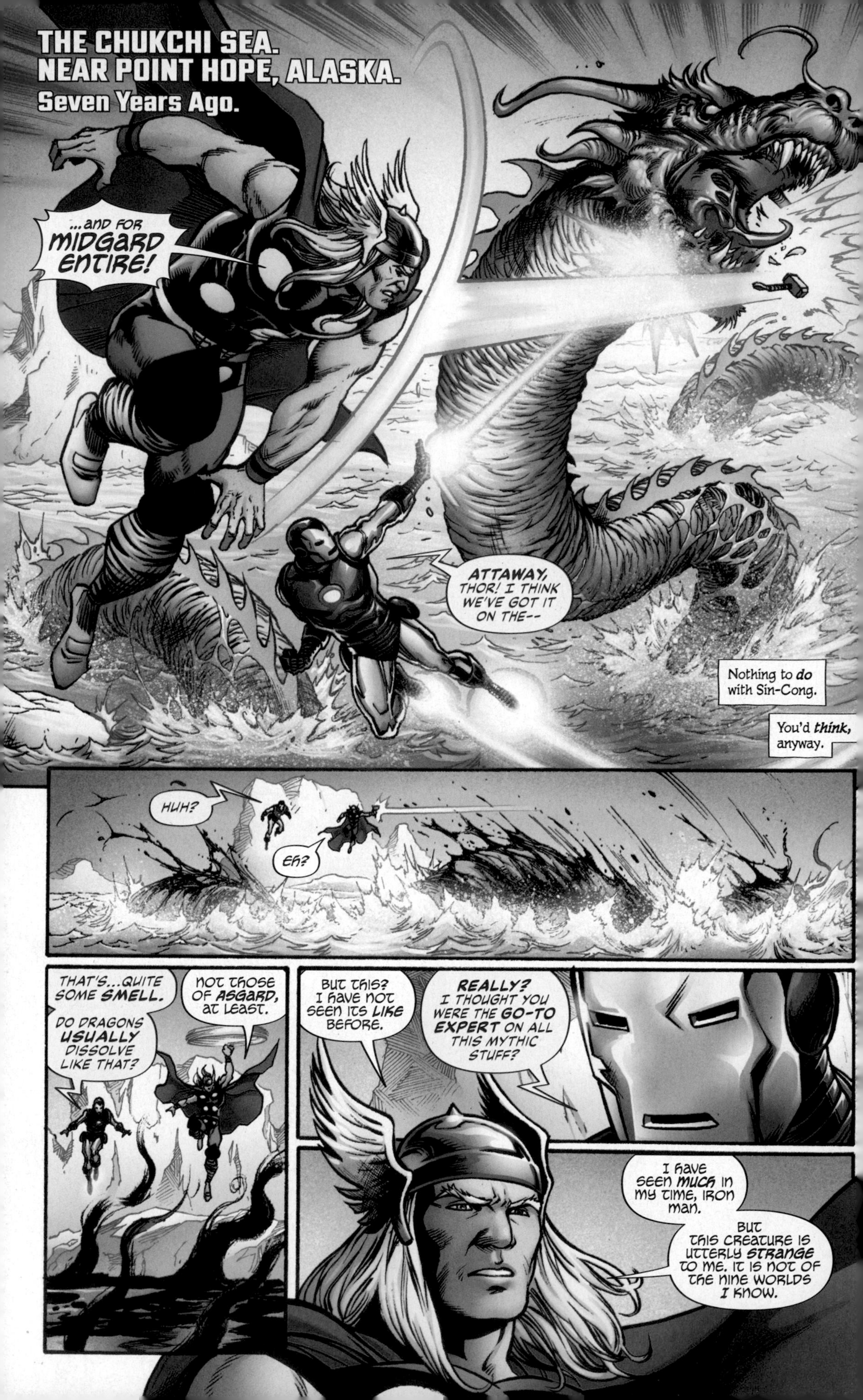
THE CHUKCHI SEA.
NEAR POINT HOPE, ALASKA.
Seven Years Ago.
...AND FOR MIDGARD ENTIRE!
ATTAWAY, THOR! I THINK WE'VE GOT IT ON THE--
Nothing to do with Sin-Cong.
You'd think, anyway.
HUH?
EH?
THAT'S...QUITE SOME SMELL.
DO DRAGONS USUALLY DISSOLVE LIKE THAT?
NOT THOSE OF ASGARD, AT LEAST.
BUT THIS? I HAVE NOT SEEN ITS LIKE BEFORE.
REALLY? I THOUGHT YOU WERE THE GO-TO EXPERT ON ALL THIS MYTHIC STUFF?
I HAVE SEEN MUCH IN MY TIME, IRON MAN.
BUT THIS CREATURE IS UTTERLY STRANGE TO ME. IT IS NOT OF THE NINE WORLDS I KNOW.

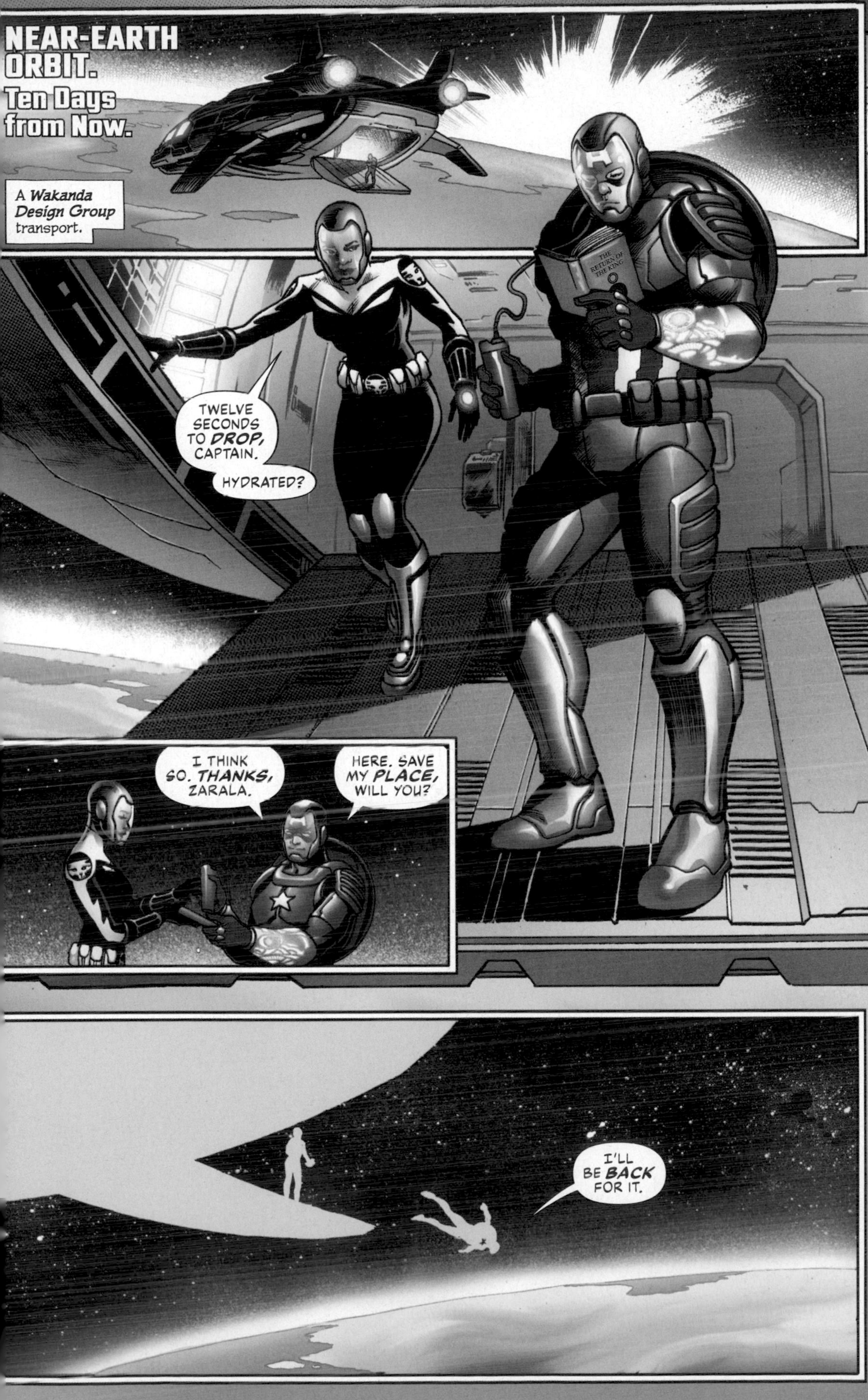
NEAR-EARTH ORBIT.
Ten Days from Now.
A Wakanda Design Group transport.
TWELVE SECONDS TO DROP, CAPTAIN.
HYDRATED?
THE RETURN OF THE KING
I THINK SO. THANKS, ZARALA.
HERE. SAVE MY PLACE, WILL YOU?
I'LL BE BACK FOR IT.

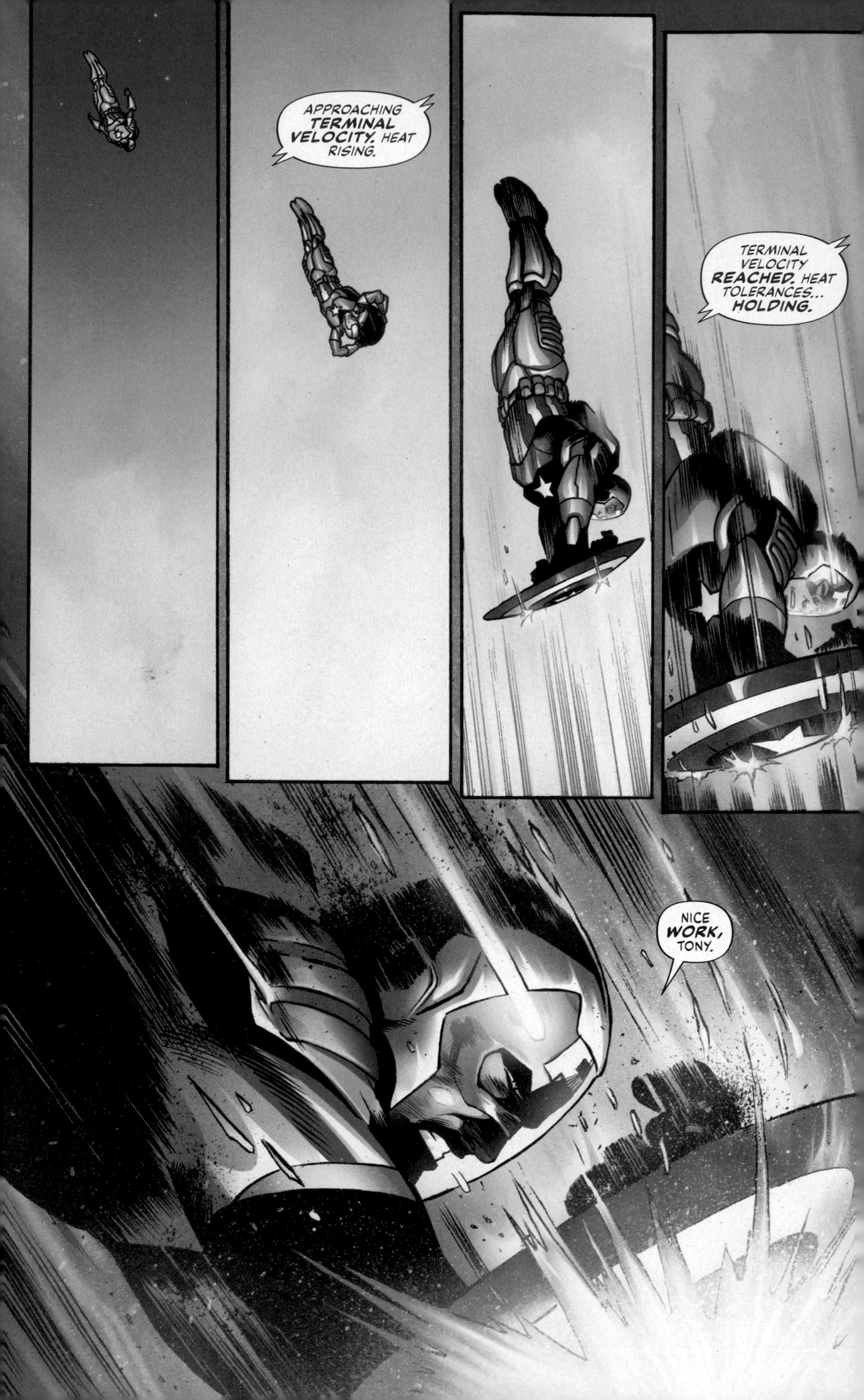
APPROACHING TERMINAL VELOCITY. HEAT RISING.
TERMINAL VELOCITY REACHED. HEAT TOLERANCES... HOLDING.
NICE WORK, TONY.

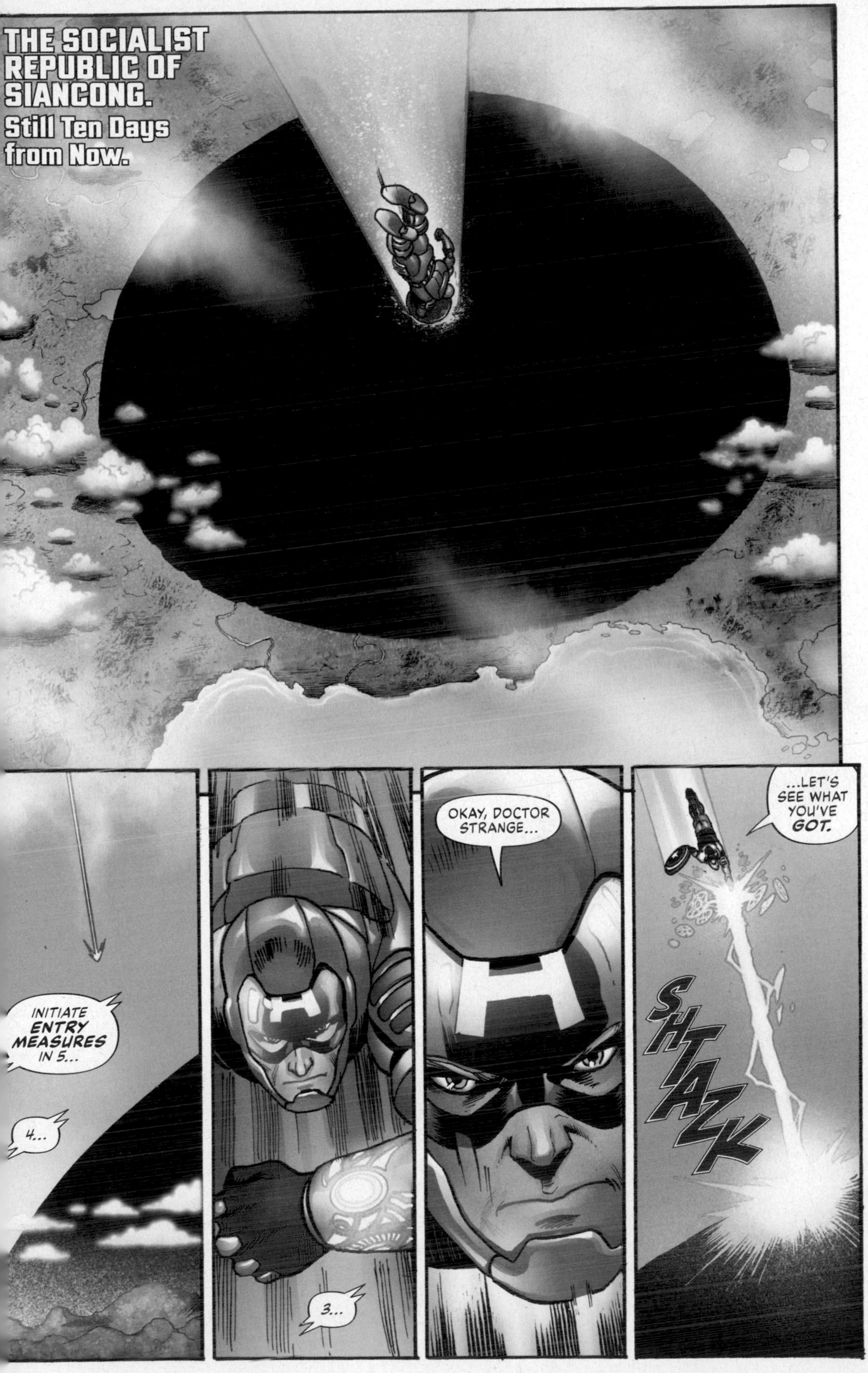
THE SOCIALIST REPUBLIC OF SIANCONG.
Still Ten Days from Now.
INITIATE ENTRY MEASURES IN 5...
4...
3...
OKAY, DOCTOR STRANGE...
...LET'S SEE WHAT YOU'VE GOT.
SHTAZK

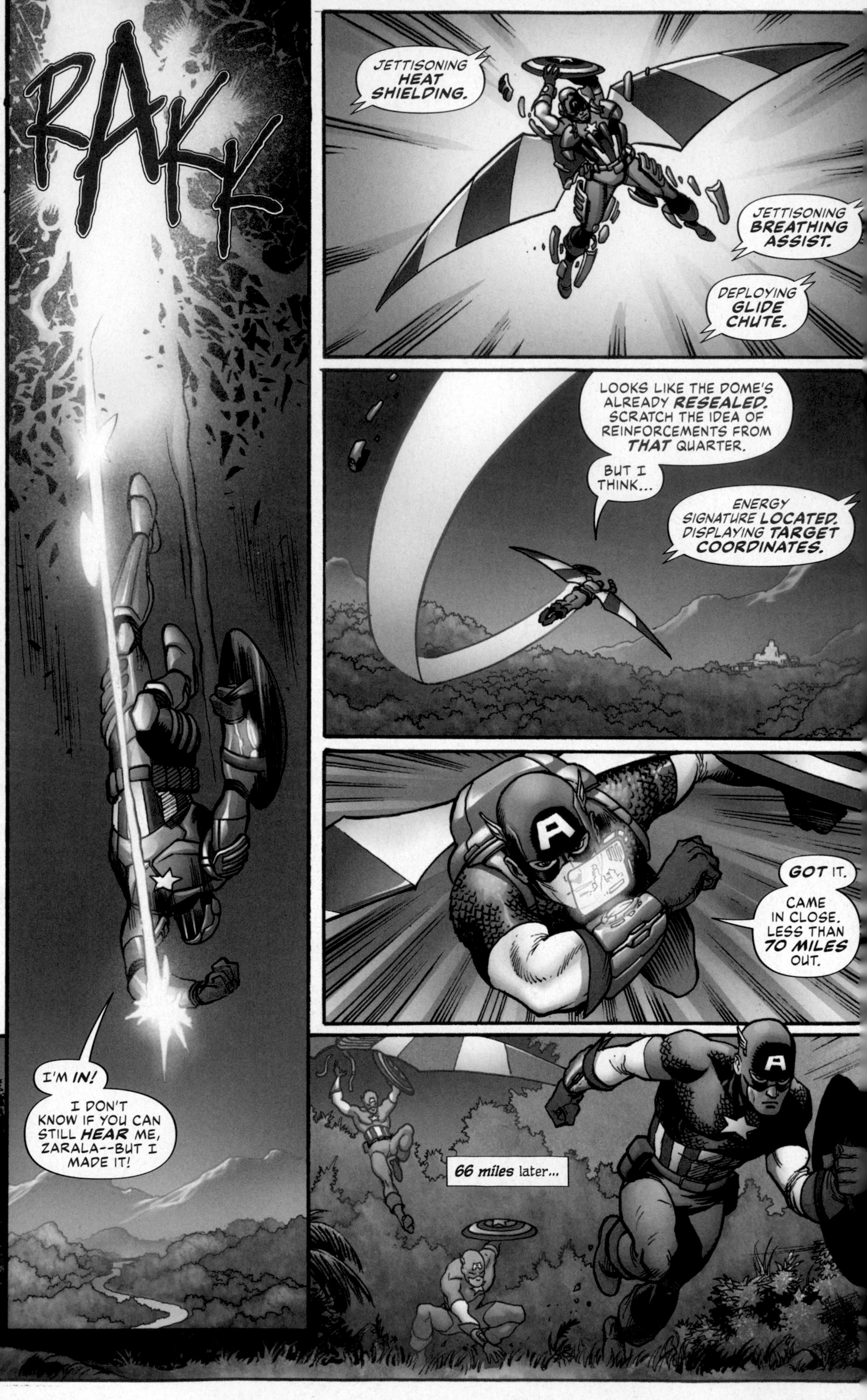
RAKK
JETTISONING HEAT SHIELDING.
JETTISONING BREATHING ASSIST.
DEPLOYING GLIDE CHUTE.
LOOKS LIKE THE DOME'S ALREADY RESEALED. SCRATCH THE IDEA OF REINFORCEMENTS FROM THAT QUARTER.
BUT I THINK...
ENERGY SIGNATURE LOCATED. DISPLAYING TARGET COORDINATES.
GOT IT.
CAME IN CLOSE. LESS THAN 70 MILES OUT.
I'M IN!
I DON'T KNOW IF YOU CAN STILL HEAR ME, ZARALA--BUT I MADE IT!
66 miles later...

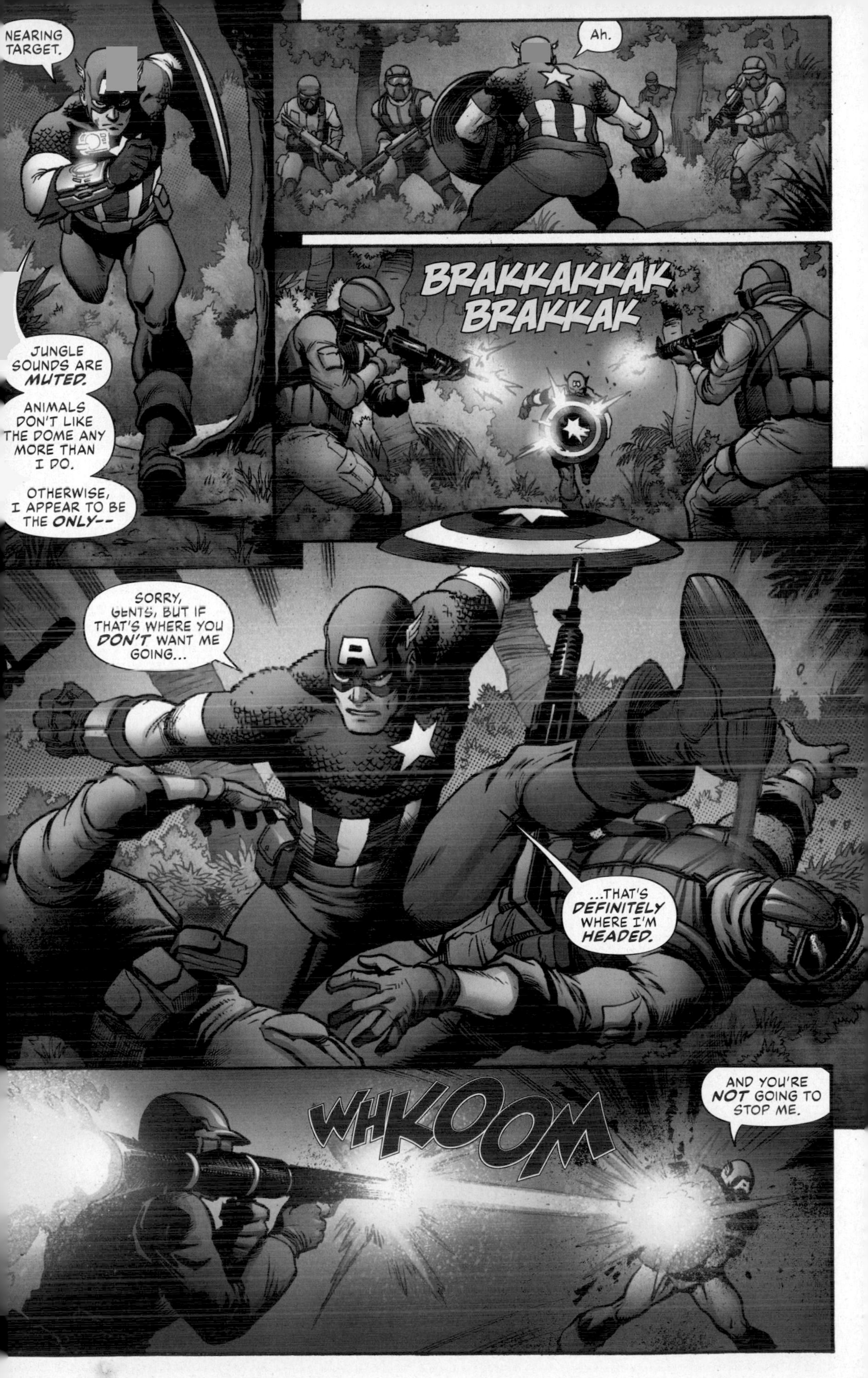

NEARING TARGET.
JUNGLE SOUNDS ARE MUTED.
ANIMALS DON'T LIKE THE DOME ANY MORE THAN I DO.
OTHERWISE, I APPEAR TO BE THE ONLY--
Ah.
BRAKKAKKAK BRAKKAK
SORRY, GENTS, BUT IF THAT'S WHERE YOU DON'T WANT ME GOING...
...THAT'S DEFINITELY WHERE I'M HEADED.
WHKOOM
AND YOU'RE NOT GOING TO STOP ME.

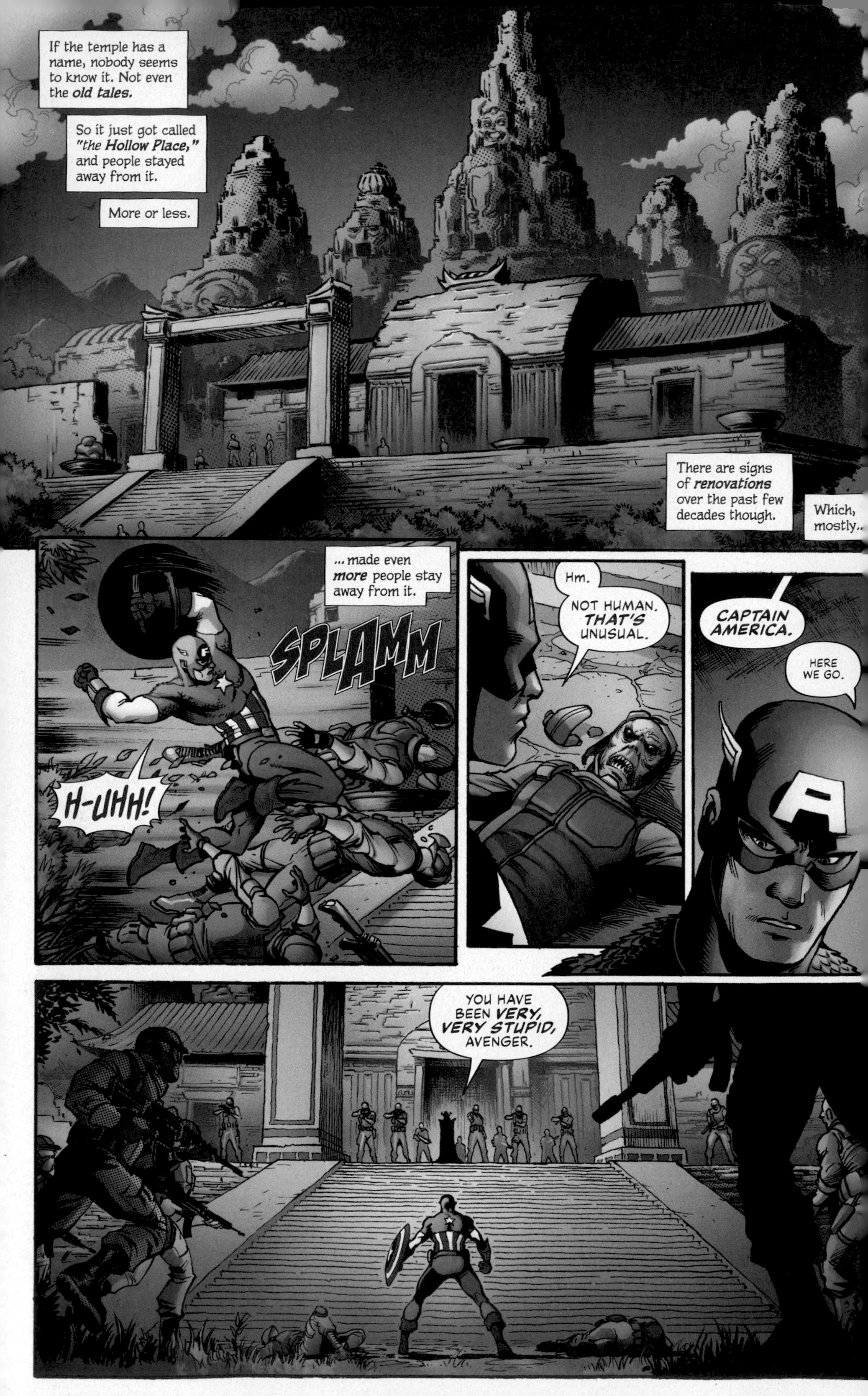
If the temple has a name, nobody seems to know it. Not even the *old tales.*
So it just got called *"the Hollow Place,"* and people stayed away from it.
More or less.
There are signs of *renovations* over the past few decades though.
Which, mostly...
...made even *more* people stay away from it.
SPLAMM
H-UHH!
Hm.
NOT HUMAN. *THAT'S* UNUSUAL.
CAPTAIN AMERICA.
HERE WE GO.
YOU HAVE BEEN *VERY, VERY STUPID,* AVENGER.

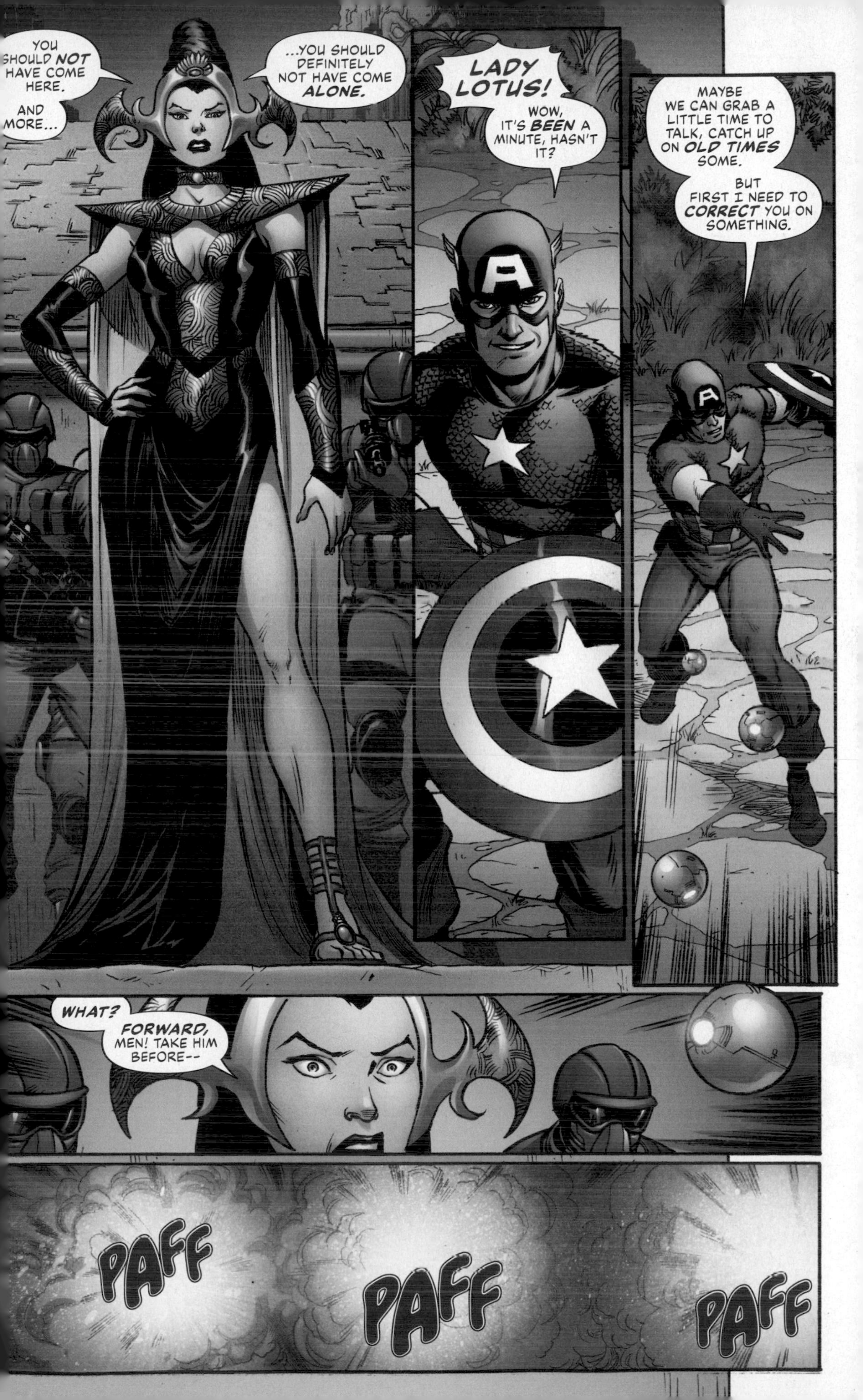
YOU SHOULD NOT HAVE COME HERE.
AND MORE...
...YOU SHOULD DEFINITELY NOT HAVE COME ALONE.
LADY LOTUS!
WOW, IT'S BEEN A MINUTE, HASN'T IT?
MAYBE WE CAN GRAB A LITTLE TIME TO TALK, CATCH UP ON OLD TIMES SOME.
BUT FIRST I NEED TO CORRECT YOU ON SOMETHING.
WHAT?
FORWARD, MEN! TAKE HIM BEFORE--
PAFF
PAFF
PAFF

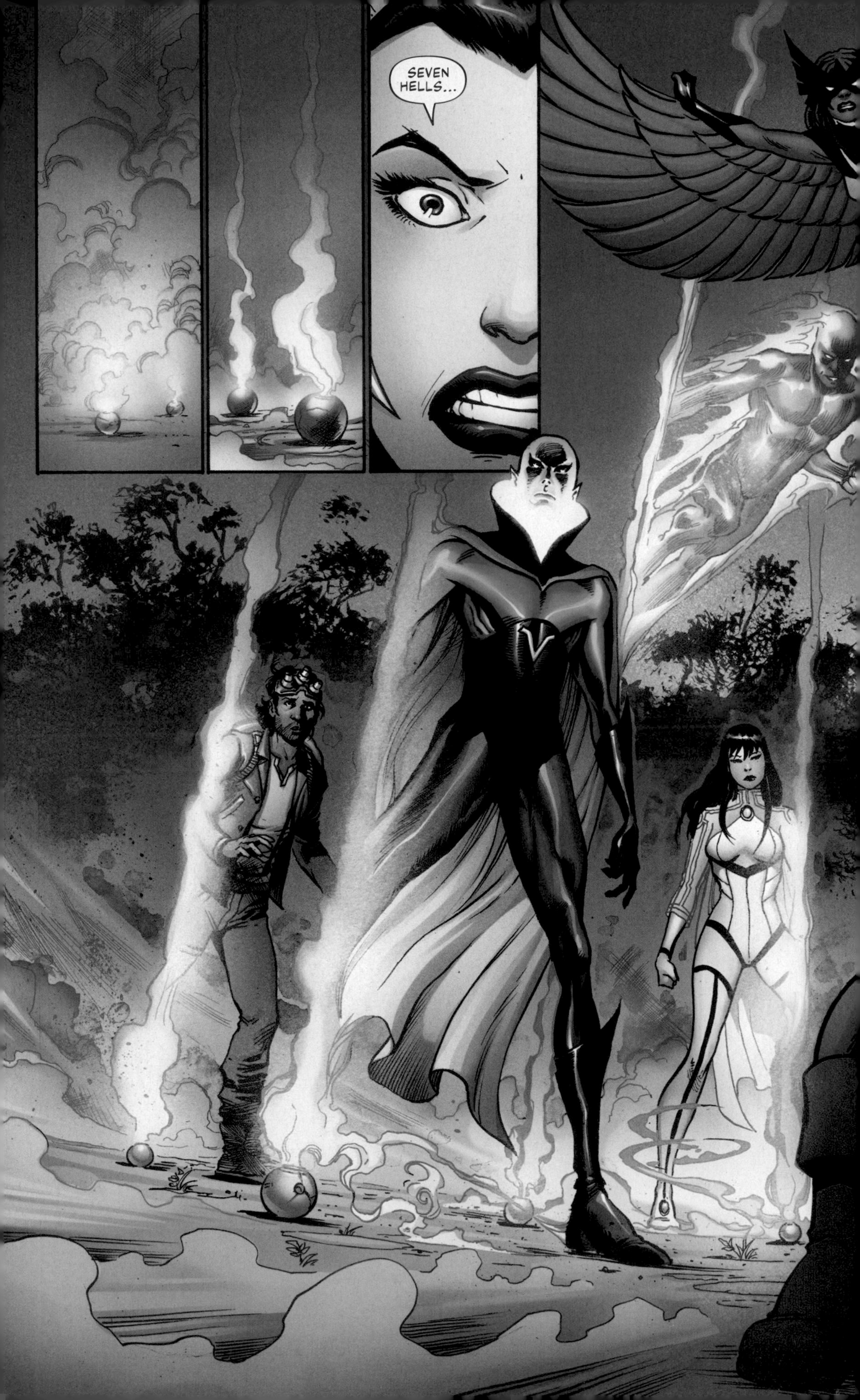
SEVEN HELLS...

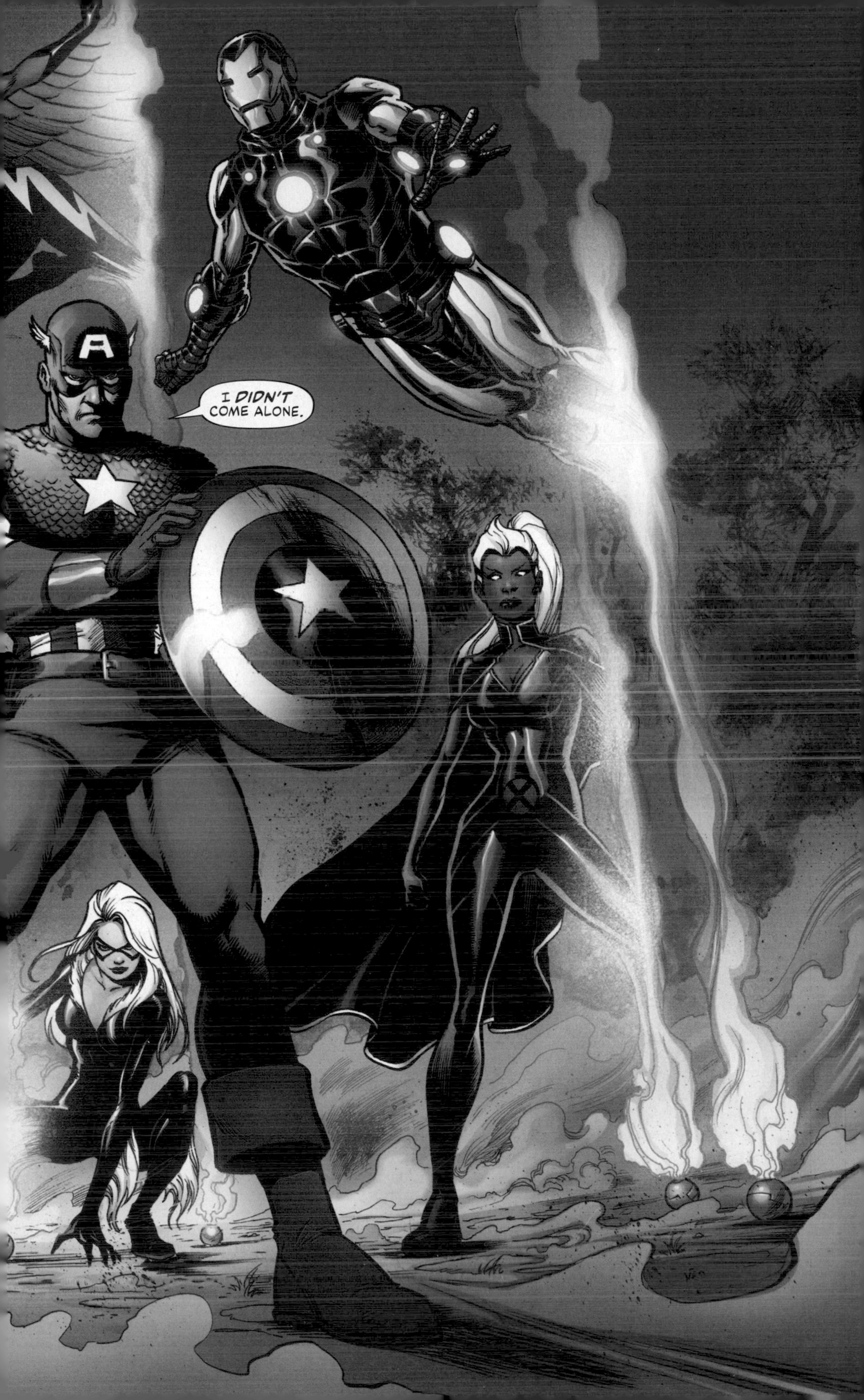
I *DIDN'T* COME ALONE.

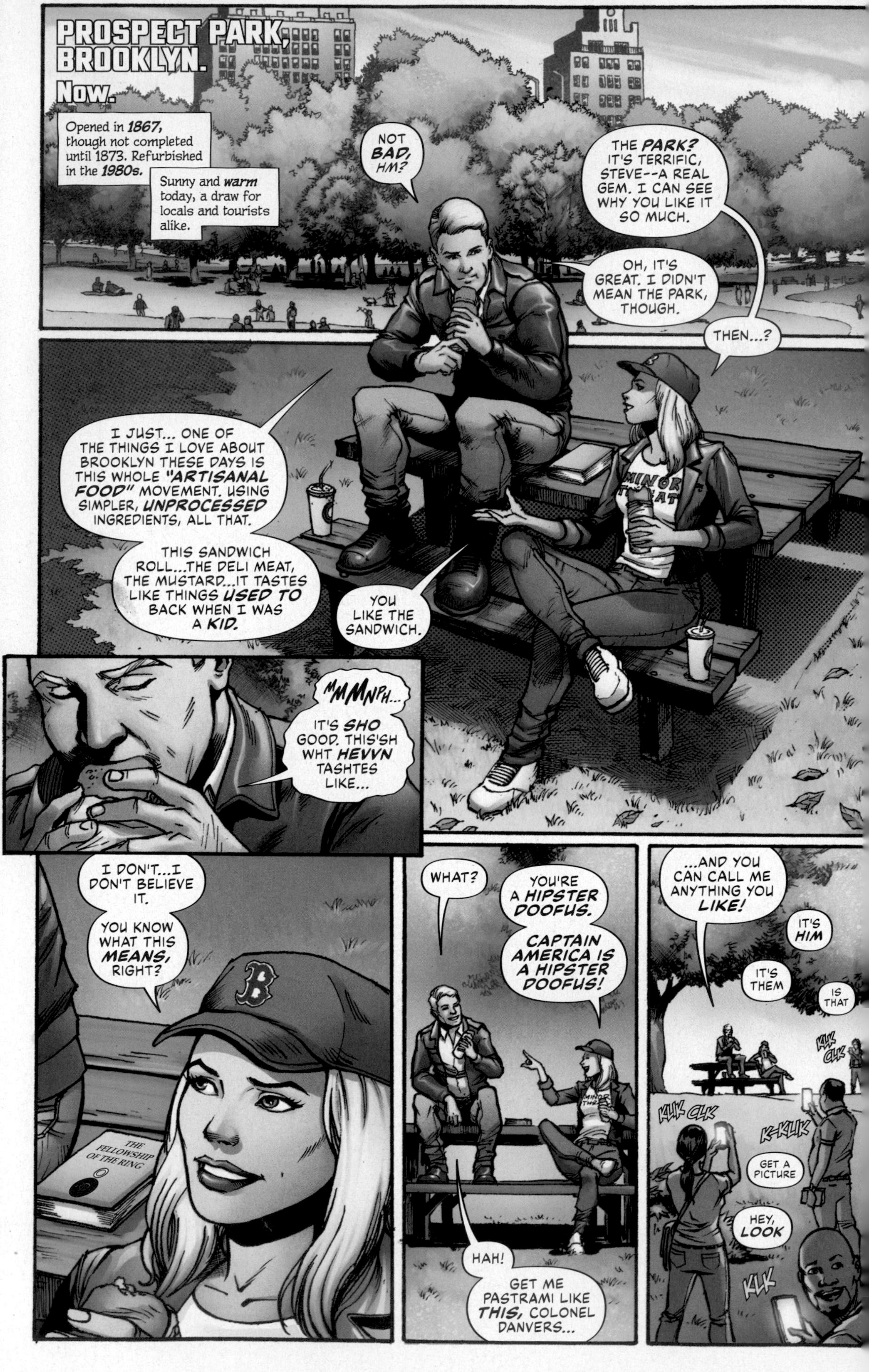
PROSPECT PARK, BROOKLYN.
Now.
Opened in 1867, though not completed until 1873. Refurbished in the 1980s.
Sunny and warm today, a draw for locals and tourists alike.
NOT BAD, HM?
THE PARK? IT'S TERRIFIC, STEVE--A REAL GEM. I CAN SEE WHY YOU LIKE IT SO MUCH.
OH, IT'S GREAT. I DIDN'T MEAN THE PARK, THOUGH.
THEN...?
I JUST... ONE OF THE THINGS I LOVE ABOUT BROOKLYN THESE DAYS IS THIS WHOLE "ARTISANAL FOOD" MOVEMENT. USING SIMPLER, UNPROCESSED INGREDIENTS, ALL THAT.
THIS SANDWICH ROLL...THE DELI MEAT, THE MUSTARD...IT TASTES LIKE THINGS USED TO BACK WHEN I WAS A KID.
YOU LIKE THE SANDWICH.
MMMNPH...
IT'S SHO GOOD. THIS'SH WHT HEVVN TASHTES LIKE...
I DON'T...I DON'T BELIEVE IT.
YOU KNOW WHAT THIS MEANS, RIGHT?
THE FELLOWSHIP OF THE RING
WHAT?
YOU'RE A HIPSTER DOOFUS.
CAPTAIN AMERICA IS A HIPSTER DOOFUS!
HAH!
GET ME PASTRAMI LIKE THIS, COLONEL DANVERS...
...AND YOU CAN CALL ME ANYTHING YOU LIKE!
IT'S HIM
IT'S THEM
IS THAT
KLK CLK
KLIK CLK
K-KLIK
GET A PICTURE
HEY, LOOK
KLK

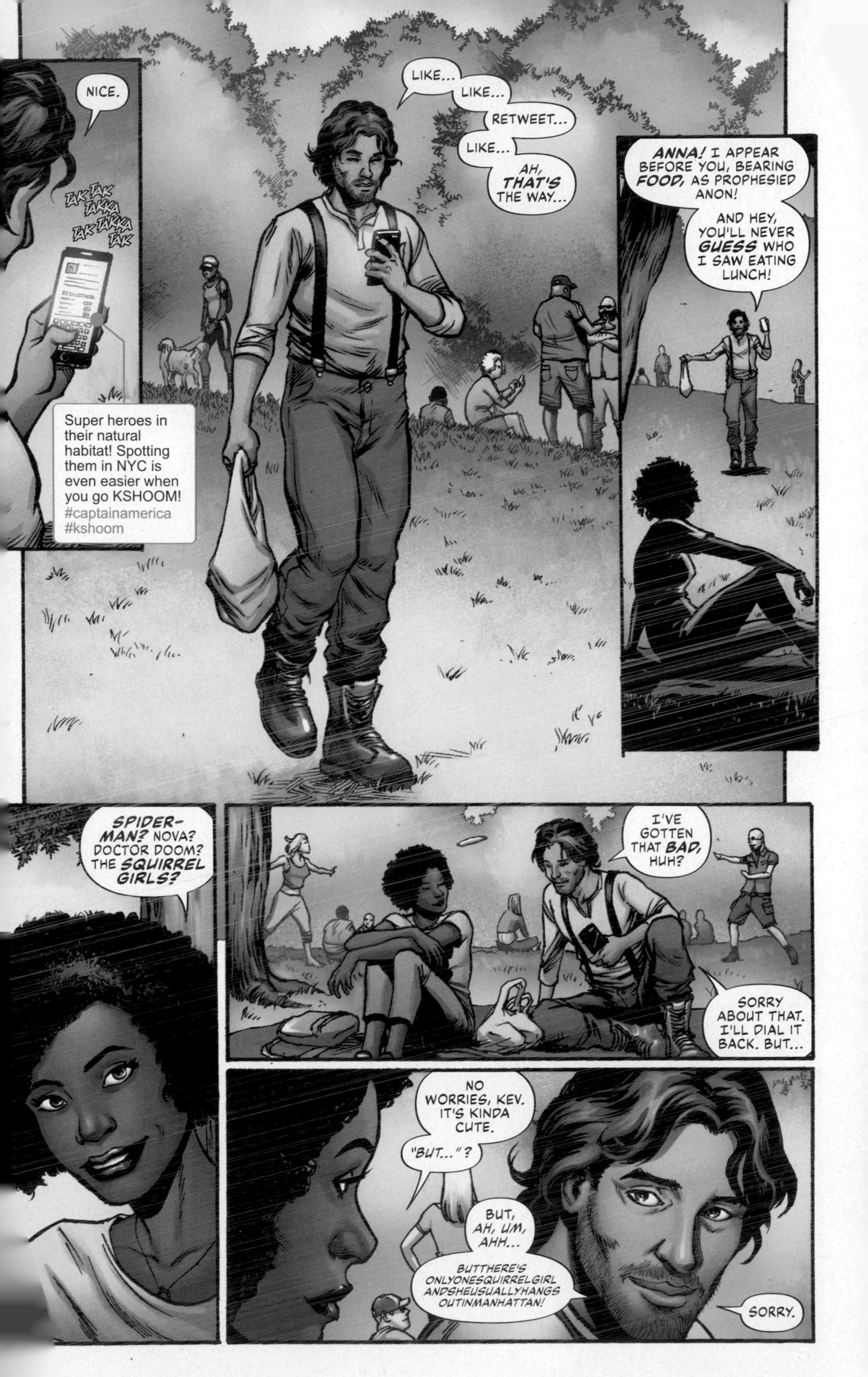
NICE.
TAK TAK TAKKA TAK TAKKA TAK
Super heroes in their natural habitat! Spotting them in NYC is even easier when you go KSHOOM! #captainamerica #kshoom
LIKE...
LIKE...
RETWEET...
LIKE...
AH, THAT'S THE WAY...
ANNA! I APPEAR BEFORE YOU, BEARING FOOD, AS PROPHESIED ANON!
AND HEY, YOU'LL NEVER GUESS WHO I SAW EATING LUNCH!
SPIDER-MAN? NOVA? DOCTOR DOOM? THE SQUIRREL GIRLS?
I'VE GOTTEN THAT BAD, HUH?
SORRY ABOUT THAT. I'LL DIAL IT BACK. BUT...
NO WORRIES, KEV. IT'S KINDA CUTE.
"BUT..."?
BUT, AH, UM, AHH...
BUTTHERE'S ONLYONESQUIRRELGIRL ANDSHEUSUALLYHANGS OUTINMANHATTAN!
SORRY.

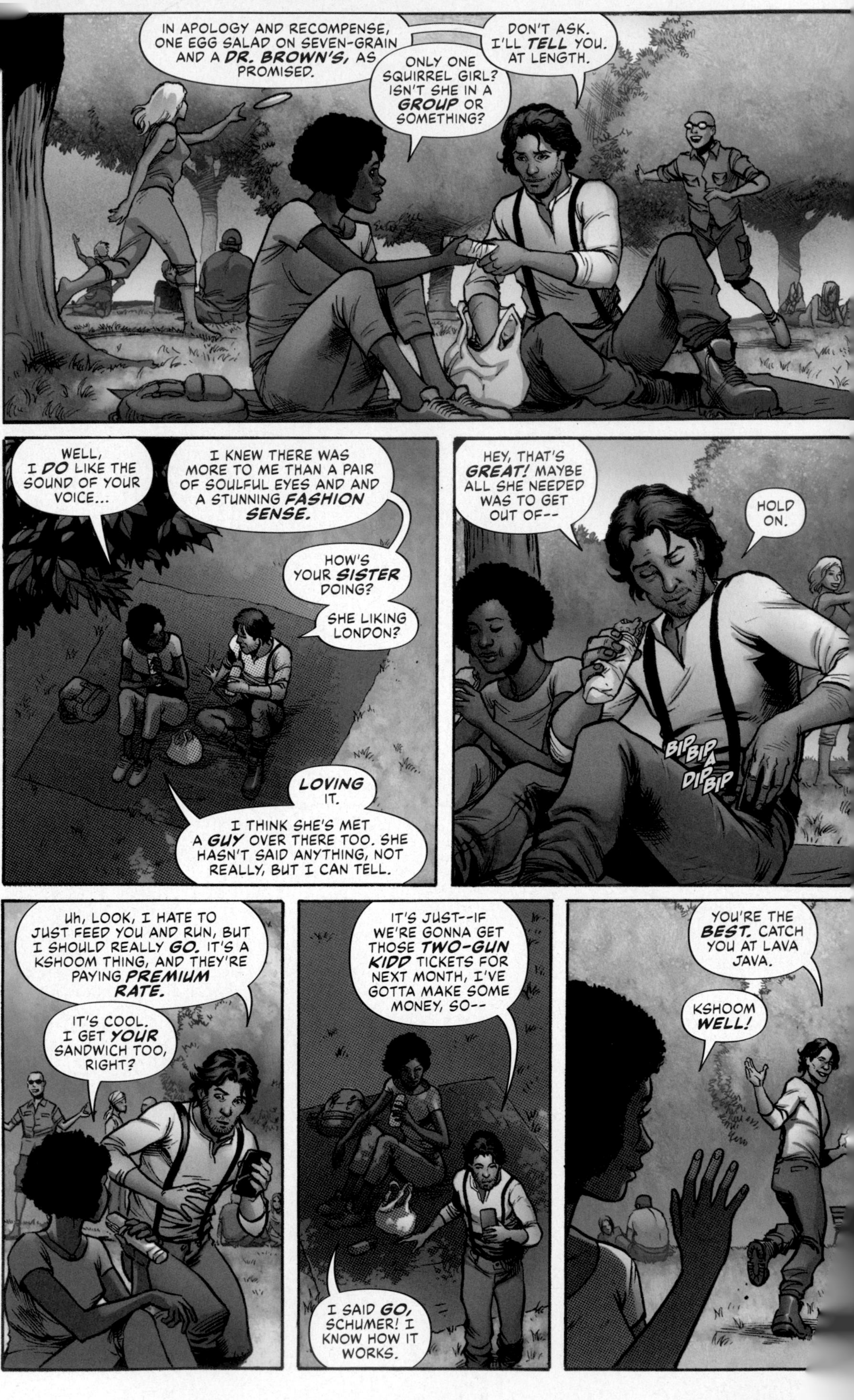
IN APOLOGY AND RECOMPENSE, ONE EGG SALAD ON SEVEN-GRAIN AND A DR. BROWN'S, AS PROMISED.
ONLY ONE SQUIRREL GIRL? ISN'T SHE IN A GROUP OR SOMETHING?
DON'T ASK. I'LL TELL YOU. AT LENGTH.
WELL, I DO LIKE THE SOUND OF YOUR VOICE...
I KNEW THERE WAS MORE TO ME THAN A PAIR OF SOULFUL EYES AND AND A STUNNING FASHION SENSE.
HOW'S YOUR SISTER DOING?
SHE LIKING LONDON?
LOVING IT.
I THINK SHE'S MET A GUY OVER THERE TOO. SHE HASN'T SAID ANYTHING, NOT REALLY, BUT I CAN TELL.
HEY, THAT'S GREAT! MAYBE ALL SHE NEEDED WAS TO GET OUT OF--
HOLD ON.
BIP BIP A DIP BIP
UH, LOOK, I HATE TO JUST FEED YOU AND RUN, BUT I SHOULD REALLY GO. IT'S A KSHOOM THING, AND THEY'RE PAYING PREMIUM RATE.
IT'S COOL. I GET YOUR SANDWICH TOO, RIGHT?
IT'S JUST--IF WE'RE GONNA GET THOSE TWO-GUN KIDD TICKETS FOR NEXT MONTH, I'VE GOTTA MAKE SOME MONEY, SO--
I SAID GO, SCHUMER! I KNOW HOW IT WORKS.
YOU'RE THE BEST. CATCH YOU AT LAVA JAVA.
KSHOOM WELL!

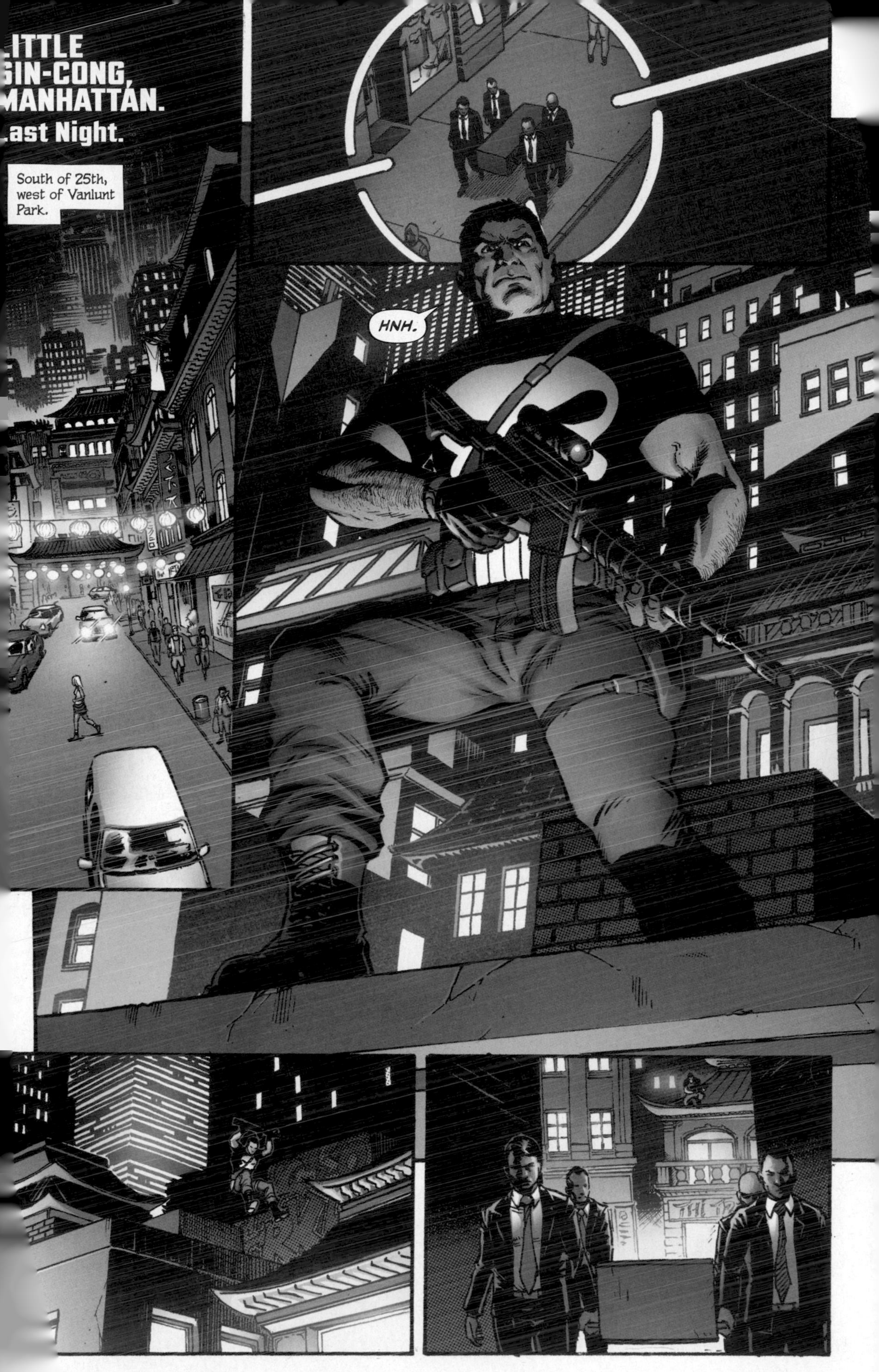
LITTLE
SIN-CONG,
MANHATTAN.
Last Night.
South of 25th, west of Vanlunt Park.
HNH.

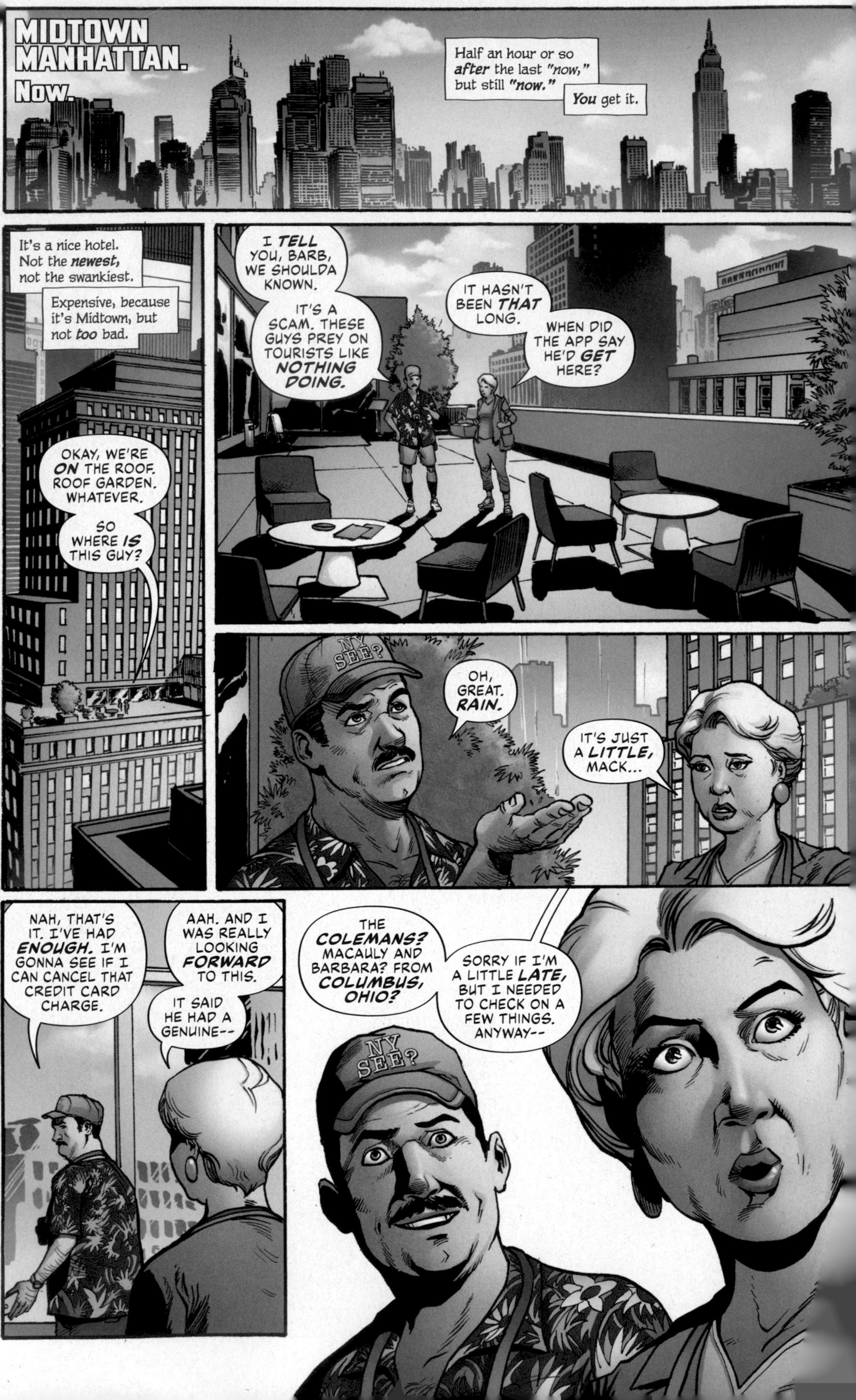
MIDTOWN MANHATTAN. Now.
Half an hour or so *after* the last "now," but still "now."
You get it.
It's a nice hotel. Not the *newest,* not the swankiest.
Expensive, because it's Midtown, but not *too* bad.
OKAY, WE'RE *ON* THE ROOF. ROOF GARDEN. WHATEVER.
SO WHERE *IS* THIS GUY?
I *TELL* YOU, BARB, WE SHOULDA KNOWN.
IT'S A SCAM. THESE GUYS PREY ON TOURISTS LIKE *NOTHING DOING.*
IT HASN'T BEEN *THAT* LONG.
WHEN DID THE APP SAY HE'D *GET* HERE?
NY SEE?
OH, GREAT. *RAIN.*
IT'S JUST A *LITTLE,* MACK...
NAH, THAT'S IT. I'VE HAD *ENOUGH.* I'M GONNA SEE IF I CAN CANCEL THAT CREDIT CARD CHARGE.
AAH. AND I WAS REALLY LOOKING *FORWARD* TO THIS.
IT SAID HE HAD A GENUINE--
THE *COLEMANS?* MACAULY AND BARBARA? FROM *COLUMBUS, OHIO?*
SORRY IF I'M A LITTLE *LATE,* BUT I NEEDED TO CHECK ON A FEW THINGS. ANYWAY--
NY SEE?

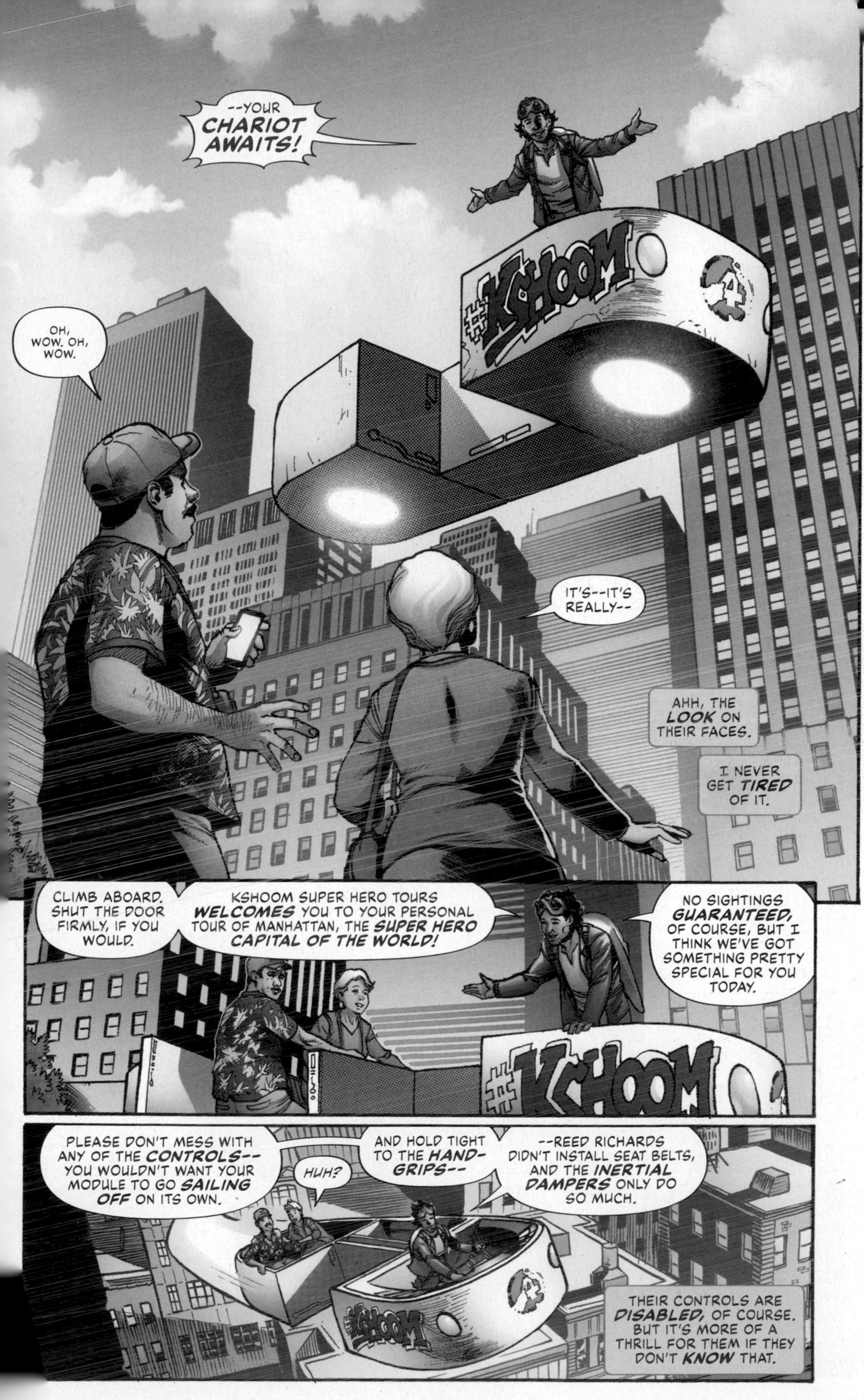
--YOUR CHARIOT AWAITS!
#KSHOOM
OH, WOW. OH, WOW.
IT'S--IT'S REALLY--
AHH, THE LOOK ON THEIR FACES.
I NEVER GET TIRED OF IT.
CLIMB ABOARD. SHUT THE DOOR FIRMLY, IF YOU WOULD.
KSHOOM SUPER HERO TOURS WELCOMES YOU TO YOUR PERSONAL TOUR OF MANHATTAN, THE SUPER HERO CAPITAL OF THE WORLD!
NO SIGHTINGS GUARANTEED, OF COURSE, BUT I THINK WE'VE GOT SOMETHING PRETTY SPECIAL FOR YOU TODAY.
#KSHOOM
PLEASE DON'T MESS WITH ANY OF THE CONTROLS-- YOU WOULDN'T WANT YOUR MODULE TO GO SAILING OFF ON ITS OWN.
HUH?
AND HOLD TIGHT TO THE HAND-GRIPS--
--REED RICHARDS DIDN'T INSTALL SEAT BELTS, AND THE INERTIAL DAMPERS ONLY DO SO MUCH.
#KSHOOM
THEIR CONTROLS ARE DISABLED, OF COURSE. BUT IT'S MORE OF A THRILL FOR THEM IF THEY DON'T KNOW THAT.

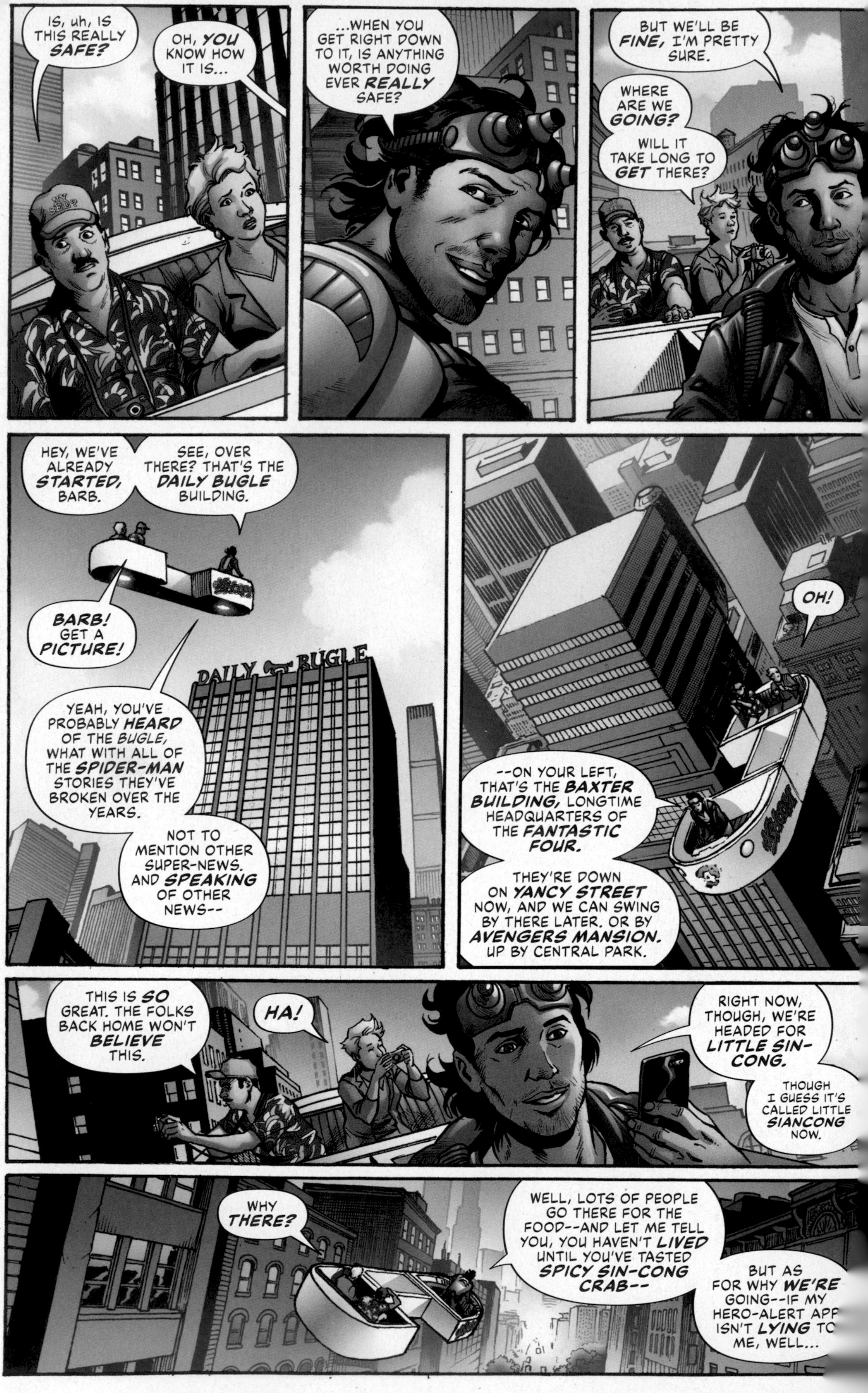
IS, uh, IS THIS REALLY SAFE?
OH, YOU KNOW HOW IT IS...
...WHEN YOU GET RIGHT DOWN TO IT, IS ANYTHING WORTH DOING EVER REALLY SAFE?
BUT WE'LL BE FINE, I'M PRETTY SURE.
WHERE ARE WE GOING?
WILL IT TAKE LONG TO GET THERE?
HEY, WE'VE ALREADY STARTED, BARB.
SEE, OVER THERE? THAT'S THE DAILY BUGLE BUILDING.
BARB! GET A PICTURE!
DAILY BUGLE
YEAH, YOU'VE PROBABLY HEARD OF THE BUGLE, WHAT WITH ALL OF THE SPIDER-MAN STORIES THEY'VE BROKEN OVER THE YEARS.
NOT TO MENTION OTHER SUPER-NEWS. AND SPEAKING OF OTHER NEWS--
OH!
--ON YOUR LEFT, THAT'S THE BAXTER BUILDING, LONGTIME HEADQUARTERS OF THE FANTASTIC FOUR.
THEY'RE DOWN ON YANCY STREET NOW, AND WE CAN SWING BY THERE LATER. OR BY AVENGERS MANSION. UP BY CENTRAL PARK.
THIS IS SO GREAT. THE FOLKS BACK HOME WON'T BELIEVE THIS.
HA!
RIGHT NOW, THOUGH, WE'RE HEADED FOR LITTLE SIN-CONG.
THOUGH I GUESS IT'S CALLED LITTLE SIANCONG NOW.
WHY THERE?
WELL, LOTS OF PEOPLE GO THERE FOR THE FOOD--AND LET ME TELL YOU, YOU HAVEN'T LIVED UNTIL YOU'VE TASTED SPICY SIN-CONG CRAB--
BUT AS FOR WHY WE'RE GOING--IF MY HERO-ALERT APP ISN'T LYING TO ME, WELL...

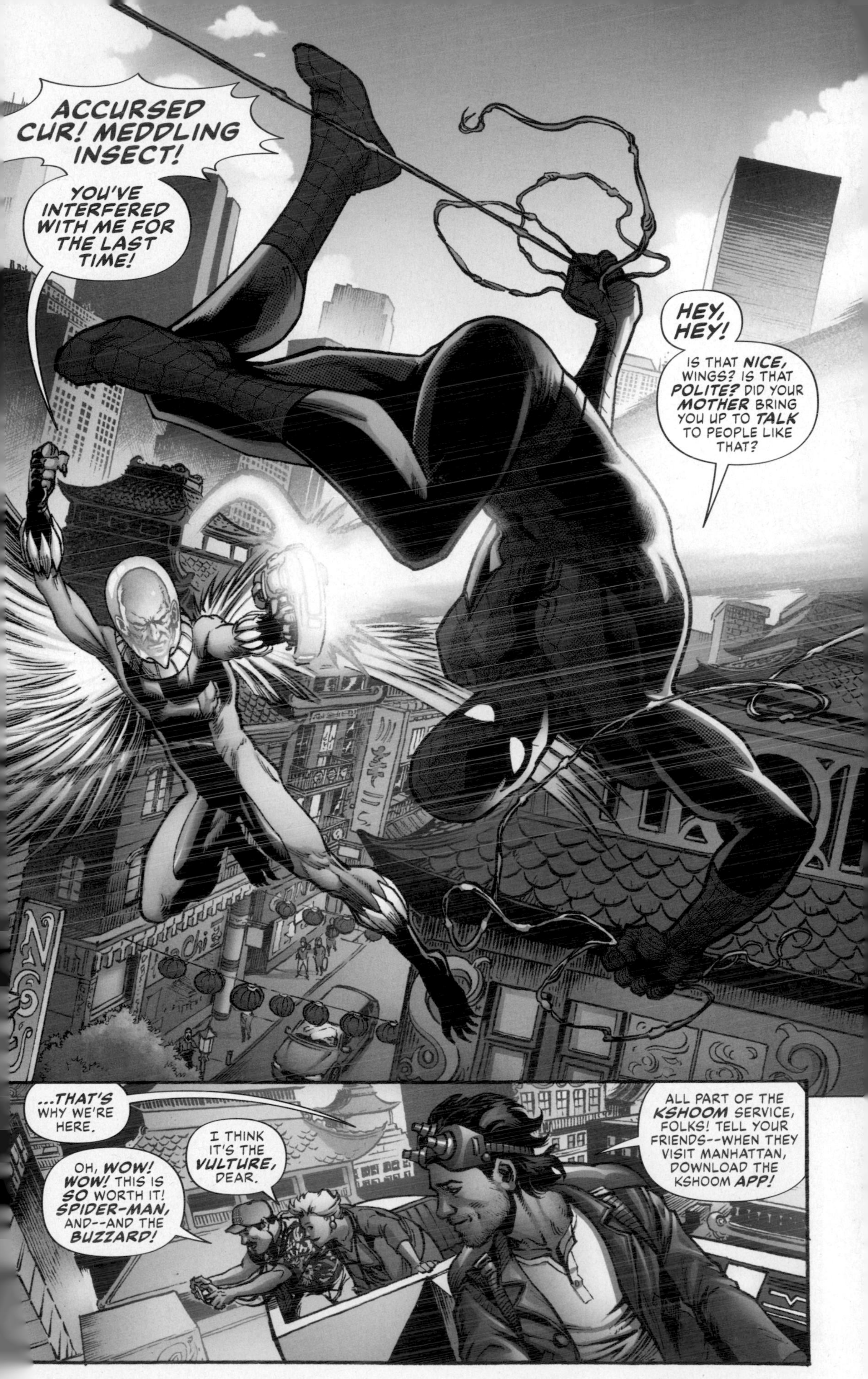
ACCURSED CUR! MEDDLING INSECT!
YOU'VE INTERFERED WITH ME FOR THE LAST TIME!
HEY, HEY!
IS THAT NICE, WINGS? IS THAT POLITE? DID YOUR MOTHER BRING YOU UP TO TALK TO PEOPLE LIKE THAT?
...THAT'S WHY WE'RE HERE.
OH, WOW! WOW! THIS IS SO WORTH IT! SPIDER-MAN, AND--AND THE BUZZARD!
I THINK IT'S THE VULTURE, DEAR.
ALL PART OF THE KSHOOM SERVICE, FOLKS! TELL YOUR FRIENDS--WHEN THEY VISIT MANHATTAN, DOWNLOAD THE KSHOOM APP!

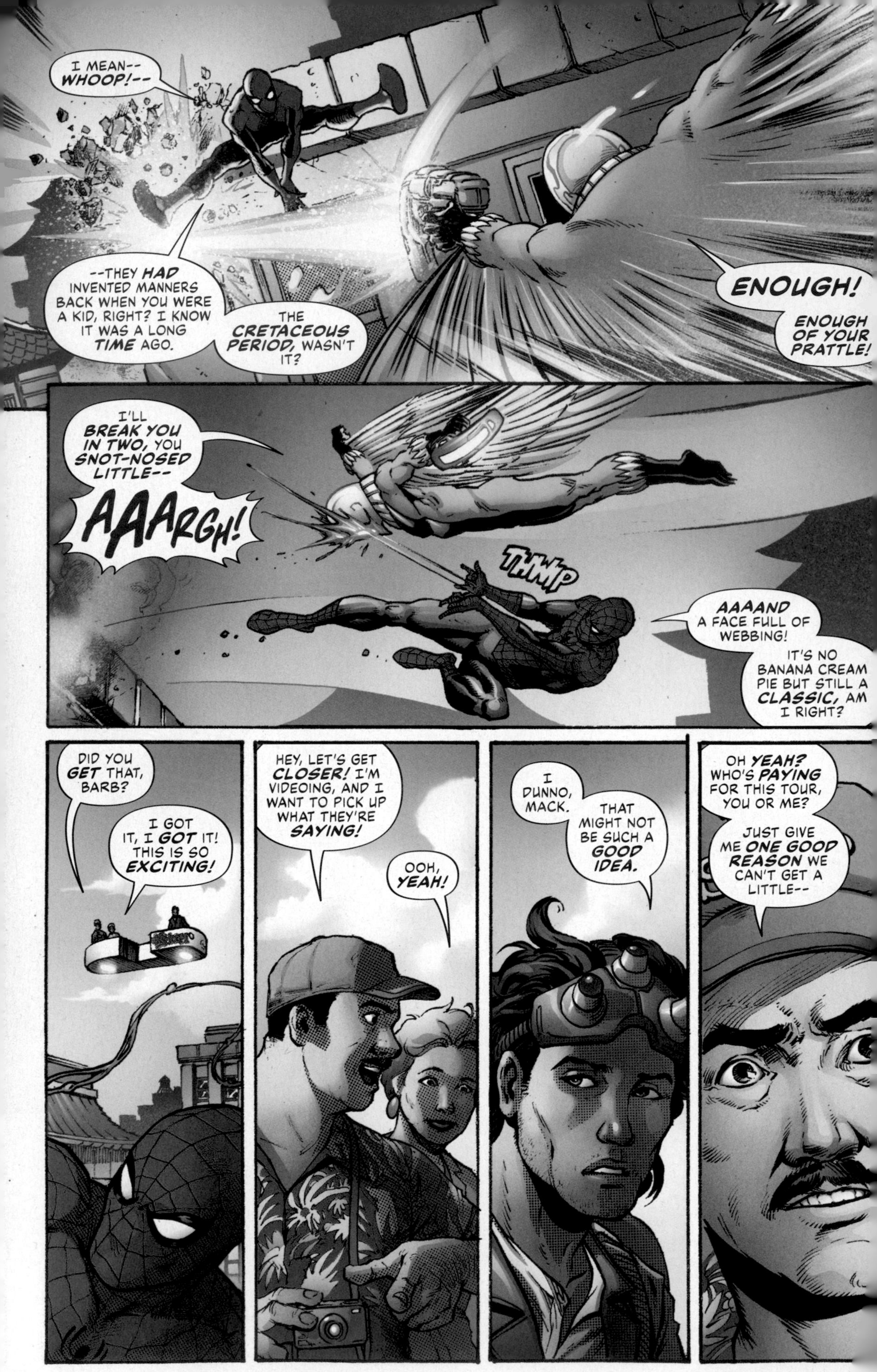

I MEAN-- WHOOP!--
--THEY HAD INVENTED MANNERS BACK WHEN YOU WERE A KID, RIGHT? I KNOW IT WAS A LONG TIME AGO.
THE CRETACEOUS PERIOD, WASN'T IT?
ENOUGH!
ENOUGH OF YOUR PRATTLE!
I'LL BREAK YOU IN TWO, YOU SNOT-NOSED LITTLE--
AAARGH!
THWIP
AAAAND A FACE FULL OF WEBBING!
IT'S NO BANANA CREAM PIE BUT STILL A CLASSIC, AM I RIGHT?
DID YOU GET THAT, BARB?
I GOT IT, I GOT IT! THIS IS SO EXCITING!
HEY, LET'S GET CLOSER! I'M VIDEOING, AND I WANT TO PICK UP WHAT THEY'RE SAYING!
OOH, YEAH!
I DUNNO, MACK.
THAT MIGHT NOT BE SUCH A GOOD IDEA.
OH YEAH? WHO'S PAYING FOR THIS TOUR, YOU OR ME?
JUST GIVE ME ONE GOOD REASON WE CAN'T GET A LITTLE--

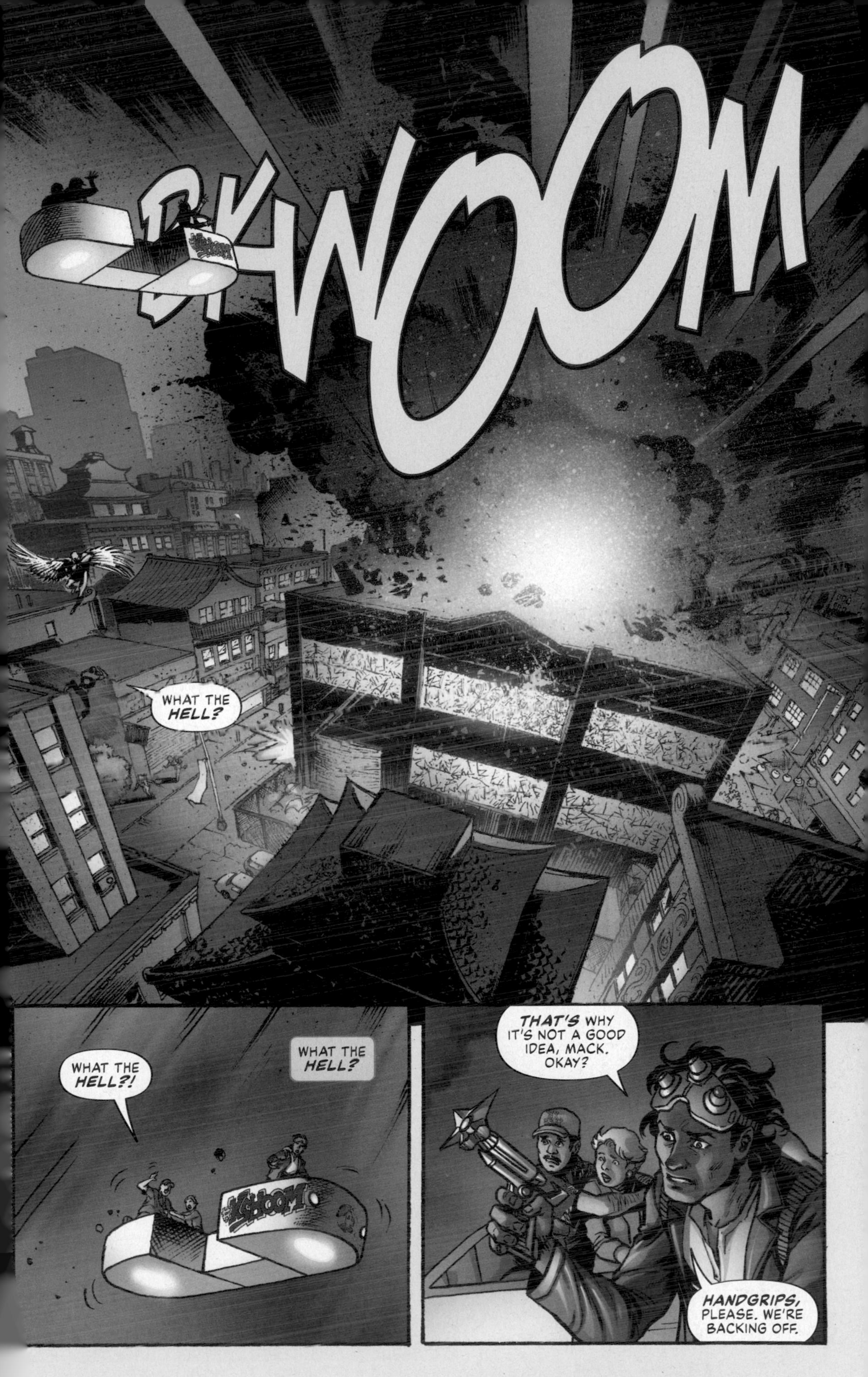
BKWOOM
WHAT THE HELL?
WHAT THE HELL?!
WHAT THE HELL?
THAT'S WHY IT'S NOT A GOOD IDEA, MACK. OKAY?
HANDGRIPS, PLEASE. WE'RE BACKING OFF.

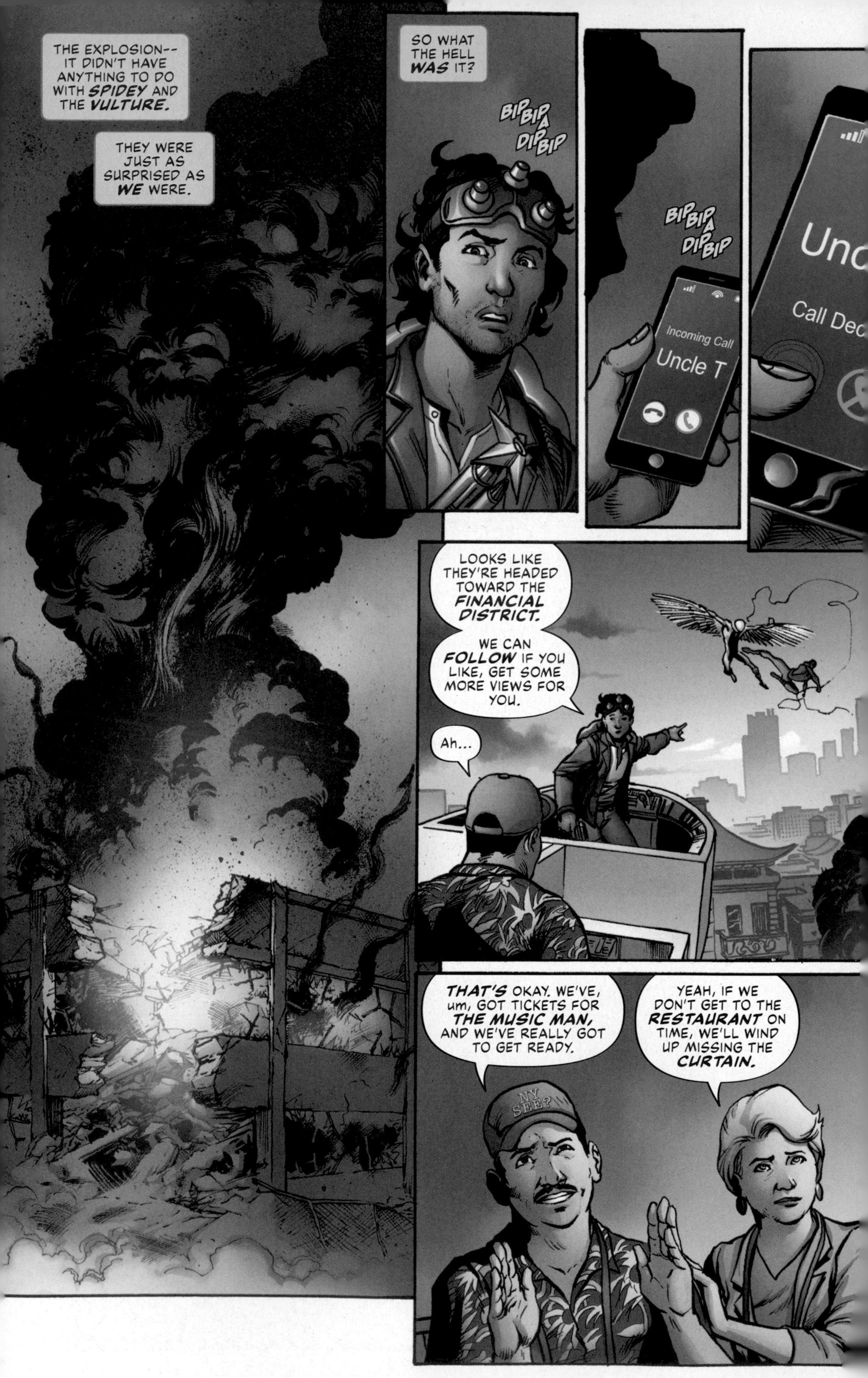
THE EXPLOSION-- IT DIDN'T HAVE ANYTHING TO DO WITH SPIDEY AND THE VULTURE.
THEY WERE JUST AS SURPRISED AS WE WERE.
SO WHAT THE HELL WAS IT?
BIP BIP A DIP BIP
BIP BIP A DIP BIP
Incoming Call
Uncle T
Unc
Call Dec
LOOKS LIKE THEY'RE HEADED TOWARD THE FINANCIAL DISTRICT.
WE CAN FOLLOW IF YOU LIKE, GET SOME MORE VIEWS FOR YOU.
Ah...
THAT'S OKAY. WE'VE, um, GOT TICKETS FOR THE MUSIC MAN, AND WE'VE REALLY GOT TO GET READY.
YEAH, IF WE DON'T GET TO THE RESTAURANT ON TIME, WE'LL WIND UP MISSING THE CURTAIN.
NY SEE?

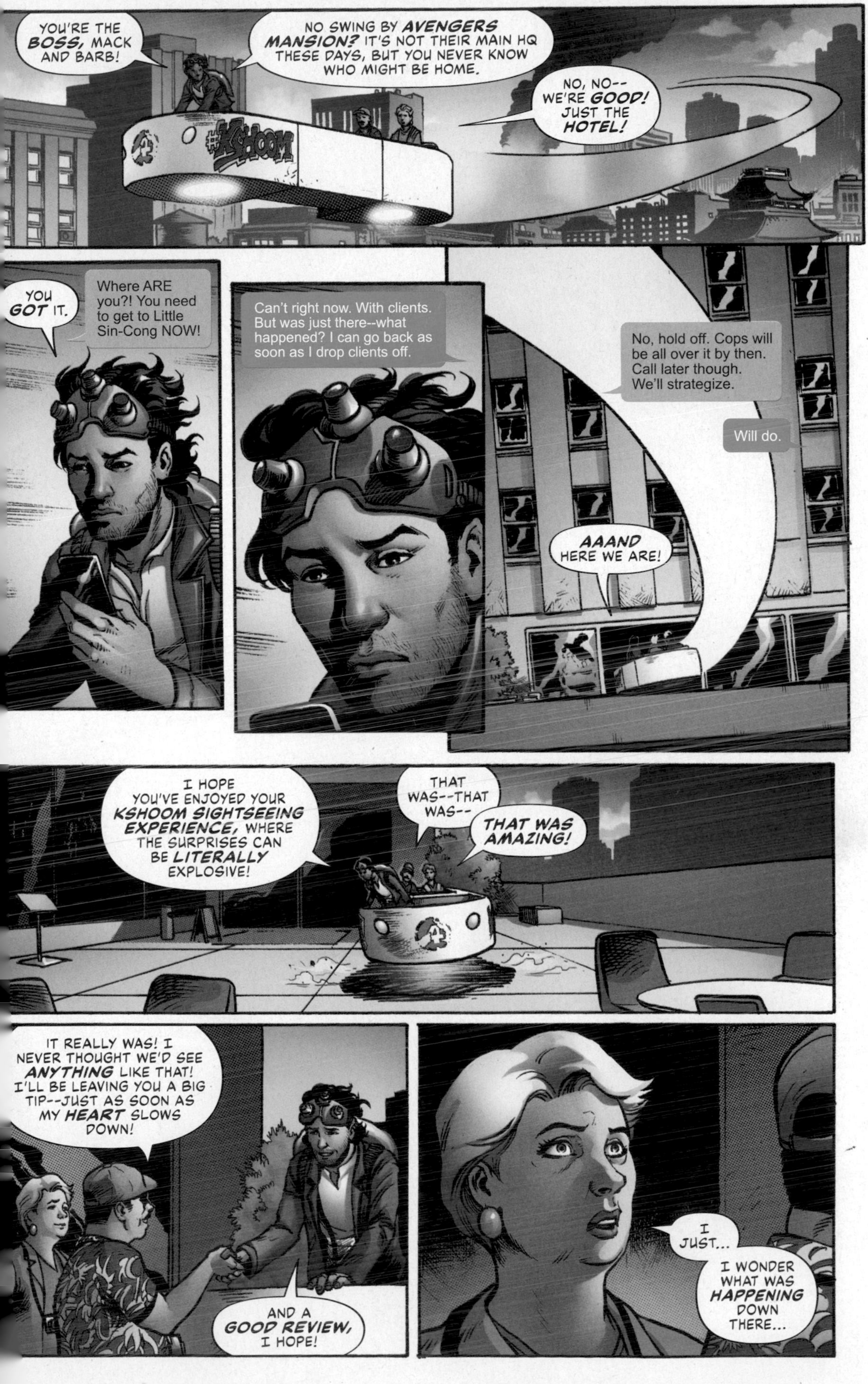
YOU'RE THE BOSS, MACK AND BARB!
NO SWING BY AVENGERS MANSION? IT'S NOT THEIR MAIN HQ THESE DAYS, BUT YOU NEVER KNOW WHO MIGHT BE HOME.
NO, NO-- WE'RE GOOD! JUST THE HOTEL!
#KSHOOM
YOU GOT IT.
Where ARE you?! You need to get to Little Sin-Cong NOW!
Can't right now. With clients. But was just there--what happened? I can go back as soon as I drop clients off.
No, hold off. Cops will be all over it by then. Call later though. We'll strategize.
Will do.
AAAND HERE WE ARE!
I HOPE YOU'VE ENJOYED YOUR KSHOOM SIGHTSEEING EXPERIENCE, WHERE THE SURPRISES CAN BE LITERALLY EXPLOSIVE!
THAT WAS--THAT WAS--
THAT WAS AMAZING!
IT REALLY WAS! I NEVER THOUGHT WE'D SEE ANYTHING LIKE THAT! I'LL BE LEAVING YOU A BIG TIP--JUST AS SOON AS MY HEART SLOWS DOWN!
AND A GOOD REVIEW, I HOPE!
I JUST...
I WONDER WHAT WAS HAPPENING DOWN THERE...

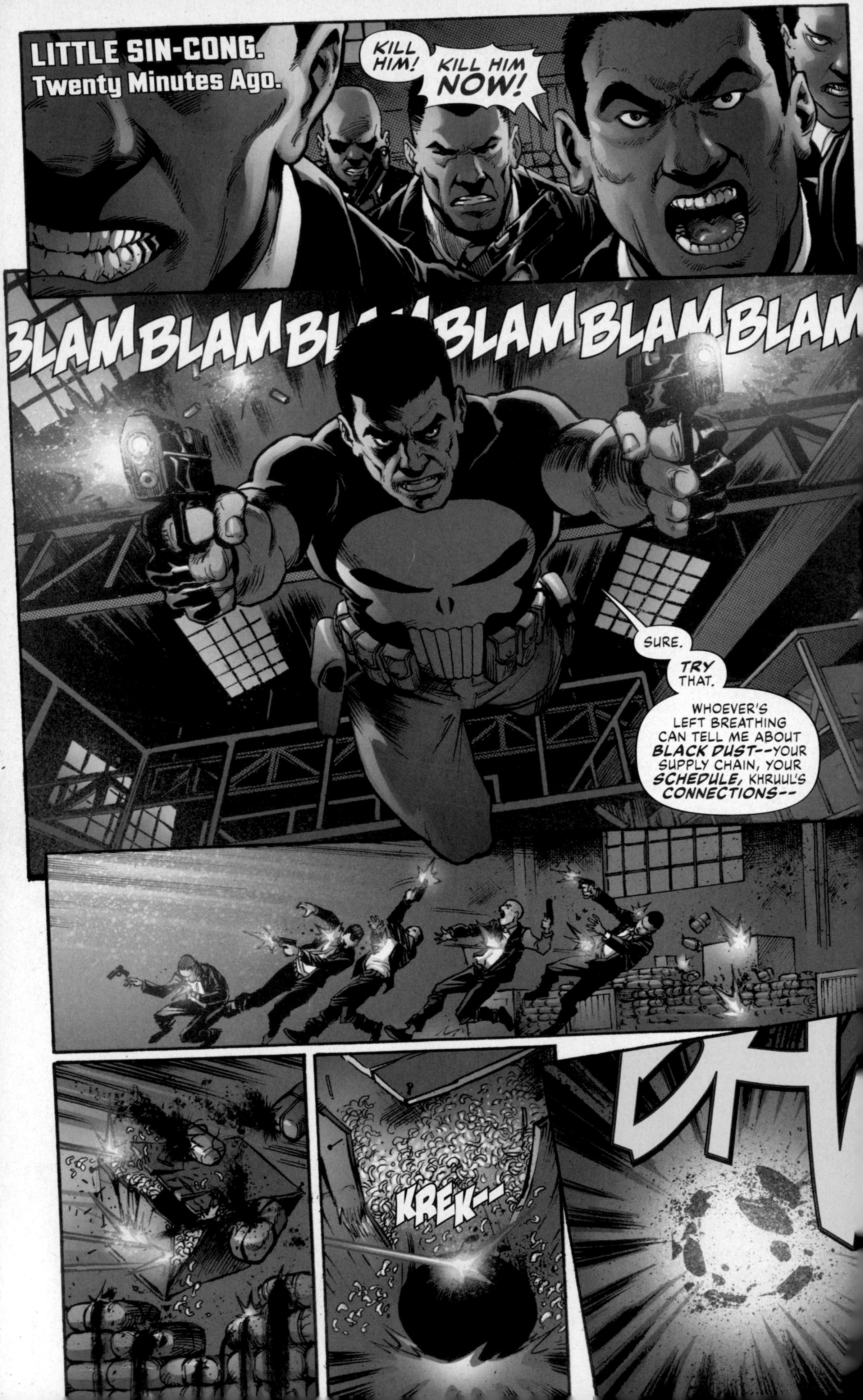

LITTLE SIN-CONG.
Twenty Minutes Ago.
KILL HIM!
KILL HIM NOW!
BLAM BLAM BLAM BLAM BLAM BLAM
SURE.
TRY THAT.
WHOEVER'S LEFT BREATHING CAN TELL ME ABOUT BLACK DUST--YOUR SUPPLY CHAIN, YOUR SCHEDULE, KHRUUL'S CONNECTIONS--
KREK--

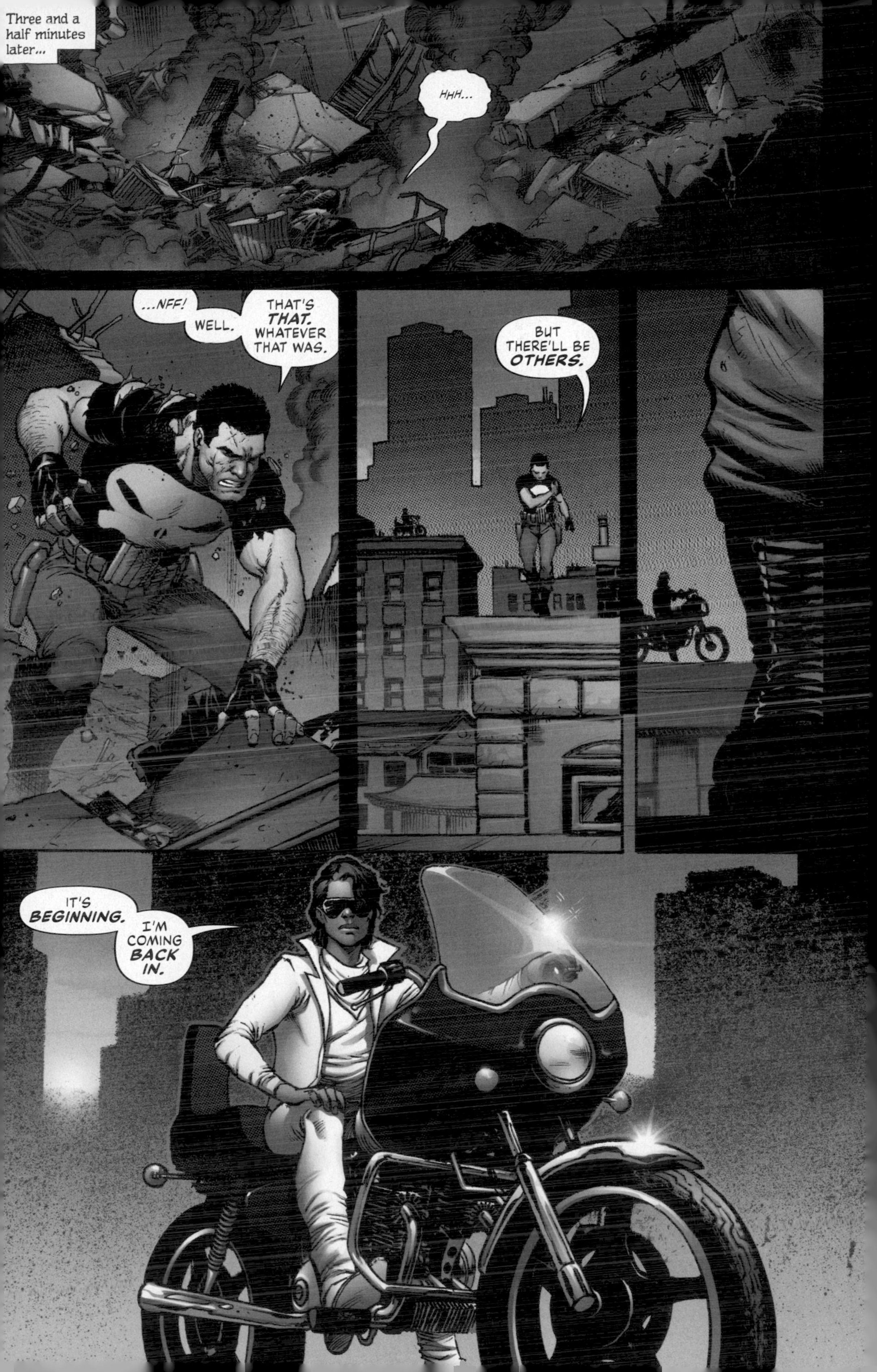

Three and a half minutes later...
HHH...
...NFF!
WELL.
THAT'S THAT. WHATEVER THAT WAS.
BUT THERE'LL BE OTHERS.
IT'S BEGINNING.
I'M COMING BACK IN.

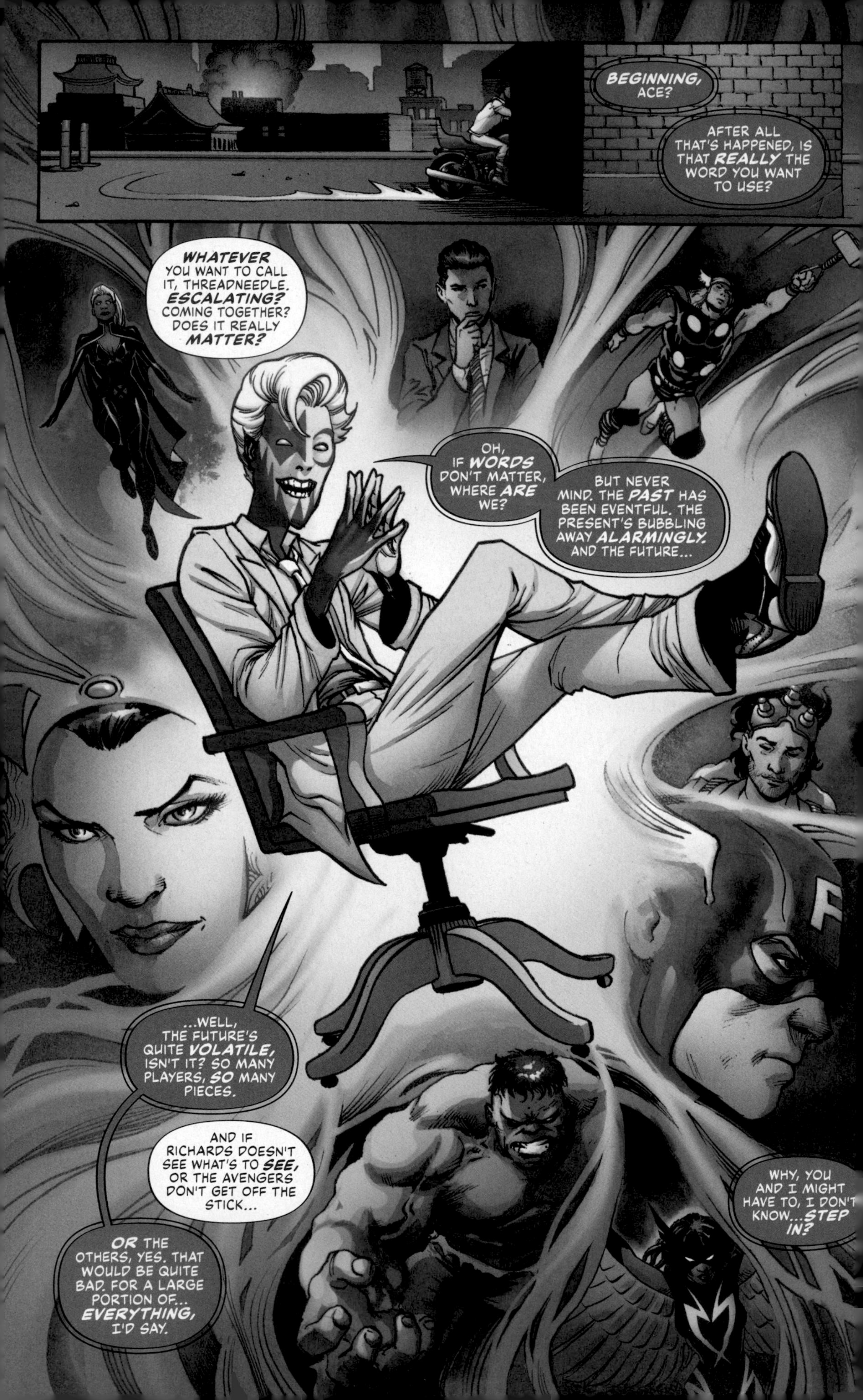

BEGINNING, ACE?
AFTER ALL THAT'S HAPPENED, IS THAT REALLY THE WORD YOU WANT TO USE?
WHATEVER YOU WANT TO CALL IT, THREADNEEDLE. ESCALATING? COMING TOGETHER? DOES IT REALLY MATTER?
OH, IF WORDS DON'T MATTER, WHERE ARE WE?
BUT NEVER MIND. THE PAST HAS BEEN EVENTFUL. THE PRESENT'S BUBBLING AWAY ALARMINGLY. AND THE FUTURE...
...WELL, THE FUTURE'S QUITE VOLATILE, ISN'T IT? SO MANY PLAYERS, SO MANY PIECES.
AND IF RICHARDS DOESN'T SEE WHAT'S TO SEE, OR THE AVENGERS DON'T GET OFF THE STICK...
OR THE OTHERS, YES. THAT WOULD BE QUITE BAD. FOR A LARGE PORTION OF... EVERYTHING, I'D SAY.
WHY, YOU AND I MIGHT HAVE TO, I DON'T KNOW...STEP IN?

#1 VARIANT BY
GABRIELE DELL'OTTO

#1 VARIANT BY
STEVE EPTING

#1 VARIANT BY
**CARLOS PACHECO, RAFAEL FONTERIZ
& FELIPE SOBREIRO**

#2 VARIANT BY
DAN PANOSIAN

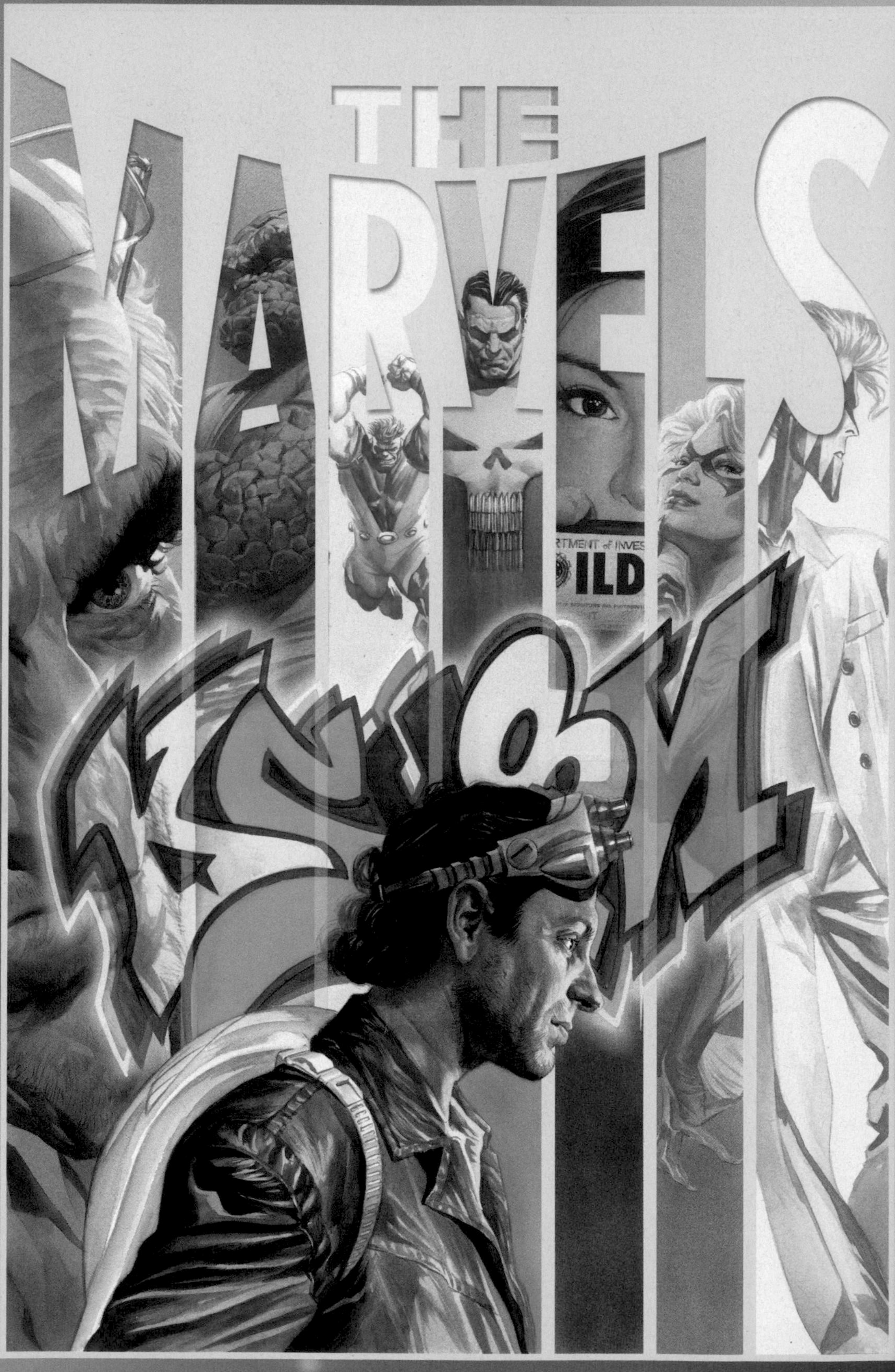
THE MARVELS

PART TWO: **"Strands and Patterns Stuff"**

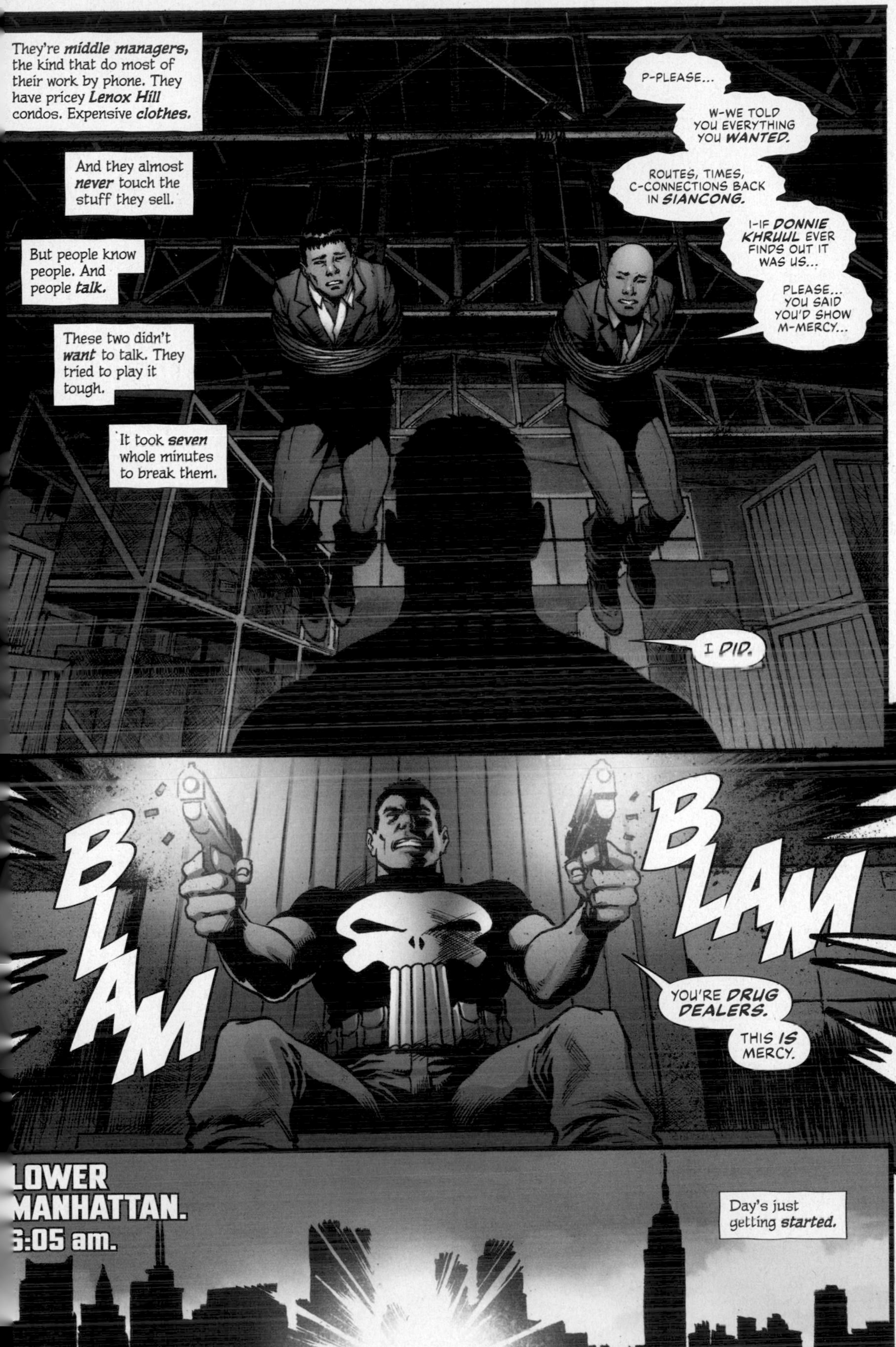
They're middle managers, the kind that do most of their work by phone. They have pricey Lenox Hill condos. Expensive clothes.
And they almost never touch the stuff they sell.
But people know people. And people talk.
These two didn't want to talk. They tried to play it tough.
It took seven whole minutes to break them.
P-PLEASE...
W-WE TOLD YOU EVERYTHING YOU WANTED.
ROUTES, TIMES, C-CONNECTIONS BACK IN SIANCONG.
I-IF DONNIE KHRUUL EVER FINDS OUT IT WAS US...
PLEASE... YOU SAID YOU'D SHOW M-MERCY...
I DID.
BLAM
BLAM
YOU'RE DRUG DEALERS.
THIS IS MERCY.
LOWER MANHATTAN. 6:05 am.
Day's just getting started.

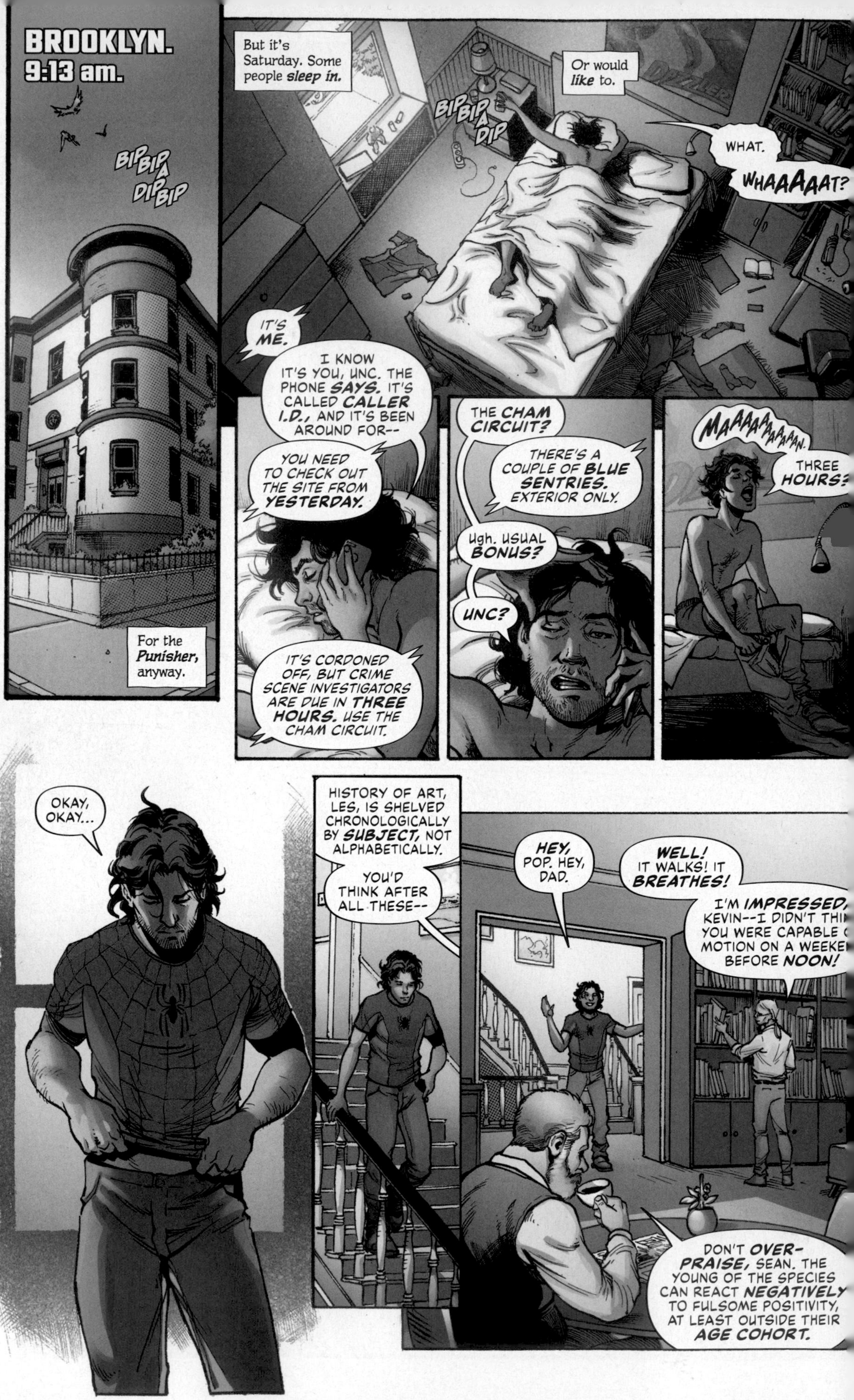
BROOKLYN.
9:13 am.
BIP BIP A DIP BIP
But it's Saturday. Some people *sleep in.*
Or would *like* to.
BIP BIP A DIP
For the *Punisher,* anyway.
WHAT.
WHAAAAAAT?
IT'S ME.
I KNOW IT'S YOU, UNC. THE PHONE SAYS. IT'S CALLED CALLER I.D., AND IT'S BEEN AROUND FOR--
YOU NEED TO CHECK OUT THE SITE FROM YESTERDAY.
IT'S CORDONED OFF, BUT CRIME SCENE INVESTIGATORS ARE DUE IN THREE HOURS. USE THE CHAM CIRCUIT.
THE CHAM CIRCUIT?
THERE'S A COUPLE OF BLUE SENTRIES. EXTERIOR ONLY.
Ugh. USUAL BONUS?
UNC?
MAAAAAAAAAAN.
THREE HOURS?
OKAY, OKAY...
HISTORY OF ART, LES, IS SHELVED CHRONOLOGICALLY BY SUBJECT, NOT ALPHABETICALLY.
YOU'D THINK AFTER ALL THESE--
HEY, POP. HEY, DAD.
WELL! IT WALKS! IT BREATHES!
I'M IMPRESSED, KEVIN--I DIDN'T THI YOU WERE CAPABLE MOTION ON A WEEKE BEFORE NOON!
DON'T OVER-PRAISE, SEAN. THE YOUNG OF THE SPECIES CAN REACT NEGATIVELY TO FULSOME POSITIVITY, AT LEAST OUTSIDE THEIR AGE COHORT.

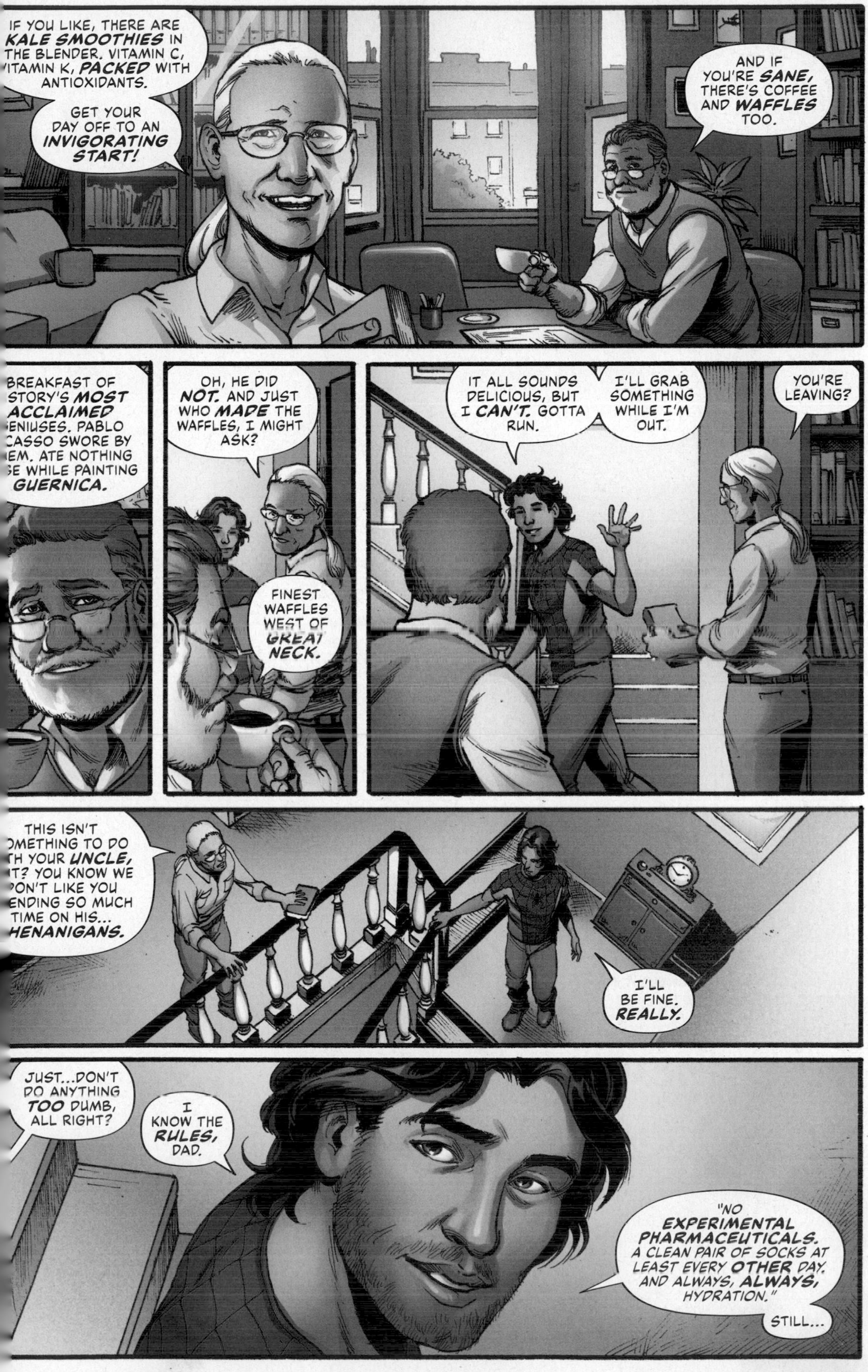

IF YOU LIKE, THERE ARE KALE SMOOTHIES IN THE BLENDER. VITAMIN C, VITAMIN K, PACKED WITH ANTIOXIDANTS.
GET YOUR DAY OFF TO AN INVIGORATING START!
AND IF YOU'RE SANE, THERE'S COFFEE AND WAFFLES TOO.
BREAKFAST OF STORY'S MOST ACCLAIMED GENIUSES. PABLO CASSO SWORE BY EM. ATE NOTHING SE WHILE PAINTING GUERNICA.
OH, HE DID NOT. AND JUST WHO MADE THE WAFFLES, I MIGHT ASK?
FINEST WAFFLES WEST OF GREAT NECK.
IT ALL SOUNDS DELICIOUS, BUT I CAN'T. GOTTA RUN.
I'LL GRAB SOMETHING WHILE I'M OUT.
YOU'RE LEAVING?
THIS ISN'T OMETHING TO DO TH YOUR UNCLE, IT? YOU KNOW WE DON'T LIKE YOU ENDING SO MUCH TIME ON HIS... HENANIGANS.
I'LL BE FINE. REALLY.
JUST...DON'T DO ANYTHING TOO DUMB, ALL RIGHT?
I KNOW THE RULES, DAD.
"NO EXPERIMENTAL PHARMACEUTICALS. A CLEAN PAIR OF SOCKS AT LEAST EVERY OTHER DAY. AND ALWAYS, ALWAYS, HYDRATION."
STILL...

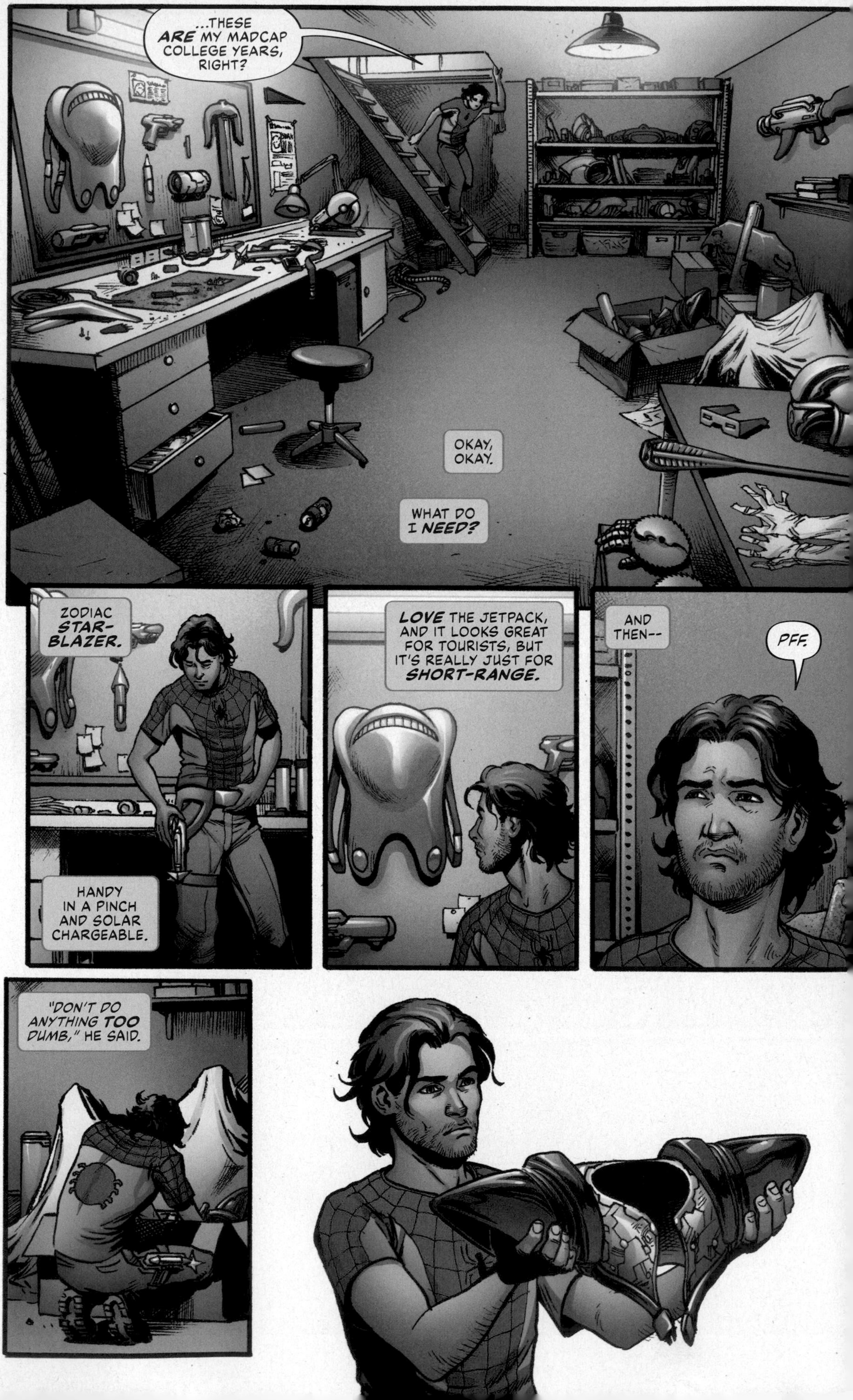

...THESE ARE MY MADCAP COLLEGE YEARS, RIGHT?
OKAY, OKAY.
WHAT DO I NEED?
ZODIAC STAR-BLAZER.
HANDY IN A PINCH AND SOLAR CHARGEABLE.
LOVE THE JETPACK, AND IT LOOKS GREAT FOR TOURISTS, BUT IT'S REALLY JUST FOR SHORT-RANGE.
AND THEN--
PFF.
"DON'T DO ANYTHING TOO DUMB," HE SAID.

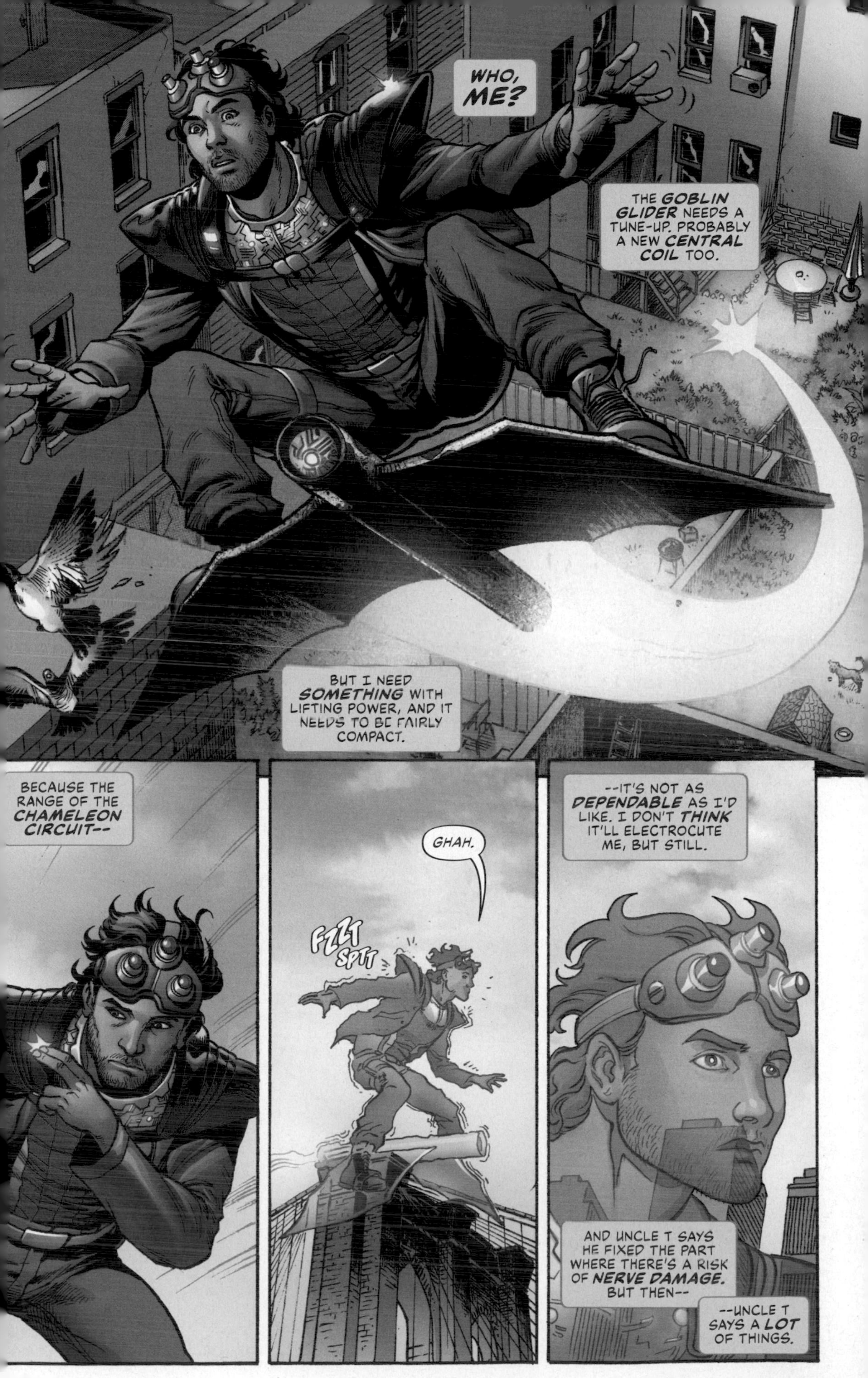
WHO, ME?
THE GOBLIN GLIDER NEEDS A TUNE-UP. PROBABLY A NEW CENTRAL COIL TOO.
BUT I NEED SOMETHING WITH LIFTING POWER, AND IT NEEDS TO BE FAIRLY COMPACT.
BECAUSE THE RANGE OF THE CHAMELEON CIRCUIT--
GHAH.
FZZT SPTT
--IT'S NOT AS DEPENDABLE AS I'D LIKE. I DON'T THINK IT'LL ELECTROCUTE ME, BUT STILL.
AND UNCLE T SAYS HE FIXED THE PART WHERE THERE'S A RISK OF NERVE DAMAGE. BUT THEN--
--UNCLE T SAYS A LOT OF THINGS.

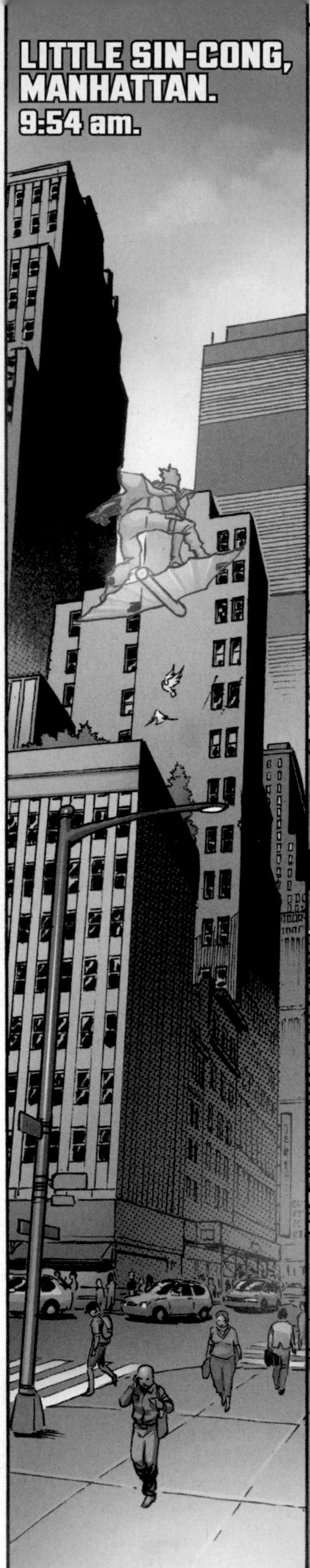
LITTLE SIN-CONG, MANHATTAN. 9:54 am.

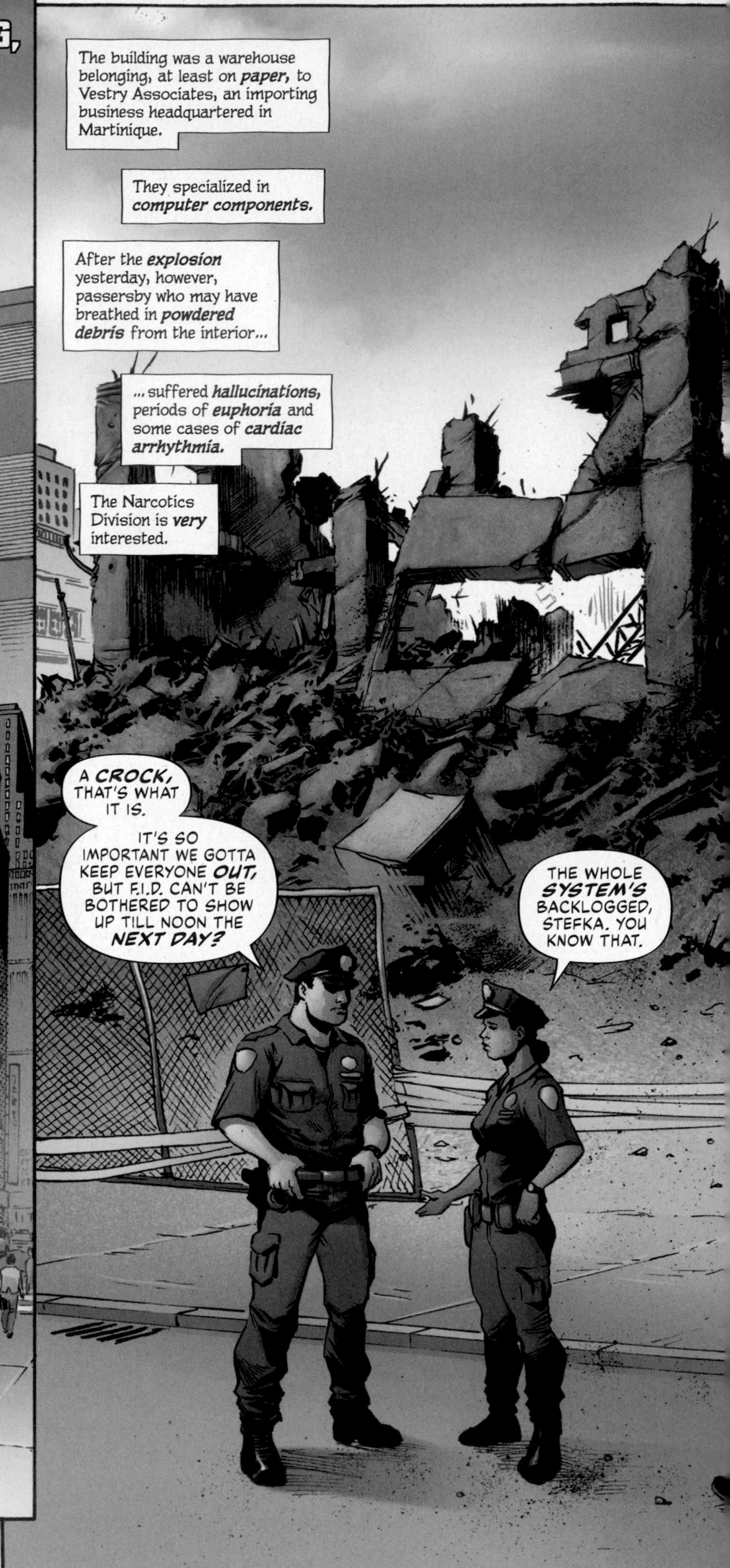
The building was a warehouse belonging, at least on paper, to Vestry Associates, an importing business headquartered in Martinique.
They specialized in computer components.
After the explosion yesterday, however, passersby who may have breathed in powdered debris from the interior...
...suffered hallucinations, periods of euphoria and some cases of cardiac arrhythmia.
The Narcotics Division is very interested.
A CROCK, THAT'S WHAT IT IS.
IT'S SO IMPORTANT WE GOTTA KEEP EVERYONE OUT, BUT F.I.D. CAN'T BE BOTHERED TO SHOW UP TILL NOON THE NEXT DAY?
THE WHOLE SYSTEM'S BACKLOGGED, STEFKA. YOU KNOW THAT.

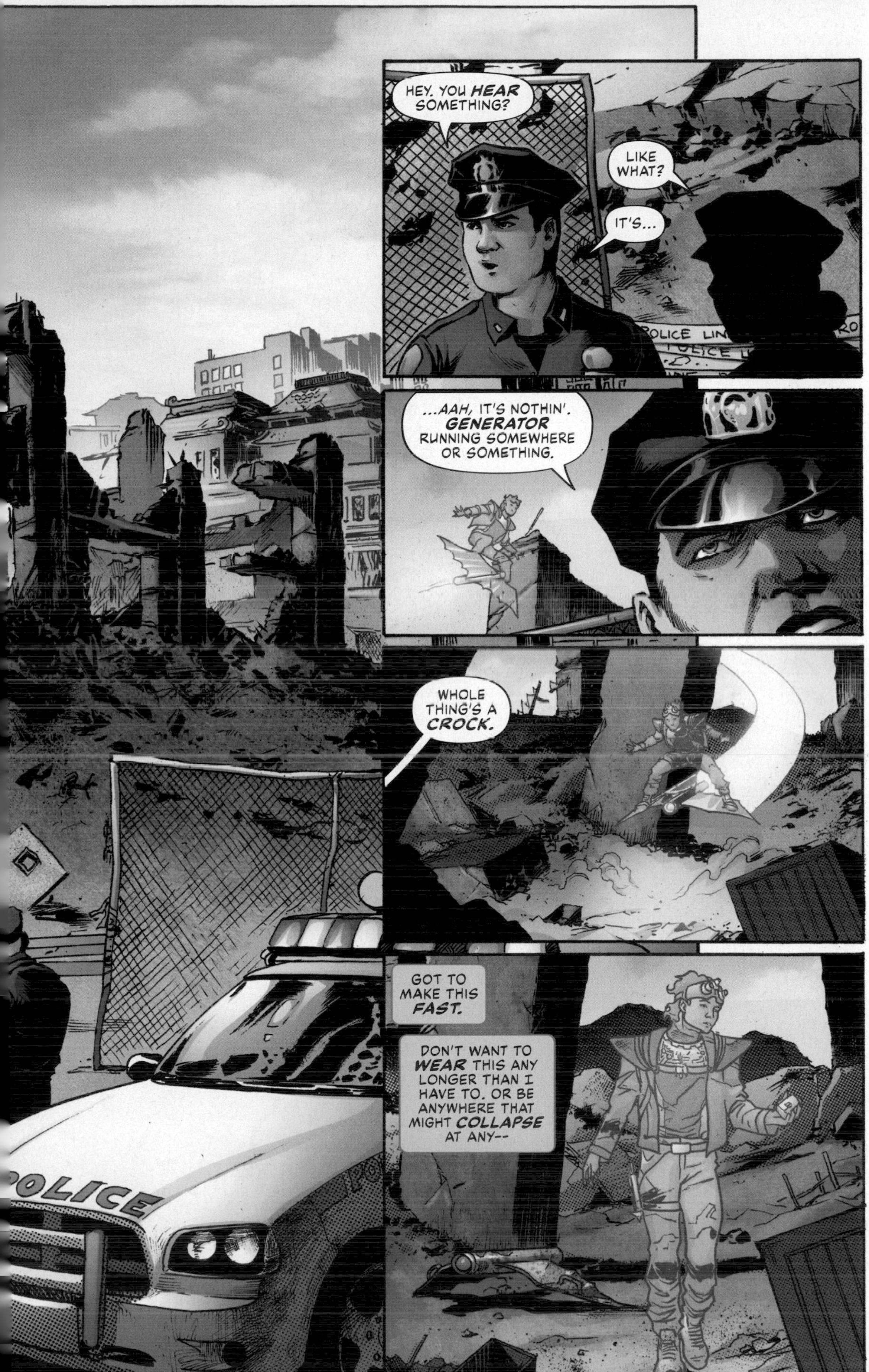
HEY. YOU HEAR SOMETHING?
LIKE WHAT?
IT'S...
POLICE LINE
...AAH, IT'S NOTHIN'. GENERATOR RUNNING SOMEWHERE OR SOMETHING.
WHOLE THING'S A CROCK.
GOT TO MAKE THIS FAST.
DON'T WANT TO WEAR THIS ANY LONGER THAN I HAVE TO. OR BE ANYWHERE THAT MIGHT COLLAPSE AT ANY--
POLICE

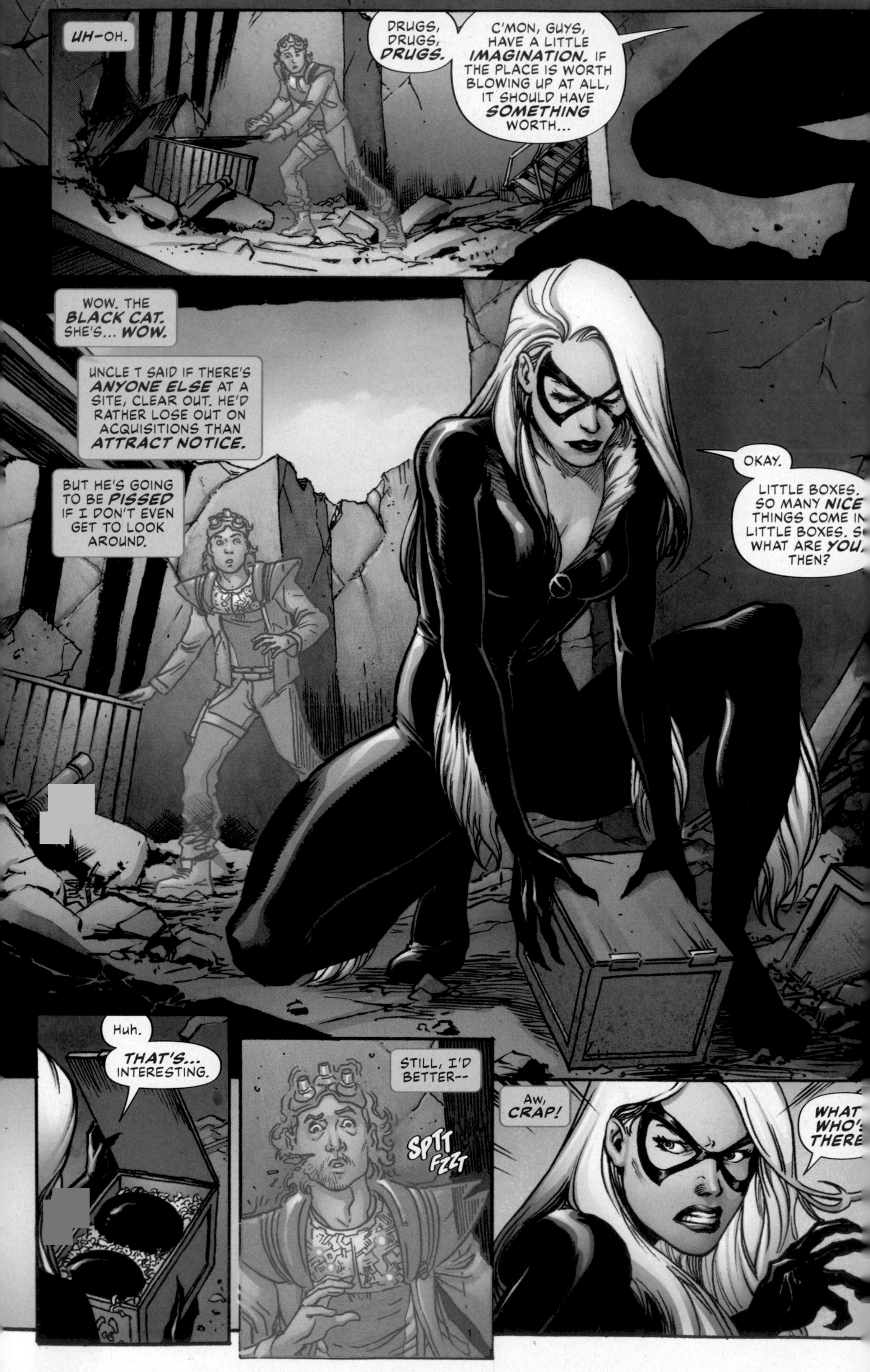
UH-OH.
DRUGS, DRUGS, DRUGS.
C'MON, GUYS, HAVE A LITTLE IMAGINATION. IF THE PLACE IS WORTH BLOWING UP AT ALL, IT SHOULD HAVE SOMETHING WORTH...
WOW. THE BLACK CAT. SHE'S... WOW.
UNCLE T SAID IF THERE'S ANYONE ELSE AT A SITE, CLEAR OUT. HE'D RATHER LOSE OUT ON ACQUISITIONS THAN ATTRACT NOTICE.
BUT HE'S GOING TO BE PISSED IF I DON'T EVEN GET TO LOOK AROUND.
OKAY.
LITTLE BOXES. SO MANY NICE THINGS COME IN LITTLE BOXES. SO WHAT ARE YOU, THEN?
Huh. THAT'S... INTERESTING.
STILL, I'D BETTER--
SPTT FZZT
Aw, CRAP!

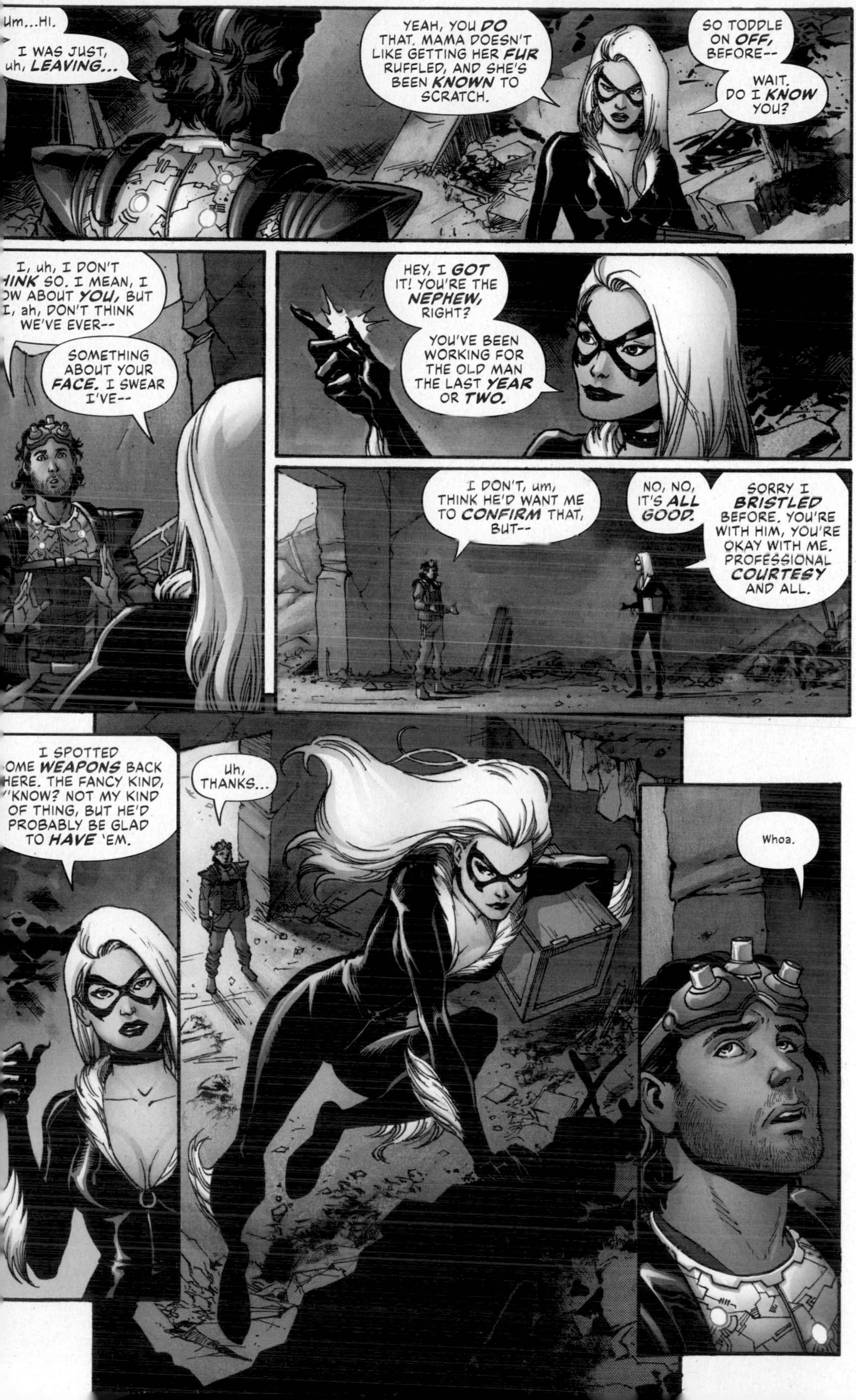
Um...Hi.
I WAS JUST, uh, LEAVING...
YEAH, YOU DO THAT. MAMA DOESN'T LIKE GETTING HER FUR RUFFLED, AND SHE'S BEEN KNOWN TO SCRATCH.
SO TODDLE ON OFF, BEFORE--
WAIT. DO I KNOW YOU?
I, uh, I DON'T HINK SO. I MEAN, I OW ABOUT YOU, BUT I, ah, DON'T THINK WE'VE EVER--
SOMETHING ABOUT YOUR FACE. I SWEAR I'VE--
HEY, I GOT IT! YOU'RE THE NEPHEW, RIGHT?
YOU'VE BEEN WORKING FOR THE OLD MAN THE LAST YEAR OR TWO.
I DON'T, um, THINK HE'D WANT ME TO CONFIRM THAT, BUT--
NO, NO, IT'S ALL GOOD.
SORRY I BRISTLED BEFORE. YOU'RE WITH HIM, YOU'RE OKAY WITH ME. PROFESSIONAL COURTESY AND ALL.
I SPOTTED OME WEAPONS BACK HERE. THE FANCY KIND, 'KNOW? NOT MY KIND OF THING, BUT HE'D PROBABLY BE GLAD TO HAVE 'EM.
Uh, THANKS...
Whoa.

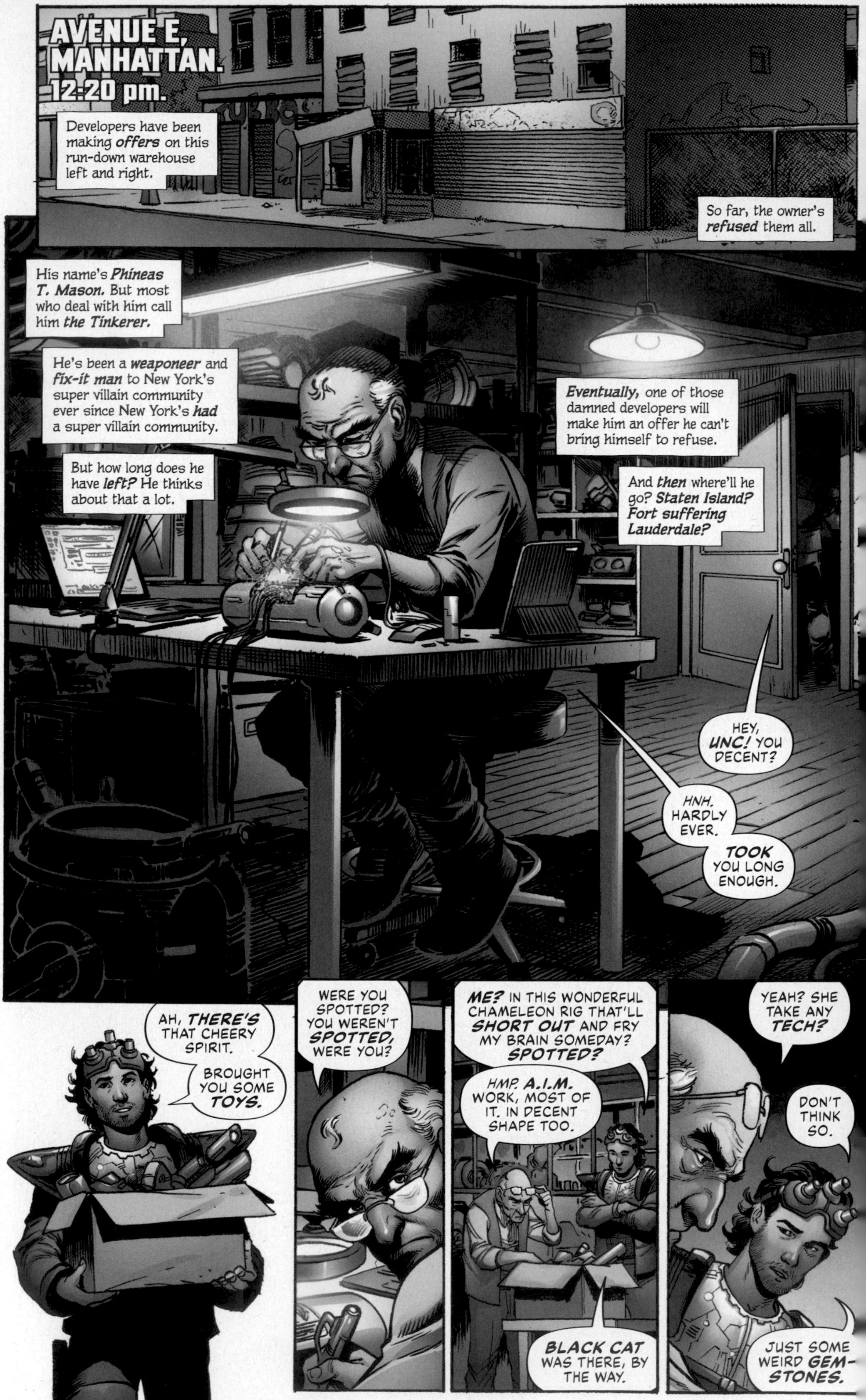
AVENUE E, MANHATTAN. 12:20 pm.
Developers have been making offers on this run-down warehouse left and right.
So far, the owner's refused them all.
His name's Phineas T. Mason. But most who deal with him call him the Tinkerer.
He's been a weaponeer and fix-it man to New York's super villain community ever since New York's had a super villain community.
But how long does he have left? He thinks about that a lot.
Eventually, one of those damned developers will make him an offer he can't bring himself to refuse.
And then where'll he go? Staten Island? Fort suffering Lauderdale?
HEY, UNC! YOU DECENT?
HNH. HARDLY EVER.
TOOK YOU LONG ENOUGH.
AH, THERE'S THAT CHEERY SPIRIT.
BROUGHT YOU SOME TOYS.
WERE YOU SPOTTED? YOU WEREN'T SPOTTED, WERE YOU?
ME? IN THIS WONDERFUL CHAMELEON RIG THAT'LL SHORT OUT AND FRY MY BRAIN SOMEDAY? SPOTTED?
HMP. A.I.M. WORK, MOST OF IT. IN DECENT SHAPE TOO.
BLACK CAT WAS THERE, BY THE WAY.
YEAH? SHE TAKE ANY TECH?
DON'T THINK SO.
JUST SOME WEIRD GEM-STONES.

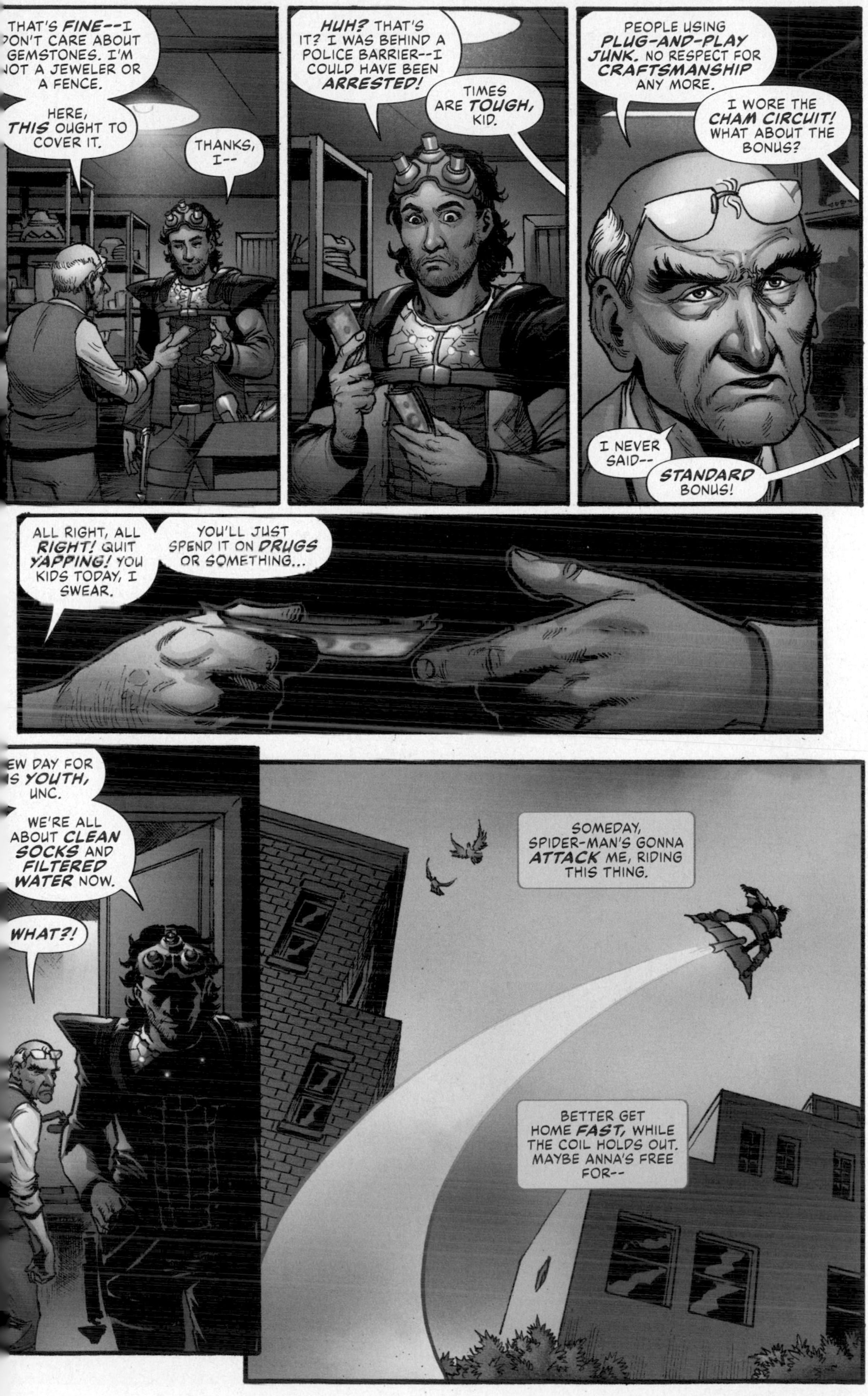

THAT'S FINE--I DON'T CARE ABOUT GEMSTONES. I'M NOT A JEWELER OR A FENCE.
HERE, THIS OUGHT TO COVER IT.
THANKS, I--
HUH? THAT'S IT? I WAS BEHIND A POLICE BARRIER--I COULD HAVE BEEN ARRESTED!
TIMES ARE TOUGH, KID.
PEOPLE USING PLUG-AND-PLAY JUNK. NO RESPECT FOR CRAFTSMANSHIP ANY MORE.
I WORE THE CHAM CIRCUIT! WHAT ABOUT THE BONUS?
I NEVER SAID--
STANDARD BONUS!
ALL RIGHT, ALL RIGHT! QUIT YAPPING! YOU KIDS TODAY, I SWEAR.
YOU'LL JUST SPEND IT ON DRUGS OR SOMETHING...
EW DAY FOR S YOUTH, UNC.
WE'RE ALL ABOUT CLEAN SOCKS AND FILTERED WATER NOW.
WHAT?!
SOMEDAY, SPIDER-MAN'S GONNA ATTACK ME, RIDING THIS THING.
BETTER GET HOME FAST, WHILE THE COIL HOLDS OUT. MAYBE ANNA'S FREE FOR--

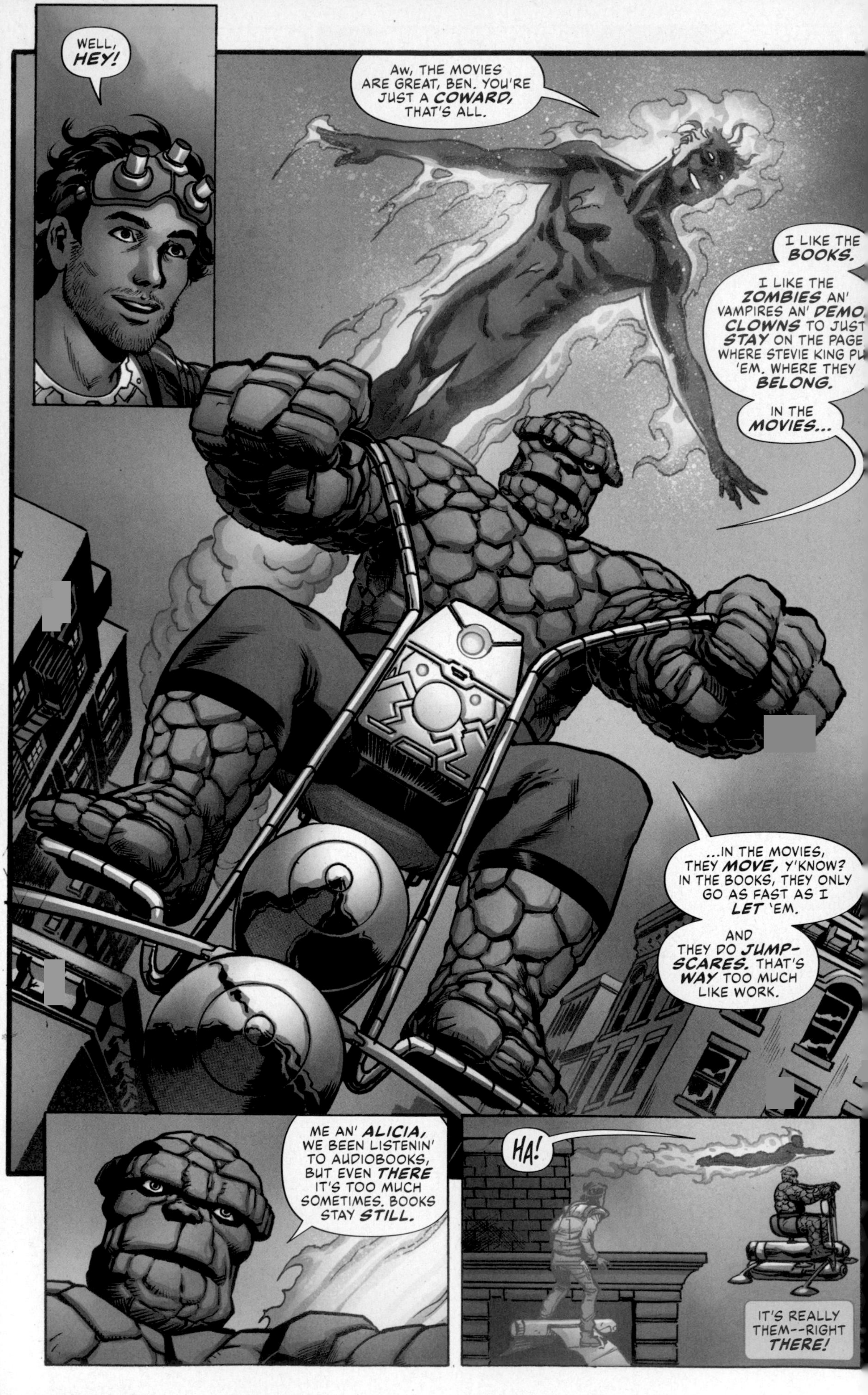
WELL, HEY!
AW, THE MOVIES ARE GREAT, BEN. YOU'RE JUST A COWARD, THAT'S ALL.
I LIKE THE BOOKS.
I LIKE THE ZOMBIES AN' VAMPIRES AN' DEMO CLOWNS TO JUST STAY ON THE PAGE WHERE STEVIE KING PU 'EM. WHERE THEY BELONG.
IN THE MOVIES...
...IN THE MOVIES, THEY MOVE, Y'KNOW? IN THE BOOKS, THEY ONLY GO AS FAST AS I LET 'EM.
AND THEY DO JUMP-SCARES. THAT'S WAY TOO MUCH LIKE WORK.
ME AN' ALICIA, WE BEEN LISTENIN' TO AUDIOBOOKS, BUT EVEN THERE IT'S TOO MUCH SOMETIMES. BOOKS STAY STILL.
HA!
IT'S REALLY THEM--RIGHT THERE!

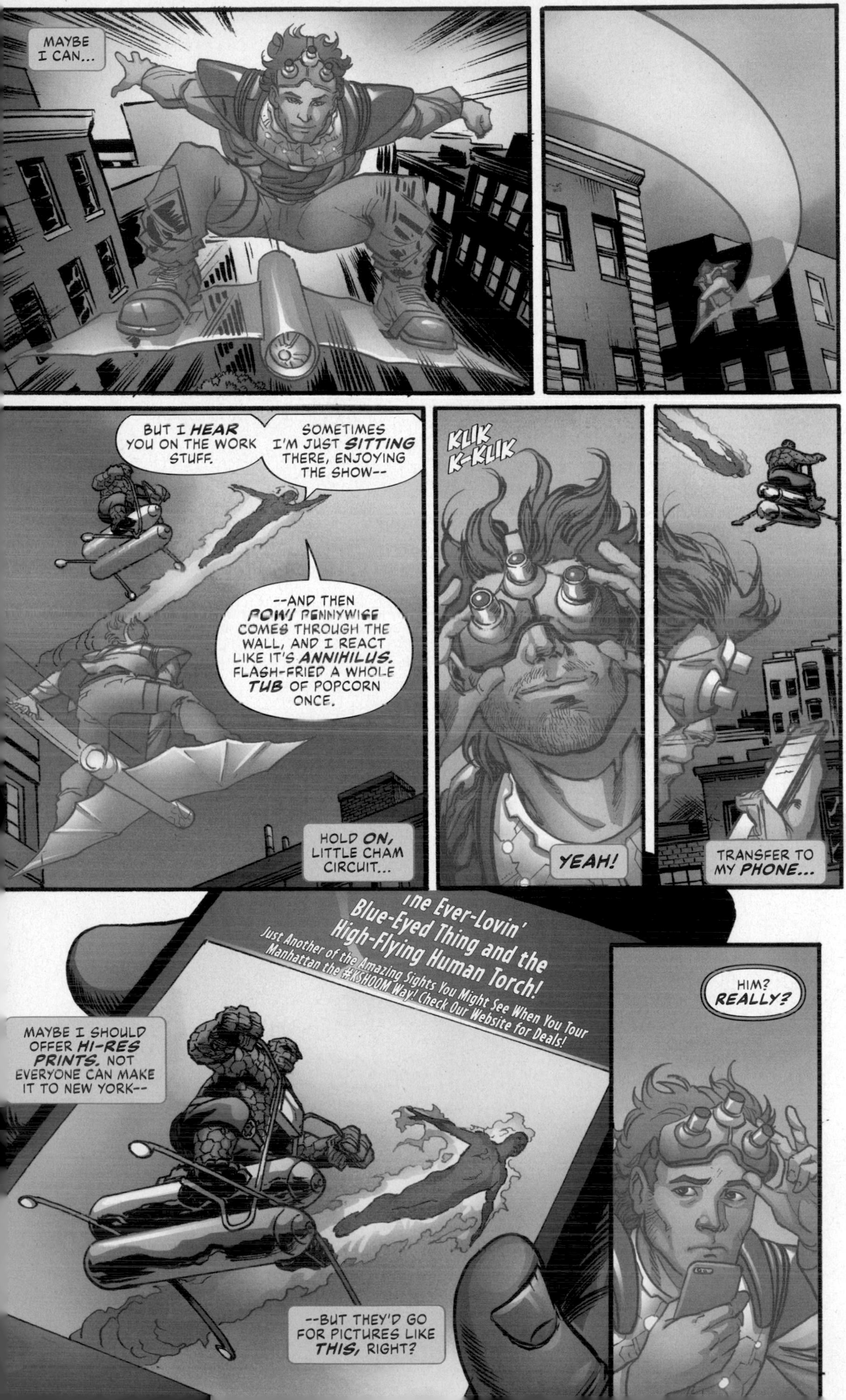
MAYBE I CAN...
BUT I HEAR YOU ON THE WORK STUFF.
SOMETIMES I'M JUST SITTING THERE, ENJOYING THE SHOW--
--AND THEN POW! PENNYWISE COMES THROUGH THE WALL, AND I REACT LIKE IT'S ANNIHILUS. FLASH-FRIED A WHOLE TUB OF POPCORN ONCE.
HOLD ON, LITTLE CHAM CIRCUIT...
KLIK K-KLIK
YEAH!
TRANSFER TO MY PHONE...
The Ever-Lovin' Blue-Eyed Thing and the High-Flying Human Torch!
Just Another of the Amazing Sights You Might See When You Tour Manhattan the #KSHOOM Way! Check Our Website for Deals!
MAYBE I SHOULD OFFER HI-RES PRINTS. NOT EVERYONE CAN MAKE IT TO NEW YORK--
--BUT THEY'D GO FOR PICTURES LIKE THIS, RIGHT?
HIM? REALLY?

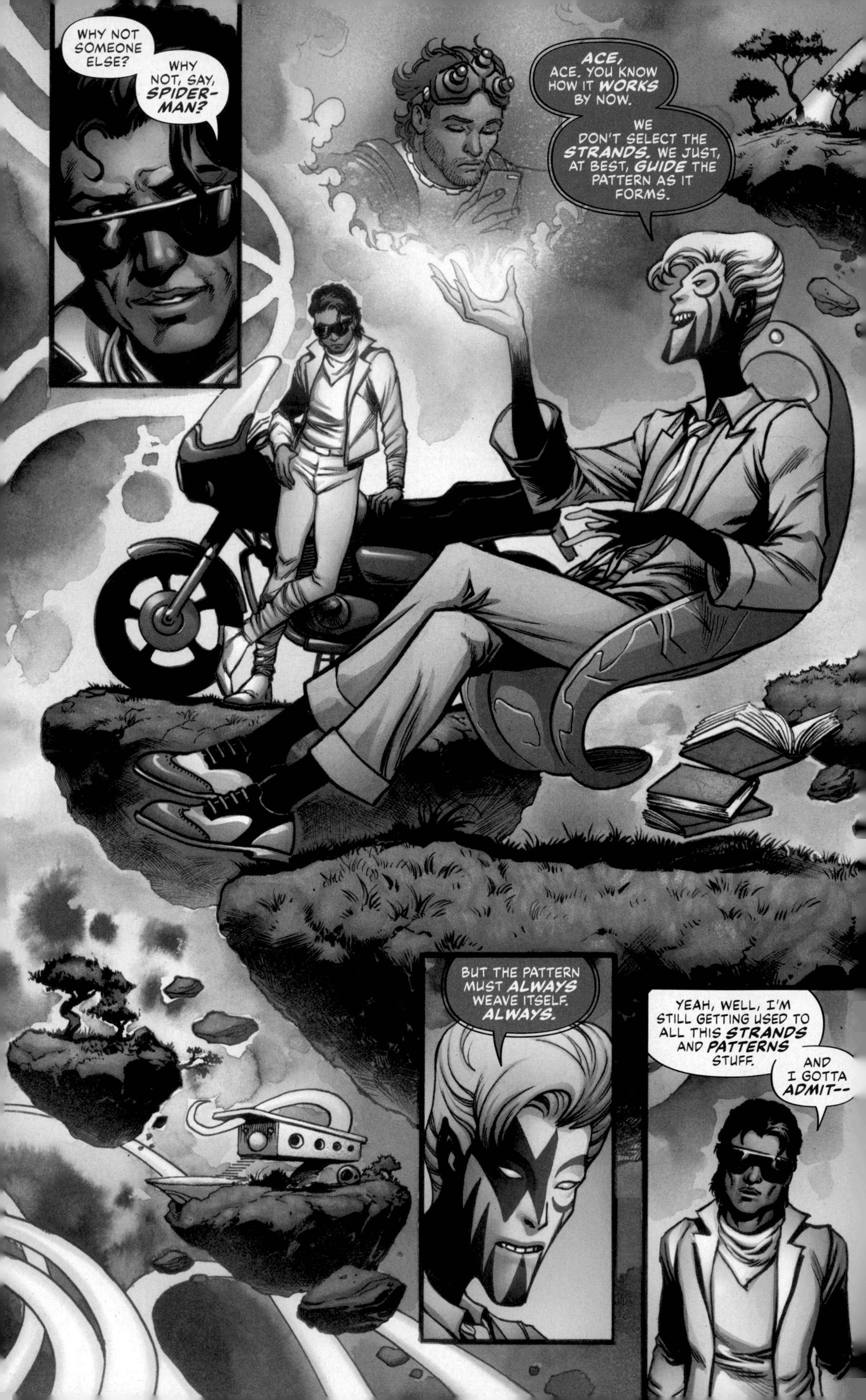
WHY NOT SOMEONE ELSE?
WHY NOT, SAY, SPIDER-MAN?
ACE, ACE. YOU KNOW HOW IT WORKS BY NOW.
WE DON'T SELECT THE STRANDS. WE JUST, AT BEST, GUIDE THE PATTERN AS IT FORMS.
BUT THE PATTERN MUST ALWAYS WEAVE ITSELF. ALWAYS.
YEAH, WELL, I'M STILL GETTING USED TO ALL THIS STRANDS AND PATTERNS STUFF.
AND I GOTTA ADMIT--

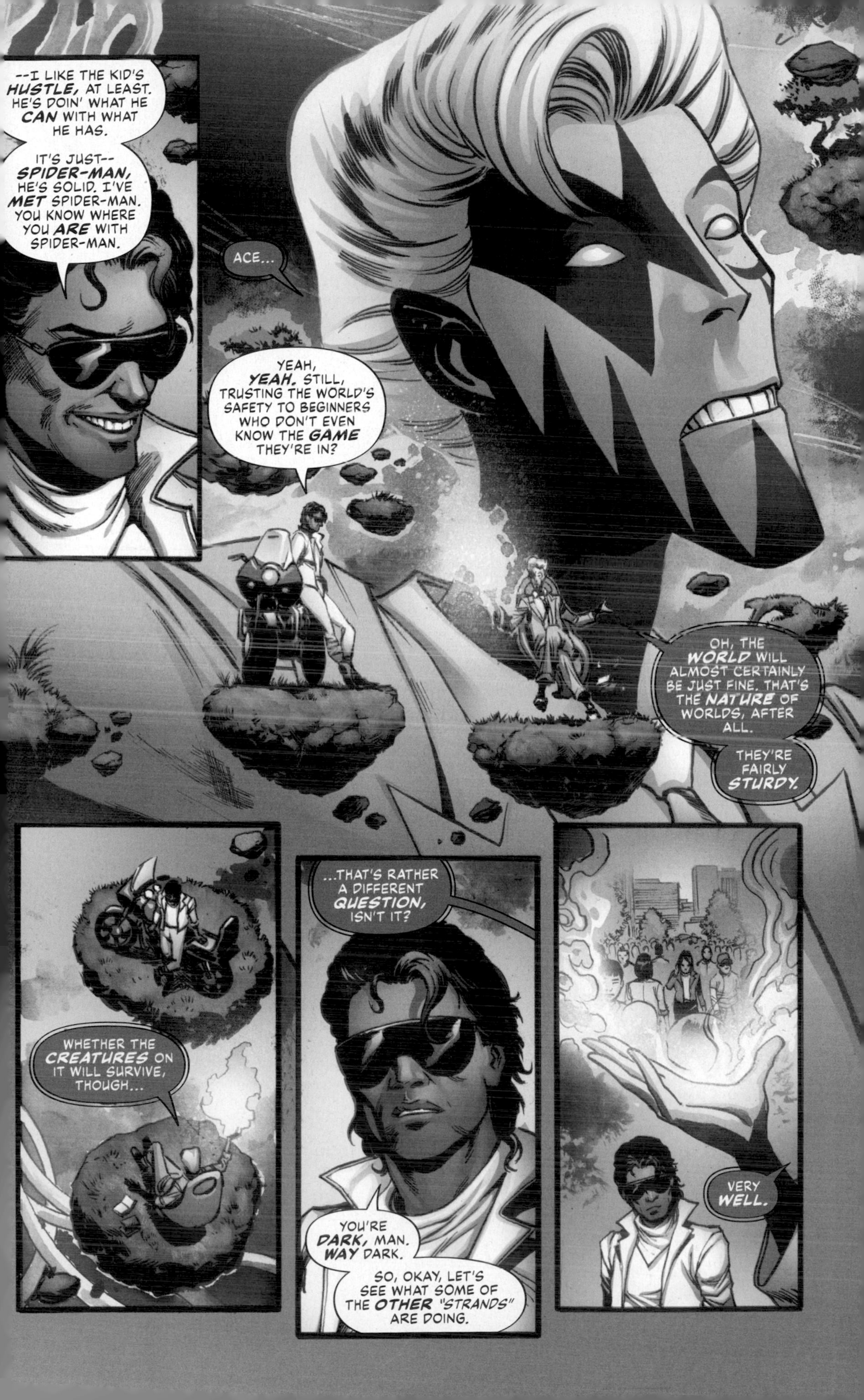
--I LIKE THE KID'S HUSTLE, AT LEAST. HE'S DOIN' WHAT HE CAN WITH WHAT HE HAS.
IT'S JUST-- SPIDER-MAN, HE'S SOLID. I'VE MET SPIDER-MAN. YOU KNOW WHERE YOU ARE WITH SPIDER-MAN.
ACE...
YEAH, YEAH. STILL, TRUSTING THE WORLD'S SAFETY TO BEGINNERS WHO DON'T EVEN KNOW THE GAME THEY'RE IN?
OH, THE WORLD WILL ALMOST CERTAINLY BE JUST FINE. THAT'S THE NATURE OF WORLDS, AFTER ALL.
THEY'RE FAIRLY STURDY.
WHETHER THE CREATURES ON IT WILL SURVIVE, THOUGH...
...THAT'S RATHER A DIFFERENT QUESTION, ISN'T IT?
YOU'RE DARK, MAN. WAY DARK.
SO, OKAY, LET'S SEE WHAT SOME OF THE OTHER "STRANDS" ARE DOING.
VERY WELL.

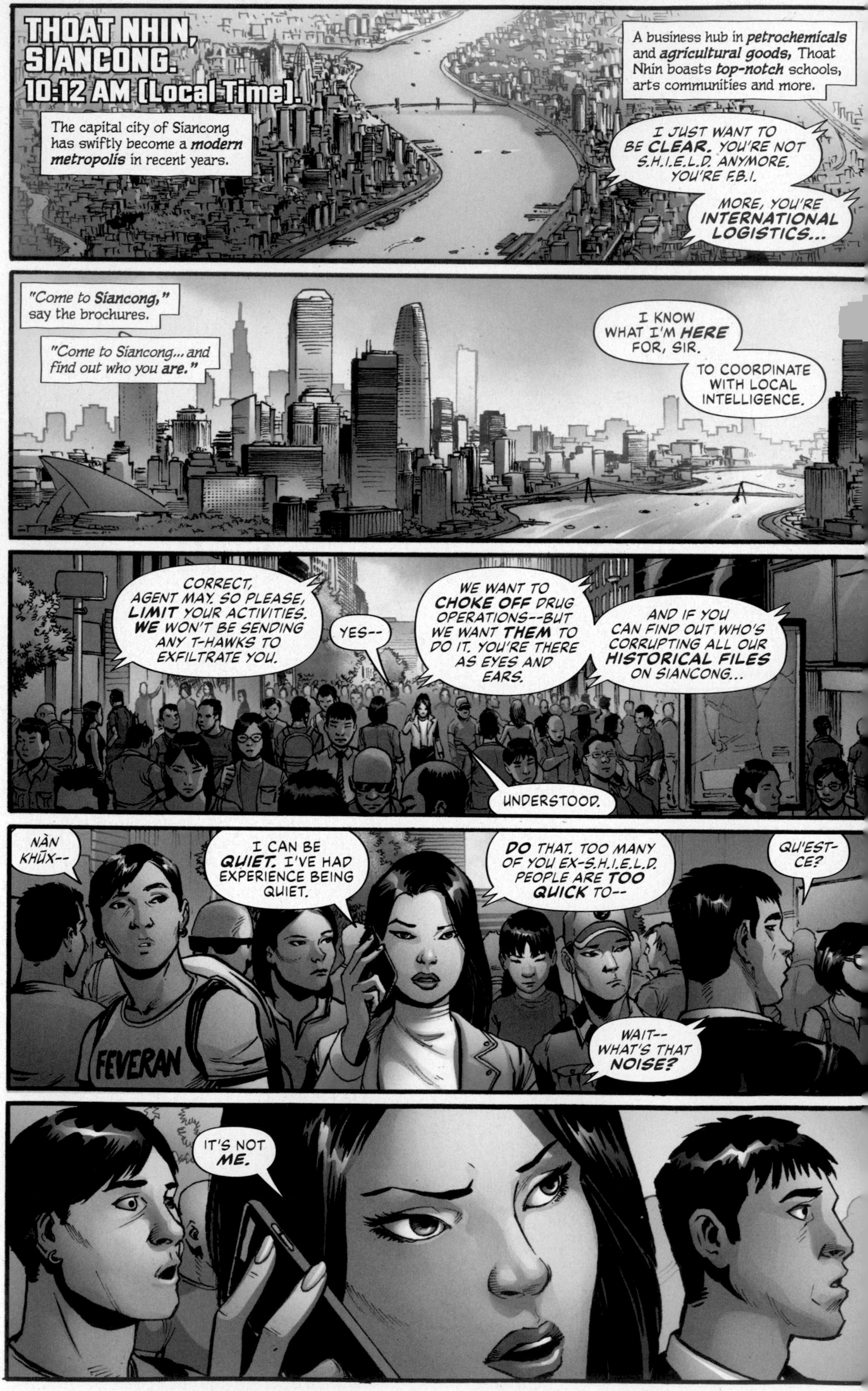
THOAT NHIN, SIANCONG. 10:12 AM (Local Time).
The capital city of Siancong has swiftly become a **modern metropolis** in recent years.
A business hub in **petrochemicals** and **agricultural goods,** Thoat Nhin boasts **top-notch** schools, arts communities and more.
I JUST WANT TO BE **CLEAR.** YOU'RE NOT S.H.I.E.L.D. ANYMORE. YOU'RE F.B.I.
MORE, YOU'RE **INTERNATIONAL LOGISTICS...**
"Come to **Siancong,**" say the brochures.
"Come to Siancong... and find out who you **are.**"
I KNOW WHAT I'M **HERE** FOR, SIR.
TO COORDINATE WITH LOCAL INTELLIGENCE.
CORRECT, AGENT MAY. SO PLEASE, **LIMIT** YOUR ACTIVITIES. **WE** WON'T BE SENDING ANY T-HAWKS TO EXFILTRATE YOU.
YES--
WE WANT TO **CHOKE OFF** DRUG OPERATIONS--BUT WE WANT **THEM** TO DO IT. YOU'RE THERE AS EYES AND EARS.
AND IF YOU CAN FIND OUT WHO'S CORRUPTING ALL OUR **HISTORICAL FILES** ON SIANCONG...
UNDERSTOOD.
NÀN KHŨX--
I CAN BE **QUIET.** I'VE HAD EXPERIENCE BEING QUIET.
DO THAT. TOO MANY OF YOU EX-S.H.I.E.L.D. PEOPLE ARE **TOO QUICK** TO--
QU'EST-CE?
FEVERAN
WAIT-- WHAT'S THAT **NOISE?**
IT'S NOT **ME.**

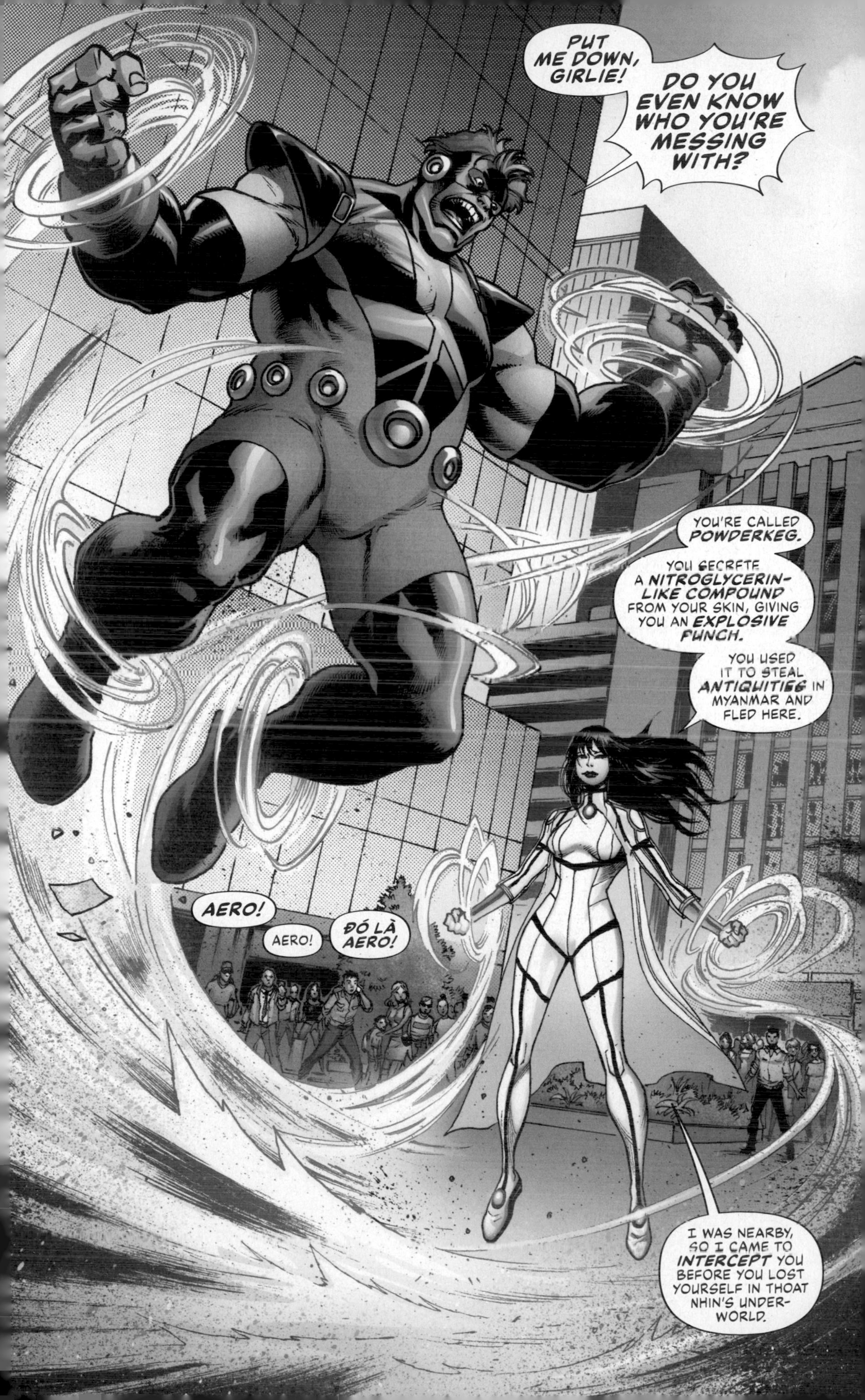
PUT ME DOWN, GIRLIE!
DO YOU EVEN KNOW WHO YOU'RE MESSING WITH?
YOU'RE CALLED POWDERKEG.
YOU SECRETE A NITROGLYCERIN-LIKE COMPOUND FROM YOUR SKIN, GIVING YOU AN EXPLOSIVE PUNCH.
YOU USED IT TO STEAL ANTIQUITIES IN MYANMAR AND FLED HERE.
AERO!
AERO!
ĐÓ LÀ AERO!
I WAS NEARBY, SO I CAME TO INTERCEPT YOU BEFORE YOU LOST YOURSELF IN THOAT NHIN'S UNDER-WORLD.

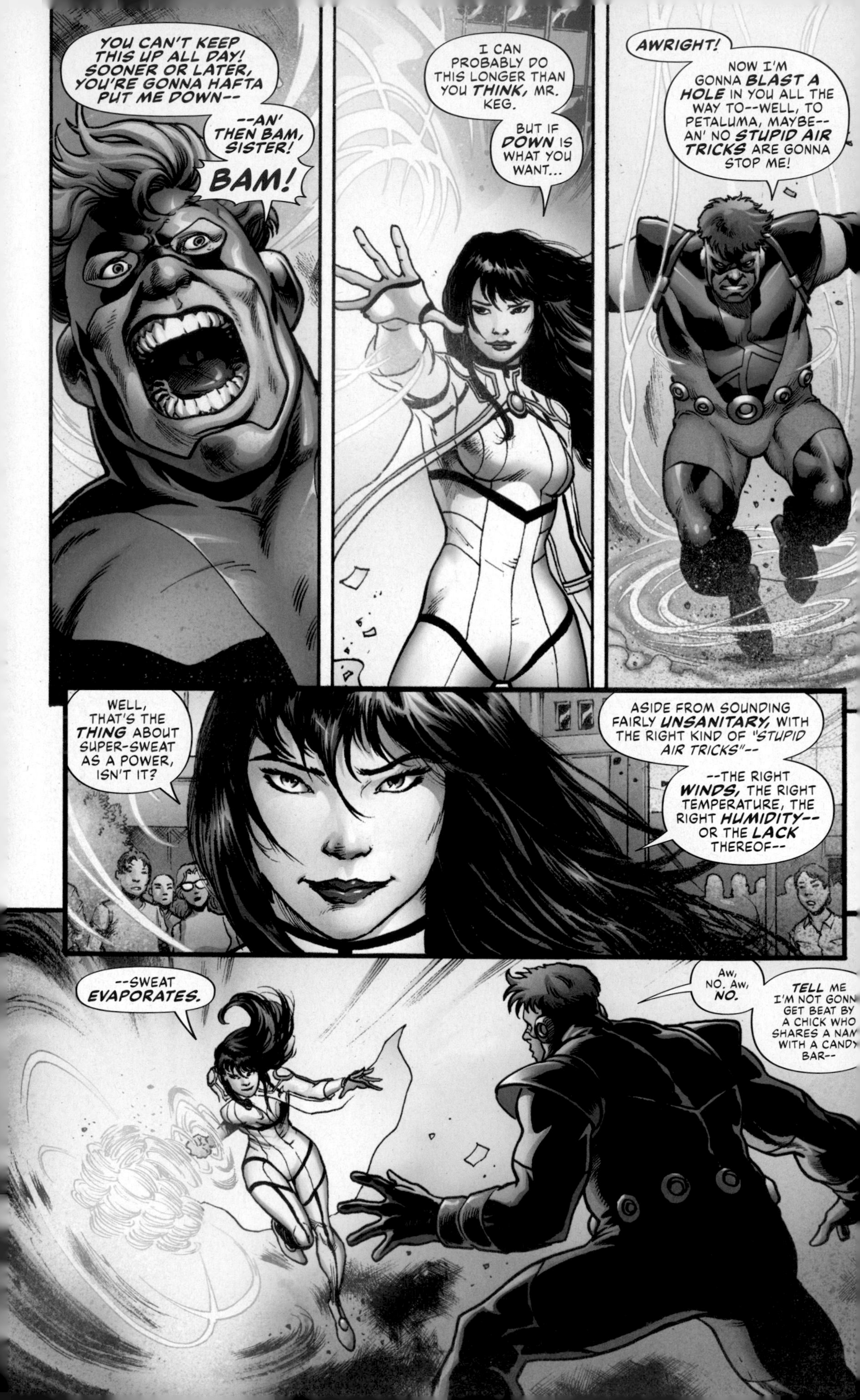
YOU CAN'T KEEP THIS UP ALL DAY! SOONER OR LATER, YOU'RE GONNA HAFTA PUT ME DOWN--
--AN' THEN BAM, SISTER!
BAM!
I CAN PROBABLY DO THIS LONGER THAN YOU THINK, MR. KEG.
BUT IF DOWN IS WHAT YOU WANT...
AWRIGHT!
NOW I'M GONNA BLAST A HOLE IN YOU ALL THE WAY TO--WELL, TO PETALUMA, MAYBE-- AN' NO STUPID AIR TRICKS ARE GONNA STOP ME!
WELL, THAT'S THE THING ABOUT SUPER-SWEAT AS A POWER, ISN'T IT?
ASIDE FROM SOUNDING FAIRLY UNSANITARY, WITH THE RIGHT KIND OF "STUPID AIR TRICKS"--
--THE RIGHT WINDS, THE RIGHT TEMPERATURE, THE RIGHT HUMIDITY-- OR THE LACK THEREOF--
--SWEAT EVAPORATES.
AW, NO. AW, NO.
TELL ME I'M NOT GONN GET BEAT BY A CHICK WHO SHARES A NAM WITH A CANDY BAR--

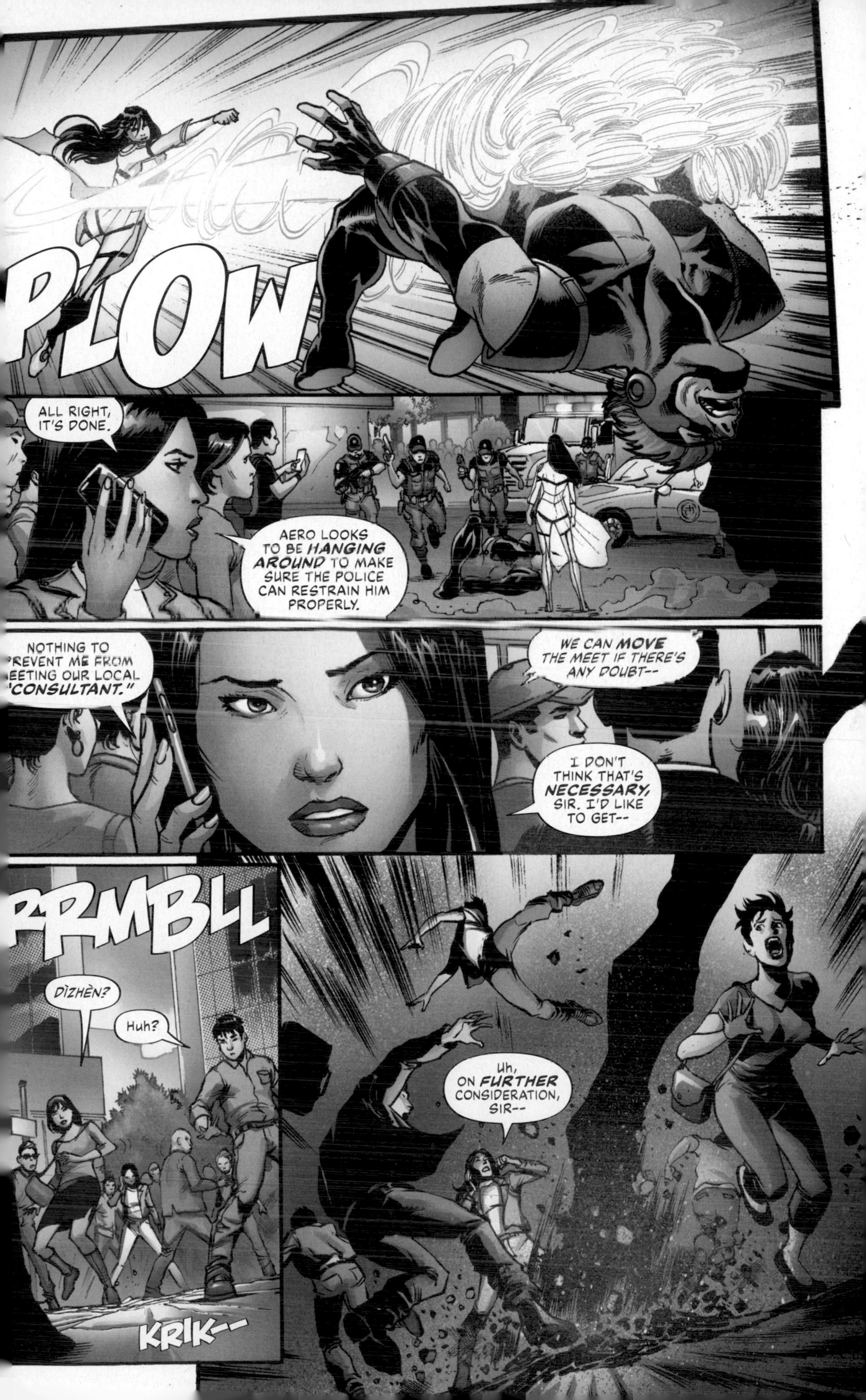
PLOW
ALL RIGHT, IT'S DONE.
AERO LOOKS TO BE HANGING AROUND TO MAKE SURE THE POLICE CAN RESTRAIN HIM PROPERLY.
NOTHING TO PREVENT ME FROM MEETING OUR LOCAL "CONSULTANT."
WE CAN MOVE THE MEET IF THERE'S ANY DOUBT--
I DON'T THINK THAT'S NECESSARY, SIR. I'D LIKE TO GET--
RRMBLL
DÌZHÈN?
Huh?
KRIK--
Uh, ON FURTHER CONSIDERATION, SIR--

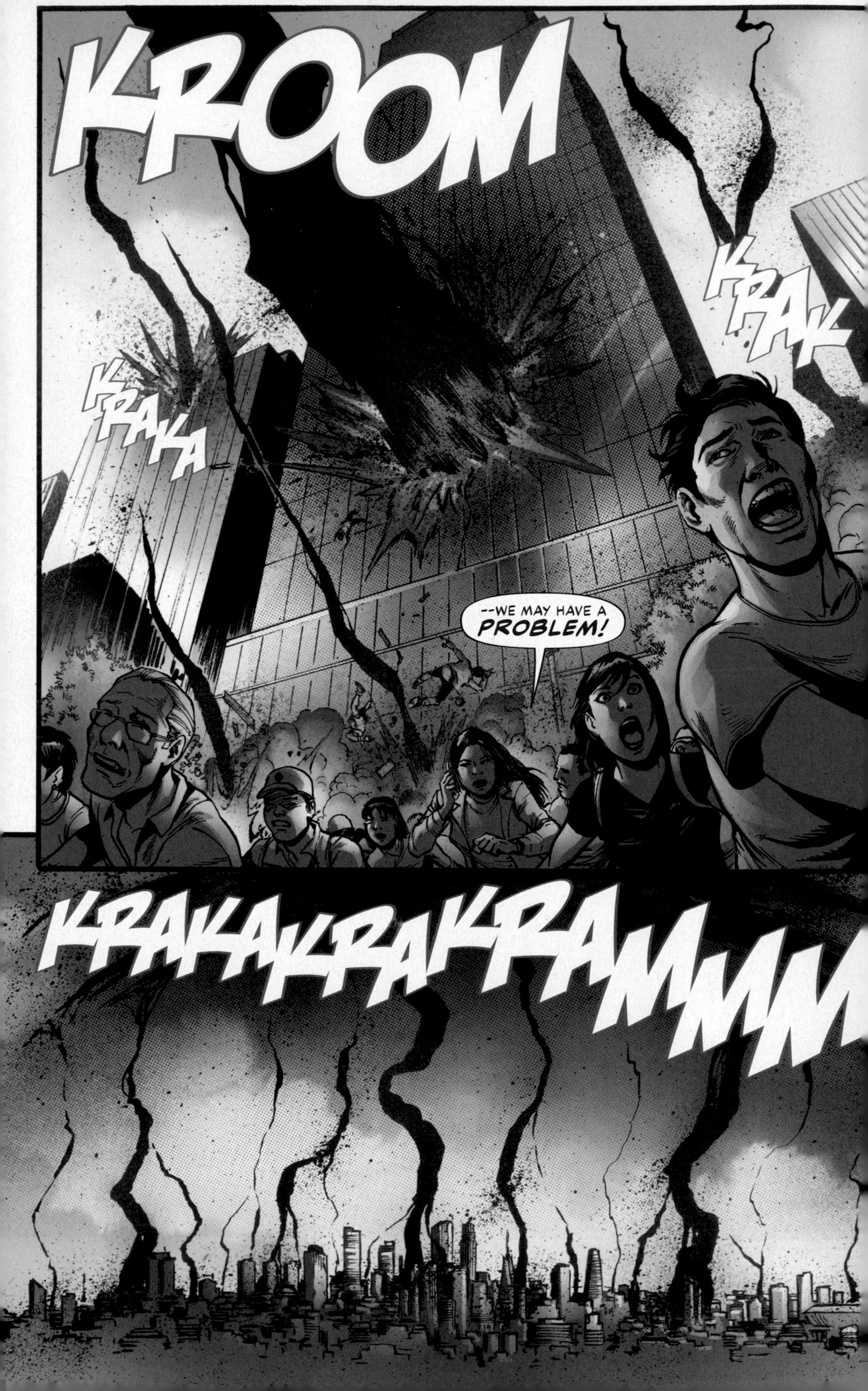
KROOM
KRAKA
KRAK
--WE MAY HAVE A PROBLEM!
KRAKAKRAKKRAMMM

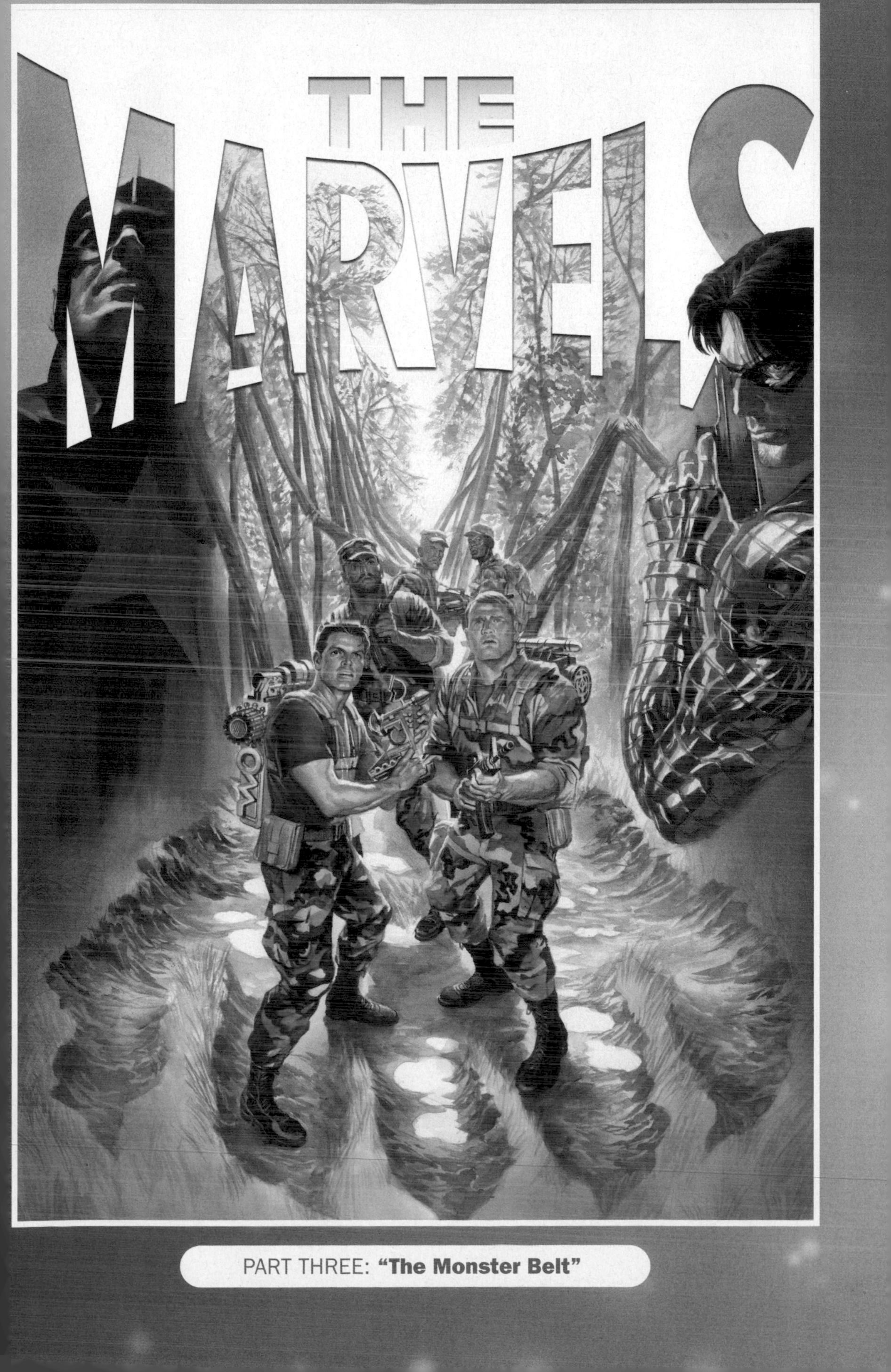
THE
MARVELS

PART THREE: **“The Monster Belt”**

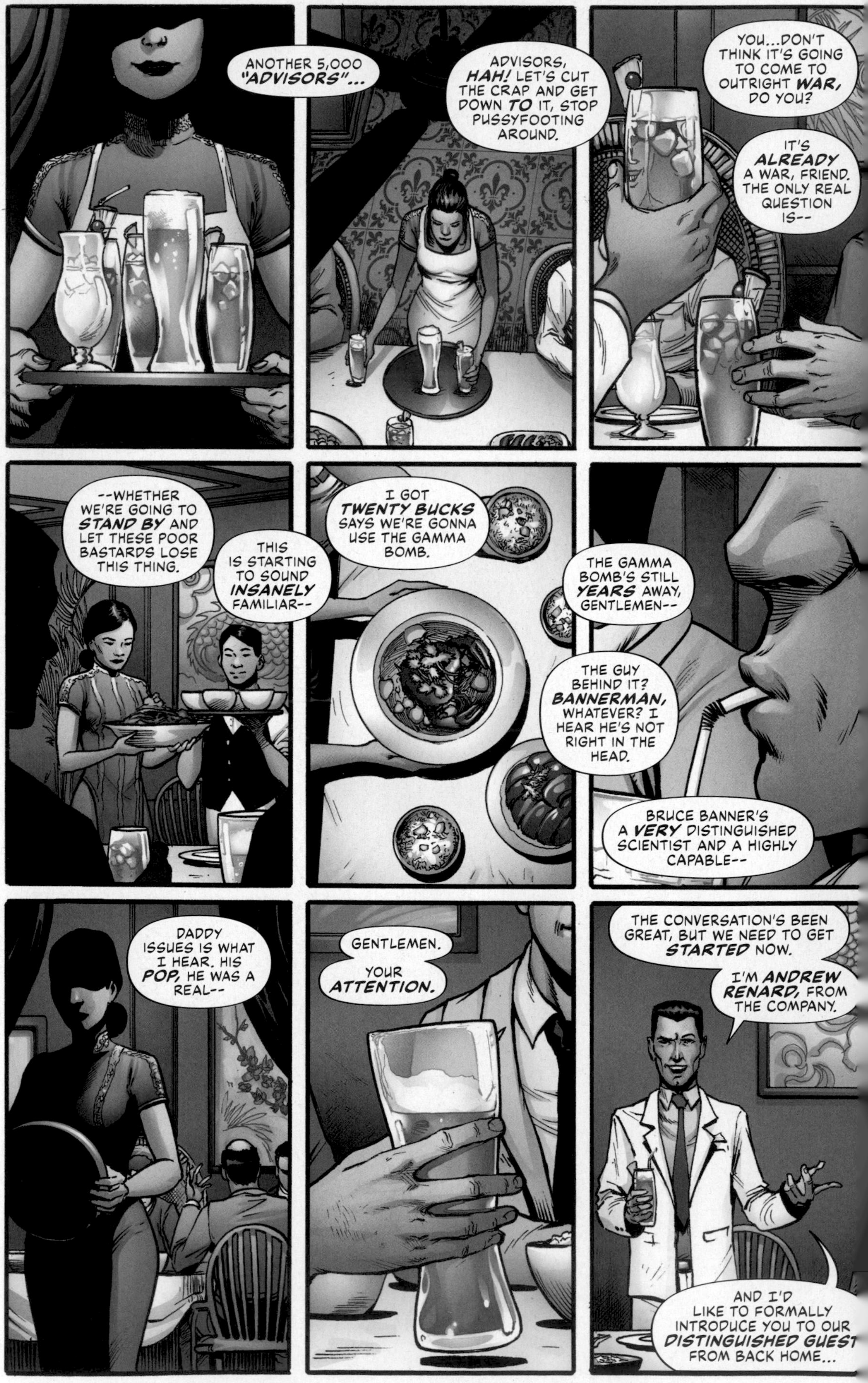
ANOTHER 5,000 "ADVISORS"...
ADVISORS, HAH! LET'S CUT THE CRAP AND GET DOWN TO IT, STOP PUSSYFOOTING AROUND.
YOU...DON'T THINK IT'S GOING TO COME TO OUTRIGHT WAR, DO YOU?
IT'S ALREADY A WAR, FRIEND. THE ONLY REAL QUESTION IS--
--WHETHER WE'RE GOING TO STAND BY AND LET THESE POOR BASTARDS LOSE THIS THING.
THIS IS STARTING TO SOUND INSANELY FAMILIAR--
I GOT TWENTY BUCKS SAYS WE'RE GONNA USE THE GAMMA BOMB.
THE GAMMA BOMB'S STILL YEARS AWAY, GENTLEMEN--
THE GUY BEHIND IT? BANNERMAN, WHATEVER? I HEAR HE'S NOT RIGHT IN THE HEAD.
BRUCE BANNER'S A VERY DISTINGUISHED SCIENTIST AND A HIGHLY CAPABLE--
DADDY ISSUES IS WHAT I HEAR. HIS POP, HE WAS A REAL--
GENTLEMEN.
YOUR ATTENTION.
THE CONVERSATION'S BEEN GREAT, BUT WE NEED TO GET STARTED NOW.
I'M ANDREW RENARD, FROM THE COMPANY.
AND I'D LIKE TO FORMALLY INTRODUCE YOU TO OUR DISTINGUISHED GUEST FROM BACK HOME...

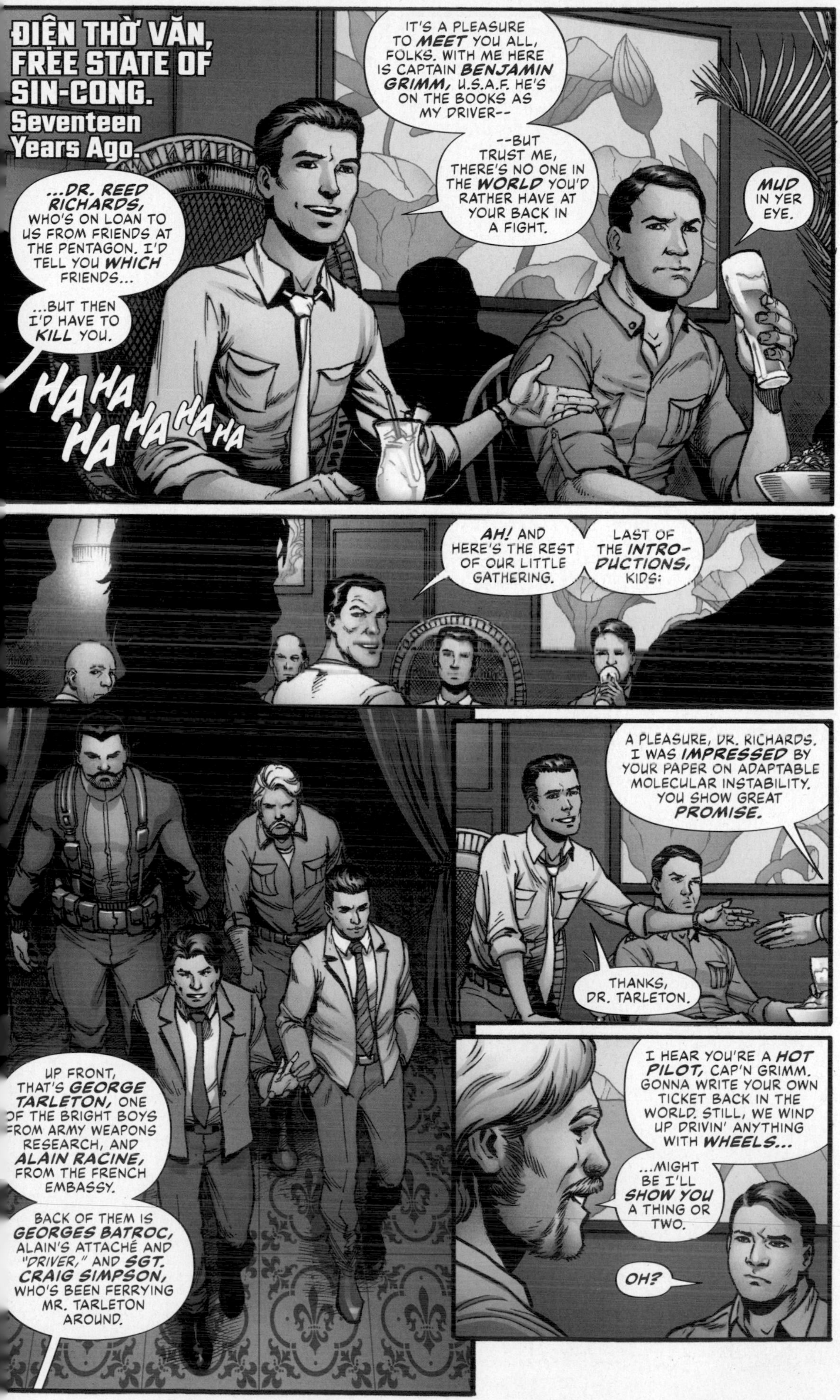
ĐIỆN THỜ VĂN, FREE STATE OF SIN-CONG.
Seventeen Years Ago.
IT'S A PLEASURE TO MEET YOU ALL, FOLKS. WITH ME HERE IS CAPTAIN BENJAMIN GRIMM, U.S.A.F. HE'S ON THE BOOKS AS MY DRIVER--
--BUT TRUST ME, THERE'S NO ONE IN THE WORLD YOU'D RATHER HAVE AT YOUR BACK IN A FIGHT.
MUD IN YER EYE.
...DR. REED RICHARDS, WHO'S ON LOAN TO US FROM FRIENDS AT THE PENTAGON. I'D TELL YOU WHICH FRIENDS...
...BUT THEN I'D HAVE TO KILL YOU.
HAHA HAHAHAHAHA
AH! AND HERE'S THE REST OF OUR LITTLE GATHERING.
LAST OF THE INTRO-DUCTIONS, KIDS:
UP FRONT, THAT'S GEORGE TARLETON, ONE OF THE BRIGHT BOYS FROM ARMY WEAPONS RESEARCH, AND ALAIN RACINE, FROM THE FRENCH EMBASSY.
BACK OF THEM IS GEORGES BATROC, ALAIN'S ATTACHÉ AND "DRIVER," AND SGT. CRAIG SIMPSON, WHO'S BEEN FERRYING MR. TARLETON AROUND.
A PLEASURE, DR. RICHARDS. I WAS IMPRESSED BY YOUR PAPER ON ADAPTABLE MOLECULAR INSTABILITY. YOU SHOW GREAT PROMISE.
THANKS, DR. TARLETON.
I HEAR YOU'RE A HOT PILOT, CAP'N GRIMM. GONNA WRITE YOUR OWN TICKET BACK IN THE WORLD. STILL, WE WIND UP DRIVIN' ANYTHING WITH WHEELS...
...MIGHT BE I'LL SHOW YOU A THING OR TWO.
OH?

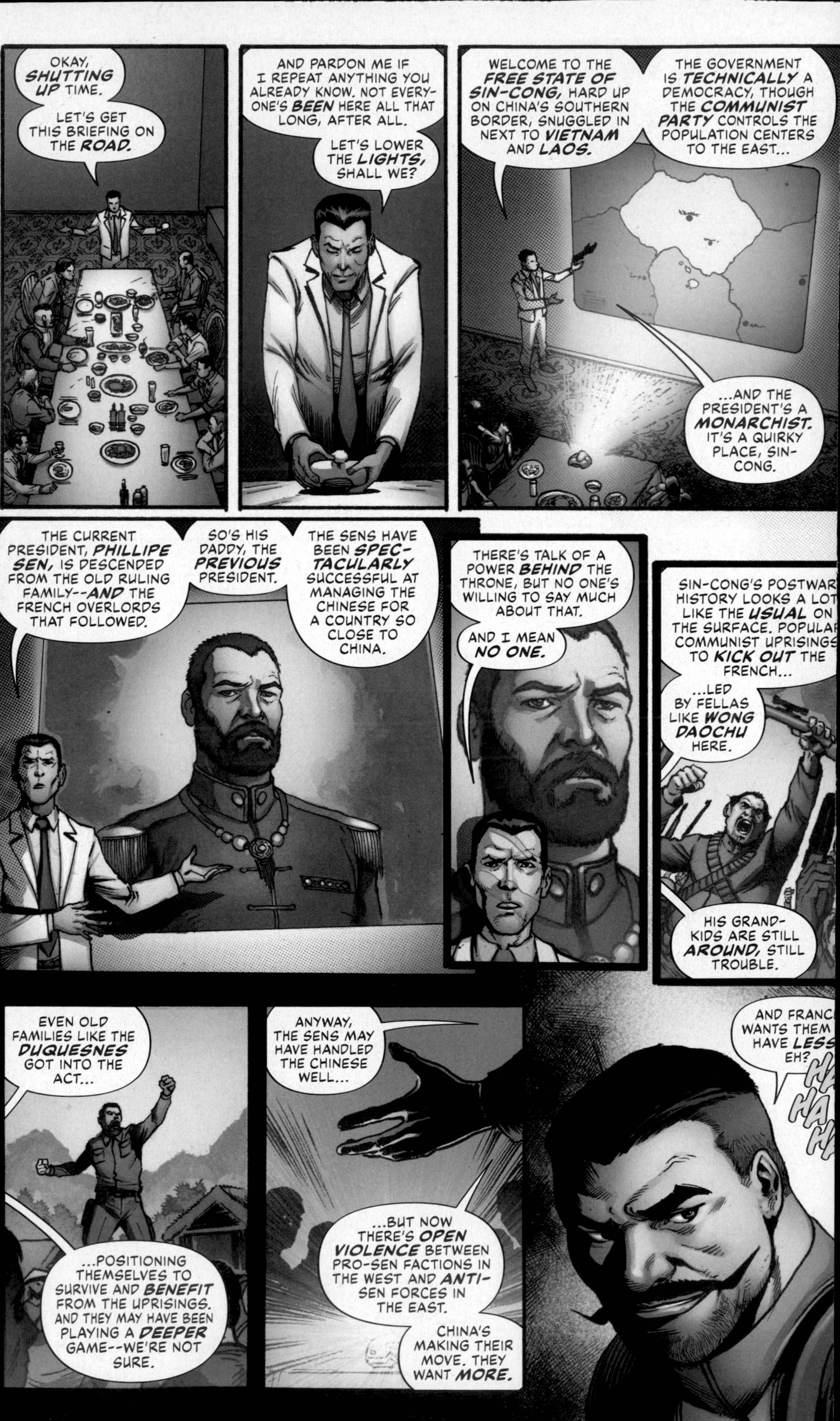

OKAY, SHUTTING UP TIME.
LET'S GET THIS BRIEFING ON THE ROAD.
AND PARDON ME IF I REPEAT ANYTHING YOU ALREADY KNOW. NOT EVERY-ONE'S BEEN HERE ALL THAT LONG, AFTER ALL.
LET'S LOWER THE LIGHTS, SHALL WE?
WELCOME TO THE FREE STATE OF SIN-CONG, HARD UP ON CHINA'S SOUTHERN BORDER, SNUGGLED IN NEXT TO VIETNAM AND LAOS.
THE GOVERNMENT IS TECHNICALLY A DEMOCRACY, THOUGH THE COMMUNIST PARTY CONTROLS THE POPULATION CENTERS TO THE EAST...
...AND THE PRESIDENT'S A MONARCHIST. IT'S A QUIRKY PLACE, SIN-CONG.
THE CURRENT PRESIDENT, PHILLIPE SEN, IS DESCENDED FROM THE OLD RULING FAMILY--AND THE FRENCH OVERLORDS THAT FOLLOWED.
SO'S HIS DADDY, THE PREVIOUS PRESIDENT.
THE SENS HAVE BEEN SPEC-TACULARLY SUCCESSFUL AT MANAGING THE CHINESE FOR A COUNTRY SO CLOSE TO CHINA.
THERE'S TALK OF A POWER BEHIND THE THRONE, BUT NO ONE'S WILLING TO SAY MUCH ABOUT THAT.
AND I MEAN NO ONE.
SIN-CONG'S POSTWAR HISTORY LOOKS A LOT LIKE THE USUAL ON THE SURFACE. POPULAR COMMUNIST UPRISINGS TO KICK OUT THE FRENCH...
...LED BY FELLAS LIKE WONG DAOCHU HERE.
HIS GRAND-KIDS ARE STILL AROUND, STILL TROUBLE.
EVEN OLD FAMILIES LIKE THE DUQUESNES GOT INTO THE ACT...
...POSITIONING THEMSELVES TO SURVIVE AND BENEFIT FROM THE UPRISINGS. AND THEY MAY HAVE BEEN PLAYING A DEEPER GAME--WE'RE NOT SURE.
ANYWAY, THE SENS MAY HAVE HANDLED THE CHINESE WELL...
...BUT NOW THERE'S OPEN VIOLENCE BETWEEN PRO-SEN FACTIONS IN THE WEST AND ANTI-SEN FORCES IN THE EAST.
CHINA'S MAKING THEIR MOVE. THEY WANT MORE.
AND FRANC WANTS THEM HAVE LESS EH?

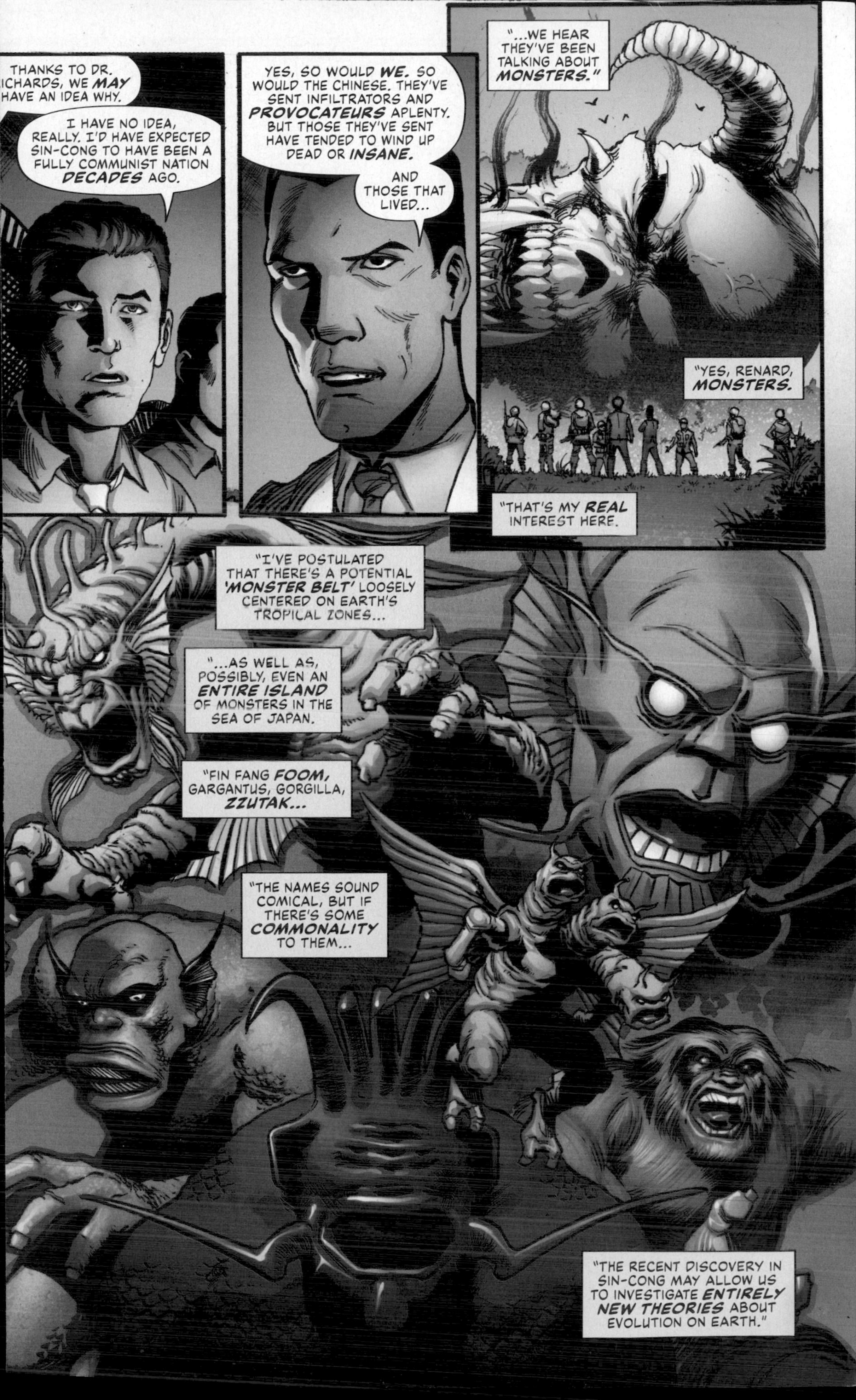
THANKS TO DR. RICHARDS, WE MAY HAVE AN IDEA WHY.
I HAVE NO IDEA, REALLY. I'D HAVE EXPECTED SIN-CONG TO HAVE BEEN A FULLY COMMUNIST NATION DECADES AGO.
YES, SO WOULD WE. SO WOULD THE CHINESE. THEY'VE SENT INFILTRATORS AND PROVOCATEURS APLENTY. BUT THOSE THEY'VE SENT HAVE TENDED TO WIND UP DEAD OR INSANE.
AND THOSE THAT LIVED...
"...WE HEAR THEY'VE BEEN TALKING ABOUT MONSTERS."
"YES, RENARD, MONSTERS.
"THAT'S MY REAL INTEREST HERE.
"I'VE POSTULATED THAT THERE'S A POTENTIAL 'MONSTER BELT' LOOSELY CENTERED ON EARTH'S TROPICAL ZONES...
"...AS WELL AS, POSSIBLY, EVEN AN ENTIRE ISLAND OF MONSTERS IN THE SEA OF JAPAN.
"FIN FANG FOOM, GARGANTUS, GORGILLA, ZZUTAK...
"THE NAMES SOUND COMICAL, BUT IF THERE'S SOME COMMONALITY TO THEM...
"THE RECENT DISCOVERY IN SIN-CONG MAY ALLOW US TO INVESTIGATE ENTIRELY NEW THEORIES ABOUT EVOLUTION ON EARTH."

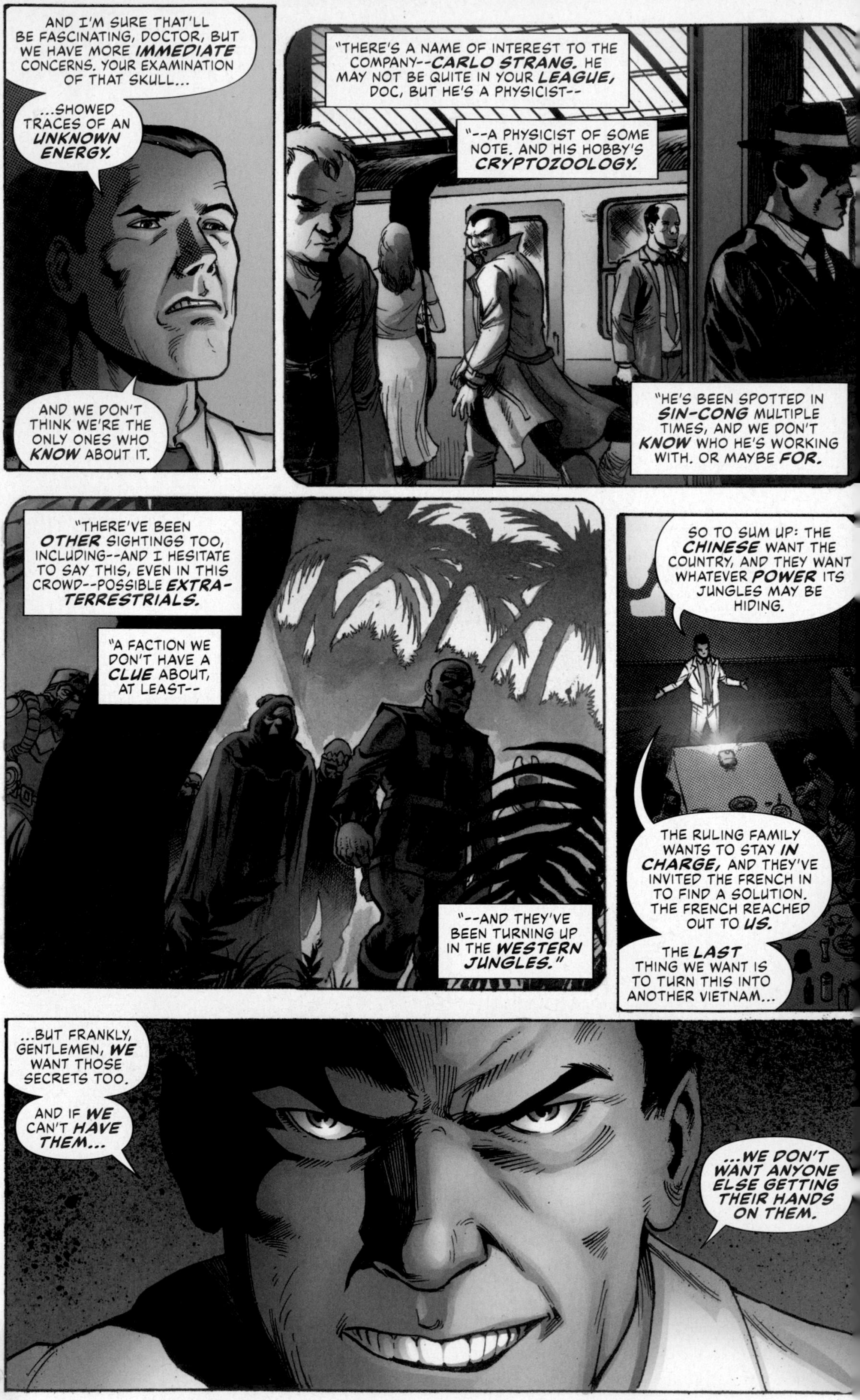
AND I'M SURE THAT'LL BE FASCINATING, DOCTOR, BUT WE HAVE MORE IMMEDIATE CONCERNS. YOUR EXAMINATION OF THAT SKULL...
...SHOWED TRACES OF AN UNKNOWN ENERGY.
AND WE DON'T THINK WE'RE THE ONLY ONES WHO KNOW ABOUT IT.
"THERE'S A NAME OF INTEREST TO THE COMPANY--CARLO STRANG. HE MAY NOT BE QUITE IN YOUR LEAGUE, DOC, BUT HE'S A PHYSICIST--
"--A PHYSICIST OF SOME NOTE. AND HIS HOBBY'S CRYPTOZOOLOGY.
"HE'S BEEN SPOTTED IN SIN-CONG MULTIPLE TIMES, AND WE DON'T KNOW WHO HE'S WORKING WITH. OR MAYBE FOR.
"THERE'VE BEEN OTHER SIGHTINGS TOO, INCLUDING--AND I HESITATE TO SAY THIS, EVEN IN THIS CROWD--POSSIBLE EXTRA-TERRESTRIALS.
"A FACTION WE DON'T HAVE A CLUE ABOUT, AT LEAST--
"--AND THEY'VE BEEN TURNING UP IN THE WESTERN JUNGLES."
SO TO SUM UP: THE CHINESE WANT THE COUNTRY, AND THEY WANT WHATEVER POWER ITS JUNGLES MAY BE HIDING.
THE RULING FAMILY WANTS TO STAY IN CHARGE, AND THEY'VE INVITED THE FRENCH IN TO FIND A SOLUTION. THE FRENCH REACHED OUT TO US.
THE LAST THING WE WANT IS TO TURN THIS INTO ANOTHER VIETNAM...
...BUT FRANKLY, GENTLEMEN, WE WANT THOSE SECRETS TOO.
AND IF WE CAN'T HAVE THEM...
...WE DON'T WANT ANYONE ELSE GETTING THEIR HANDS ON THEM.

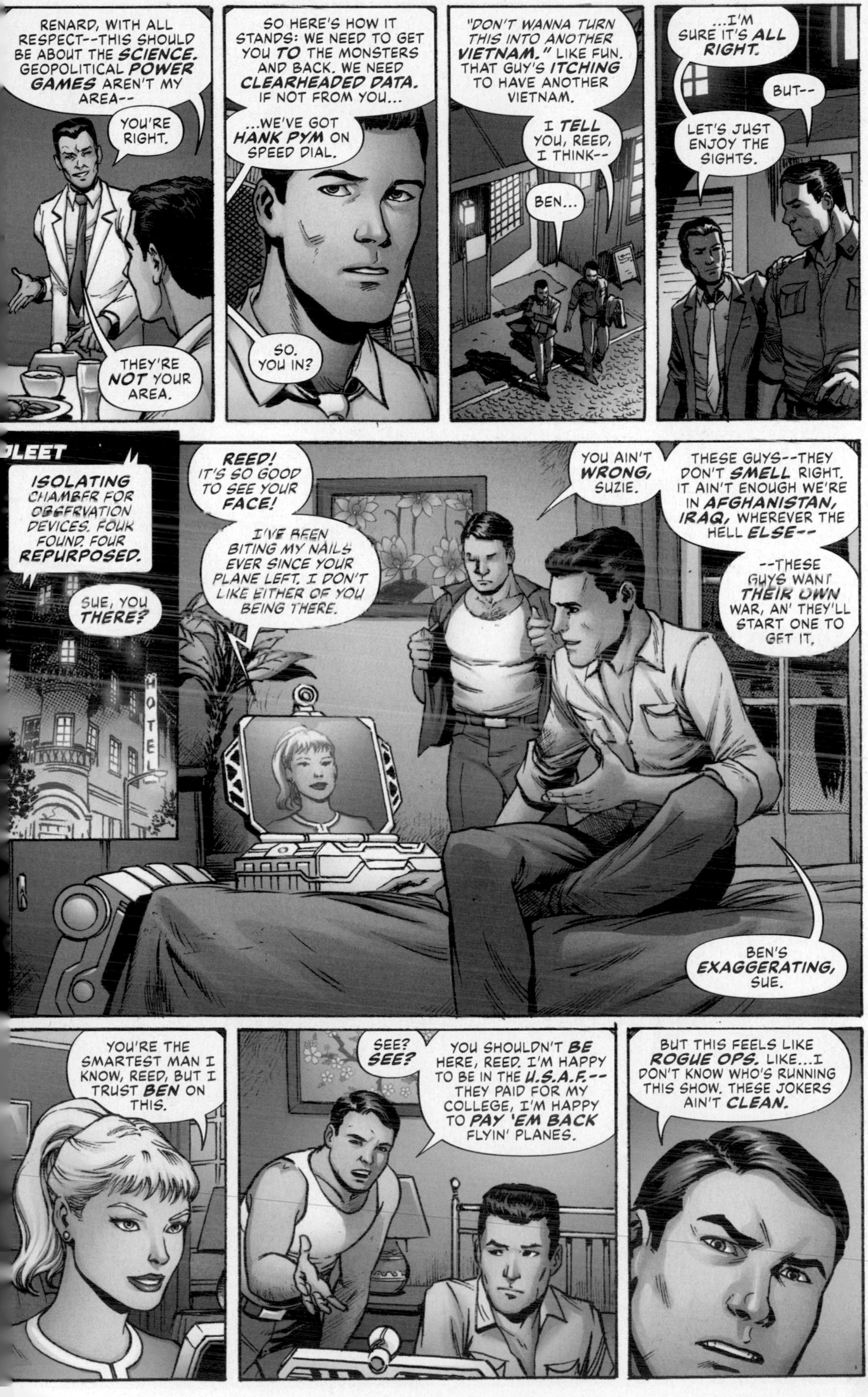
RENARD, WITH ALL RESPECT--THIS SHOULD BE ABOUT THE SCIENCE. GEOPOLITICAL POWER GAMES AREN'T MY AREA--
YOU'RE RIGHT.
THEY'RE NOT YOUR AREA.
SO HERE'S HOW IT STANDS: WE NEED TO GET YOU TO THE MONSTERS AND BACK. WE NEED CLEARHEADED DATA. IF NOT FROM YOU...
...WE'VE GOT HANK PYM ON SPEED DIAL.
SO. YOU IN?
"DON'T WANNA TURN THIS INTO ANOTHER VIETNAM." LIKE FUN. THAT GUY'S ITCHING TO HAVE ANOTHER VIETNAM.
I TELL YOU, REED, I THINK--
BEN...
...I'M SURE IT'S ALL RIGHT.
BUT--
LET'S JUST ENJOY THE SIGHTS.
ISOLATING CHAMBER FOR OBSERVATION DEVICES. FOUR FOUND. FOUR REPURPOSED.
SUE, YOU THERE?
REED! IT'S SO GOOD TO SEE YOUR FACE!
I'VE BEEN BITING MY NAILS EVER SINCE YOUR PLANE LEFT. I DON'T LIKE EITHER OF YOU BEING THERE.
YOU AIN'T WRONG, SUZIE.
THESE GUYS--THEY DON'T SMELL RIGHT. IT AIN'T ENOUGH WE'RE IN AFGHANISTAN, IRAQ, WHEREVER THE HELL ELSE--
--THESE GUYS WANT THEIR OWN WAR, AN' THEY'LL START ONE TO GET IT.
BEN'S EXAGGERATING, SUE.
HOTEL
YOU'RE THE SMARTEST MAN I KNOW, REED, BUT I TRUST BEN ON THIS.
SEE? SEE?
YOU SHOULDN'T BE HERE, REED. I'M HAPPY TO BE IN THE U.S.A.F.--THEY PAID FOR MY COLLEGE, I'M HAPPY TO PAY 'EM BACK FLYIN' PLANES.
BUT THIS FEELS LIKE ROGUE OPS. LIKE...I DON'T KNOW WHO'S RUNNING THIS SHOW. THESE JOKERS AIN'T CLEAN.

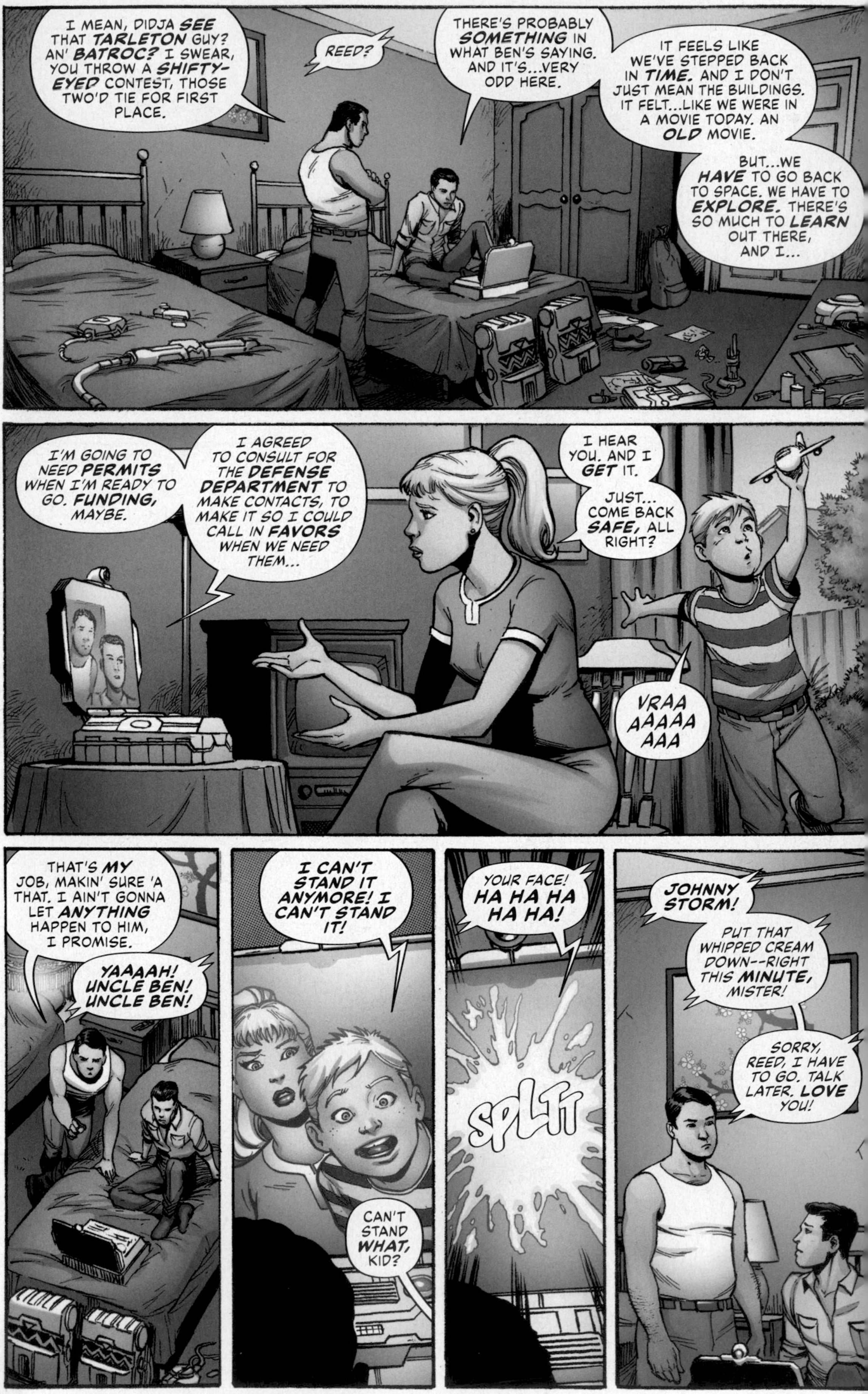
I MEAN, DIDJA SEE THAT TARLETON GUY? AN' BATROC? I SWEAR, YOU THROW A SHIFTY-EYED CONTEST, THOSE TWO'D TIE FOR FIRST PLACE.
REED?
THERE'S PROBABLY SOMETHING IN WHAT BEN'S SAYING. AND IT'S...VERY ODD HERE.
IT FEELS LIKE WE'VE STEPPED BACK IN TIME. AND I DON'T JUST MEAN THE BUILDINGS. IT FELT...LIKE WE WERE IN A MOVIE TODAY. AN OLD MOVIE.
BUT...WE HAVE TO GO BACK TO SPACE. WE HAVE TO EXPLORE. THERE'S SO MUCH TO LEARN OUT THERE, AND I...
I'M GOING TO NEED PERMITS WHEN I'M READY TO GO. FUNDING, MAYBE.
I AGREED TO CONSULT FOR THE DEFENSE DEPARTMENT TO MAKE CONTACTS, TO MAKE IT SO I COULD CALL IN FAVORS WHEN WE NEED THEM...
I HEAR YOU. AND I GET IT.
JUST... COME BACK SAFE, ALL RIGHT?
VRAA AAAAA AAA
THAT'S MY JOB, MAKIN' SURE 'A THAT. I AIN'T GONNA LET ANYTHING HAPPEN TO HIM, I PROMISE.
YAAAAH! UNCLE BEN! UNCLE BEN!
I CAN'T STAND IT ANYMORE! I CAN'T STAND IT!
CAN'T STAND WHAT, KID?
YOUR FACE! HA HA HA HA HA!
SPLTT
JOHNNY STORM!
PUT THAT WHIPPED CREAM DOWN--RIGHT THIS MINUTE, MISTER!
SORRY, REED, I HAVE TO GO. TALK LATER. LOVE YOU!

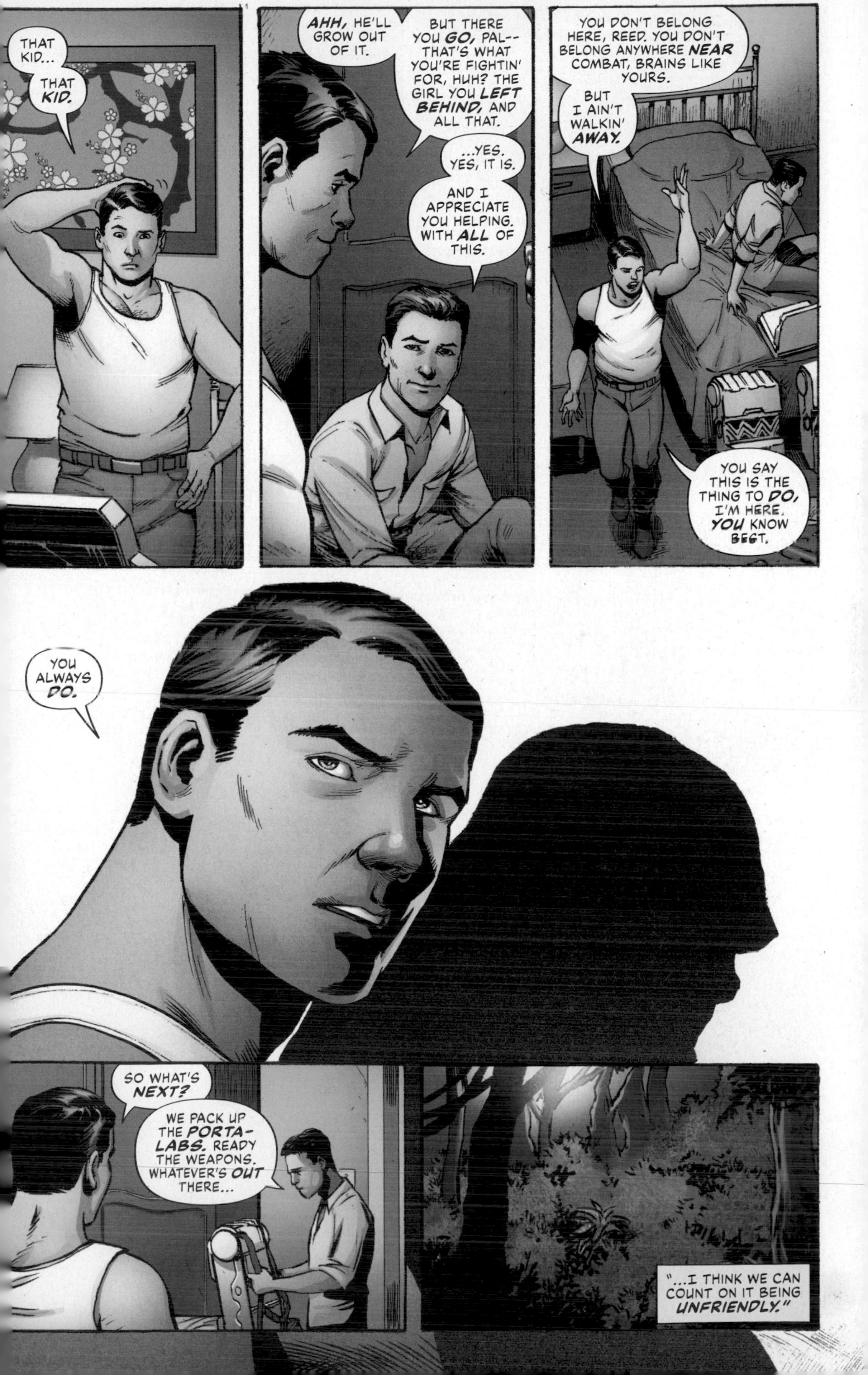
THAT KID...
THAT KID.
AHH, HE'LL GROW OUT OF IT.
BUT THERE YOU GO, PAL-- THAT'S WHAT YOU'RE FIGHTIN' FOR, HUH? THE GIRL YOU LEFT BEHIND, AND ALL THAT.
...YES. YES, IT IS.
AND I APPRECIATE YOU HELPING. WITH ALL OF THIS.
YOU DON'T BELONG HERE, REED. YOU DON'T BELONG ANYWHERE NEAR COMBAT, BRAINS LIKE YOURS.
BUT I AIN'T WALKIN' AWAY.
YOU SAY THIS IS THE THING TO DO, I'M HERE. YOU KNOW BEST.
YOU ALWAYS DO.
SO WHAT'S NEXT?
WE PACK UP THE PORTA-LABS. READY THE WEAPONS. WHATEVER'S OUT THERE...
"...I THINK WE CAN COUNT ON IT BEING UNFRIENDLY."

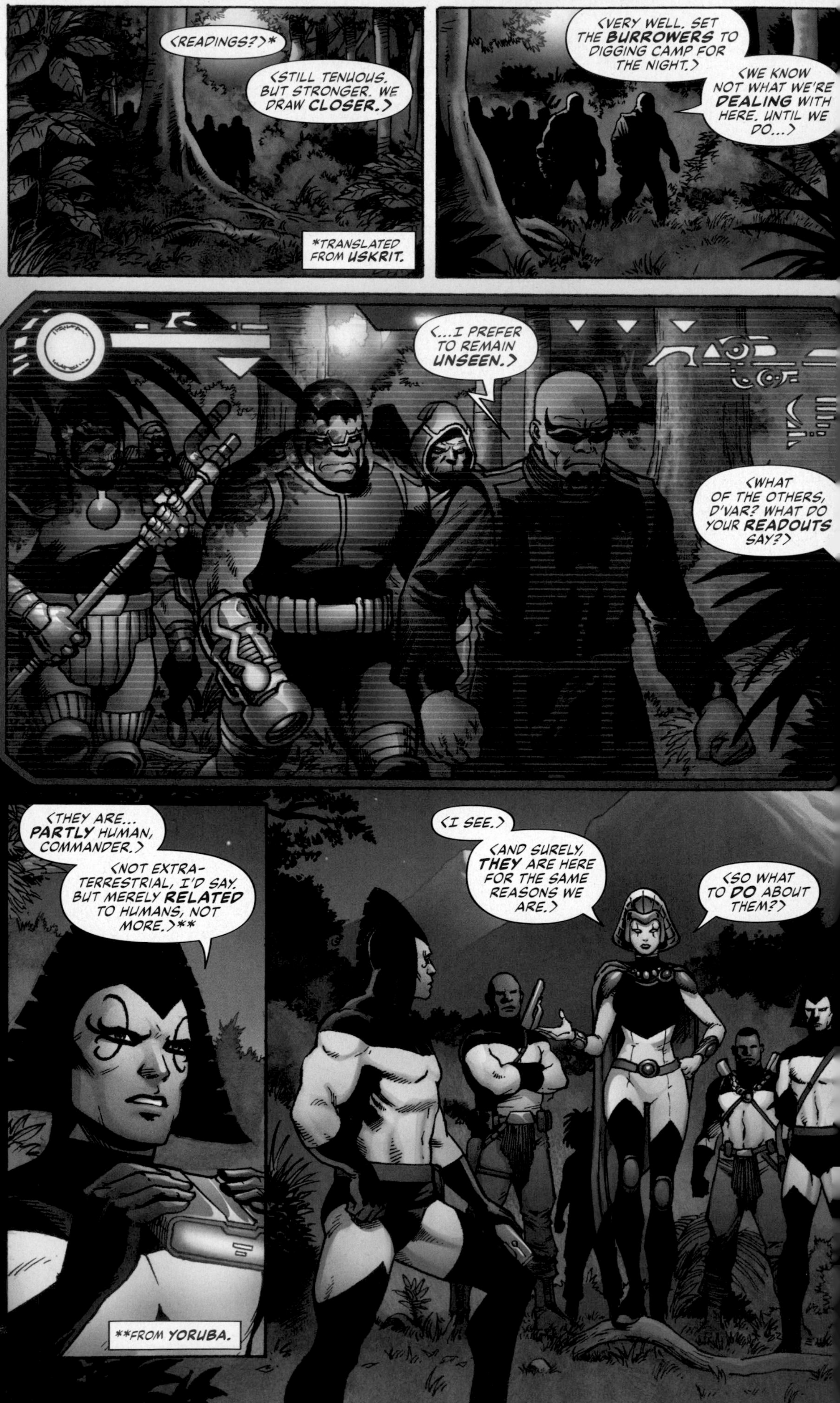
<READINGS?>*
<STILL TENUOUS. BUT STRONGER. WE DRAW CLOSER.>
*TRANSLATED FROM USKRIT.
<VERY WELL. SET THE BURROWERS TO DIGGING CAMP FOR THE NIGHT.>
<WE KNOW NOT WHAT WE'RE DEALING WITH HERE. UNTIL WE DO...>
<...I PREFER TO REMAIN UNSEEN.>
<WHAT OF THE OTHERS, D'VAR? WHAT DO YOUR READOUTS SAY?>
<THEY ARE... PARTLY HUMAN, COMMANDER.>
<NOT EXTRA-TERRESTRIAL, I'D SAY. BUT MERELY RELATED TO HUMANS, NOT MORE.>**
**FROM YORUBA.
<I SEE.>
<AND SURELY, THEY ARE HERE FOR THE SAME REASONS WE ARE.>
<SO WHAT TO DO ABOUT THEM?>

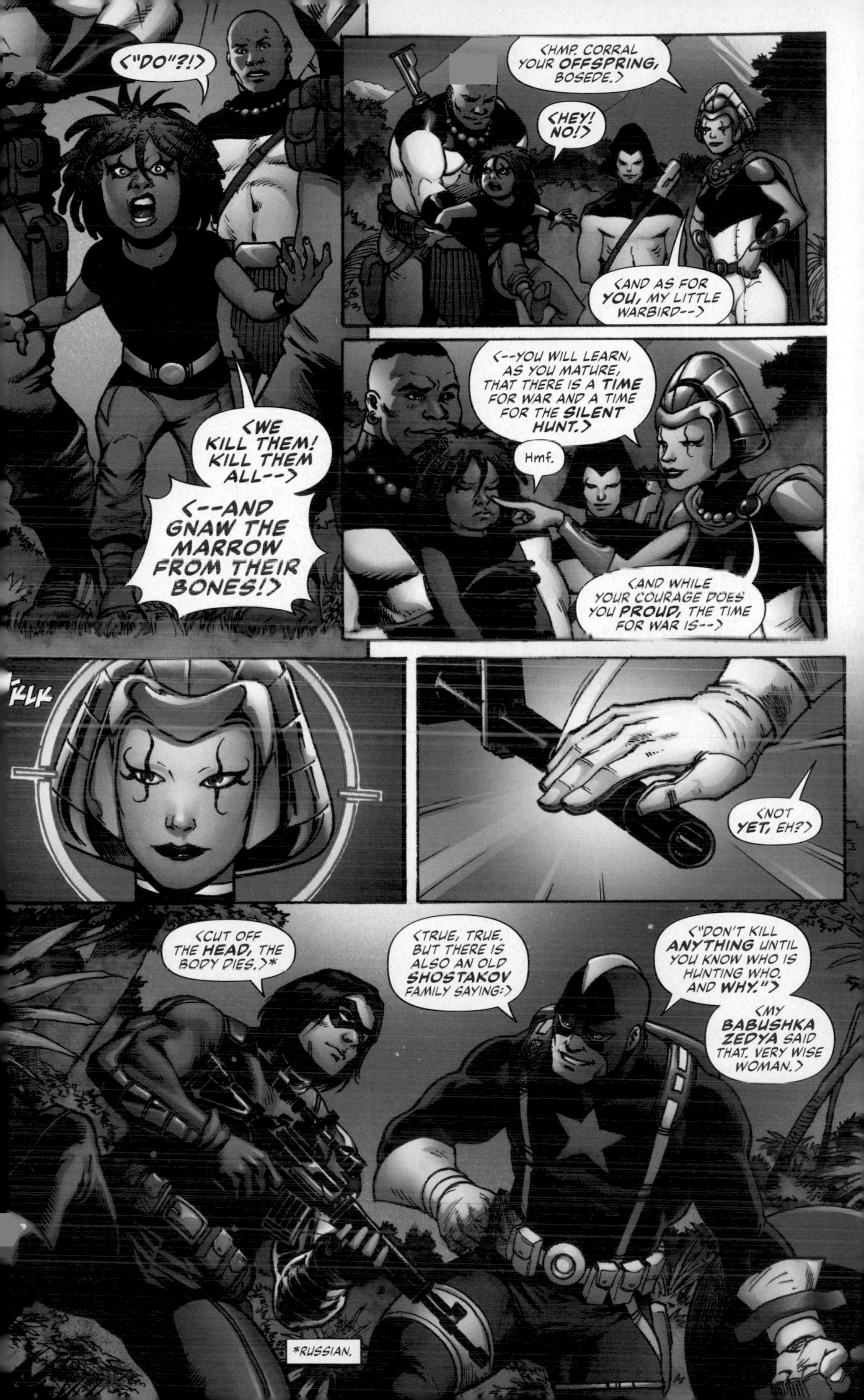

<"DO"?!>
<WE KILL THEM! KILL THEM ALL-->
<--AND GNAW THE MARROW FROM THEIR BONES!>
<HMP. CORRAL YOUR OFFSPRING, BOSEDE.>
<HEY! NO!>
<AND AS FOR YOU, MY LITTLE WARBIRD-->
<--YOU WILL LEARN, AS YOU MATURE, THAT THERE IS A TIME FOR WAR AND A TIME FOR THE SILENT HUNT.>
Hmf.
<AND WHILE YOUR COURAGE DOES YOU PROUD, THE TIME FOR WAR IS-->
KLK
<NOT YET, EH?>
<CUT OFF THE HEAD, THE BODY DIES.>*
<TRUE, TRUE, BUT THERE IS ALSO AN OLD SHOSTAKOV FAMILY SAYING:>
<"DON'T KILL ANYTHING UNTIL YOU KNOW WHO IS HUNTING WHO, AND WHY.">
<MY BABUSHKA ZEDYA SAID THAT. VERY WISE WOMAN.>
*RUSSIAN.

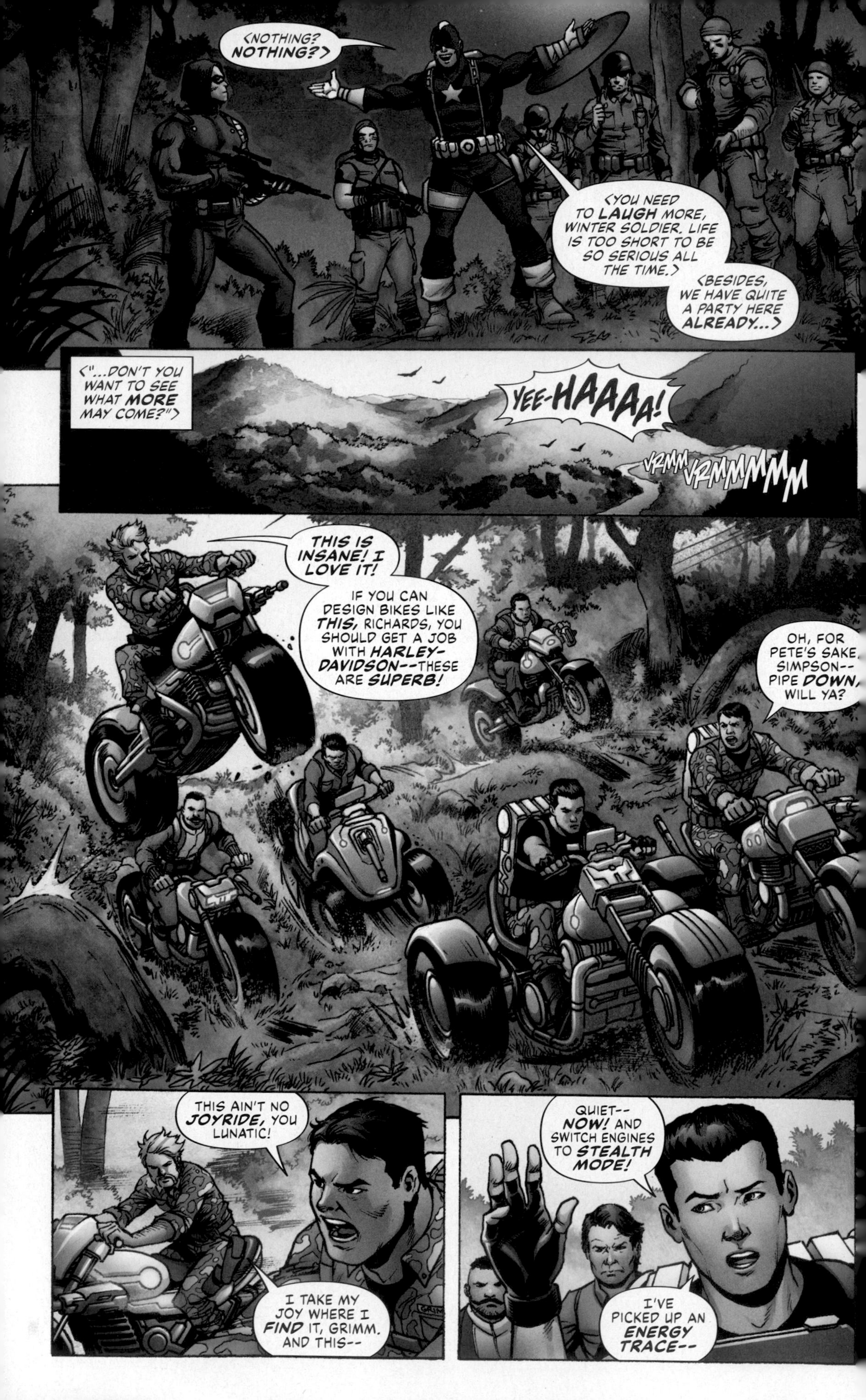

<NOTHING? NOTHING?>
<YOU NEED TO LAUGH MORE, WINTER SOLDIER. LIFE IS TOO SHORT TO BE SO SERIOUS ALL THE TIME.>
<BESIDES, WE HAVE QUITE A PARTY HERE ALREADY...>
<"...DON'T YOU WANT TO SEE WHAT MORE MAY COME?">
YEE-HAAAA!
VRMM VRMMMMMM
THIS IS INSANE! I LOVE IT!
IF YOU CAN DESIGN BIKES LIKE THIS, RICHARDS, YOU SHOULD GET A JOB WITH HARLEY-DAVIDSON--THESE ARE SUPERB!
OH, FOR PETE'S SAKE, SIMPSON--PIPE DOWN, WILL YA?
THIS AIN'T NO JOYRIDE, YOU LUNATIC!
I TAKE MY JOY WHERE I FIND IT, GRIMM. AND THIS--
QUIET--NOW! AND SWITCH ENGINES TO STEALTH MODE!
I'VE PICKED UP AN ENERGY TRACE--

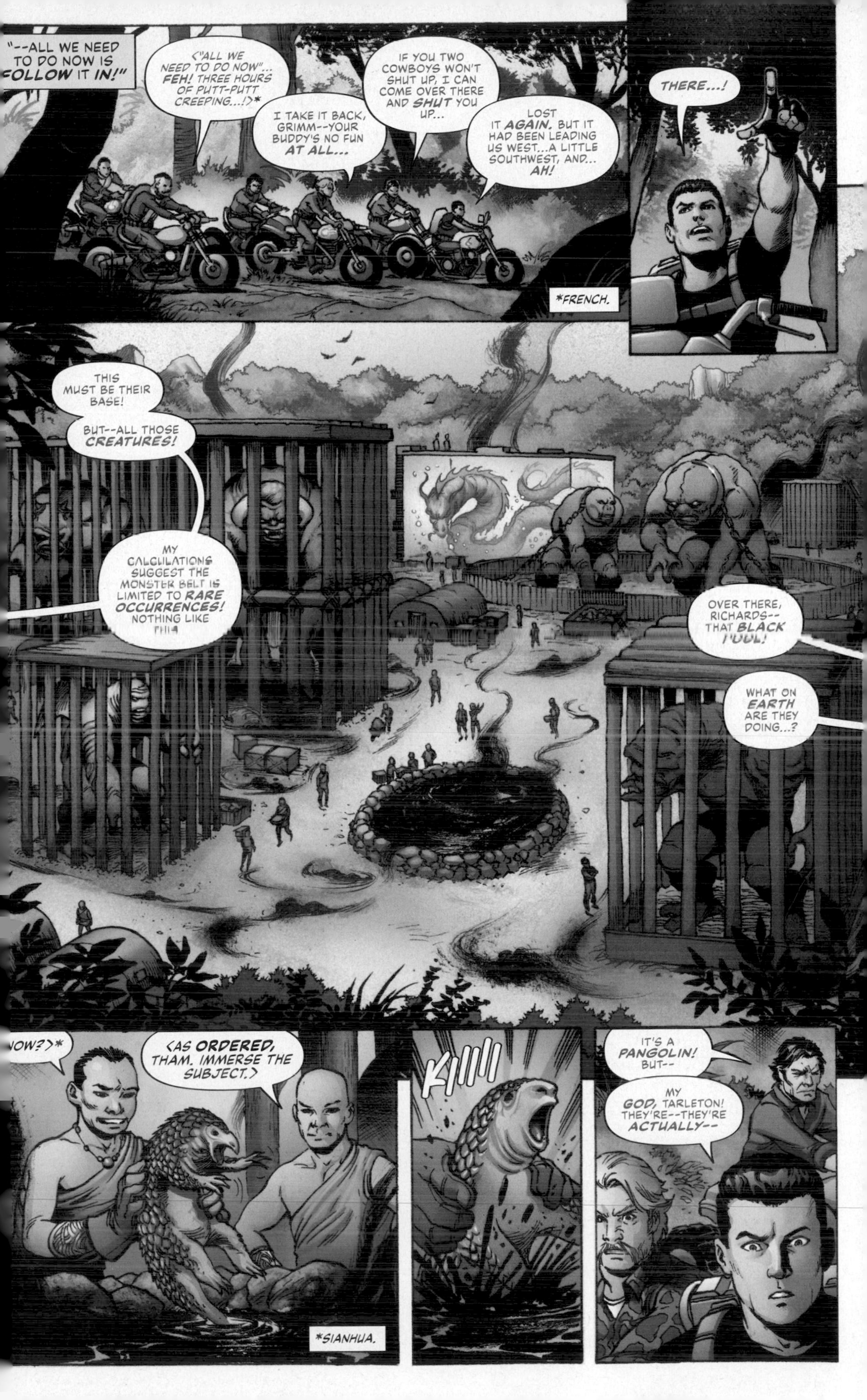

"--ALL WE NEED TO DO NOW IS FOLLOW IT IN!"
<"ALL WE NEED TO DO NOW"... FEH! THREE HOURS OF PUTT-PUTT CREEPING...!>*
I TAKE IT BACK, GRIMM--YOUR BUDDY'S NO FUN AT ALL...
IF YOU TWO COWBOYS WON'T SHUT UP, I CAN COME OVER THERE AND SHUT YOU UP...
LOST IT AGAIN. BUT IT HAD BEEN LEADING US WEST...A LITTLE SOUTHWEST, AND... AH!
*FRENCH.
THERE...!
THIS MUST BE THEIR BASE!
BUT--ALL THOSE CREATURES!
MY CALCULATIONS SUGGEST THE MONSTER BELT IS LIMITED TO RARE OCCURRENCES! NOTHING LIKE
OVER THERE, RICHARDS--THAT BLACK
WHAT ON EARTH ARE THEY DOING...?
NOW?>*
<AS ORDERED, THAM. IMMERSE THE SUBJECT.>
*SIANHUA.
KIIIII
IT'S A PANGOLIN! BUT--
MY GOD, TARLETON! THEY'RE--THEY'RE ACTUALLY--

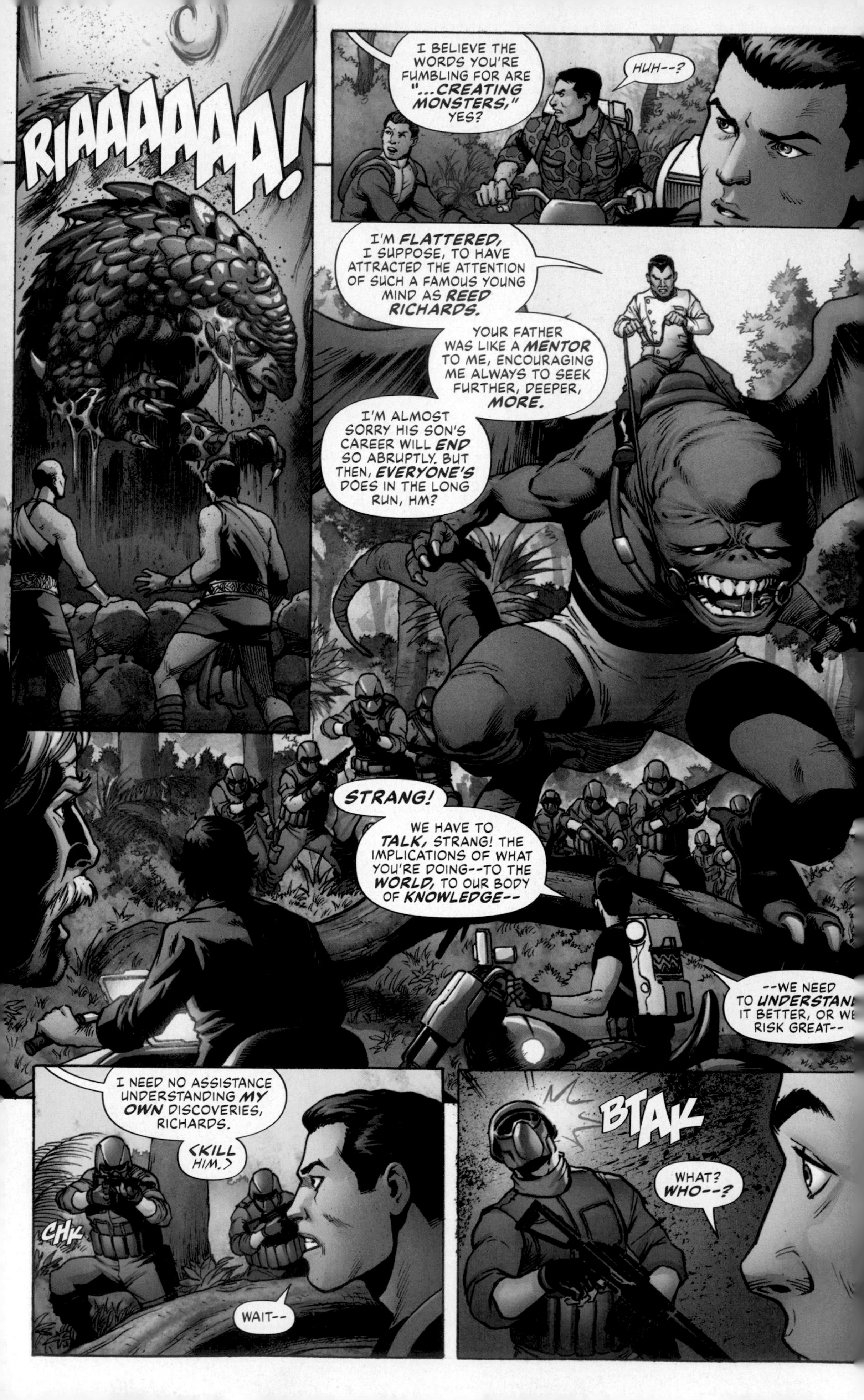
RIAAAAAA!
I BELIEVE THE WORDS YOU'RE FUMBLING FOR ARE "...CREATING MONSTERS," YES?
HUH--?
I'M FLATTERED, I SUPPOSE, TO HAVE ATTRACTED THE ATTENTION OF SUCH A FAMOUS YOUNG MIND AS REED RICHARDS.
YOUR FATHER WAS LIKE A MENTOR TO ME, ENCOURAGING ME ALWAYS TO SEEK FURTHER, DEEPER, MORE.
I'M ALMOST SORRY HIS SON'S CAREER WILL END SO ABRUPTLY. BUT THEN, EVERYONE'S DOES IN THE LONG RUN, HM?
STRANG!
WE HAVE TO TALK, STRANG! THE IMPLICATIONS OF WHAT YOU'RE DOING--TO THE WORLD, TO OUR BODY OF KNOWLEDGE--
--WE NEED TO UNDERSTAND IT BETTER, OR WE RISK GREAT--
I NEED NO ASSISTANCE UNDERSTANDING MY OWN DISCOVERIES, RICHARDS.
<KILL HIM.>
CHK
WAIT--
BTAK
WHAT? WHO--?

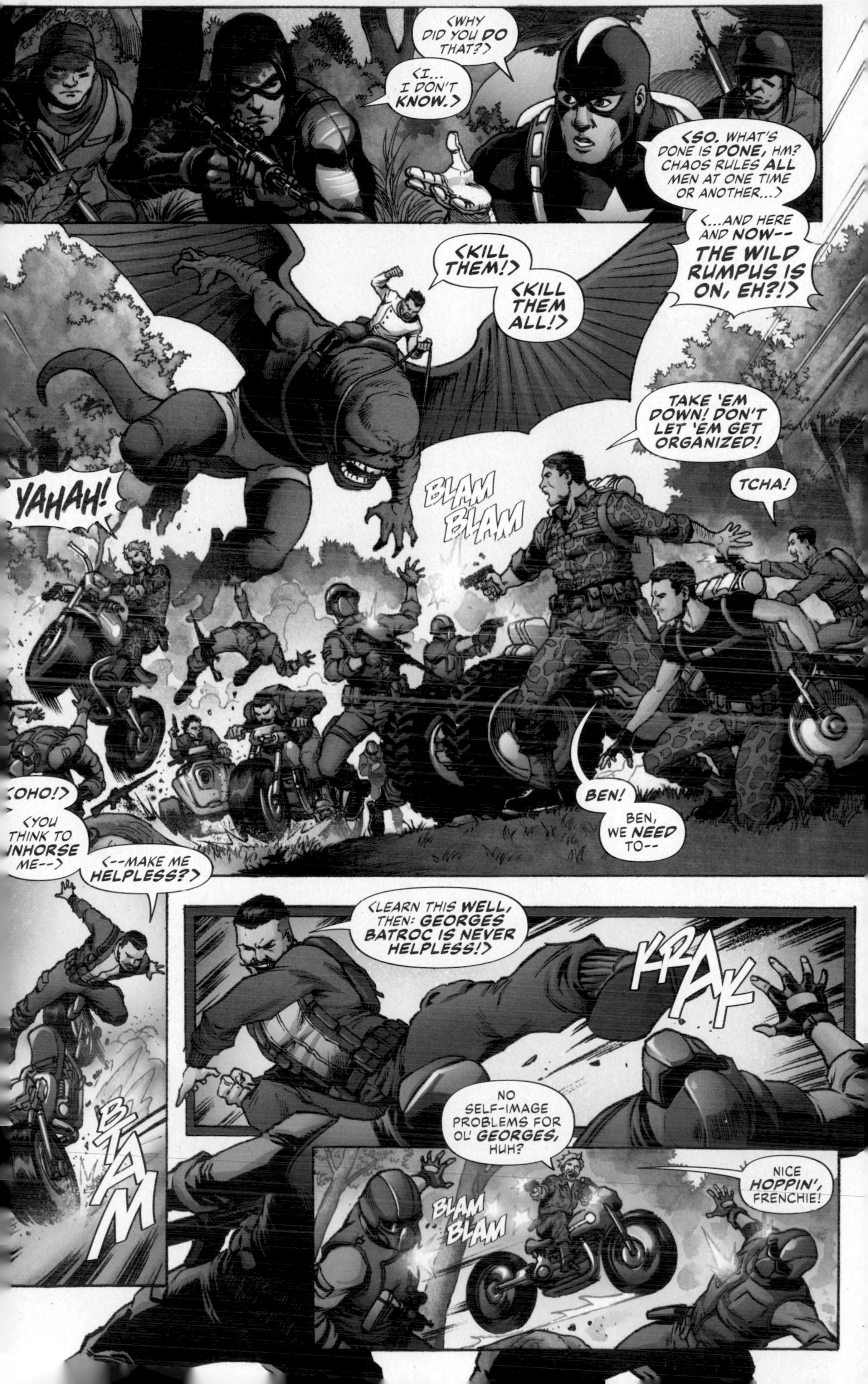

<WHY DID YOU DO THAT?>
<I... I DON'T KNOW.>
<SO. WHAT'S DONE IS DONE, HM? CHAOS RULES ALL MEN AT ONE TIME OR ANOTHER...>
<...AND HERE AND NOW-- THE WILD RUMPUS IS ON, EH?!>
<KILL THEM!>
<KILL THEM ALL!>
TAKE 'EM DOWN! DON'T LET 'EM GET ORGANIZED!
YAHAH!
BLAM BLAM
TCHA!
<OHO!>
<YOU THINK TO UNHORSE ME-->
<--MAKE ME HELPLESS?>
BEN!
BEN, WE NEED TO--
<LEARN THIS WELL, THEN: GEORGES BATROC IS NEVER HELPLESS!>
KRAK
BLAM
NO SELF-IMAGE PROBLEMS FOR OL' GEORGES, HUH?
NICE HOPPIN', FRENCHIE!
BLAM BLAM

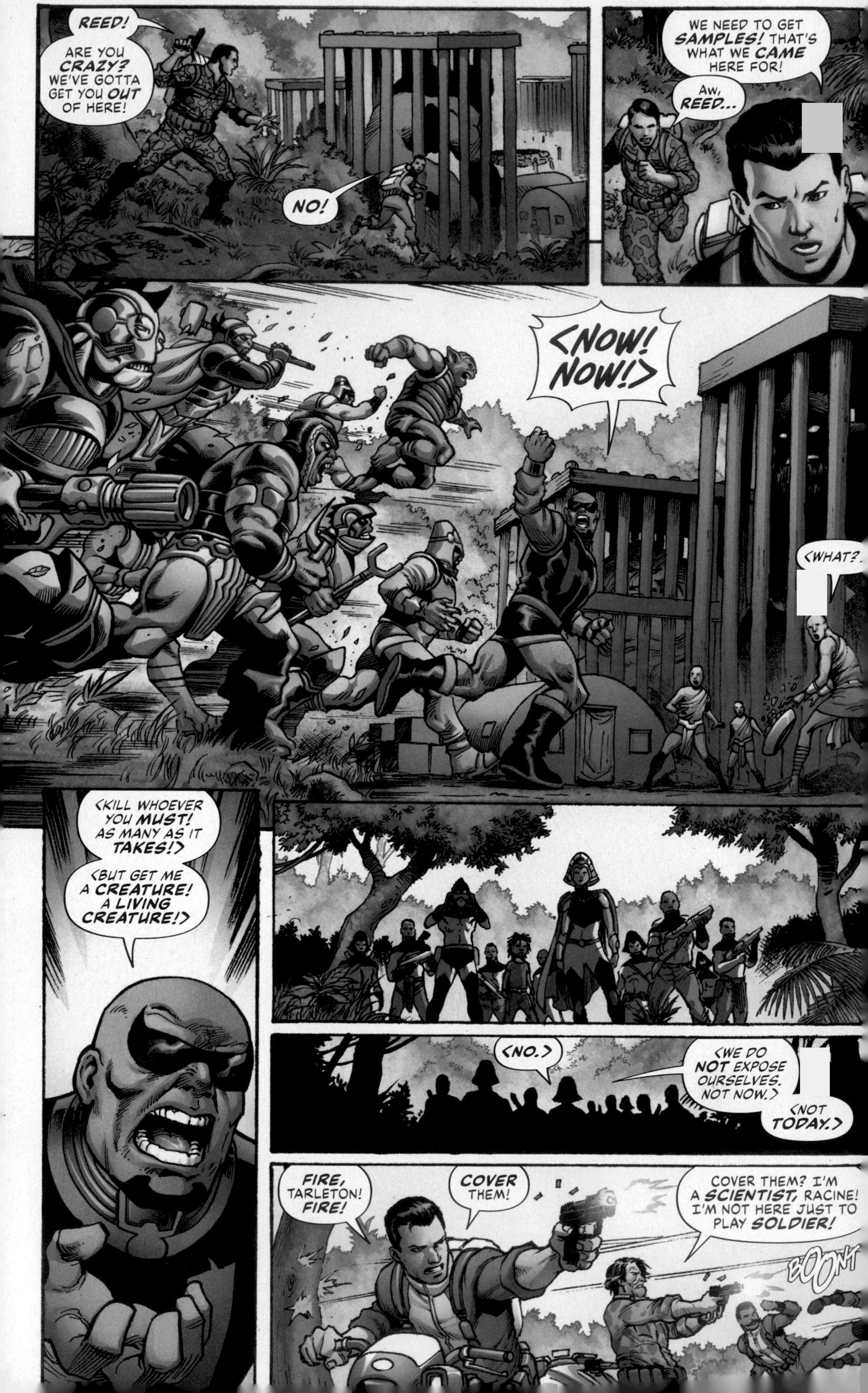
REED!
ARE YOU CRAZY? WE'VE GOTTA GET YOU OUT OF HERE!
NO!
WE NEED TO GET SAMPLES! THAT'S WHAT WE CAME HERE FOR!
AW, REED...
<NOW! NOW!>
<WHAT?
<KILL WHOEVER YOU MUST! AS MANY AS IT TAKES!>
<BUT GET ME A CREATURE! A LIVING CREATURE!>
<NO.>
<WE DO NOT EXPOSE OURSELVES. NOT NOW.>
<NOT TODAY.>
FIRE, TARLETON! FIRE!
COVER THEM!
COVER THEM? I'M A SCIENTIST, RACINE! I'M NOT HERE JUST TO PLAY SOLDIER!

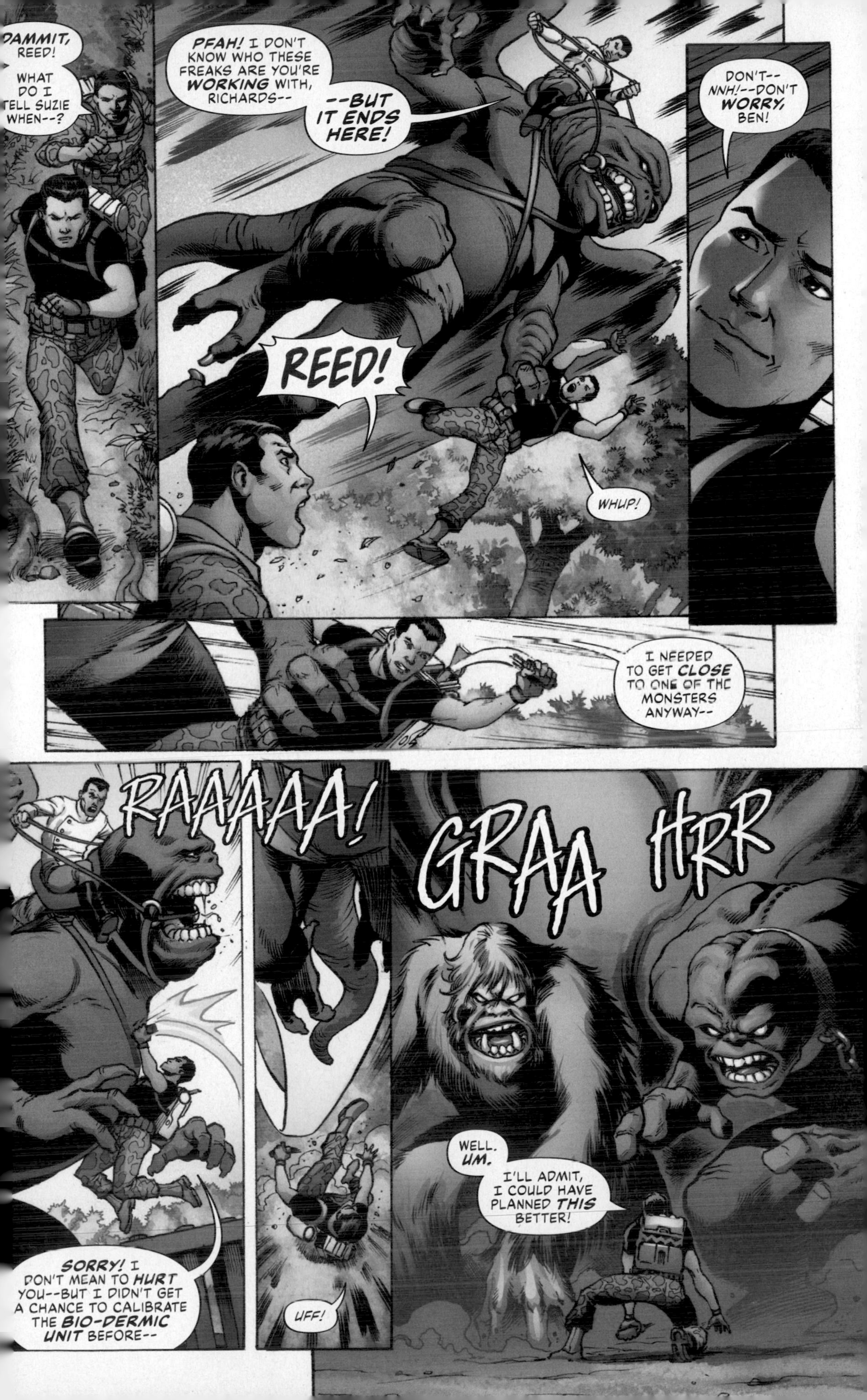
DAMMIT, REED!
WHAT DO I TELL SUZIE WHEN--?
PFAH! I DON'T KNOW WHO THESE FREAKS ARE YOU'RE WORKING WITH, RICHARDS--
--BUT IT ENDS HERE!
REED!
WHUP!
DON'T-- NNH!--DON'T WORRY, BEN!
I NEEDED TO GET CLOSE TO ONE OF THE MONSTERS ANYWAY--
RAAAAAA!
SORRY! I DON'T MEAN TO HURT YOU--BUT I DIDN'T GET A CHANCE TO CALIBRATE THE BIO-DERMIC UNIT BEFORE--
UFF!
GRAA HRR
WELL. UM.
I'LL ADMIT, I COULD HAVE PLANNED THIS BETTER!

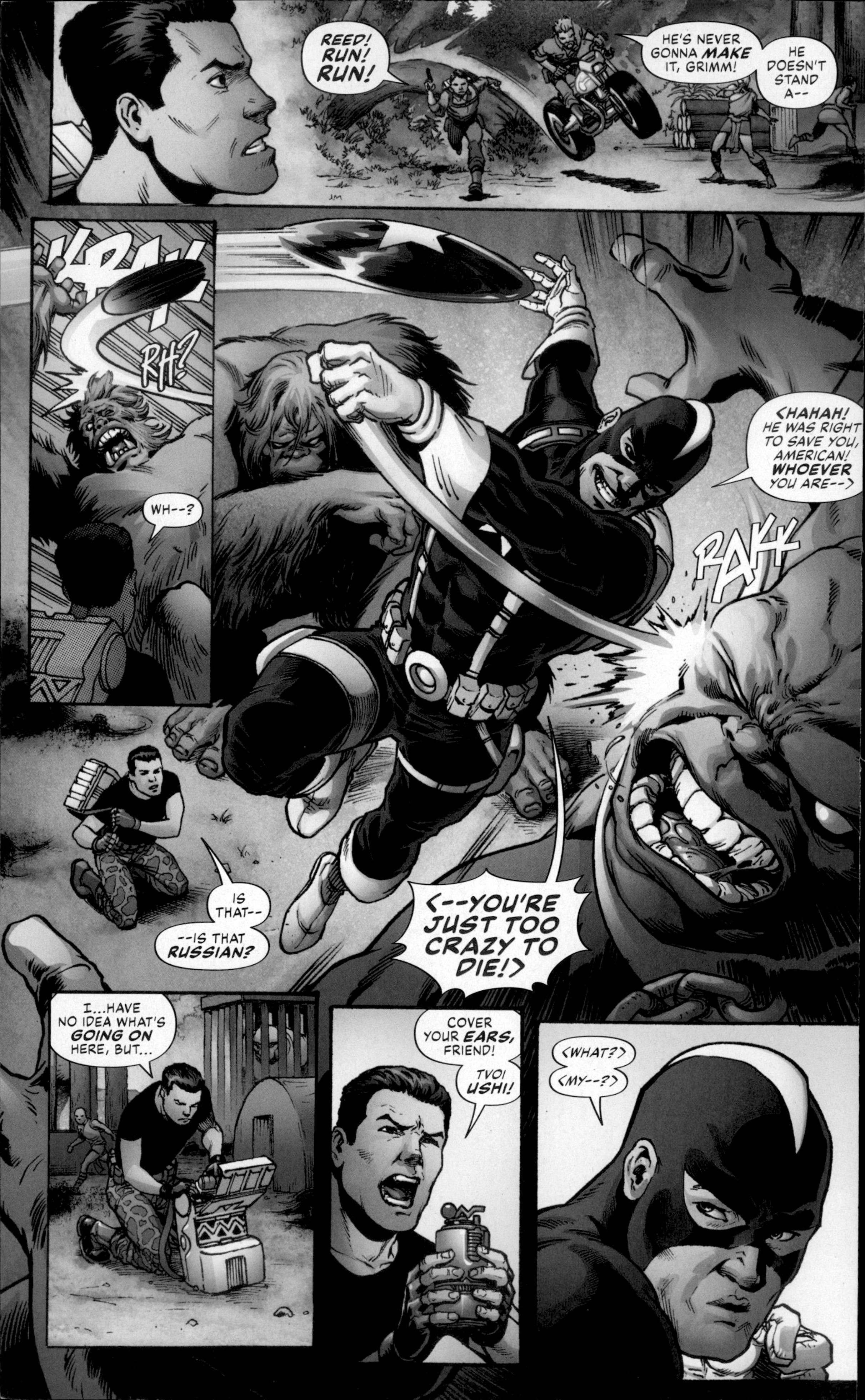

REED! RUN! RUN!
HE'S NEVER GONNA MAKE IT, GRIMM!
HE DOESN'T STAND A--
RH?
WH--?
<HAHAH! HE WAS RIGHT TO SAVE YOU, AMERICAN! WHOEVER YOU ARE-->
RAKK
IS THAT--
--IS THAT RUSSIAN?
<--YOU'RE JUST TOO CRAZY TO DIE!>
I...HAVE NO IDEA WHAT'S GOING ON HERE, BUT...
COVER YOUR EARS, FRIEND!
TVOI USHI!
<WHAT?>
<MY--?>

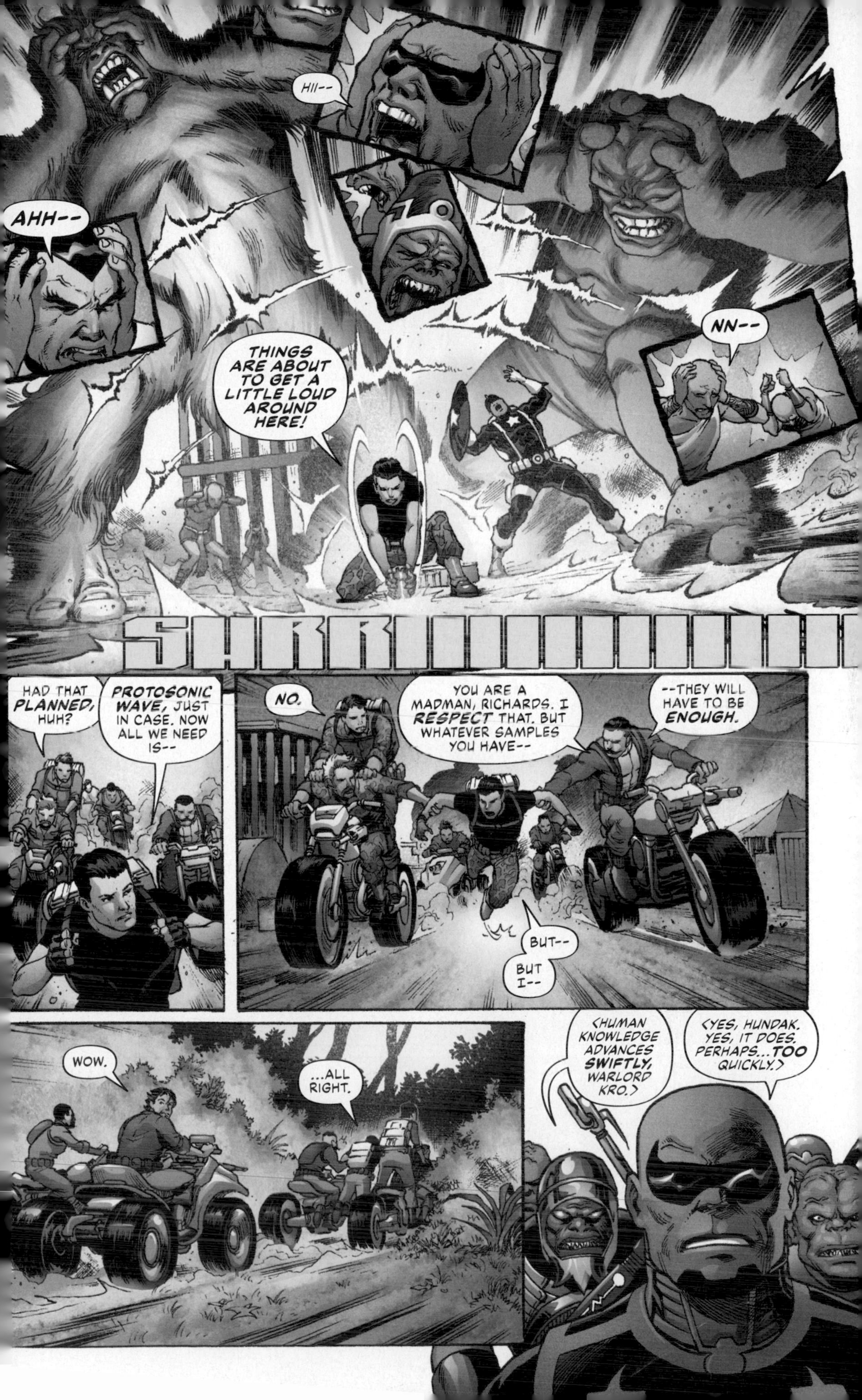
HII--
AHH--
THINGS ARE ABOUT TO GET A LITTLE LOUD AROUND HERE!
NN--
SHRIIIIIIIIIIII
HAD THAT PLANNED, HUH?
PROTOSONIC WAVE, JUST IN CASE. NOW ALL WE NEED IS--
NO.
YOU ARE A MADMAN, RICHARDS. I RESPECT THAT. BUT WHATEVER SAMPLES YOU HAVE--
--THEY WILL HAVE TO BE ENOUGH.
BUT--
BUT I--
WOW.
...ALL RIGHT.
<HUMAN KNOWLEDGE ADVANCES SWIFTLY, WARLORD KRO.>
<YES, HUNDAK. YES, IT DOES. PERHAPS...TOO QUICKLY.>

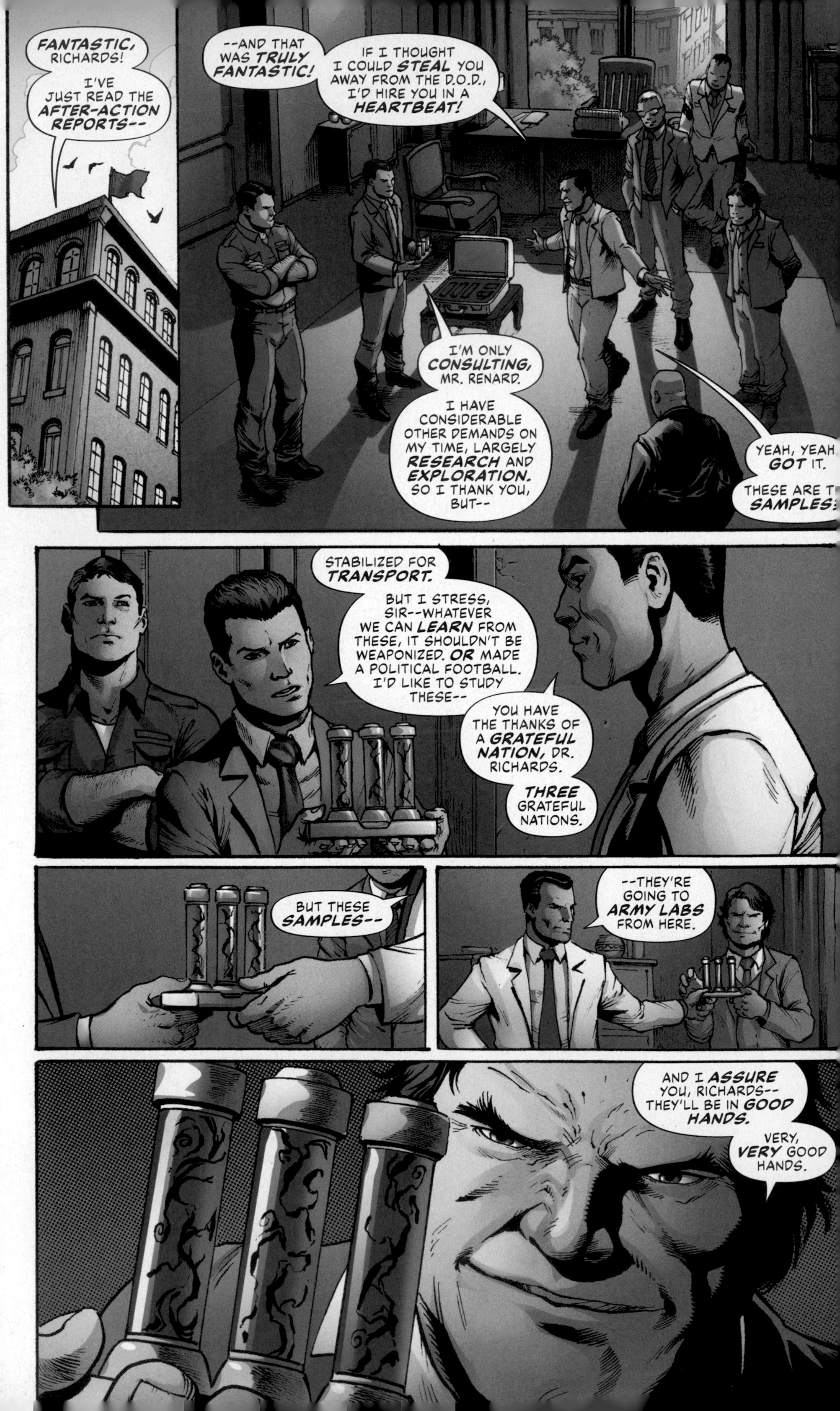
FANTASTIC, RICHARDS!
I'VE JUST READ THE AFTER-ACTION REPORTS--
--AND THAT WAS TRULY FANTASTIC!
IF I THOUGHT I COULD STEAL YOU AWAY FROM THE D.O.D., I'D HIRE YOU IN A HEARTBEAT!
I'M ONLY CONSULTING, MR. RENARD.
I HAVE CONSIDERABLE OTHER DEMANDS ON MY TIME, LARGELY RESEARCH AND EXPLORATION. SO I THANK YOU, BUT--
YEAH, YEAH GOT IT.
STABILIZED FOR TRANSPORT.
BUT I STRESS, SIR--WHATEVER WE CAN LEARN FROM THESE, IT SHOULDN'T BE WEAPONIZED. OR MADE A POLITICAL FOOTBALL. I'D LIKE TO STUDY THESE--
YOU HAVE THE THANKS OF A GRATEFUL NATION, DR. RICHARDS.
THREE GRATEFUL NATIONS.
BUT THESE SAMPLES--
--THEY'RE GOING TO ARMY LABS FROM HERE.
AND I ASSURE YOU, RICHARDS-- THEY'LL BE IN GOOD HANDS.
VERY, VERY GOOD HANDS.

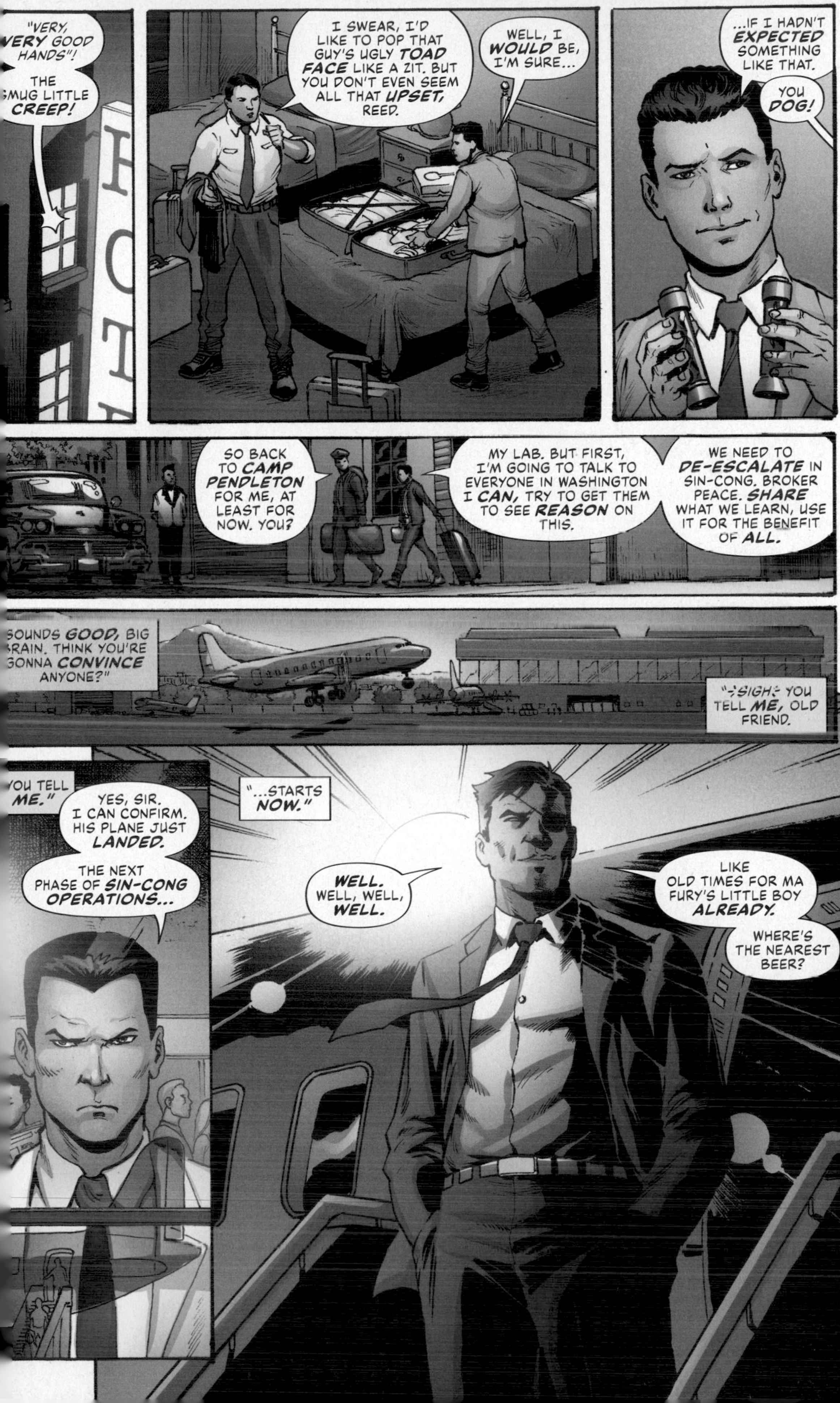
"VERY, VERY GOOD HANDS"!
THE SMUG LITTLE CREEP!
I SWEAR, I'D LIKE TO POP THAT GUY'S UGLY TOAD FACE LIKE A ZIT. BUT YOU DON'T EVEN SEEM ALL THAT UPSET, REED.
WELL, I WOULD BE, I'M SURE...
...IF I HADN'T EXPECTED SOMETHING LIKE THAT.
YOU DOG!
SO BACK TO CAMP PENDLETON FOR ME, AT LEAST FOR NOW. YOU?
MY LAB. BUT FIRST, I'M GOING TO TALK TO EVERYONE IN WASHINGTON I CAN, TRY TO GET THEM TO SEE REASON ON THIS.
WE NEED TO DE-ESCALATE IN SIN-CONG. BROKER PEACE. SHARE WHAT WE LEARN, USE IT FOR THE BENEFIT OF ALL.
SOUNDS GOOD, BIG BRAIN. THINK YOU'RE GONNA CONVINCE ANYONE?"
"-SIGH- YOU TELL ME, OLD FRIEND.
YOU TELL ME."
YES, SIR. I CAN CONFIRM. HIS PLANE JUST LANDED.
THE NEXT PHASE OF SIN-CONG OPERATIONS...
"...STARTS NOW."
WELL. WELL, WELL, WELL.
LIKE OLD TIMES FOR MA FURY'S LITTLE BOY ALREADY.
WHERE'S THE NEAREST BEER?

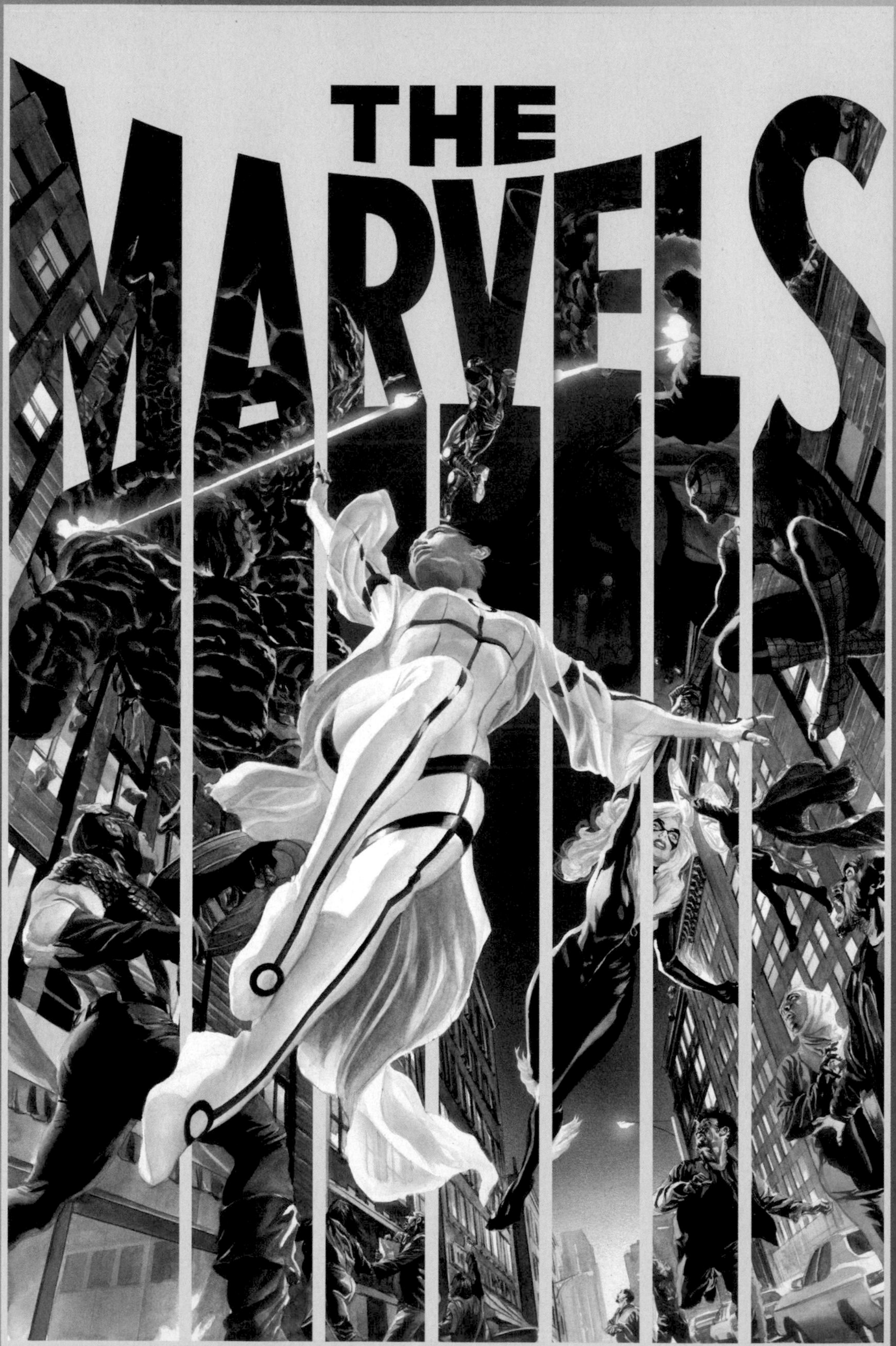
THE
MARVELS

PART FOUR: **"Ohio's Fine"**

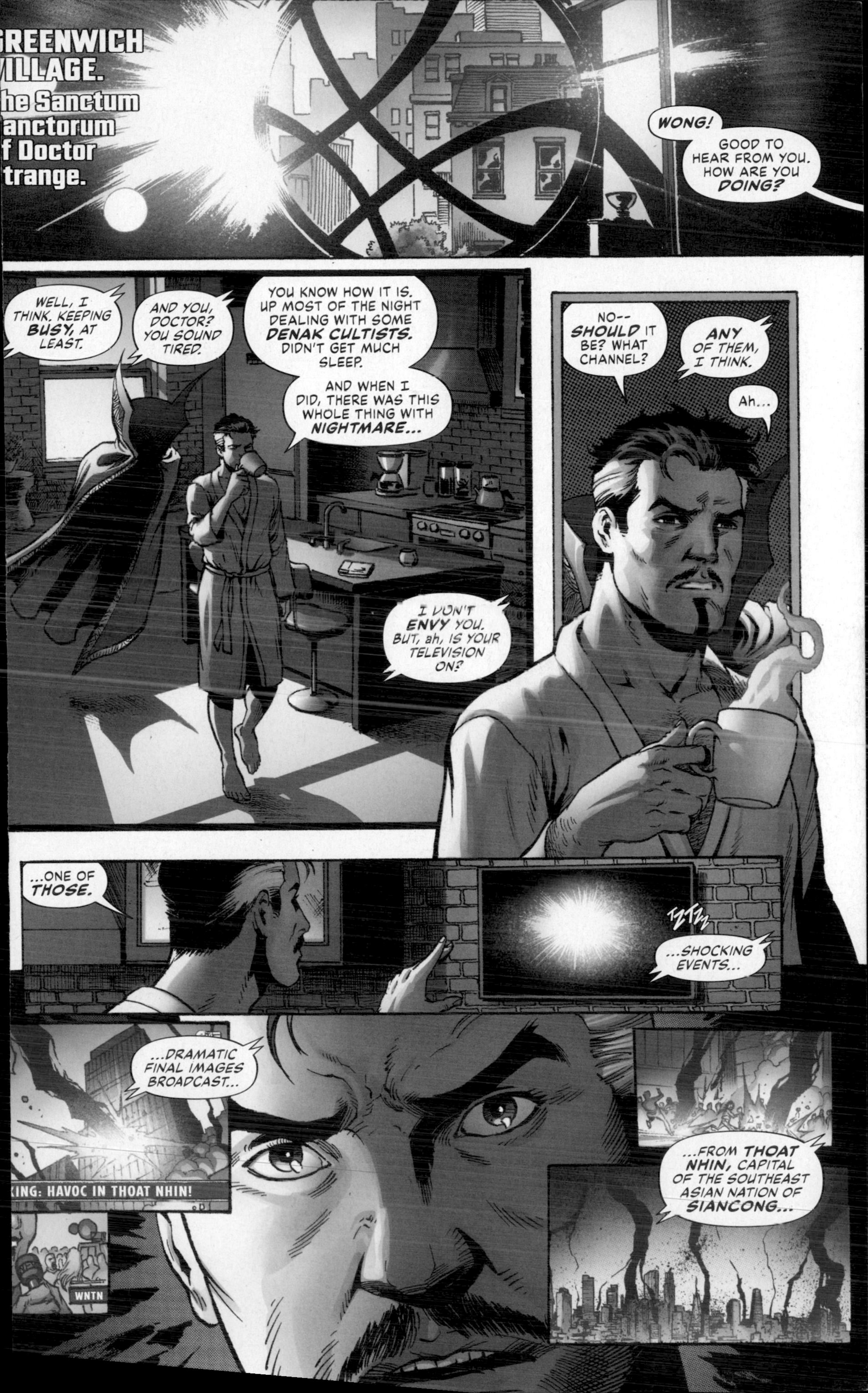

GREENWICH VILLAGE.
The Sanctum Sanctorum of Doctor Strange.
WONG!
GOOD TO HEAR FROM YOU. HOW ARE YOU DOING?
WELL, I THINK. KEEPING BUSY, AT LEAST.
AND YOU, DOCTOR? YOU SOUND TIRED.
YOU KNOW HOW IT IS. UP MOST OF THE NIGHT DEALING WITH SOME DENAK CULTISTS. DIDN'T GET MUCH SLEEP.
AND WHEN I DID, THERE WAS THIS WHOLE THING WITH NIGHTMARE...
I DON'T ENVY YOU. BUT, ah, IS YOUR TELEVISION ON?
NO-- SHOULD IT BE? WHAT CHANNEL?
ANY OF THEM, I THINK.
Ah...
...ONE OF THOSE.
TZTZZ
...SHOCKING EVENTS...
...DRAMATIC FINAL IMAGES BROADCAST...
KING: HAVOC IN THOAT NHIN!
WNTN
...FROM THOAT NHIN, CAPITAL OF THE SOUTHEAST ASIAN NATION OF SIANCONG...

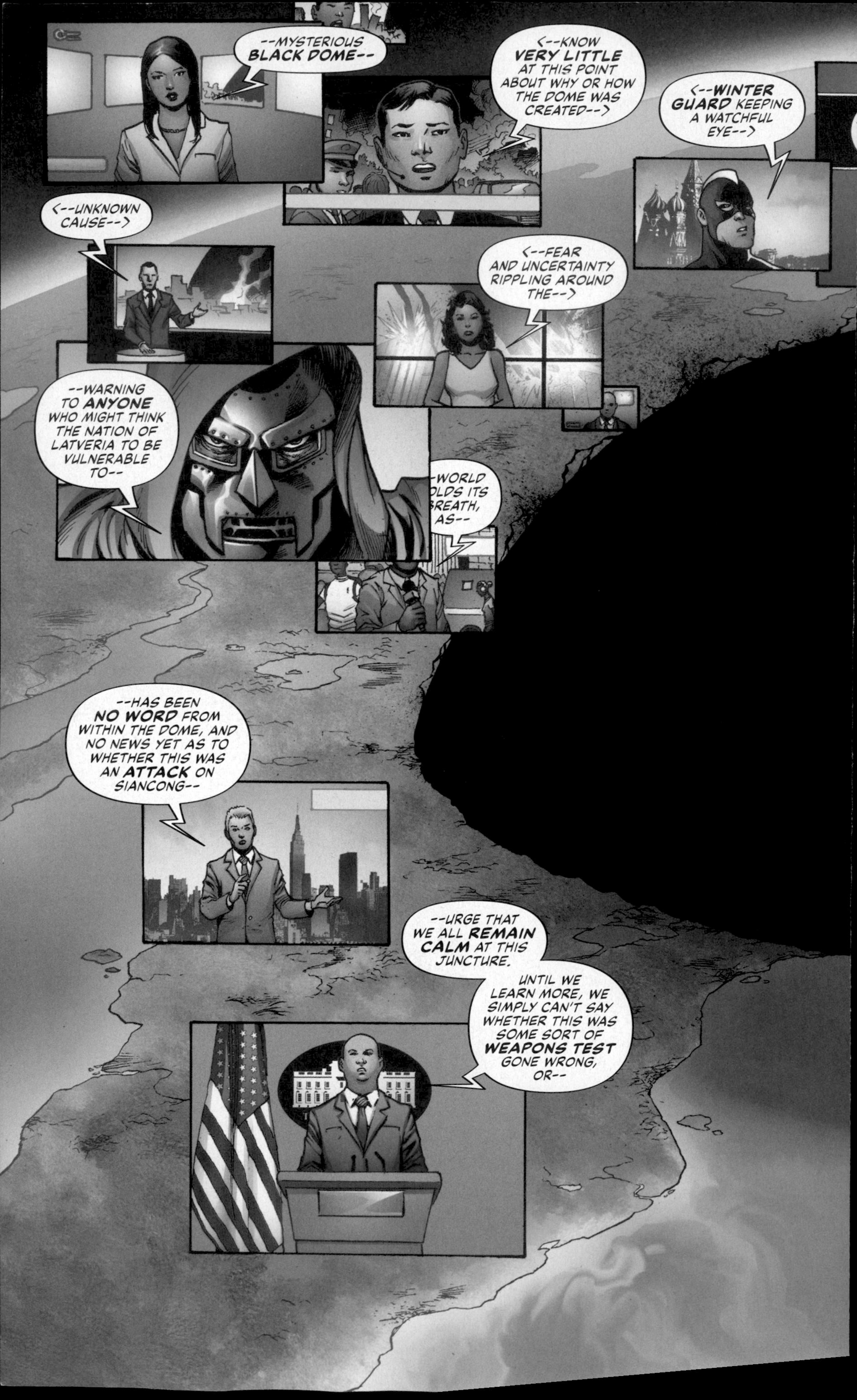
--MYSTERIOUS BLACK DOME--
<--KNOW VERY LITTLE AT THIS POINT ABOUT WHY OR HOW THE DOME WAS CREATED-->
<--WINTER GUARD KEEPING A WATCHFUL EYE-->
<--UNKNOWN CAUSE-->
<--FEAR AND UNCERTAINTY RIPPLING AROUND THE-->
--WARNING TO ANYONE WHO MIGHT THINK THE NATION OF LATVERIA TO BE VULNERABLE TO--
-WORLD OLDS ITS REATH, AS--
--HAS BEEN NO WORD FROM WITHIN THE DOME, AND NO NEWS YET AS TO WHETHER THIS WAS AN ATTACK ON SIANCONG--
--URGE THAT WE ALL REMAIN CALM AT THIS JUNCTURE.
UNTIL WE LEARN MORE, WE SIMPLY CAN'T SAY WHETHER THIS WAS SOME SORT OF WEAPONS TEST GONE WRONG, OR--

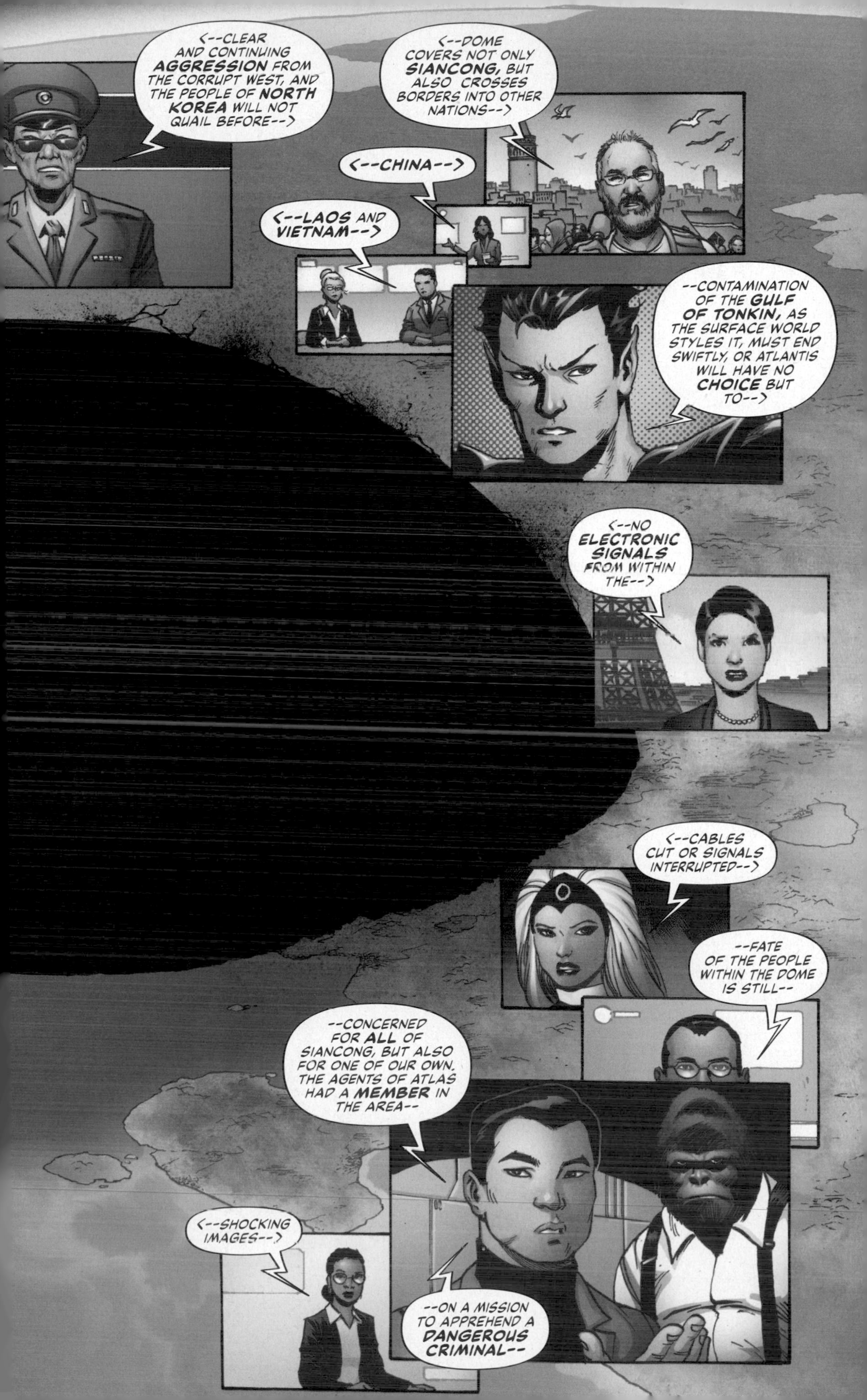

<--CLEAR AND CONTINUING AGGRESSION FROM THE CORRUPT WEST, AND THE PEOPLE OF NORTH KOREA WILL NOT QUAIL BEFORE-->
<--DOME COVERS NOT ONLY SIANCONG, BUT ALSO CROSSES BORDERS INTO OTHER NATIONS-->
<--CHINA-->
<--LAOS AND VIETNAM-->
--CONTAMINATION OF THE GULF OF TONKIN, AS THE SURFACE WORLD STYLES IT, MUST END SWIFTLY, OR ATLANTIS WILL HAVE NO CHOICE BUT TO-->
<--NO ELECTRONIC SIGNALS FROM WITHIN THE-->
<--CABLES CUT OR SIGNALS INTERRUPTED-->
--FATE OF THE PEOPLE WITHIN THE DOME IS STILL--
--CONCERNED FOR ALL OF SIANCONG, BUT ALSO FOR ONE OF OUR OWN. THE AGENTS OF ATLAS HAD A MEMBER IN THE AREA--
<--SHOCKING IMAGES-->
--ON A MISSION TO APPREHEND A DANGEROUS CRIMINAL--

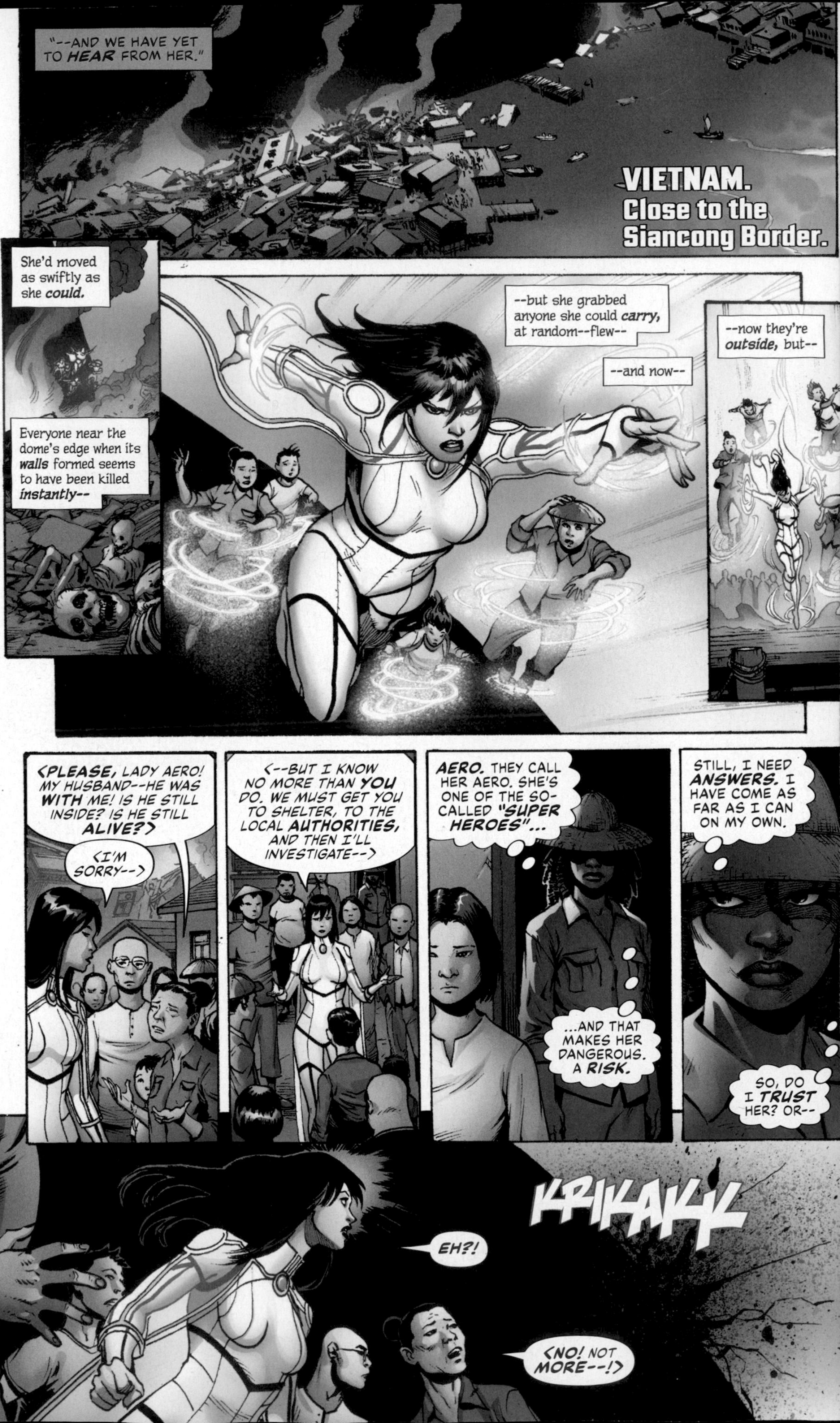
"--AND WE HAVE YET TO HEAR FROM HER."
VIETNAM. Close to the Siancong Border.
She'd moved as swiftly as she could.
Everyone near the dome's edge when its walls formed seems to have been killed instantly--
--but she grabbed anyone she could carry, at random--flew--
--and now--
--now they're outside, but--
<PLEASE, LADY AERO! MY HUSBAND--HE WAS WITH ME! IS HE STILL INSIDE? IS HE STILL ALIVE?>
<I'M SORRY-->
<--BUT I KNOW NO MORE THAN YOU DO. WE MUST GET YOU TO SHELTER, TO THE LOCAL AUTHORITIES, AND THEN I'LL INVESTIGATE-->
AERO. THEY CALL HER AERO. SHE'S ONE OF THE SO-CALLED "SUPER HEROES"...
...AND THAT MAKES HER DANGEROUS. A RISK.
STILL, I NEED ANSWERS. I HAVE COME AS FAR AS I CAN ON MY OWN.
SO, DO I TRUST HER? OR--
KRIKAKK
EH?!
<NO! NOT MORE--!>

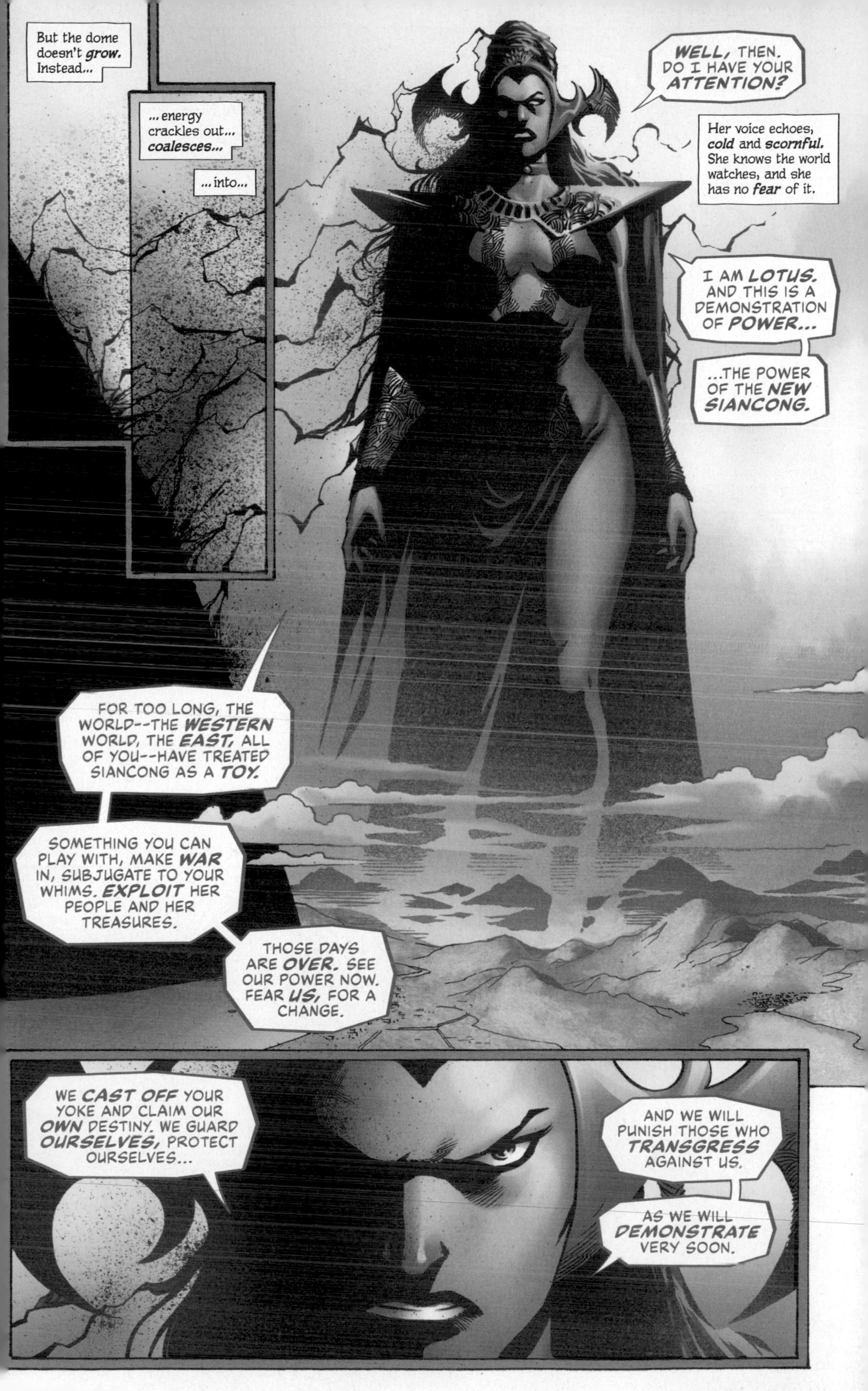

But the dome doesn't *grow.* Instead...
...energy crackles out... *coalesces...*
...into...
WELL, THEN. DO I HAVE YOUR *ATTENTION?*
Her voice echoes, *cold* and *scornful.* She knows the world watches, and she has no *fear* of it.
I AM *LOTUS.* AND THIS IS A DEMONSTRATION OF *POWER...*
...THE POWER OF THE *NEW SIANCONG.*
FOR TOO LONG, THE WORLD--THE *WESTERN* WORLD, THE *EAST,* ALL OF YOU--HAVE TREATED SIANCONG AS A *TOY.*
SOMETHING YOU CAN PLAY WITH, MAKE *WAR* IN, SUBJUGATE TO YOUR WHIMS. *EXPLOIT* HER PEOPLE AND HER TREASURES.
THOSE DAYS ARE *OVER.* SEE OUR POWER NOW. FEAR *US,* FOR A CHANGE.
WE *CAST OFF* YOUR YOKE AND CLAIM OUR *OWN* DESTINY. WE GUARD *OURSELVES,* PROTECT OURSELVES...
AND WE WILL PUNISH THOSE WHO *TRANSGRESS* AGAINST US.
AS WE WILL *DEMONSTRATE* VERY SOON.

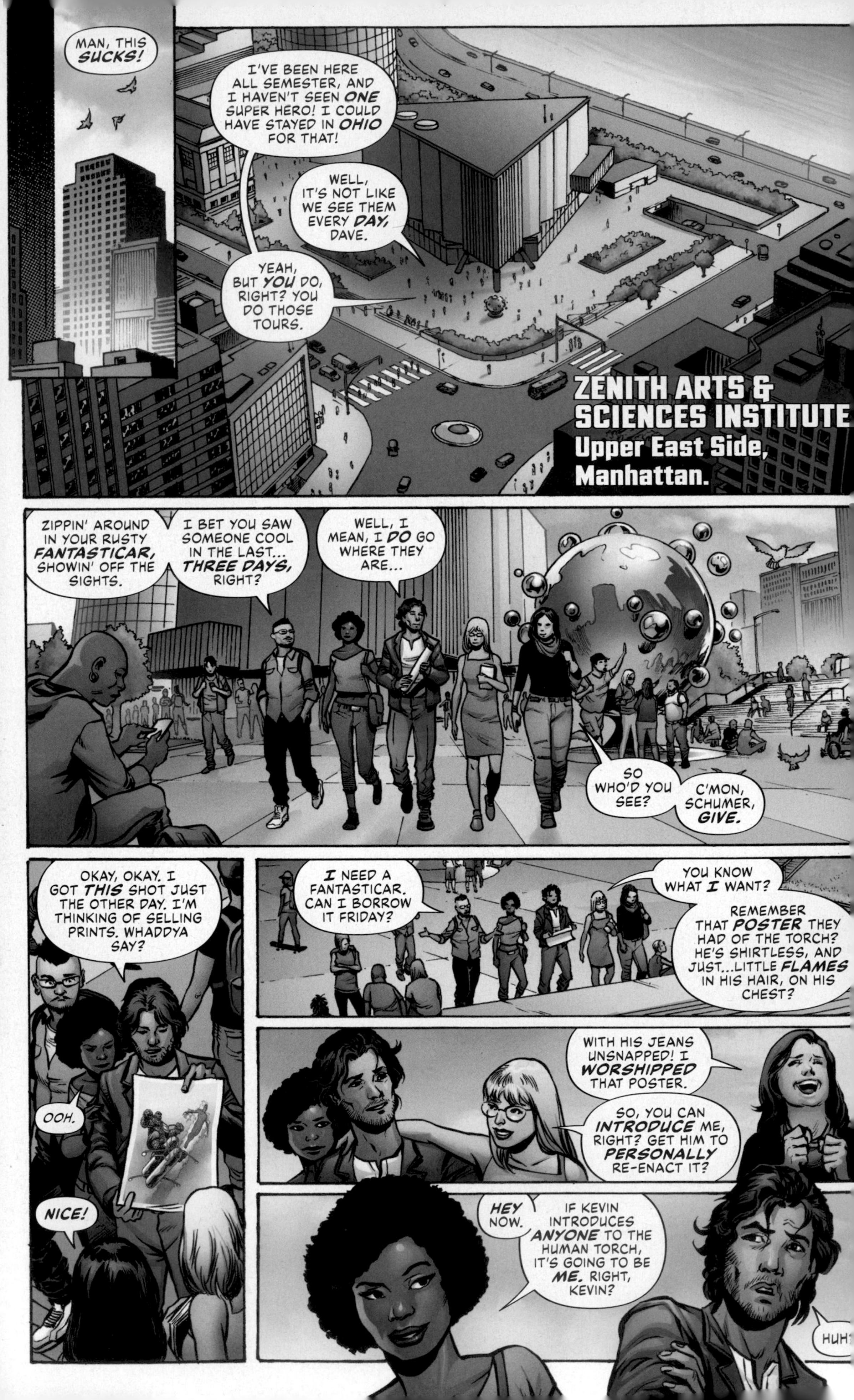
MAN, THIS SUCKS!
I'VE BEEN HERE ALL SEMESTER, AND I HAVEN'T SEEN ONE SUPER HERO! I COULD HAVE STAYED IN OHIO FOR THAT!
WELL, IT'S NOT LIKE WE SEE THEM EVERY DAY, DAVE.
YEAH, BUT YOU DO, RIGHT? YOU DO THOSE TOURS.
ZENITH ARTS & SCIENCES INSTITUTE
Upper East Side, Manhattan.
ZIPPIN' AROUND IN YOUR RUSTY FANTASTICAR, SHOWIN' OFF THE SIGHTS.
I BET YOU SAW SOMEONE COOL IN THE LAST... THREE DAYS, RIGHT?
WELL, I MEAN, I DO GO WHERE THEY ARE...
SO WHO'D YOU SEE?
C'MON, SCHUMER, GIVE.
OKAY, OKAY. I GOT THIS SHOT JUST THE OTHER DAY. I'M THINKING OF SELLING PRINTS. WHADDYA SAY?
OOH.
NICE!
I NEED A FANTASTICAR. CAN I BORROW IT FRIDAY?
YOU KNOW WHAT I WANT?
REMEMBER THAT POSTER THEY HAD OF THE TORCH? HE'S SHIRTLESS, AND JUST...LITTLE FLAMES IN HIS HAIR, ON HIS CHEST?
WITH HIS JEANS UNSNAPPED! I WORSHIPPED THAT POSTER.
SO, YOU CAN INTRODUCE ME, RIGHT? GET HIM TO PERSONALLY RE-ENACT IT?
HEY NOW.
IF KEVIN INTRODUCES ANYONE TO THE HUMAN TORCH, IT'S GOING TO BE ME. RIGHT, KEVIN?
HUH?

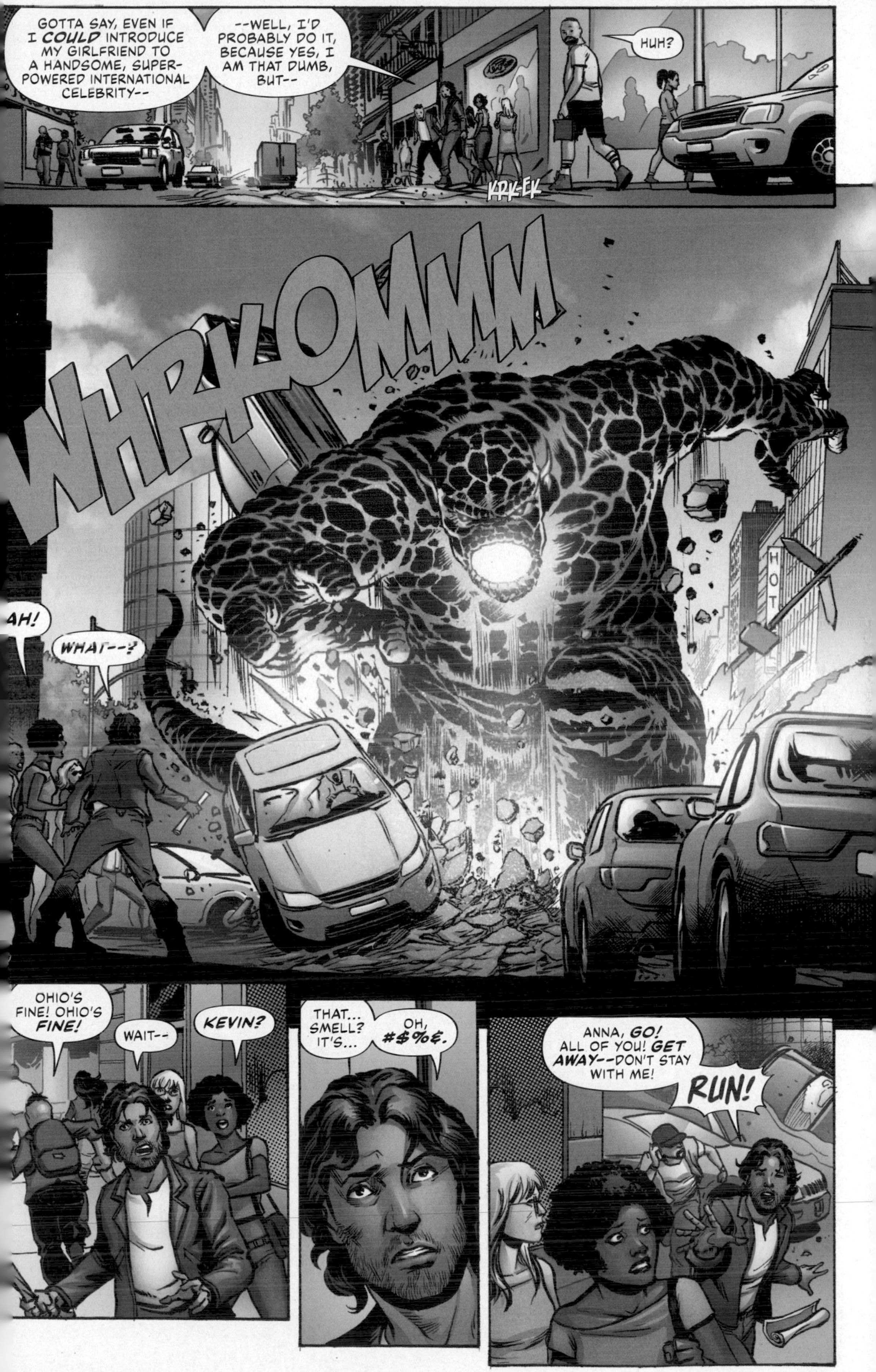
GOTTA SAY, EVEN IF I COULD INTRODUCE MY GIRLFRIEND TO A HANDSOME, SUPER-POWERED INTERNATIONAL CELEBRITY--
--WELL, I'D PROBABLY DO IT, BECAUSE YES, I AM THAT DUMB, BUT--
HUH?
KRK-EK
WHRKOMMM
AH!
WHAT--?
OHIO'S FINE! OHIO'S FINE!
WAIT--
KEVIN?
THAT... SMELL? IT'S...
OH, #$%&.
ANNA, GO! ALL OF YOU! GET AWAY--DON'T STAY WITH ME!
RUN!

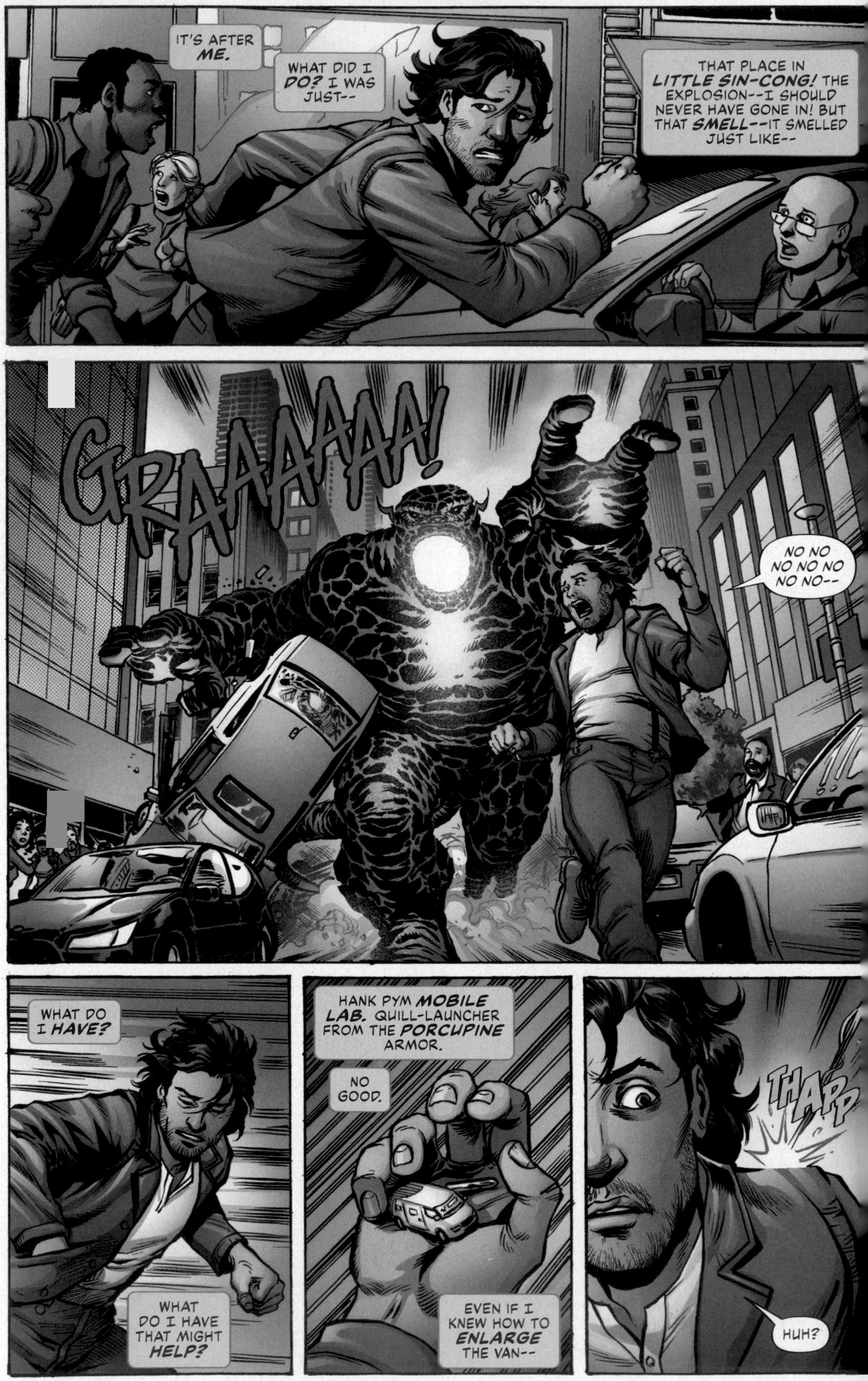
IT'S AFTER ME.
WHAT DID I DO? I WAS JUST--
THAT PLACE IN LITTLE SIN-CONG! THE EXPLOSION--I SHOULD NEVER HAVE GONE IN! BUT THAT SMELL--IT SMELLED JUST LIKE--
GRAAAAAA!
NO NO NO NO NO NO NO--
WHAT DO I HAVE?
WHAT DO I HAVE THAT MIGHT HELP?
HANK PYM MOBILE LAB. QUILL-LAUNCHER FROM THE PORCUPINE ARMOR.
NO GOOD.
EVEN IF I KNEW HOW TO ENLARGE THE VAN--
THAPP
HUH?

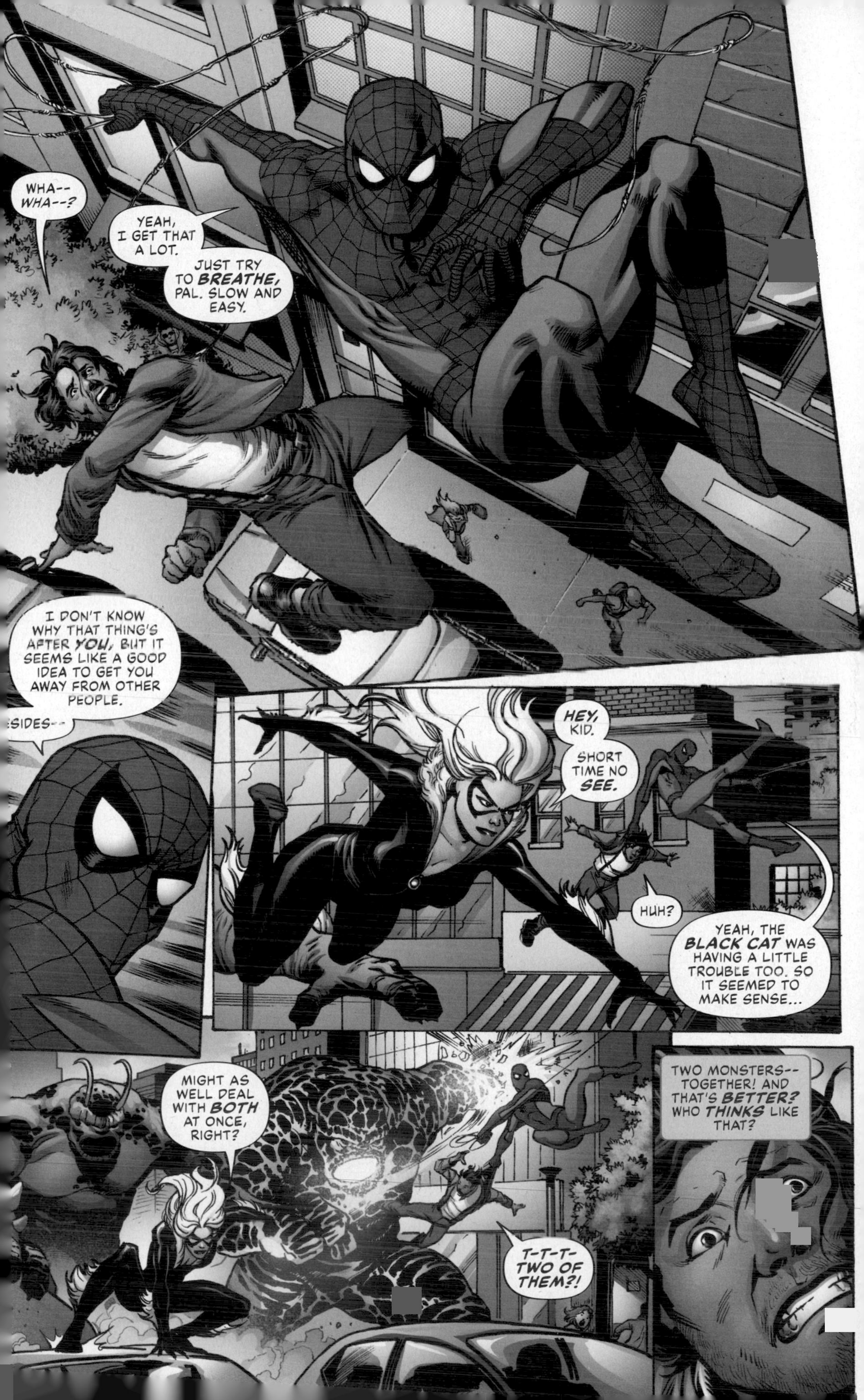
WHA-- WHA--?
YEAH, I GET THAT A LOT.
JUST TRY TO BREATHE, PAL. SLOW AND EASY.
I DON'T KNOW WHY THAT THING'S AFTER YOU, BUT IT SEEMS LIKE A GOOD IDEA TO GET YOU AWAY FROM OTHER PEOPLE.
ESIDES--
HEY, KID.
SHORT TIME NO SEE.
HUH?
YEAH, THE BLACK CAT WAS HAVING A LITTLE TROUBLE TOO. SO IT SEEMED TO MAKE SENSE...
MIGHT AS WELL DEAL WITH BOTH AT ONCE, RIGHT?
T-T-T-TWO OF THEM?!
TWO MONSTERS--TOGETHER! AND THAT'S BETTER? WHO THINKS LIKE THAT?

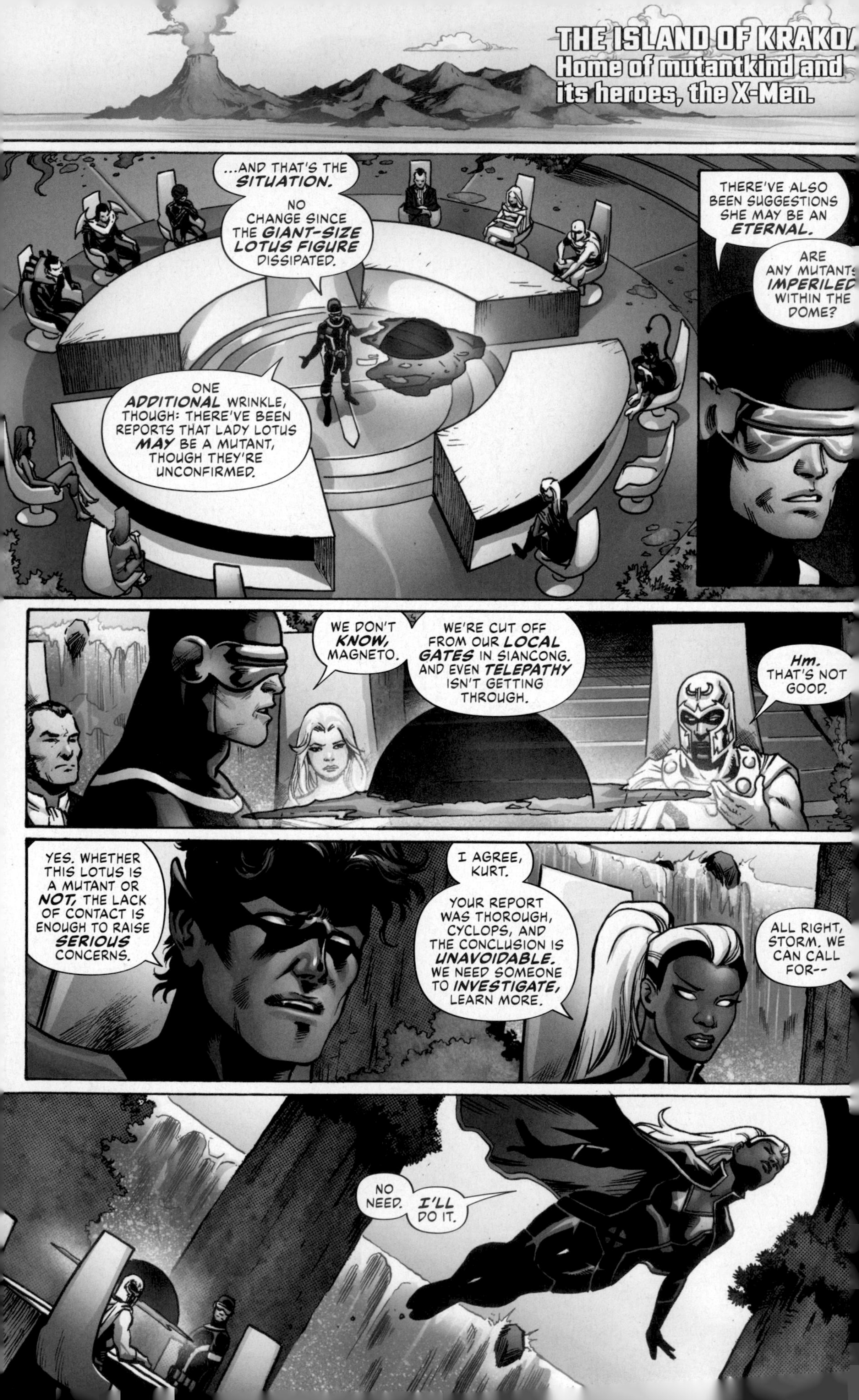
THE ISLAND OF KRAKOA
Home of mutantkind and its heroes, the X-Men.
...AND THAT'S THE SITUATION.
NO CHANGE SINCE THE GIANT-SIZE LOTUS FIGURE DISSIPATED.
ONE ADDITIONAL WRINKLE, THOUGH: THERE'VE BEEN REPORTS THAT LADY LOTUS MAY BE A MUTANT, THOUGH THEY'RE UNCONFIRMED.
THERE'VE ALSO BEEN SUGGESTIONS SHE MAY BE AN ETERNAL.
ARE ANY MUTANTS IMPERILED WITHIN THE DOME?
WE DON'T KNOW, MAGNETO.
WE'RE CUT OFF FROM OUR LOCAL GATES IN SIANCONG. AND EVEN TELEPATHY ISN'T GETTING THROUGH.
Hm. THAT'S NOT GOOD.
YES. WHETHER THIS LOTUS IS A MUTANT OR NOT, THE LACK OF CONTACT IS ENOUGH TO RAISE SERIOUS CONCERNS.
I AGREE, KURT.
YOUR REPORT WAS THOROUGH, CYCLOPS, AND THE CONCLUSION IS UNAVOIDABLE. WE NEED SOMEONE TO INVESTIGATE, LEARN MORE.
ALL RIGHT, STORM. WE CAN CALL FOR--
NO NEED. I'LL DO IT.

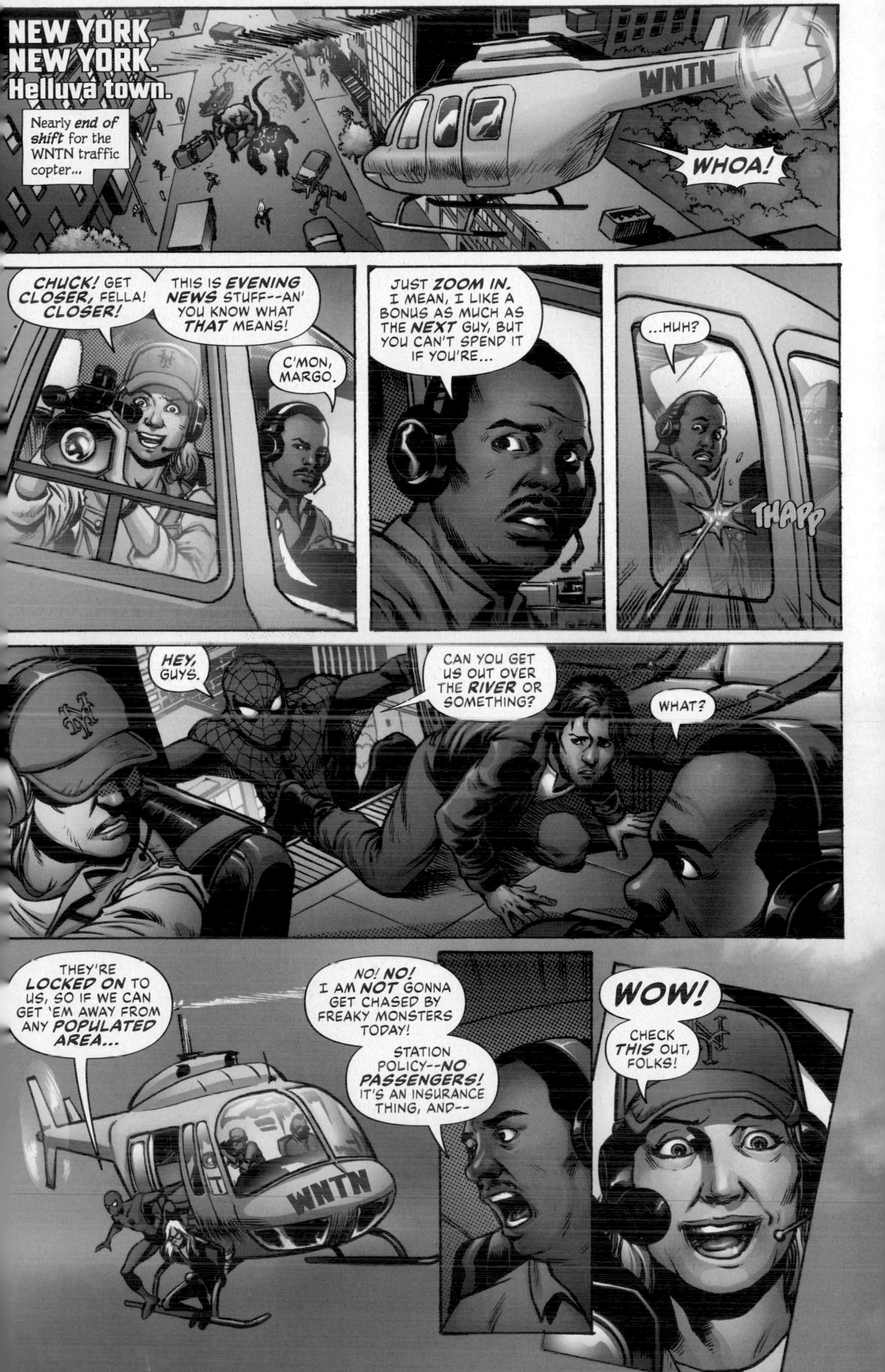
NEW YORK, NEW YORK. Helluva town.
Nearly end of shift for the WNTN traffic copter...
WNTN
WHOA!
CHUCK! GET CLOSER, FELLA! CLOSER!
THIS IS EVENING NEWS STUFF--AN' YOU KNOW WHAT THAT MEANS!
C'MON, MARGO.
JUST ZOOM IN. I MEAN, I LIKE A BONUS AS MUCH AS THE NEXT GUY, BUT YOU CAN'T SPEND IT IF YOU'RE...
...HUH?
THAPP
HEY, GUYS.
CAN YOU GET US OUT OVER THE RIVER OR SOMETHING?
WHAT?
THEY'RE LOCKED ON TO US, SO IF WE CAN GET 'EM AWAY FROM ANY POPULATED AREA...
WNTN
NO! NO! I AM NOT GONNA GET CHASED BY FREAKY MONSTERS TODAY!
STATION POLICY--NO PASSENGERS! IT'S AN INSURANCE THING, AND--
WOW!
CHECK THIS OUT, FOLKS!

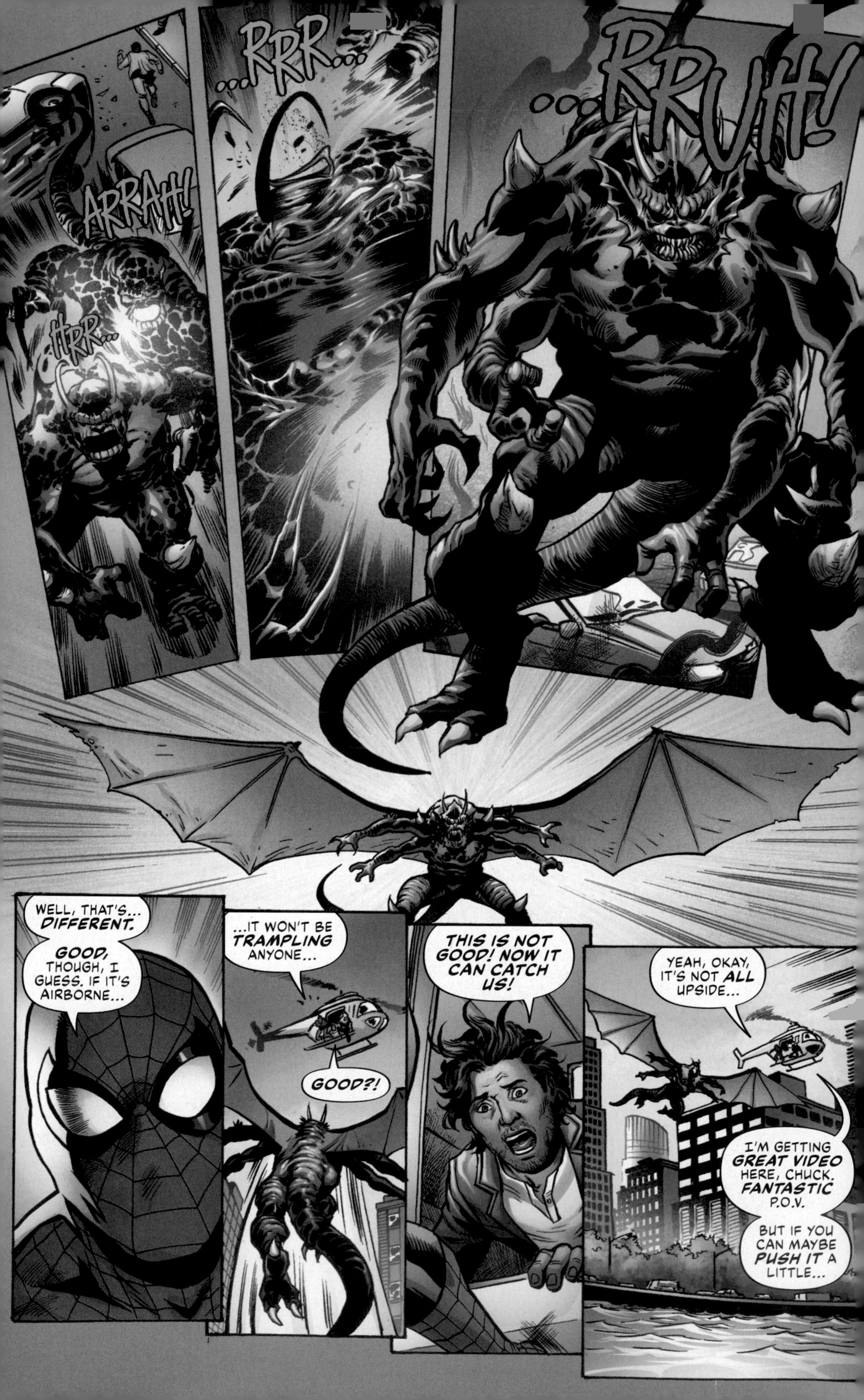
ARRAH!
HRR...
...RRR...
...RRUH!
WELL, THAT'S... DIFFERENT.
GOOD, THOUGH, I GUESS. IF IT'S AIRBORNE...
...IT WON'T BE TRAMPLING ANYONE...
GOOD?!
THIS IS NOT GOOD! NOW IT CAN CATCH US!
YEAH, OKAY, IT'S NOT ALL UPSIDE...
I'M GETTING GREAT VIDEO HERE, CHUCK. FANTASTIC P.O.V.
BUT IF YOU CAN MAYBE PUSH IT A LITTLE...

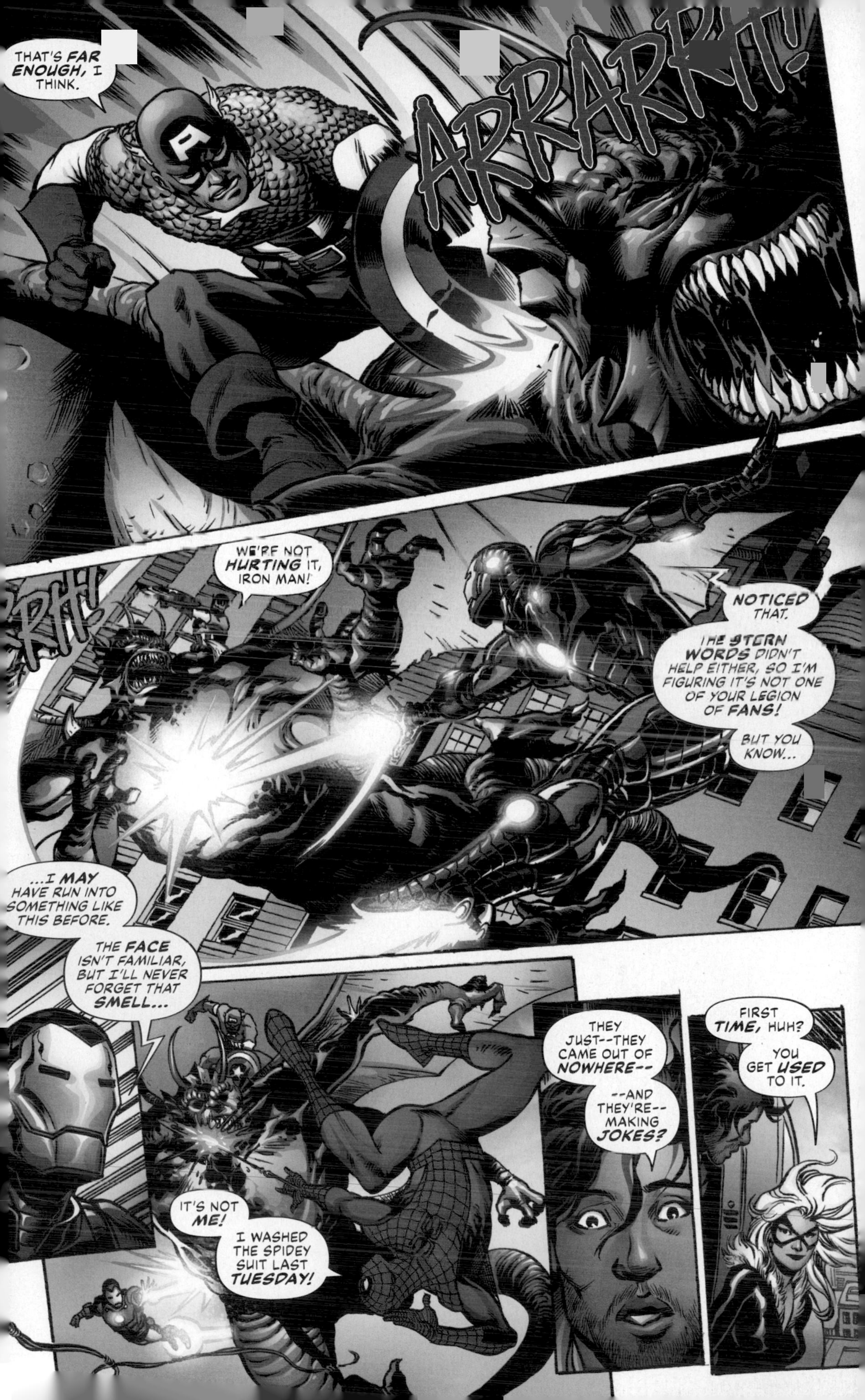
THAT'S FAR ENOUGH, I THINK.
ARRAR
WE'RE NOT HURTING IT, IRON MAN!
NOTICED THAT.
THE STERN WORDS DIDN'T HELP EITHER, SO I'M FIGURING IT'S NOT ONE OF YOUR LEGION OF FANS!
BUT YOU KNOW...
...I MAY HAVE RUN INTO SOMETHING LIKE THIS BEFORE.
THE FACE ISN'T FAMILIAR, BUT I'LL NEVER FORGET THAT SMELL...
IT'S NOT ME!
I WASHED THE SPIDEY SUIT LAST TUESDAY!
THEY JUST--THEY CAME OUT OF NOWHERE--
--AND THEY'RE--MAKING JOKES?
FIRST TIME, HUH?
YOU GET USED TO IT.

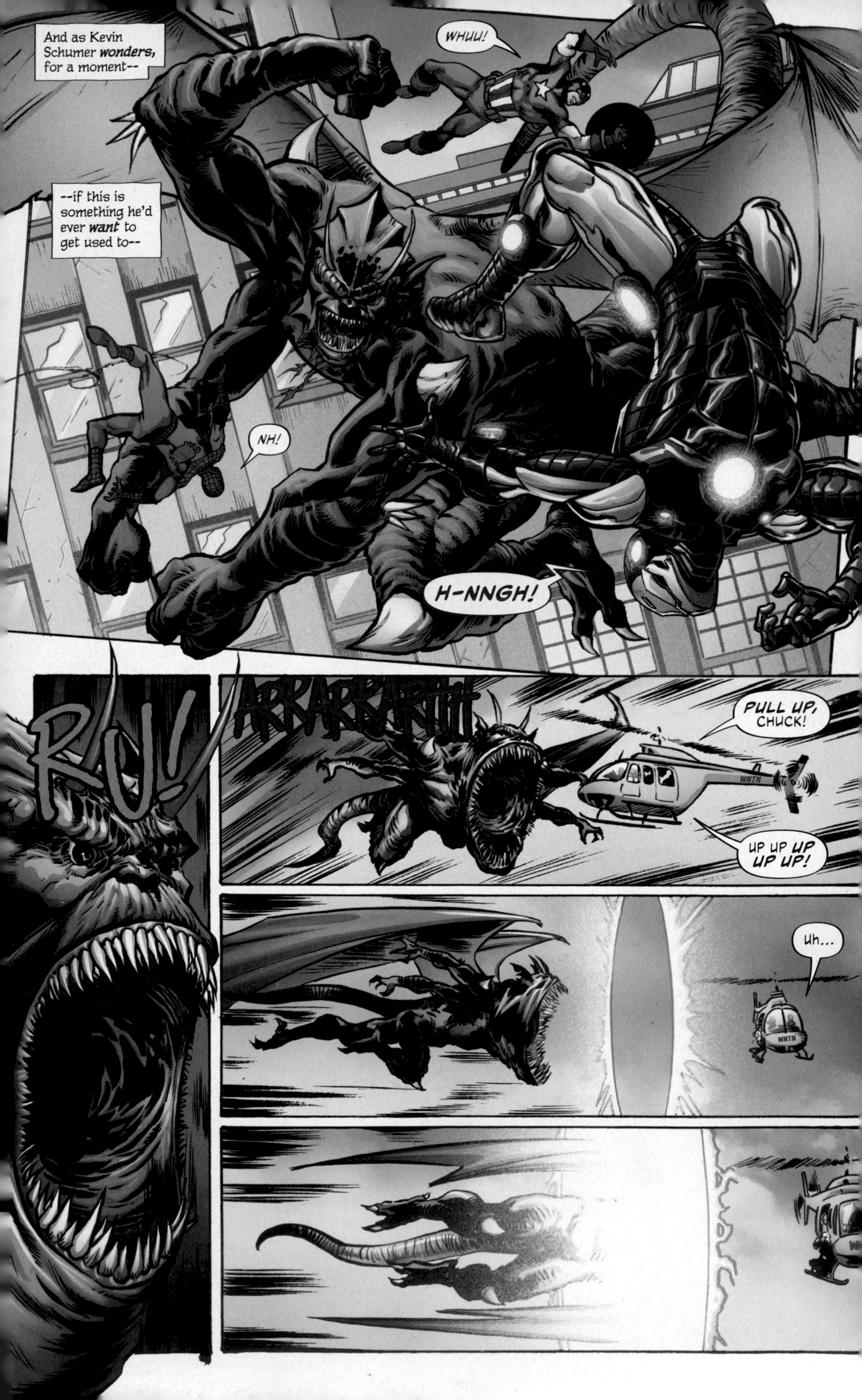
And as Kevin Schumer **wonders,** for a moment--
WHUU!
--if this is something he'd ever **want** to get used to--
NH!
H-NNGH!
RU!
ARRARRARRH!
PULL UP, CHUCK!
UP UP **UP UP UP!**
WNTN
Uh...
WNTN

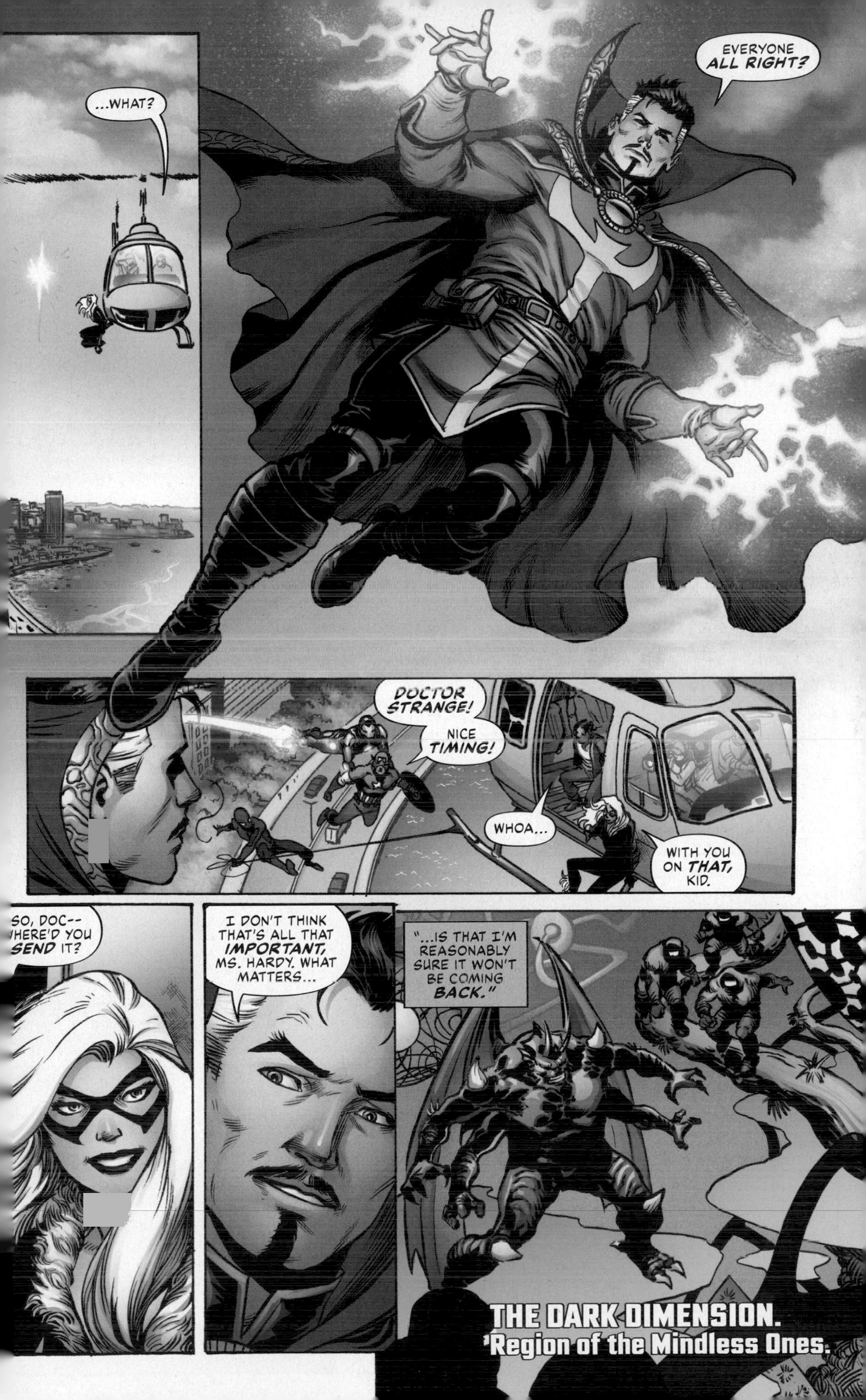
...WHAT?
EVERYONE ALL RIGHT?
DOCTOR STRANGE!
NICE TIMING!
WHOA...
WITH YOU ON THAT, KID.
SO, DOC-- HERE'D YOU SEND IT?
I DON'T THINK THAT'S ALL THAT IMPORTANT, MS. HARDY. WHAT MATTERS...
"...IS THAT I'M REASONABLY SURE IT WON'T BE COMING BACK."
THE DARK DIMENSION.
'Region of the Mindless Ones.

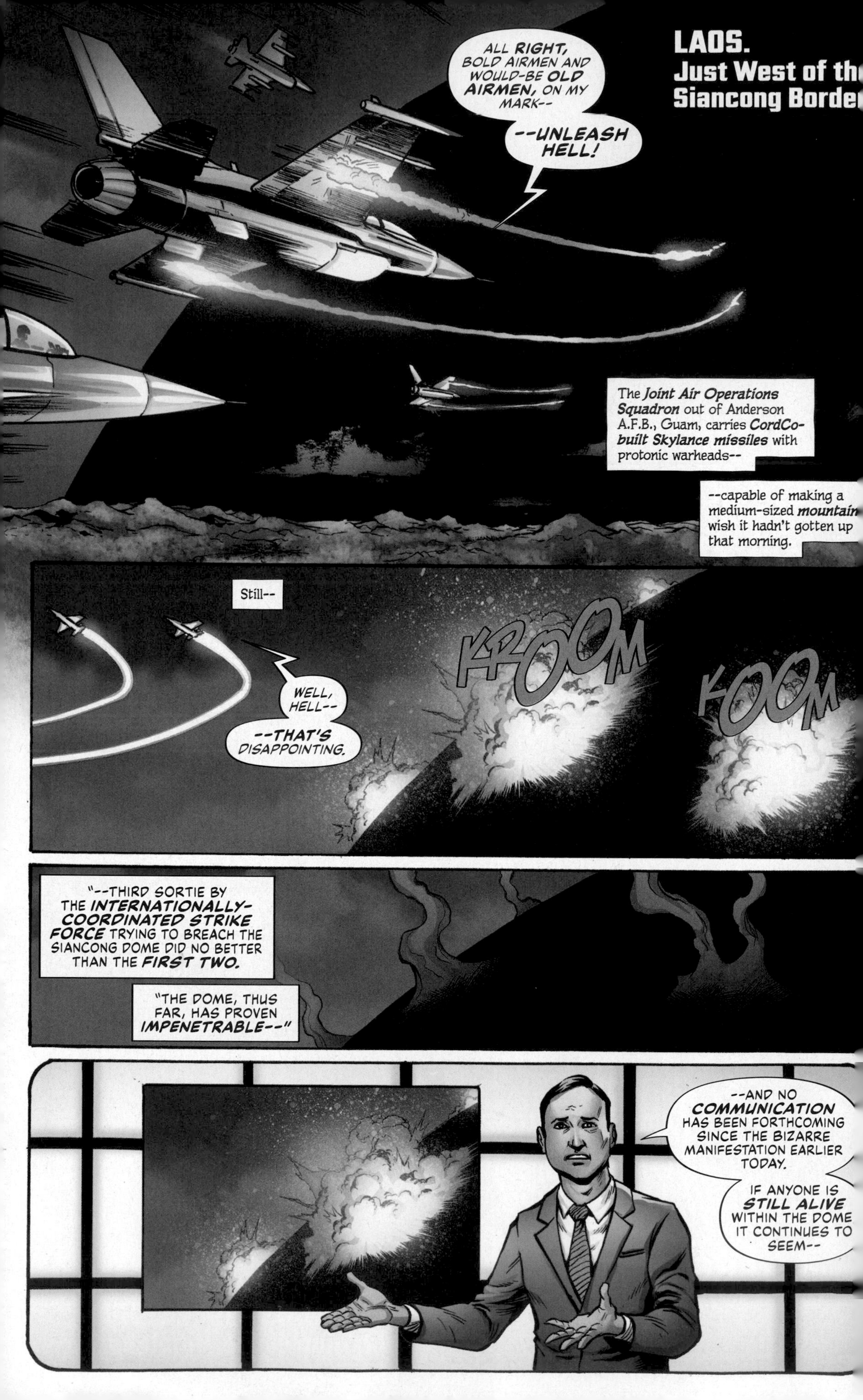
LAOS. Just West of the Siancong Border
ALL RIGHT, BOLD AIRMEN AND WOULD-BE OLD AIRMEN, ON MY MARK--
--UNLEASH HELL!
The Joint Air Operations Squadron out of Anderson A.F.B., Guam, carries CordCo-built Skylance missiles with protonic warheads--
--capable of making a medium-sized mountain wish it hadn't gotten up that morning.
Still--
WELL, HELL--
--THAT'S DISAPPOINTING.
KROOOM
KOOOM
"--THIRD SORTIE BY THE INTERNATIONALLY-COORDINATED STRIKE FORCE TRYING TO BREACH THE SIANCONG DOME DID NO BETTER THAN THE FIRST TWO.
"THE DOME, THUS FAR, HAS PROVEN IMPENETRABLE--"
--AND NO COMMUNICATION HAS BEEN FORTHCOMING SINCE THE BIZARRE MANIFESTATION EARLIER TODAY.
IF ANYONE IS STILL ALIVE WITHIN THE DOME IT CONTINUES TO SEEM--

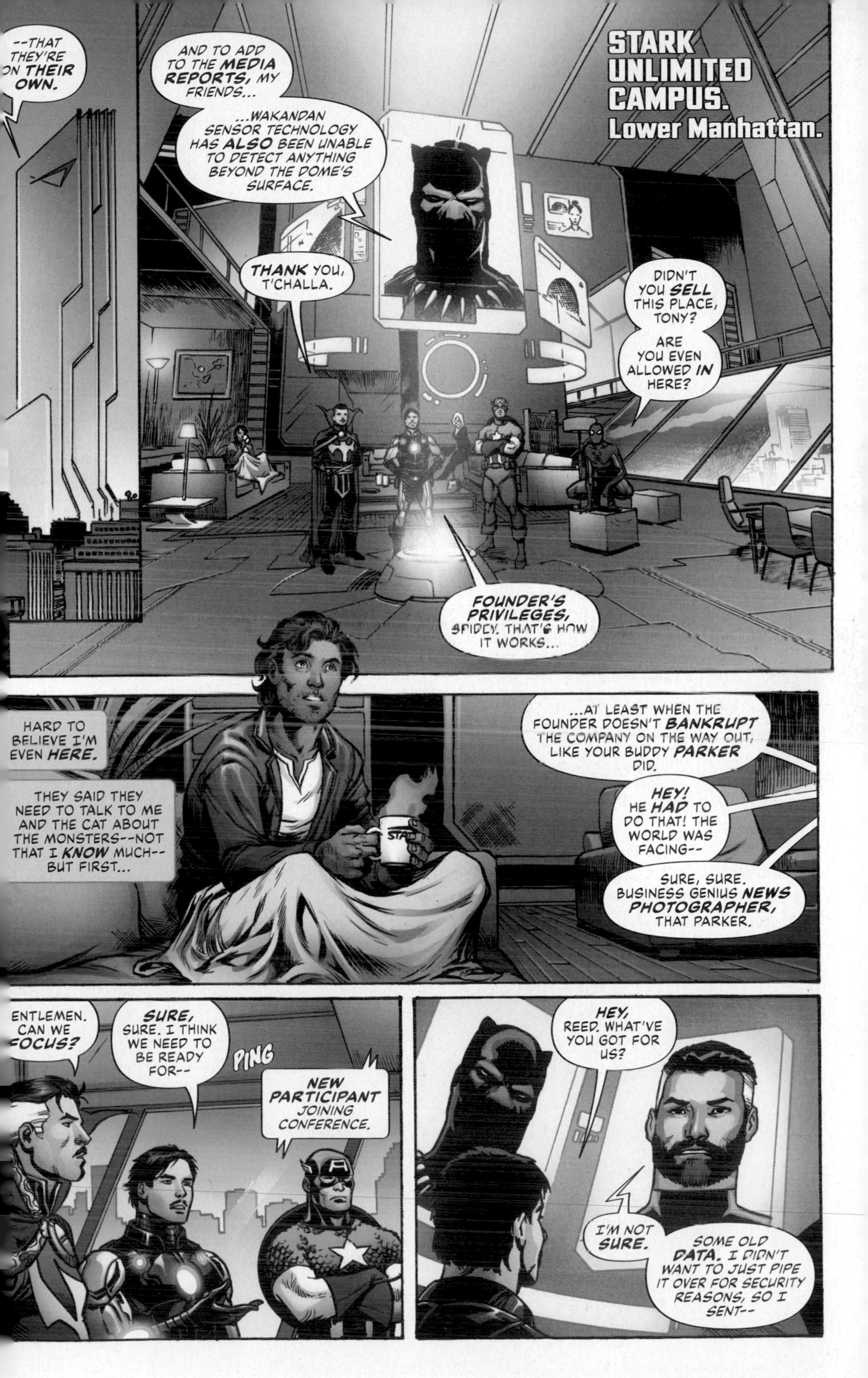
STARK UNLIMITED CAMPUS. Lower Manhattan.
--THAT THEY'RE ON THEIR OWN.
AND TO ADD TO THE MEDIA REPORTS, MY FRIENDS...
...WAKANDAN SENSOR TECHNOLOGY HAS ALSO BEEN UNABLE TO DETECT ANYTHING BEYOND THE DOME'S SURFACE.
THANK YOU, T'CHALLA.
DIDN'T YOU SELL THIS PLACE, TONY?
ARE YOU EVEN ALLOWED IN HERE?
FOUNDER'S PRIVILEGES, SPIDEY. THAT'S HOW IT WORKS...
HARD TO BELIEVE I'M EVEN HERE.
THEY SAID THEY NEED TO TALK TO ME AND THE CAT ABOUT THE MONSTERS--NOT THAT I KNOW MUCH--BUT FIRST...
...AT LEAST WHEN THE FOUNDER DOESN'T BANKRUPT THE COMPANY ON THE WAY OUT, LIKE YOUR BUDDY PARKER DID.
HEY! HE HAD TO DO THAT! THE WORLD WAS FACING--
SURE, SURE. BUSINESS GENIUS NEWS PHOTOGRAPHER, THAT PARKER.
ENTLEMEN. CAN WE FOCUS?
SURE, SURE. I THINK WE NEED TO BE READY FOR--
PING
NEW PARTICIPANT JOINING CONFERENCE.
HEY, REED. WHAT'VE YOU GOT FOR US?
I'M NOT SURE.
SOME OLD DATA. I DIDN'T WANT TO JUST PIPE IT OVER FOR SECURITY REASONS, SO I SENT--

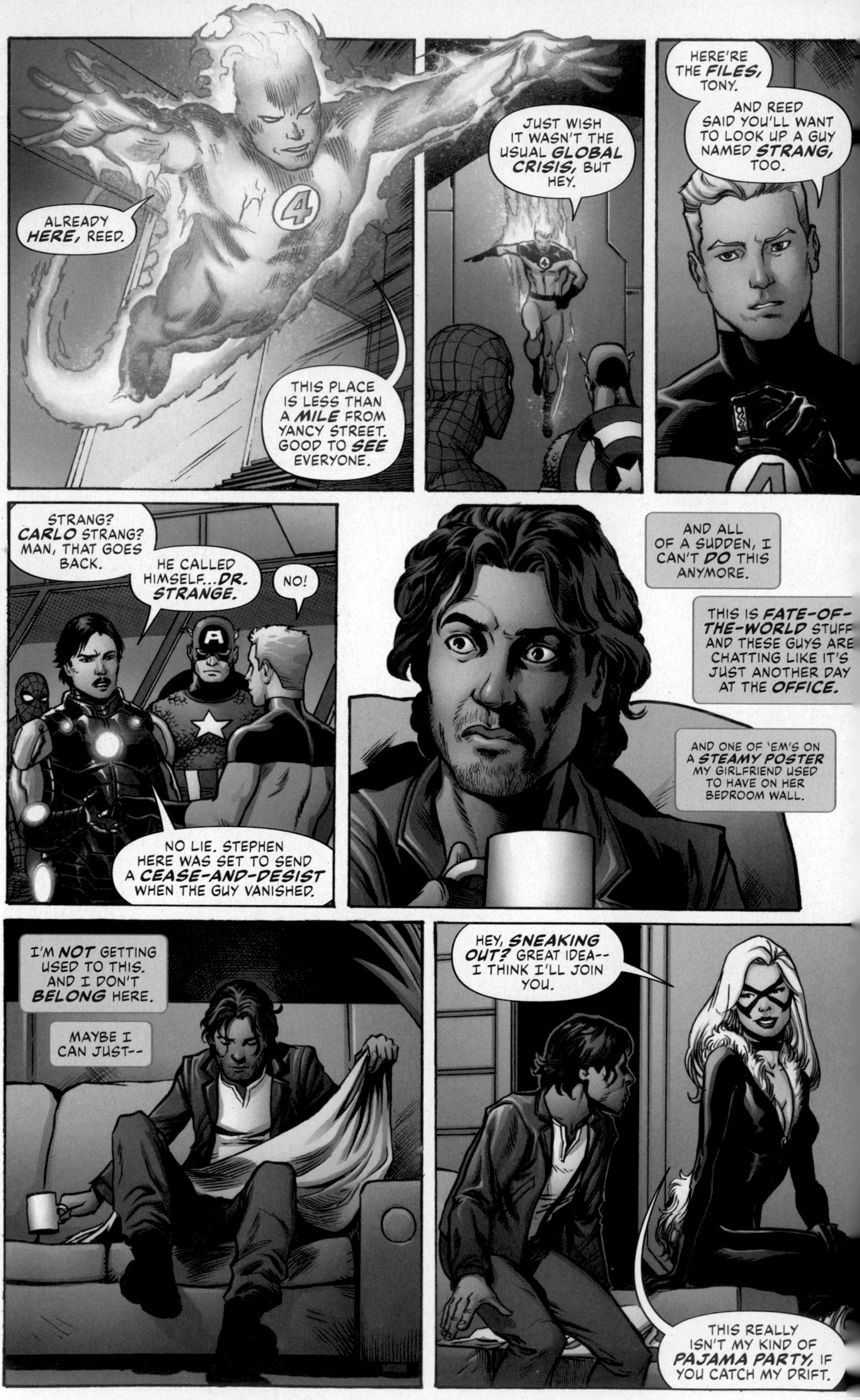
ALREADY HERE, REED.
THIS PLACE IS LESS THAN A MILE FROM YANCY STREET. GOOD TO SEE EVERYONE.
JUST WISH IT WASN'T THE USUAL GLOBAL CRISIS, BUT HEY.
HERE'RE THE FILES, TONY.
AND REED SAID YOU'LL WANT TO LOOK UP A GUY NAMED STRANG, TOO.
STRANG? CARLO STRANG? MAN, THAT GOES BACK.
HE CALLED HIMSELF...DR. STRANGE.
NO!
NO LIE. STEPHEN HERE WAS SET TO SEND A CEASE-AND-DESIST WHEN THE GUY VANISHED.
AND ALL OF A SUDDEN, I CAN'T DO THIS ANYMORE.
THIS IS FATE-OF-THE-WORLD STUFF AND THESE GUYS ARE CHATTING LIKE IT'S JUST ANOTHER DAY AT THE OFFICE.
AND ONE OF 'EM'S ON A STEAMY POSTER MY GIRLFRIEND USED TO HAVE ON HER BEDROOM WALL.
I'M NOT GETTING USED TO THIS. AND I DON'T BELONG HERE.
MAYBE I CAN JUST--
HEY, SNEAKING OUT? GREAT IDEA-- I THINK I'LL JOIN YOU.
THIS REALLY ISN'T MY KIND OF PAJAMA PARTY, IF YOU CATCH MY DRIFT.

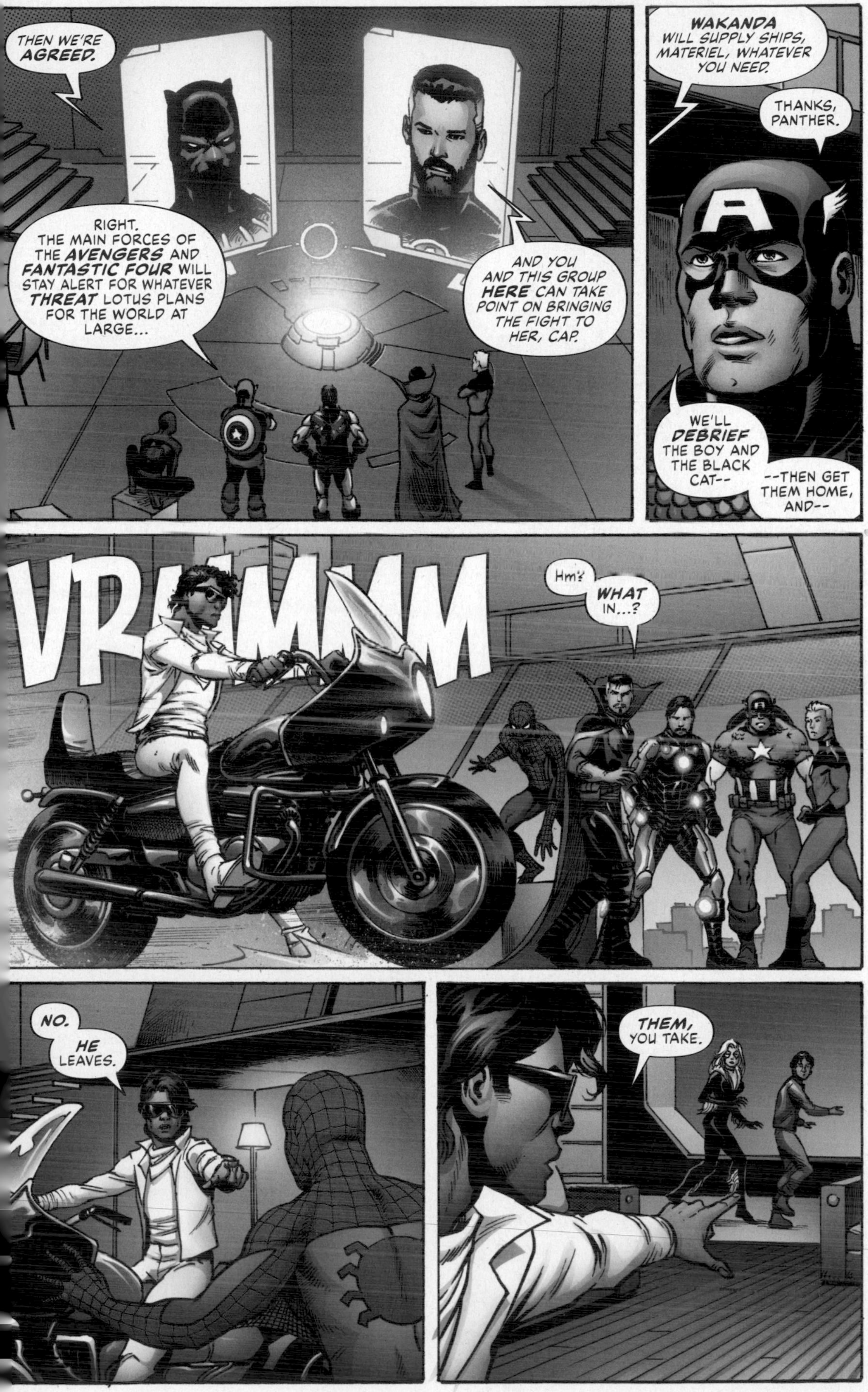
THEN WE'RE AGREED.
RIGHT. THE MAIN FORCES OF THE AVENGERS AND FANTASTIC FOUR WILL STAY ALERT FOR WHATEVER THREAT LOTUS PLANS FOR THE WORLD AT LARGE...
AND YOU AND THIS GROUP HERE CAN TAKE POINT ON BRINGING THE FIGHT TO HER, CAP.
WAKANDA WILL SUPPLY SHIPS, MATERIEL, WHATEVER YOU NEED.
THANKS, PANTHER.
WE'LL DEBRIEF THE BOY AND THE BLACK CAT--
--THEN GET THEM HOME, AND--
VRMMMM
Hm? WHAT IN...?
NO. HE LEAVES.
THEM, YOU TAKE.

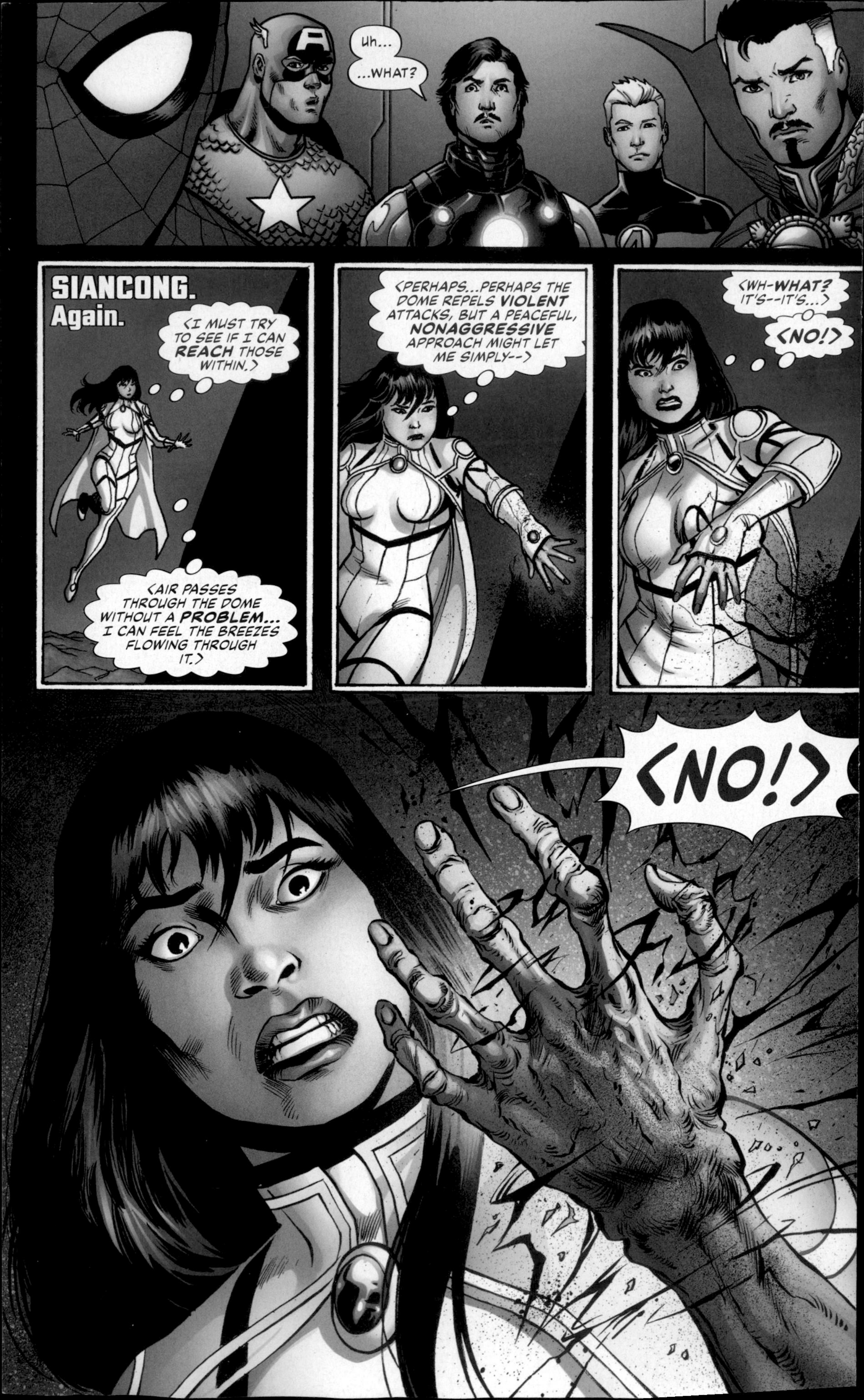
Uh...
...WHAT?
SIANCONG.
Again.
<I MUST TRY TO SEE IF I CAN REACH THOSE WITHIN.>
<AIR PASSES THROUGH THE DOME WITHOUT A PROBLEM... I CAN FEEL THE BREEZES FLOWING THROUGH IT.>
<PERHAPS...PERHAPS THE DOME REPELS VIOLENT ATTACKS, BUT A PEACEFUL, NONAGGRESSIVE APPROACH MIGHT LET ME SIMPLY-->
<WH-WHAT? IT'S--IT'S...>
<NO!>
<NO!>

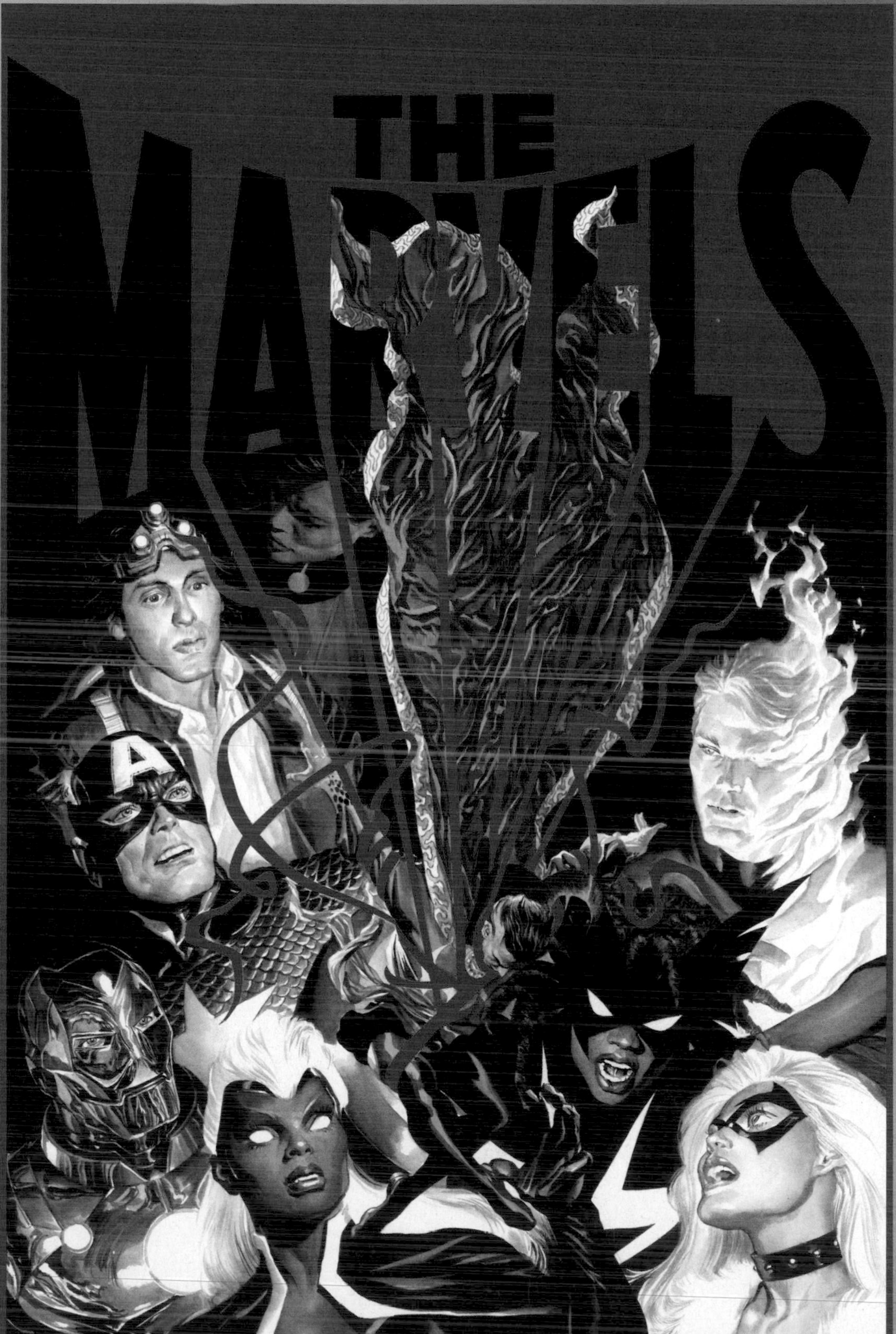
THE MARVELS

PART FIVE: **"I Might Know a Guy"**

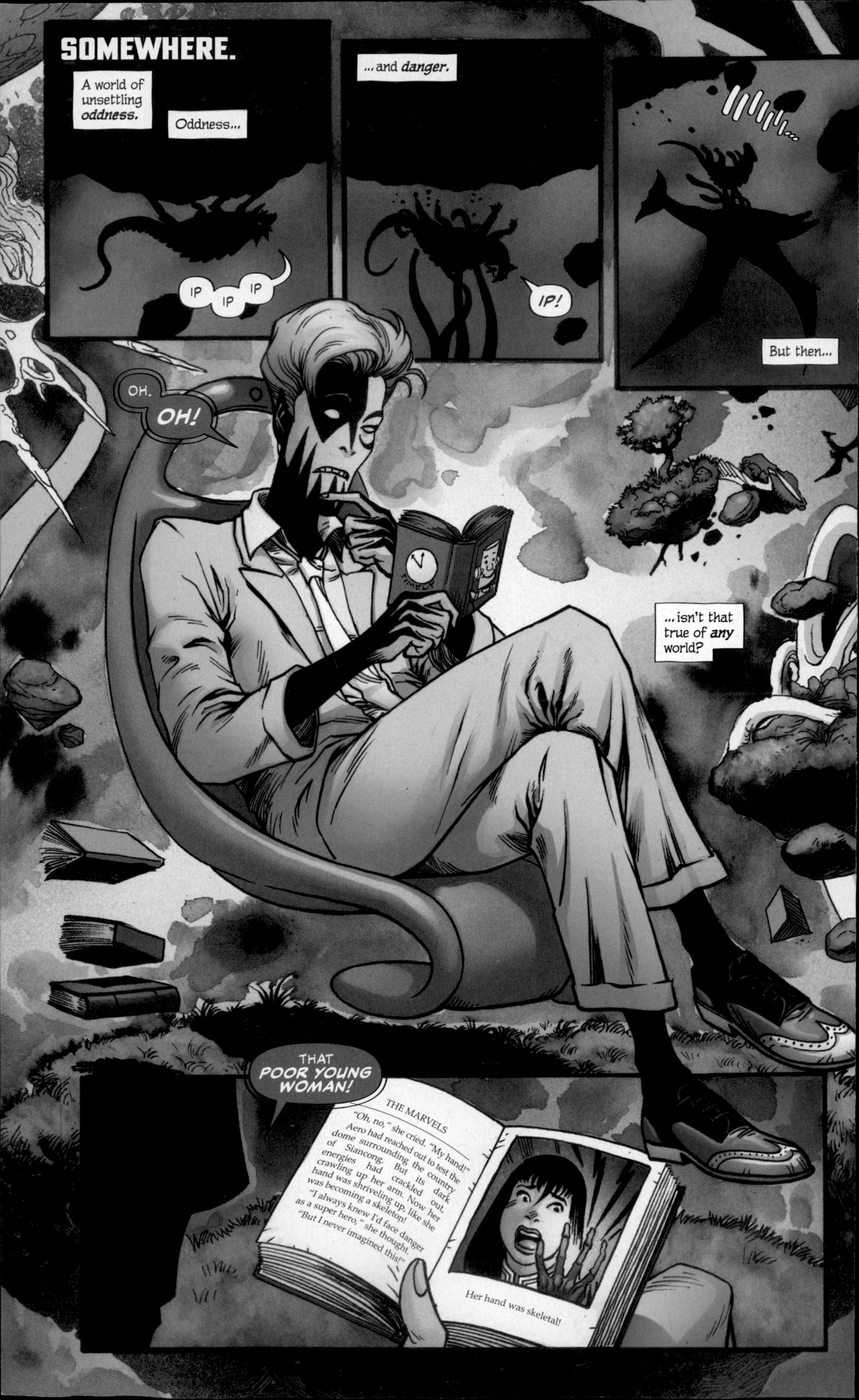
SOMEWHERE.
A world of unsettling oddness.
Oddness...
IP IP IP
...and danger.
IP!
But then...
OH. OH!
...isn't that true of any world?
THAT POOR YOUNG WOMAN!
THE MARVELS
"Oh, no," she cried. "My hand!"
Aero had reached out to test the dome surrounding the country of Siancong. But its dark energies had crackled out, crawling up her arm. Now her hand was shriveling up, like she was becoming a skeleton!
"I always knew I'd face danger as a super hero," she thought. "But I never imagined this!"
Her hand was skeletal!

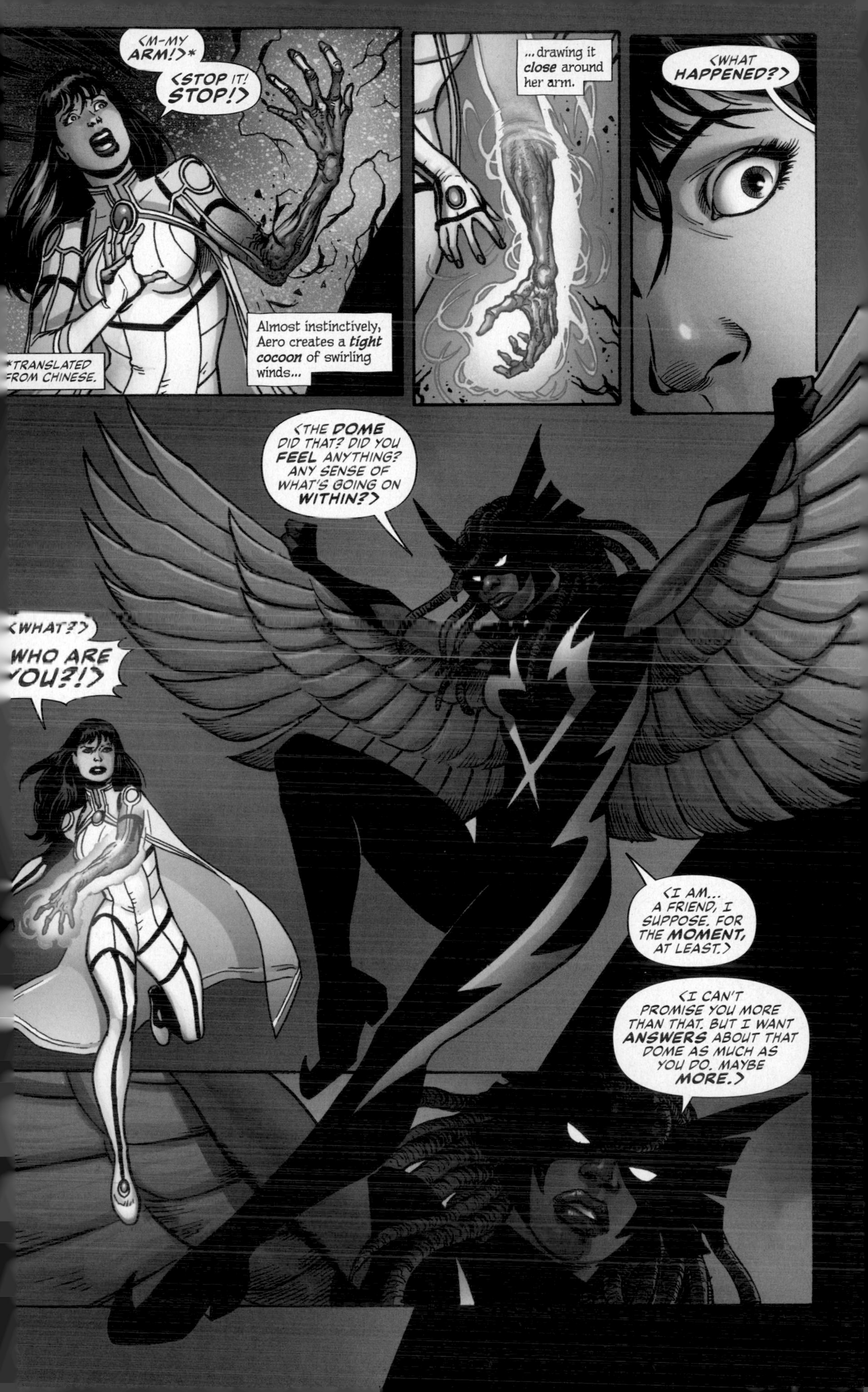

<M-MY ARM!>*
<STOP IT! STOP!>
*TRANSLATED FROM CHINESE.
Almost instinctively, Aero creates a tight cocoon of swirling winds...
...drawing it close around her arm.
<WHAT HAPPENED?>
<THE DOME DID THAT? DID YOU FEEL ANYTHING? ANY SENSE OF WHAT'S GOING ON WITHIN?>
<WHAT?>
WHO ARE YOU?!>
<I AM... A FRIEND, I SUPPOSE. FOR THE MOMENT, AT LEAST.>
<I CAN'T PROMISE YOU MORE THAN THAT. BUT I WANT ANSWERS ABOUT THAT DOME AS MUCH AS YOU DO. MAYBE MORE.>

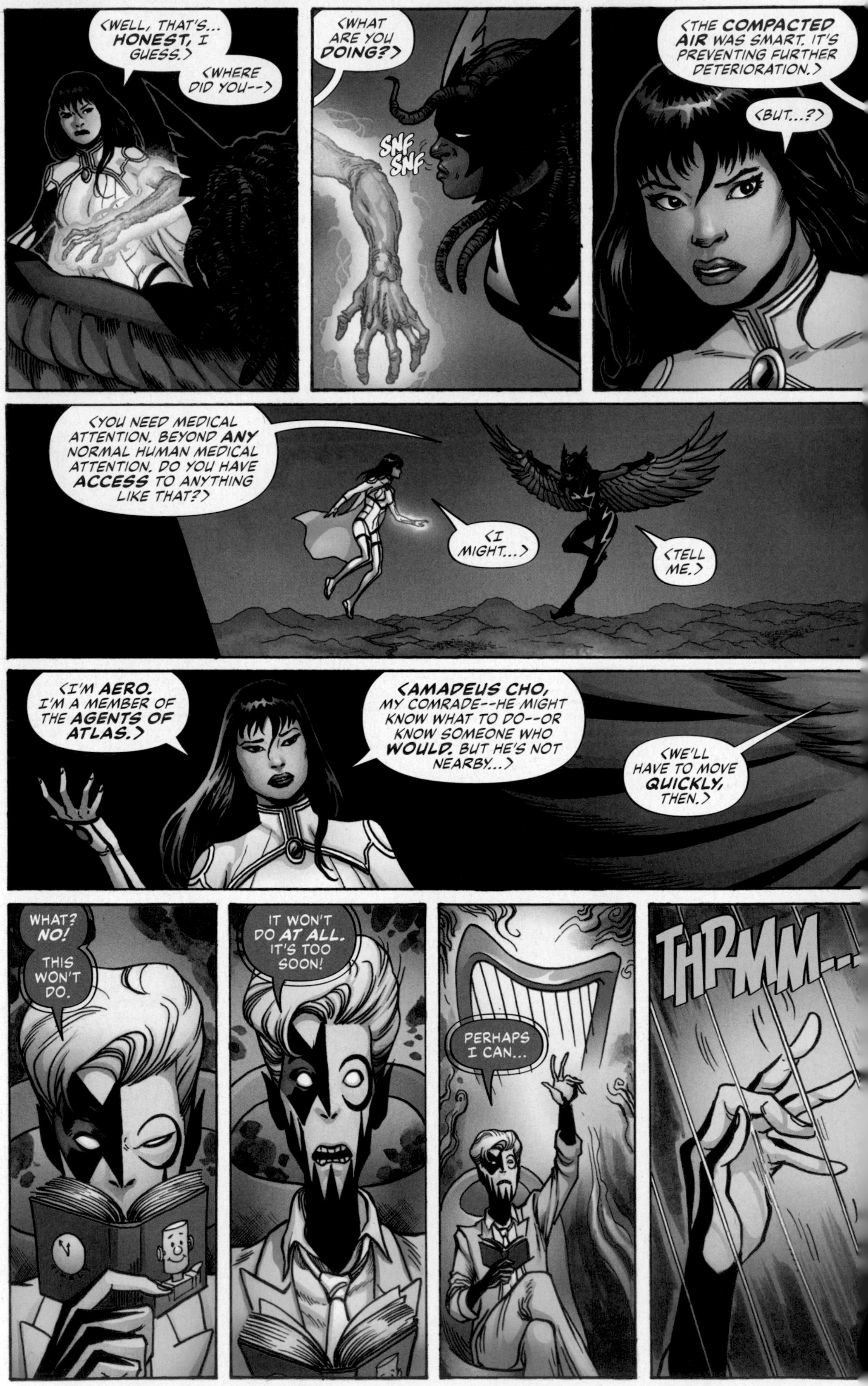

<WELL, THAT'S... HONEST, I GUESS.>
<WHERE DID YOU-->
<WHAT ARE YOU DOING?>
SNF SNF
<THE COMPACTED AIR WAS SMART. IT'S PREVENTING FURTHER DETERIORATION.>
<BUT...?>
<YOU NEED MEDICAL ATTENTION. BEYOND ANY NORMAL HUMAN MEDICAL ATTENTION. DO YOU HAVE ACCESS TO ANYTHING LIKE THAT?>
<I MIGHT...>
<TELL ME.>
<I'M AERO. I'M A MEMBER OF THE AGENTS OF ATLAS.>
<AMADEUS CHO, MY COMRADE--HE MIGHT KNOW WHAT TO DO--OR KNOW SOMEONE WHO WOULD. BUT HE'S NOT NEARBY...>
<WE'LL HAVE TO MOVE QUICKLY, THEN.>
WHAT? NO!
THIS WON'T DO.
IT WON'T DO AT ALL. IT'S TOO SOON!
PERHAPS I CAN...
THRMM...

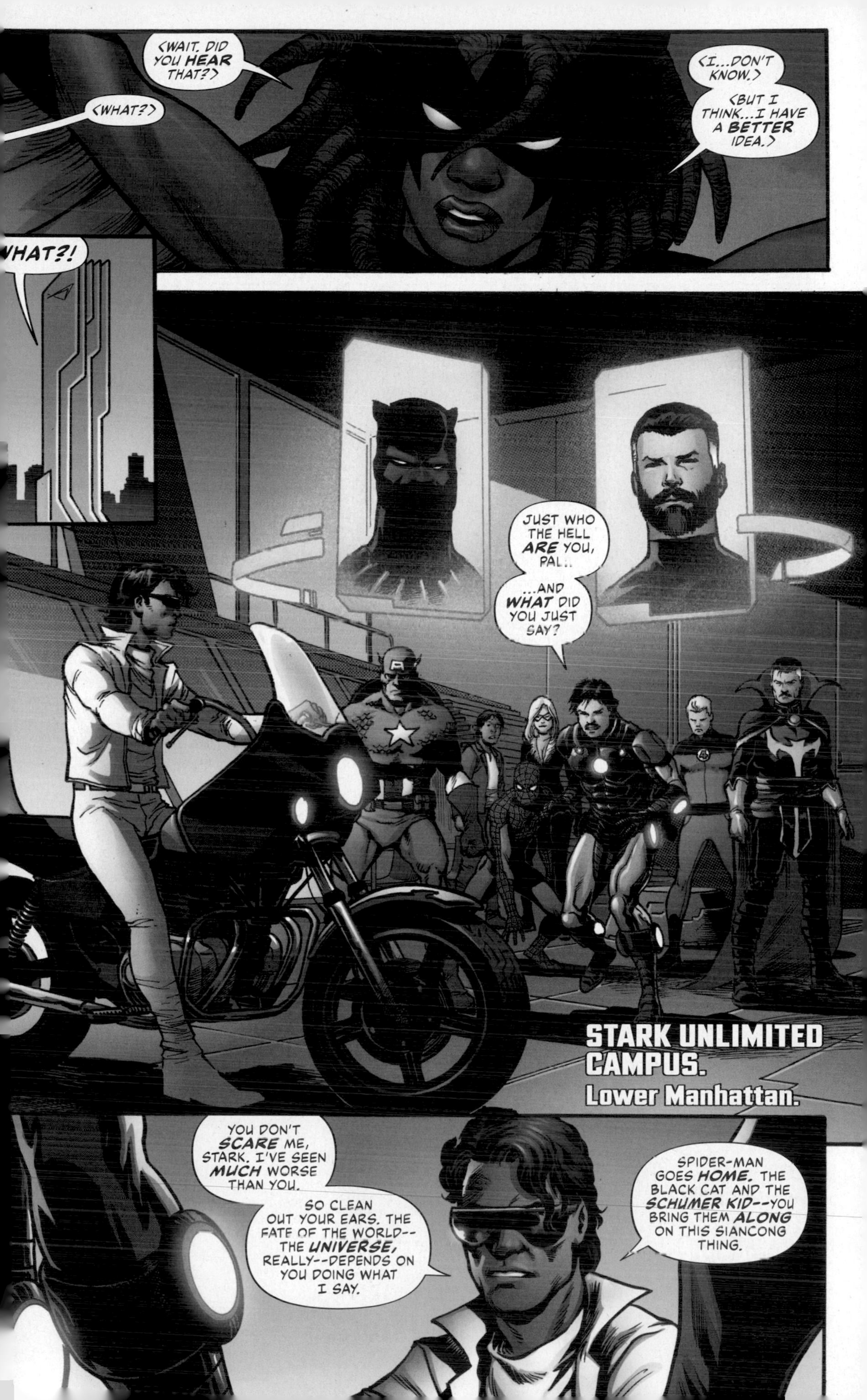

<WAIT. DID YOU HEAR THAT?>
<WHAT?>
<I...DON'T KNOW.>
<BUT I THINK...I HAVE A BETTER IDEA.>
WHAT?!
JUST WHO THE HELL ARE YOU, PAL?
...AND WHAT DID YOU JUST SAY?
STARK UNLIMITED CAMPUS.
Lower Manhattan.
YOU DON'T SCARE ME, STARK. I'VE SEEN MUCH WORSE THAN YOU.
SO CLEAN OUT YOUR EARS. THE FATE OF THE WORLD-- THE UNIVERSE, REALLY--DEPENDS ON YOU DOING WHAT I SAY.
SPIDER-MAN GOES HOME. THE BLACK CAT AND THE SCHUMER KID--YOU BRING THEM ALONG ON THIS SIANCONG THING.

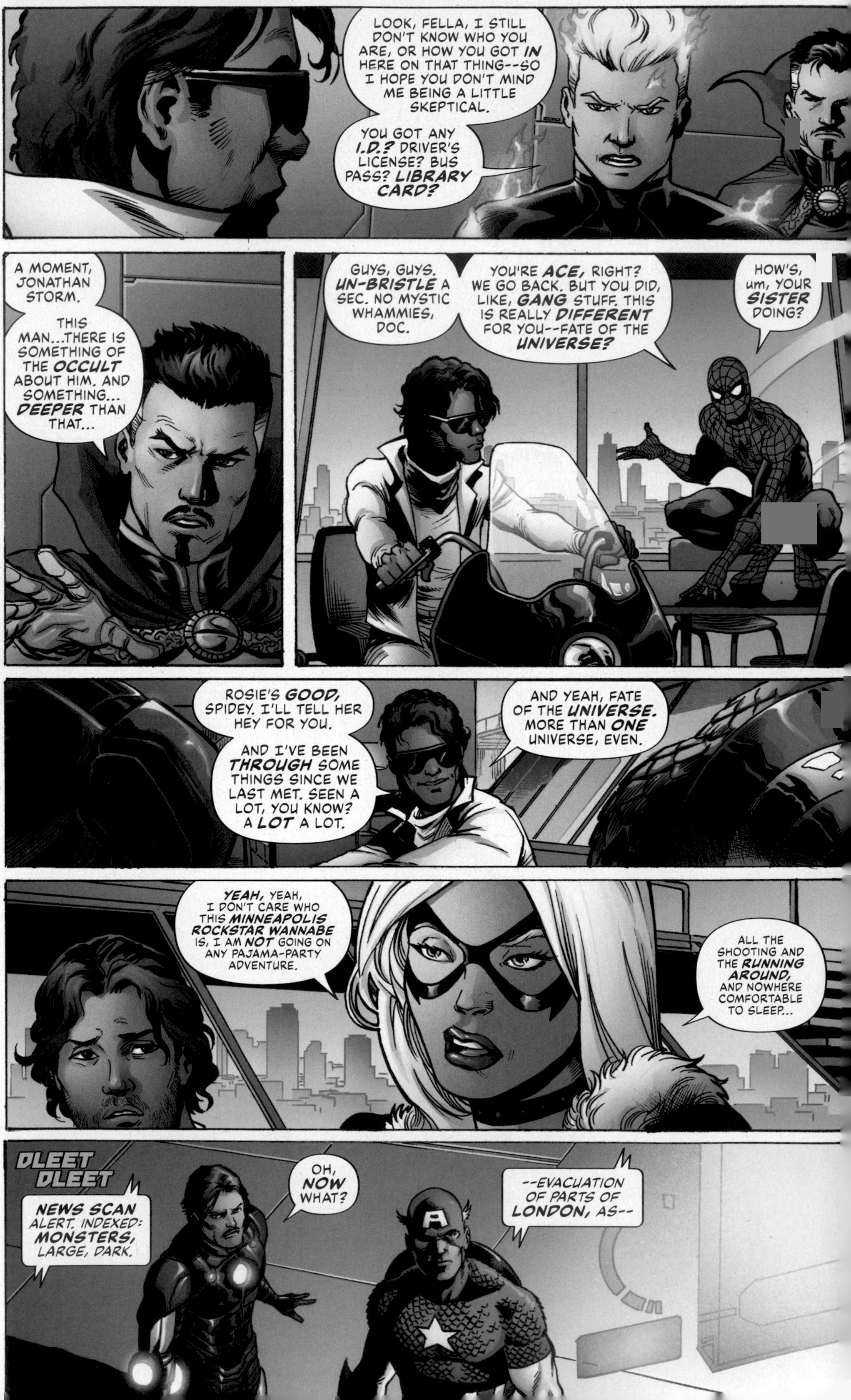
LOOK, FELLA, I STILL DON'T KNOW WHO YOU ARE, OR HOW YOU GOT IN HERE ON THAT THING--SO I HOPE YOU DON'T MIND ME BEING A LITTLE SKEPTICAL.
YOU GOT ANY I.D.? DRIVER'S LICENSE? BUS PASS? LIBRARY CARD?
A MOMENT, JONATHAN STORM.
THIS MAN...THERE IS SOMETHING OF THE OCCULT ABOUT HIM. AND SOMETHING... DEEPER THAN THAT...
GUYS, GUYS. UN-BRISTLE A SEC. NO MYSTIC WHAMMIES, DOC.
YOU'RE ACE, RIGHT? WE GO BACK. BUT YOU DID, LIKE, GANG STUFF. THIS IS REALLY DIFFERENT FOR YOU--FATE OF THE UNIVERSE?
HOW'S, um, YOUR SISTER DOING?
ROSIE'S GOOD, SPIDEY. I'LL TELL HER HEY FOR YOU.
AND I'VE BEEN THROUGH SOME THINGS SINCE WE LAST MET. SEEN A LOT, YOU KNOW? A LOT A LOT.
AND YEAH, FATE OF THE UNIVERSE. MORE THAN ONE UNIVERSE, EVEN.
YEAH, YEAH, I DON'T CARE WHO THIS MINNEAPOLIS ROCKSTAR WANNABE IS, I AM NOT GOING ON ANY PAJAMA-PARTY ADVENTURE.
ALL THE SHOOTING AND THE RUNNING AROUND, AND NOWHERE COMFORTABLE TO SLEEP...
DLEET DLEET
NEWS SCAN ALERT. INDEXED: MONSTERS, LARGE, DARK.
OH, NOW WHAT?
--EVACUATION OF PARTS OF LONDON, AS--

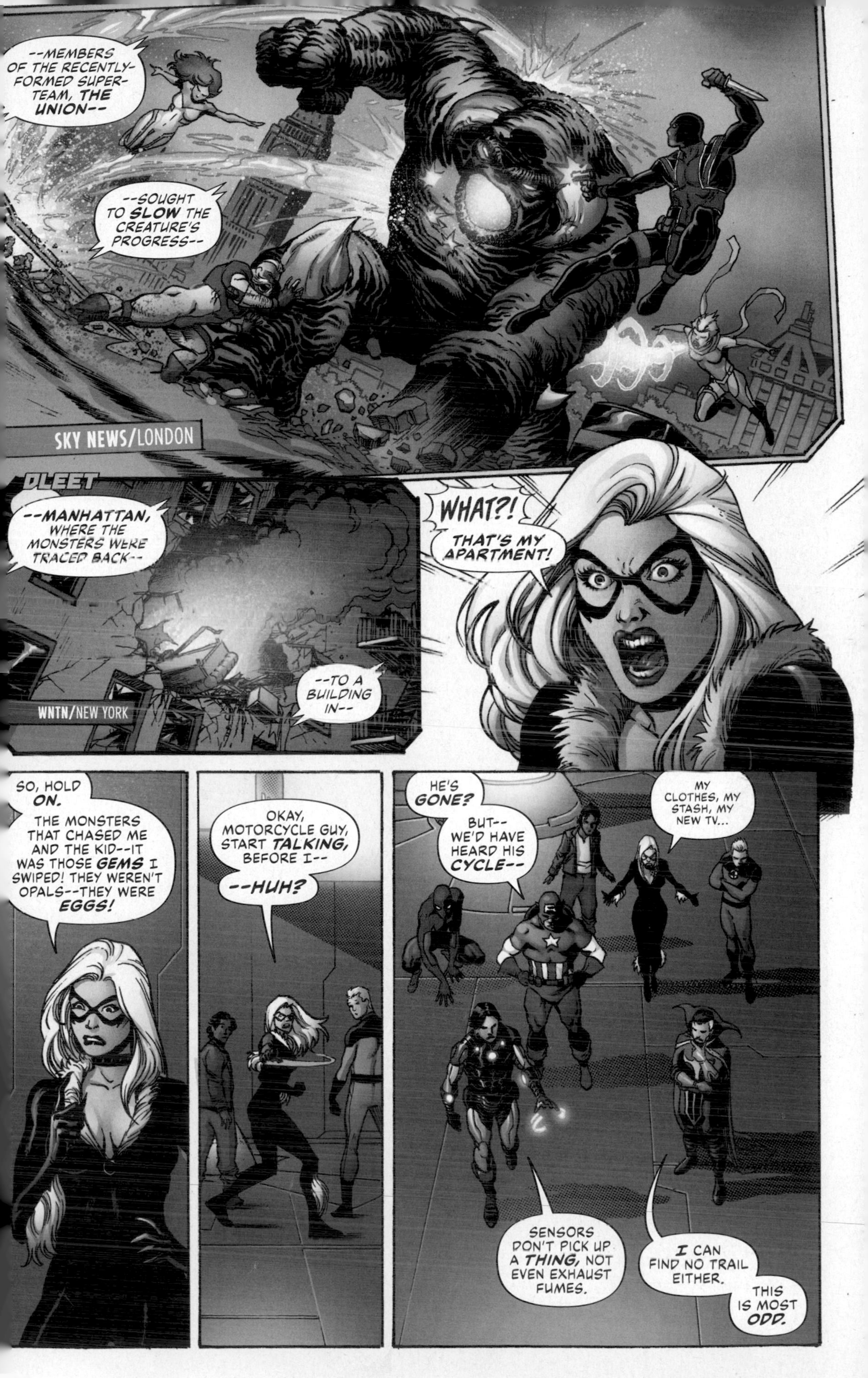
--MEMBERS OF THE RECENTLY-FORMED SUPER-TEAM, THE UNION--
--SOUGHT TO SLOW THE CREATURE'S PROGRESS--
SKY NEWS/LONDON
BLEET
--MANHATTAN, WHERE THE MONSTERS WERE TRACED BACK--
--TO A BUILDING IN--
WNTN/NEW YORK
WHAT?!
THAT'S MY APARTMENT!
SO, HOLD ON.
THE MONSTERS THAT CHASED ME AND THE KID--IT WAS THOSE GEMS I SWIPED! THEY WEREN'T OPALS--THEY WERE EGGS!
OKAY, MOTORCYCLE GUY, START TALKING, BEFORE I--
--HUH?
HE'S GONE?
BUT--WE'D HAVE HEARD HIS CYCLE--
MY CLOTHES, MY STASH, MY NEW TV...
SENSORS DON'T PICK UP A THING, NOT EVEN EXHAUST FUMES.
I CAN FIND NO TRAIL EITHER.
THIS IS MOST ODD.

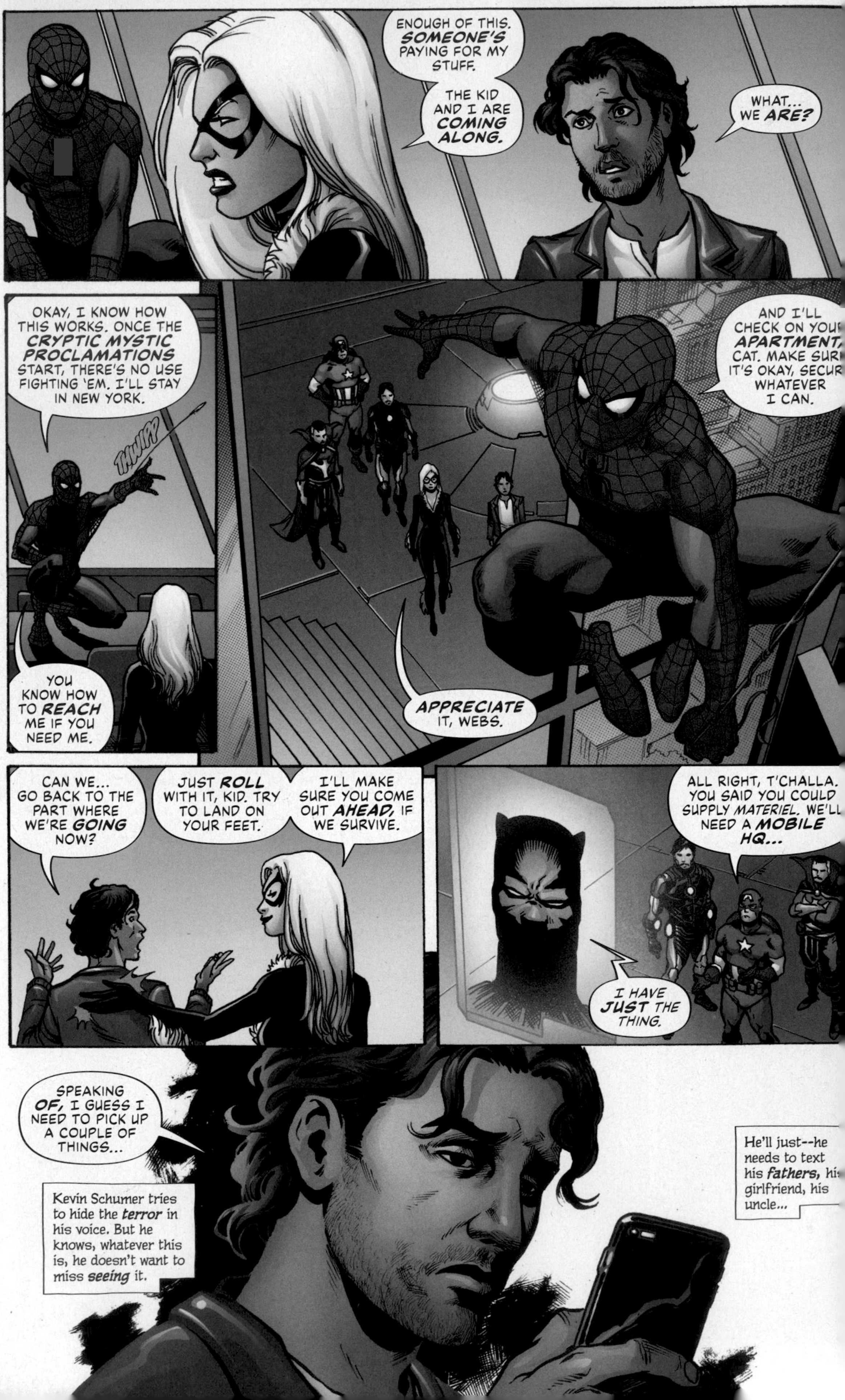

ENOUGH OF THIS. SOMEONE'S PAYING FOR MY STUFF.
THE KID AND I ARE COMING ALONG.
WHAT... WE ARE?
OKAY, I KNOW HOW THIS WORKS. ONCE THE CRYPTIC MYSTIC PROCLAMATIONS START, THERE'S NO USE FIGHTING 'EM. I'LL STAY IN NEW YORK.
THWIPP
YOU KNOW HOW TO REACH ME IF YOU NEED ME.
AND I'LL CHECK ON YOUR APARTMENT, CAT. MAKE SURE IT'S OKAY, SECURE WHATEVER I CAN.
APPRECIATE IT, WEBS.
CAN WE... GO BACK TO THE PART WHERE WE'RE GOING NOW?
JUST ROLL WITH IT, KID. TRY TO LAND ON YOUR FEET.
I'LL MAKE SURE YOU COME OUT AHEAD, IF WE SURVIVE.
ALL RIGHT, T'CHALLA. YOU SAID YOU COULD SUPPLY MATERIEL. WE'LL NEED A MOBILE HQ...
I HAVE JUST THE THING.
SPEAKING OF, I GUESS I NEED TO PICK UP A COUPLE OF THINGS...
Kevin Schumer tries to hide the terror in his voice. But he knows, whatever this is, he doesn't want to miss seeing it.
He'll just--he needs to text his fathers, his girlfriend, his uncle...

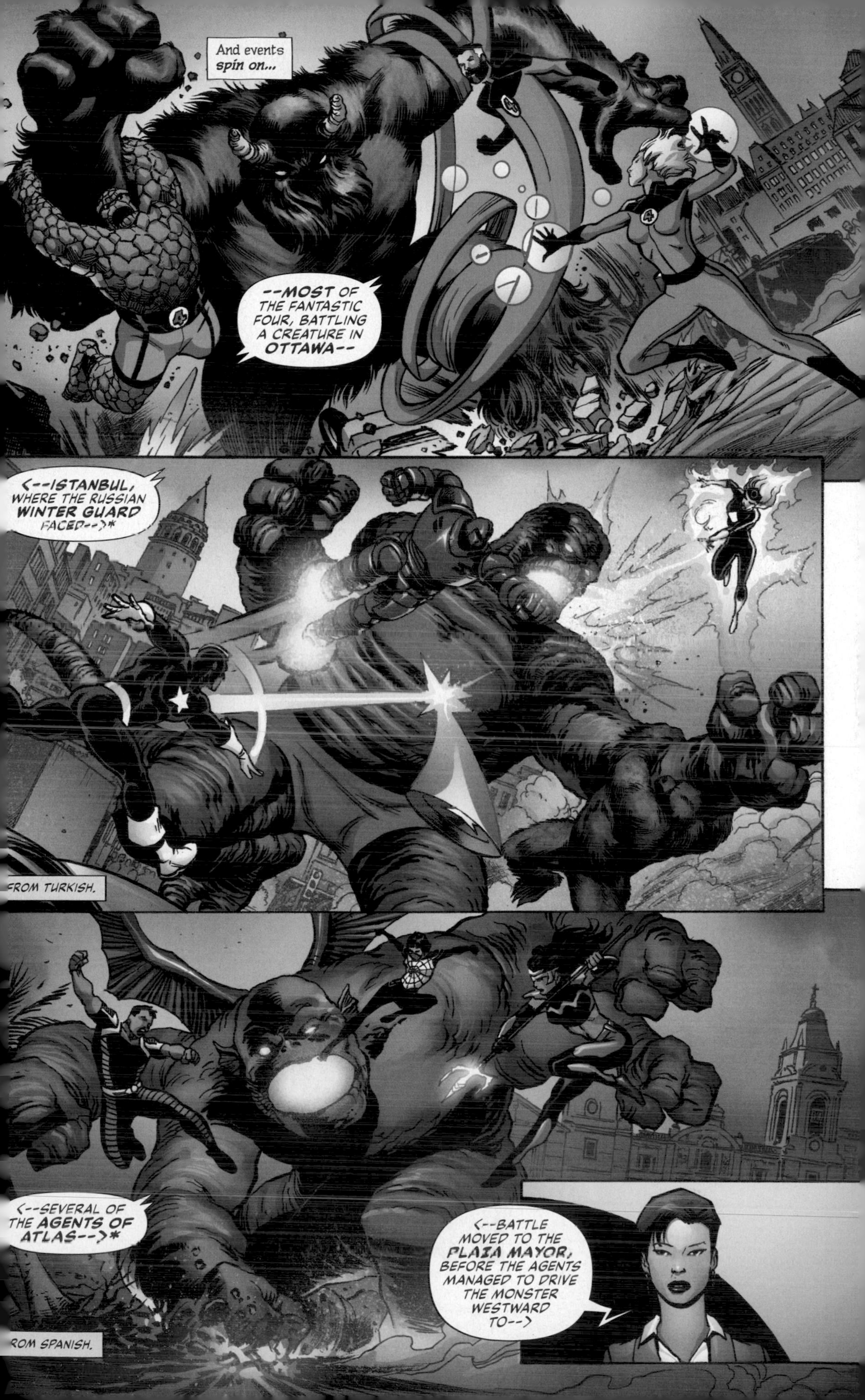
And events spin on...
--MOST OF THE FANTASTIC FOUR, BATTLING A CREATURE IN OTTAWA--
<--ISTANBUL, WHERE THE RUSSIAN WINTER GUARD FACED-->*
FROM TURKISH.
<--SEVERAL OF THE AGENTS OF ATLAS-->*
<--BATTLE MOVED TO THE PLAZA MAYOR, BEFORE THE AGENTS MANAGED TO DRIVE THE MONSTER WESTWARD TO-->
ROM SPANISH.

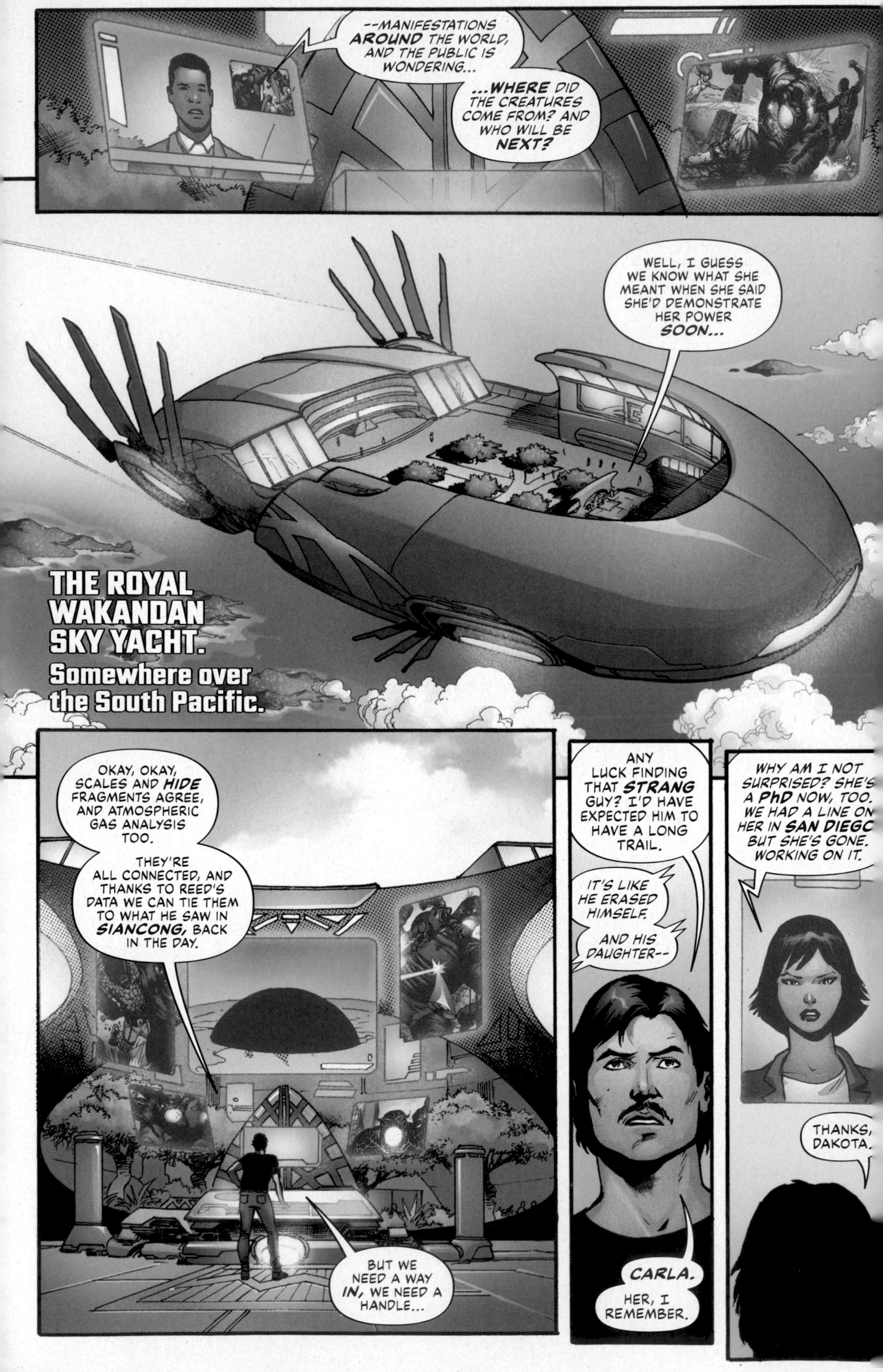
--MANIFESTATIONS AROUND THE WORLD, AND THE PUBLIC IS WONDERING...
...WHERE DID THE CREATURES COME FROM? AND WHO WILL BE NEXT?
THE ROYAL WAKANDAN SKY YACHT. Somewhere over the South Pacific.
WELL, I GUESS WE KNOW WHAT SHE MEANT WHEN SHE SAID SHE'D DEMONSTRATE HER POWER SOON...
OKAY, OKAY, SCALES AND HIDE FRAGMENTS AGREE, AND ATMOSPHERIC GAS ANALYSIS TOO.
THEY'RE ALL CONNECTED, AND THANKS TO REED'S DATA WE CAN TIE THEM TO WHAT HE SAW IN SIANCONG, BACK IN THE DAY.
BUT WE NEED A WAY IN, WE NEED A HANDLE...
ANY LUCK FINDING THAT STRANG GUY? I'D HAVE EXPECTED HIM TO HAVE A LONG TRAIL.
IT'S LIKE HE ERASED HIMSELF.
AND HIS DAUGHTER--
CARLA.
HER, I REMEMBER.
WHY AM I NOT SURPRISED? SHE'S A PhD NOW, TOO. WE HAD A LINE ON HER IN SAN DIEGO BUT SHE'S GONE. WORKING ON IT.
THANKS, DAKOTA.

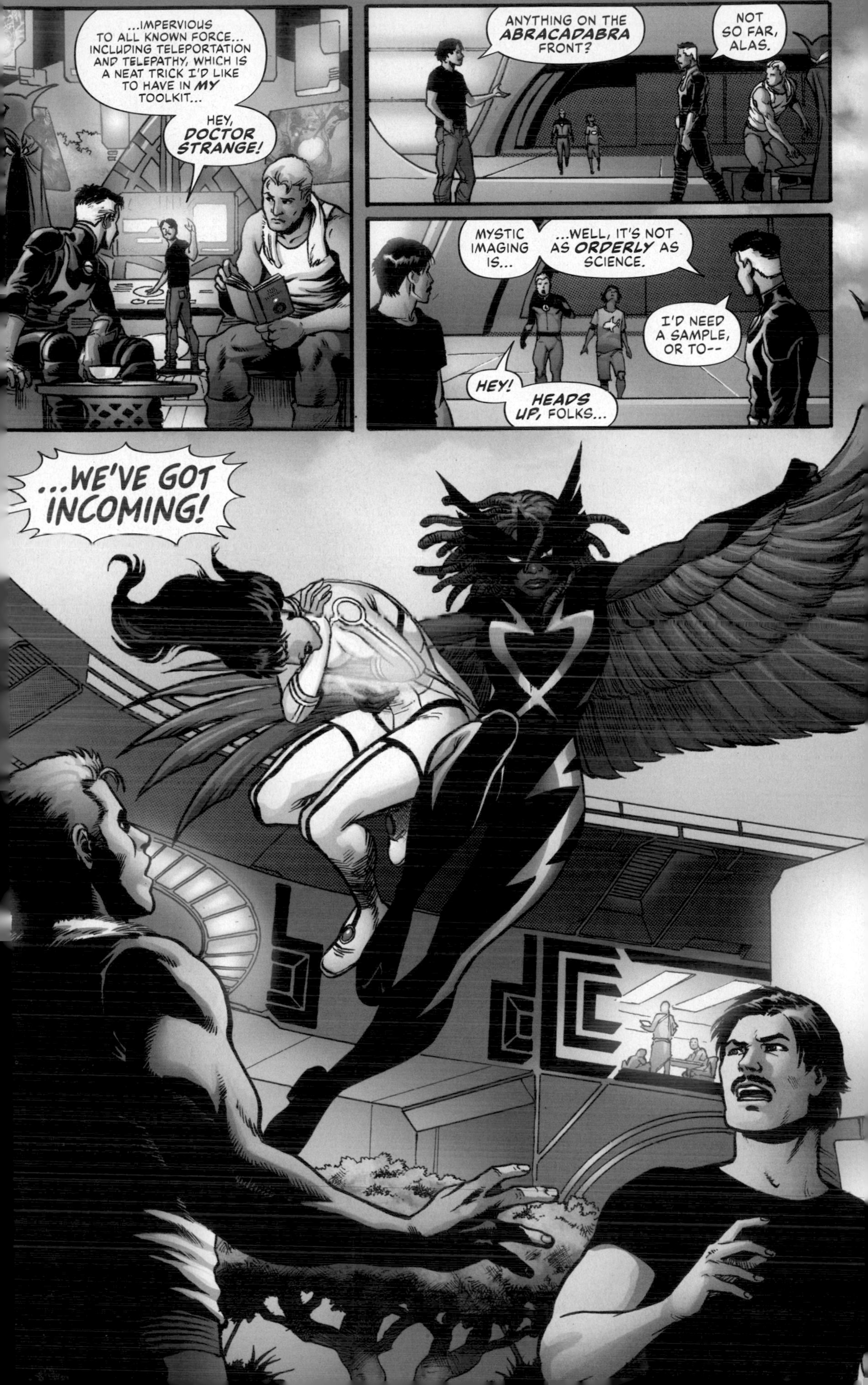
...IMPERVIOUS TO ALL KNOWN FORCE... INCLUDING TELEPORTATION AND TELEPATHY, WHICH IS A NEAT TRICK I'D LIKE TO HAVE IN MY TOOLKIT...
HEY, DOCTOR STRANGE!
ANYTHING ON THE ABRACADABRA FRONT?
NOT SO FAR, ALAS.
MYSTIC IMAGING IS...
...WELL, IT'S NOT AS ORDERLY AS SCIENCE.
I'D NEED A SAMPLE, OR TO--
HEY!
HEADS UP, FOLKS...
...WE'VE GOT INCOMING!

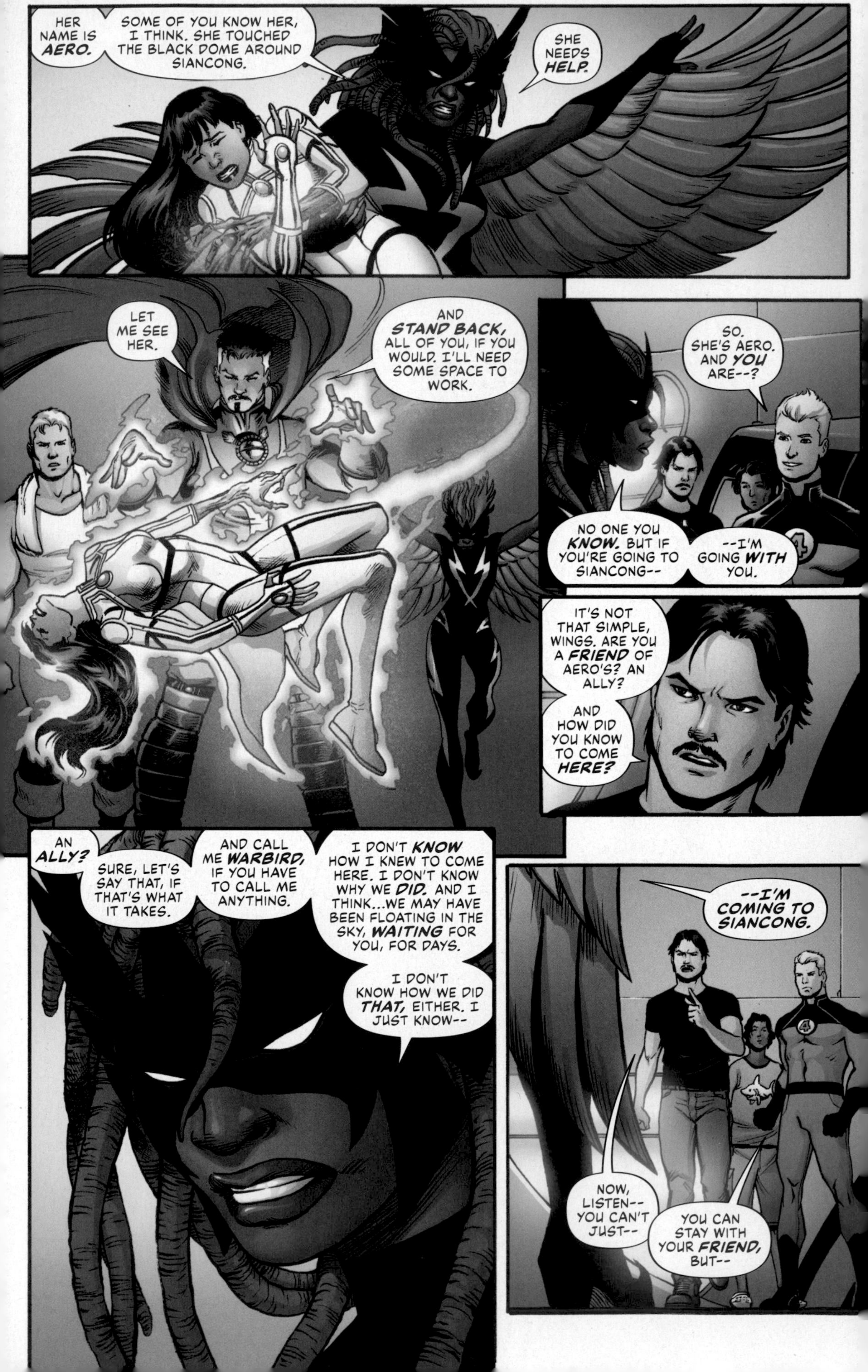
HER NAME IS AERO.
SOME OF YOU KNOW HER, I THINK. SHE TOUCHED THE BLACK DOME AROUND SIANCONG.
SHE NEEDS HELP.
LET ME SEE HER.
AND STAND BACK, ALL OF YOU, IF YOU WOULD. I'LL NEED SOME SPACE TO WORK.
SO. SHE'S AERO. AND YOU ARE--?
NO ONE YOU KNOW. BUT IF YOU'RE GOING TO SIANCONG--
--I'M GOING WITH YOU.
IT'S NOT THAT SIMPLE, WINGS. ARE YOU A FRIEND OF AERO'S? AN ALLY?
AND HOW DID YOU KNOW TO COME HERE?
AN ALLY?
SURE, LET'S SAY THAT, IF THAT'S WHAT IT TAKES.
AND CALL ME WARBIRD, IF YOU HAVE TO CALL ME ANYTHING.
I DON'T KNOW HOW I KNEW TO COME HERE. I DON'T KNOW WHY WE DID. AND I THINK...WE MAY HAVE BEEN FLOATING IN THE SKY, WAITING FOR YOU, FOR DAYS.
I DON'T KNOW HOW WE DID THAT, EITHER. I JUST KNOW--
--I'M COMING TO SIANCONG.
NOW, LISTEN-- YOU CAN'T JUST--
YOU CAN STAY WITH YOUR FRIEND, BUT--

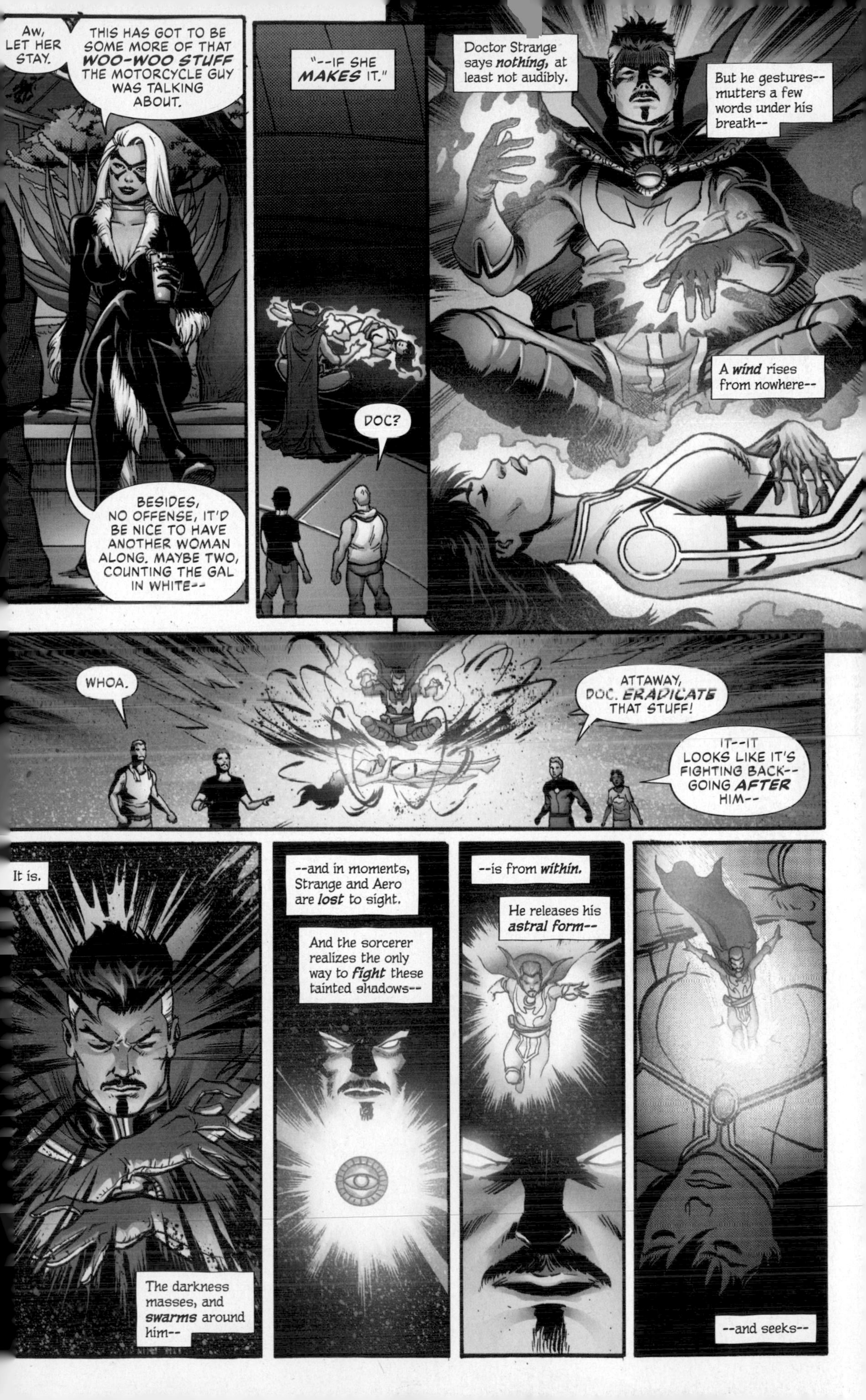
AW, LET HER STAY.
THIS HAS GOT TO BE SOME MORE OF THAT WOO-WOO STUFF THE MOTORCYCLE GUY WAS TALKING ABOUT.
BESIDES, NO OFFENSE, IT'D BE NICE TO HAVE ANOTHER WOMAN ALONG. MAYBE TWO, COUNTING THE GAL IN WHITE--
"--IF SHE MAKES IT."
DOC?
Doctor Strange says nothing, at least not audibly.
But he gestures--mutters a few words under his breath--
A wind rises from nowhere--
WHOA.
ATTAWAY, DOC. ERADICATE THAT STUFF!
IT--IT LOOKS LIKE IT'S FIGHTING BACK--GOING AFTER HIM--
It is.
The darkness masses, and swarms around him--
--and in moments, Strange and Aero are lost to sight.
And the sorcerer realizes the only way to fight these tainted shadows--
--is from within.
He releases his astral form--
--and seeks--

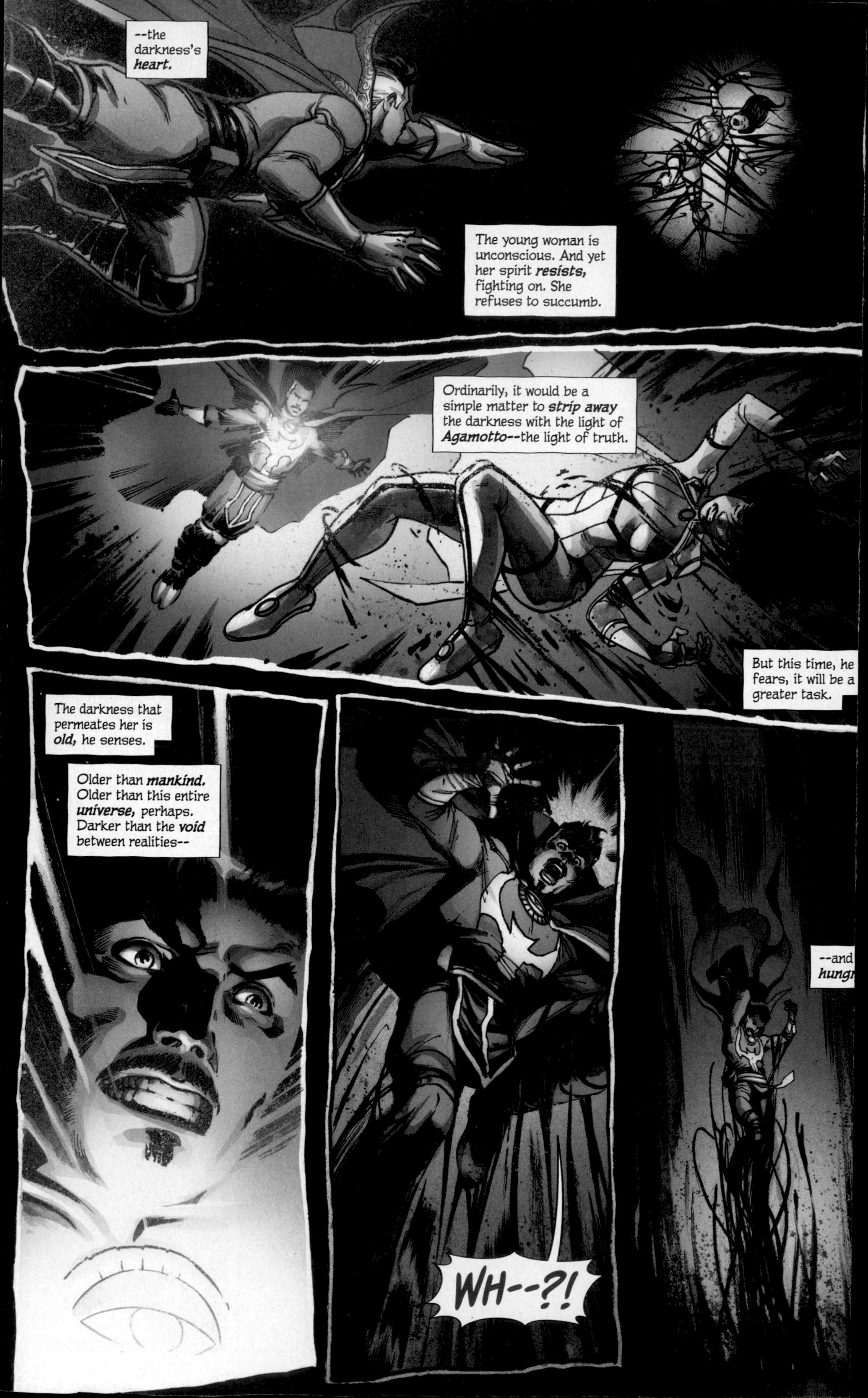
--the darkness's *heart.*
The young woman is unconscious. And yet her spirit *resists,* fighting on. She refuses to succumb.
Ordinarily, it would be a simple matter to *strip away* the darkness with the light of *Agamotto*--the light of truth.
But this time, he fears, it will be a greater task.
The darkness that permeates her is *old,* he senses.
Older than *mankind.* Older than this entire *universe,* perhaps. Darker than the *void* between realities--
WH--?!
--and

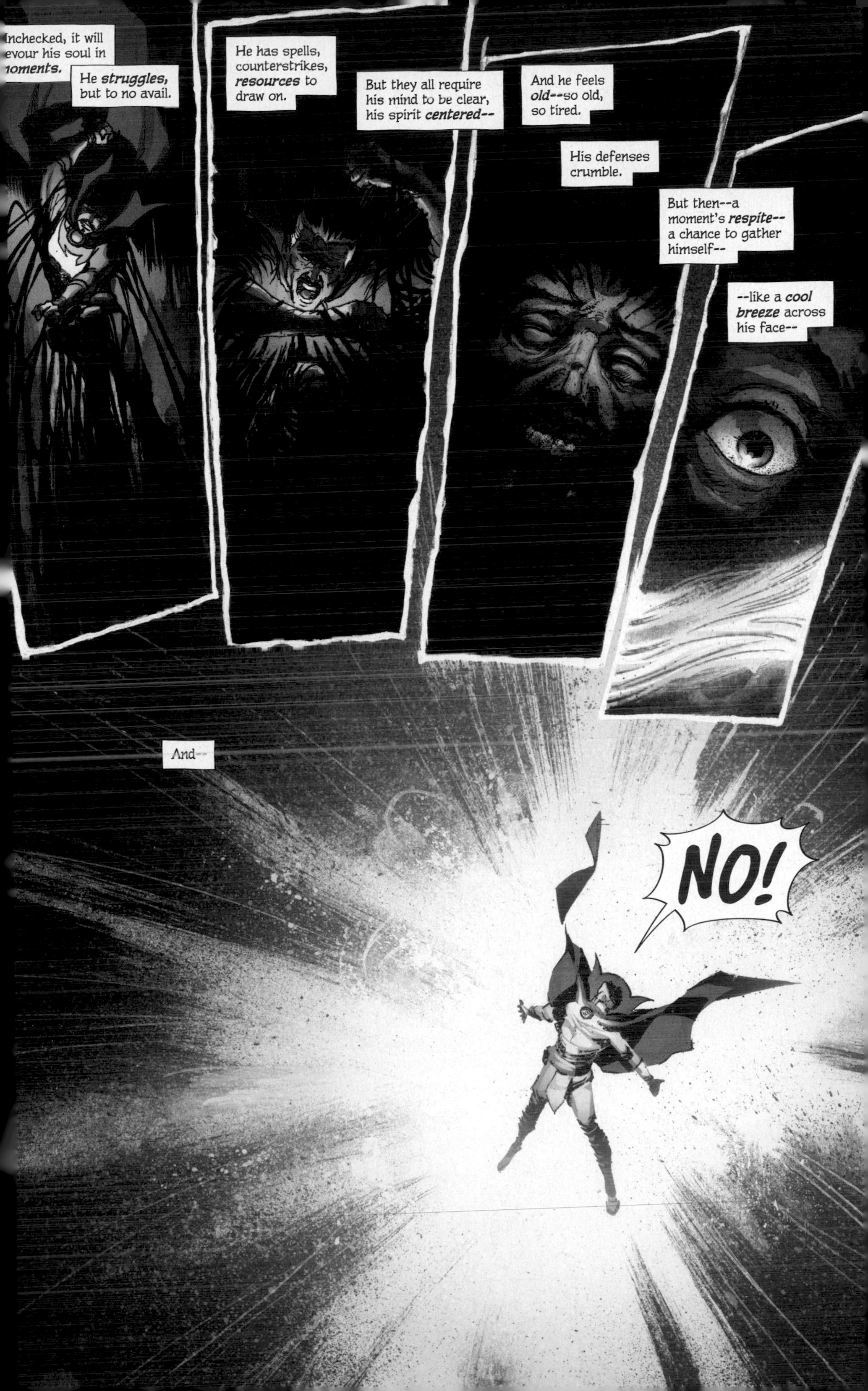
nchecked, it will
evour his soul in
moments.
He struggles, but to no avail.
He has spells, counterstrikes, resources to draw on.
But they all require his mind to be clear, his spirit centered--
And he feels old--so old, so tired.
His defenses crumble.
But then--a moment's respite--a chance to gather himself--
--like a cool breeze across his face--
And--
NO!

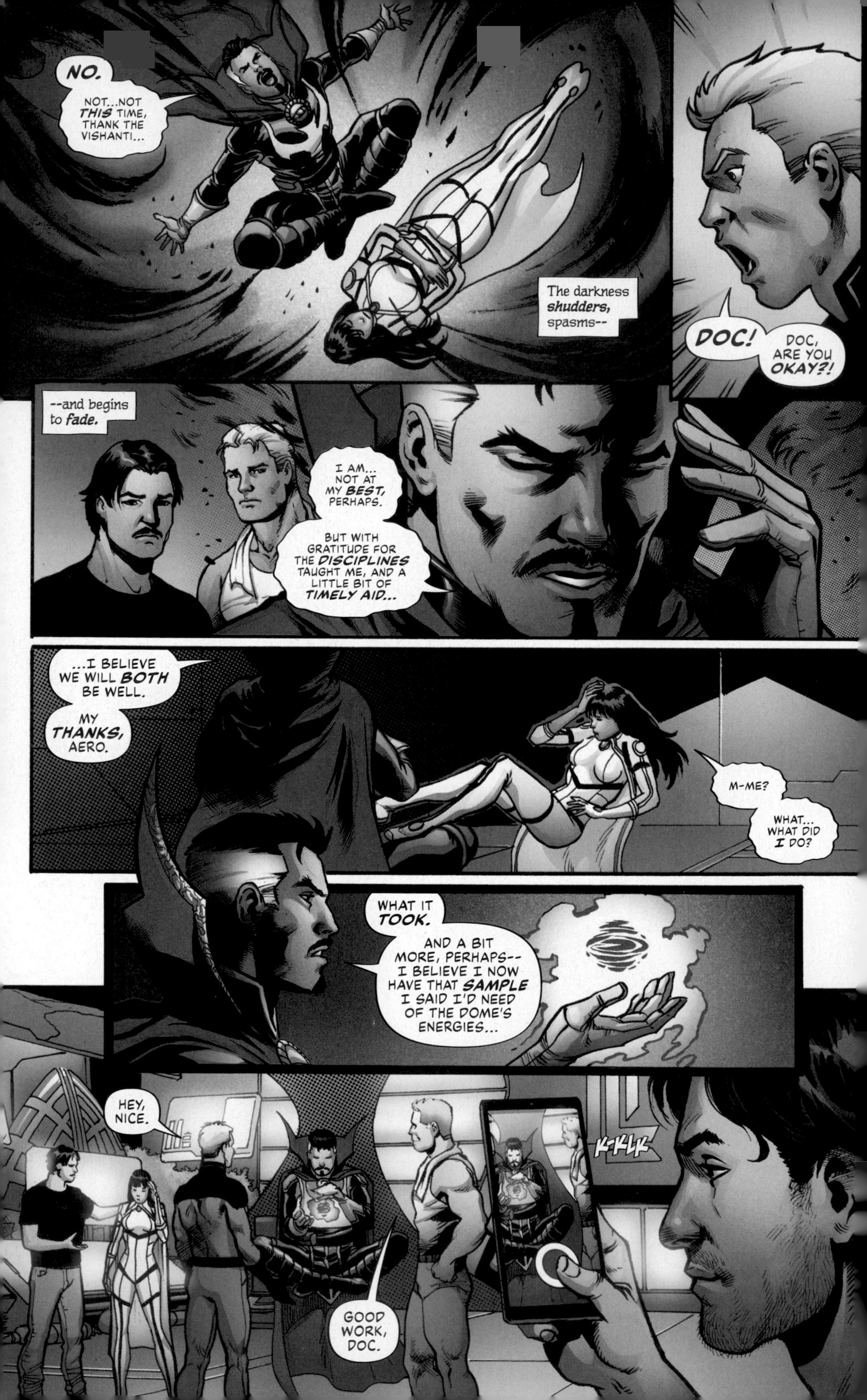
NO.
NOT...NOT THIS TIME, THANK THE VISHANTI...
The darkness shudders, spasms--
DOC!
DOC, ARE YOU OKAY?!
--and begins to fade.
I AM... NOT AT MY BEST, PERHAPS.
BUT WITH GRATITUDE FOR THE DISCIPLINES TAUGHT ME, AND A LITTLE BIT OF TIMELY AID...
...I BELIEVE WE WILL BOTH BE WELL.
MY THANKS, AERO.
M-ME?
WHAT... WHAT DID I DO?
WHAT IT TOOK.
AND A BIT MORE, PERHAPS-- I BELIEVE I NOW HAVE THAT SAMPLE I SAID I'D NEED OF THE DOME'S ENERGIES...
HEY, NICE.
K-KLIK
GOOD WORK, DOC.

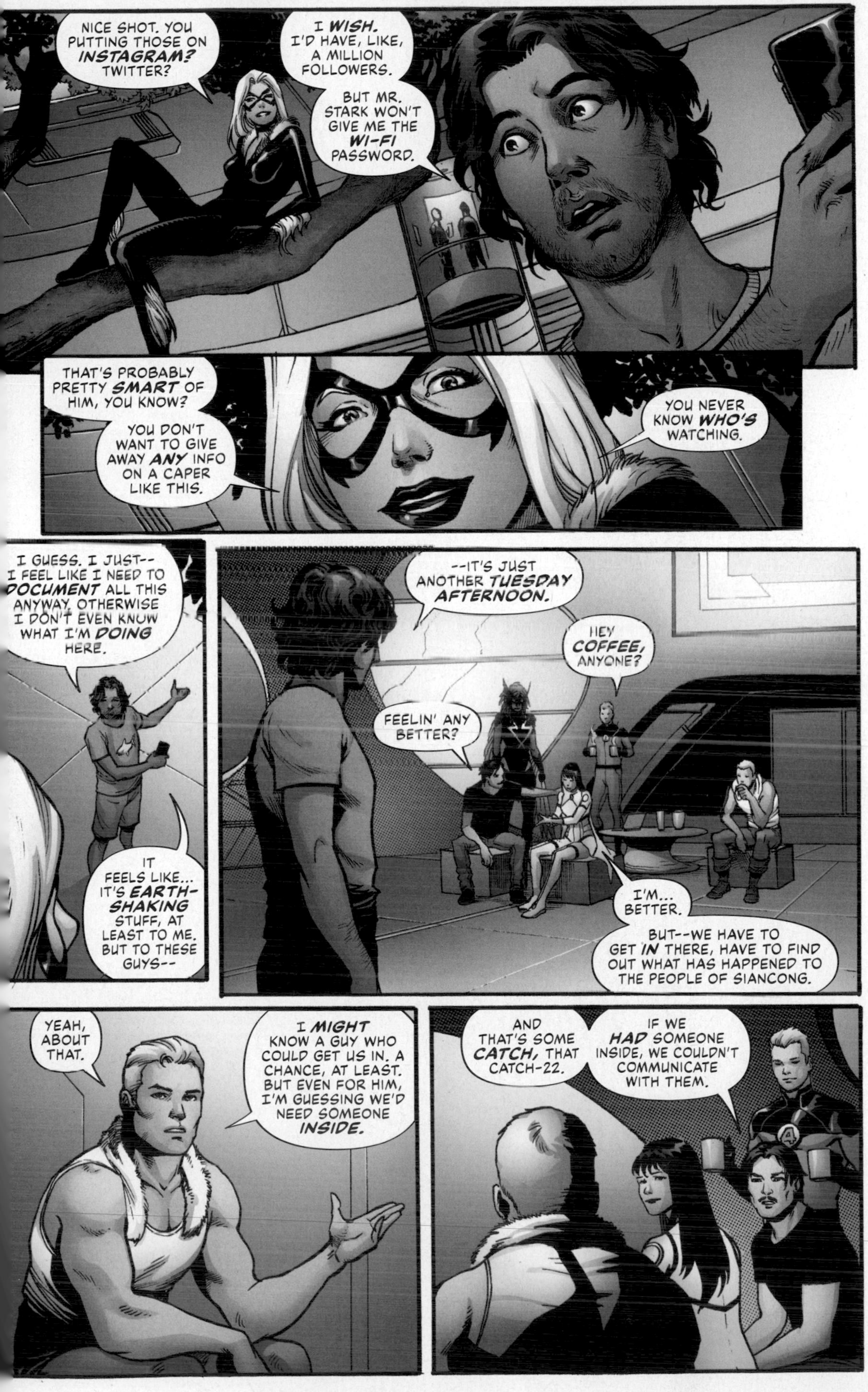
NICE SHOT. YOU PUTTING THOSE ON INSTAGRAM? TWITTER?
I WISH. I'D HAVE, LIKE, A MILLION FOLLOWERS.
BUT MR. STARK WON'T GIVE ME THE WI-FI PASSWORD.
THAT'S PROBABLY PRETTY SMART OF HIM, YOU KNOW?
YOU DON'T WANT TO GIVE AWAY ANY INFO ON A CAPER LIKE THIS.
YOU NEVER KNOW WHO'S WATCHING.
I GUESS. I JUST-- I FEEL LIKE I NEED TO DOCUMENT ALL THIS ANYWAY. OTHERWISE I DON'T EVEN KNOW WHAT I'M DOING HERE.
IT FEELS LIKE... IT'S EARTH-SHAKING STUFF, AT LEAST TO ME. BUT TO THESE GUYS--
--IT'S JUST ANOTHER TUESDAY AFTERNOON.
HEY COFFEE, ANYONE?
FEELIN' ANY BETTER?
I'M... BETTER.
BUT--WE HAVE TO GET IN THERE, HAVE TO FIND OUT WHAT HAS HAPPENED TO THE PEOPLE OF SIANCONG.
YEAH, ABOUT THAT.
I MIGHT KNOW A GUY WHO COULD GET US IN. A CHANCE, AT LEAST. BUT EVEN FOR HIM, I'M GUESSING WE'D NEED SOMEONE INSIDE.
AND THAT'S SOME CATCH, THAT CATCH-22.
IF WE HAD SOMEONE INSIDE, WE COULDN'T COMMUNICATE WITH THEM.

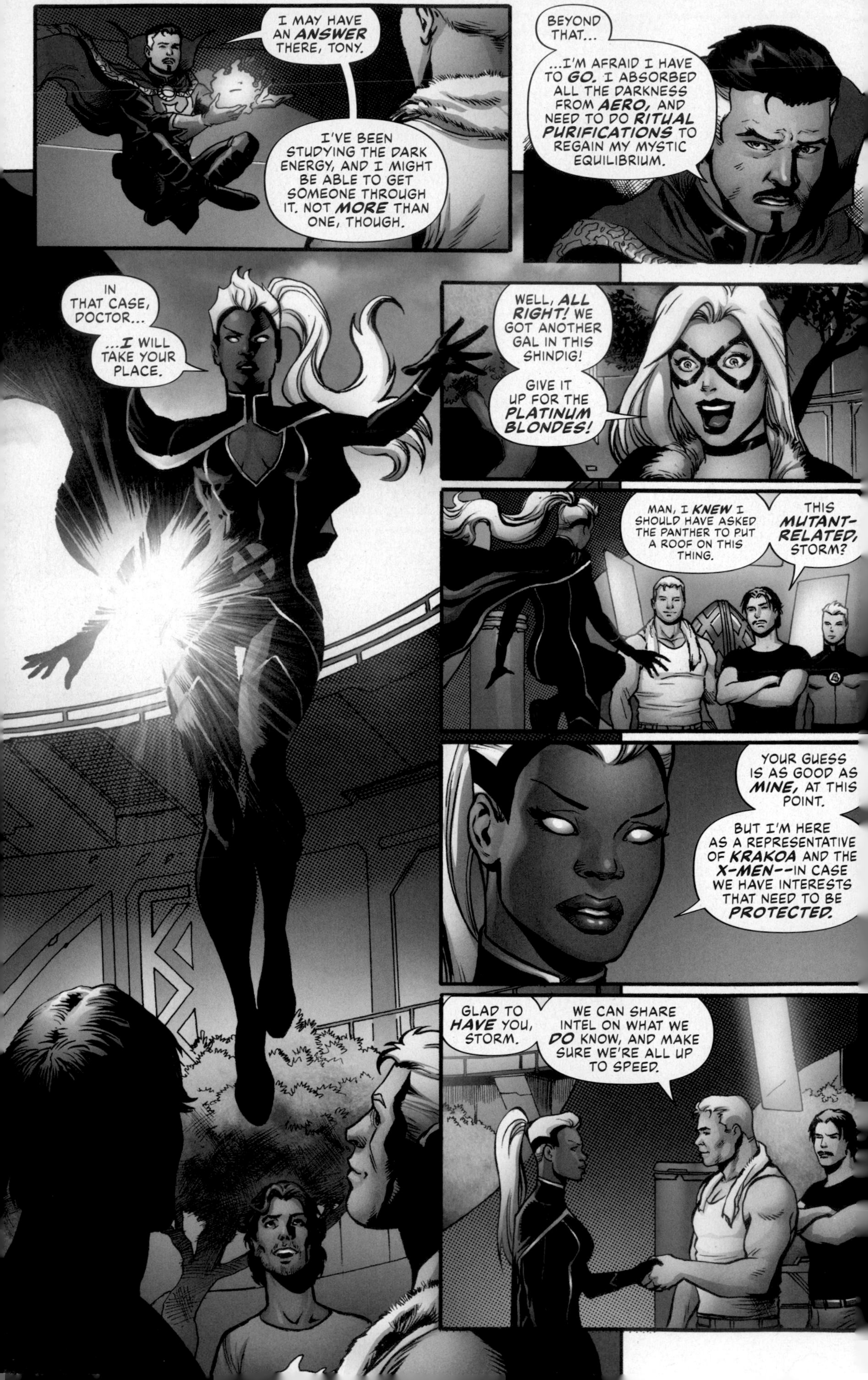
I MAY HAVE AN ANSWER THERE, TONY.
I'VE BEEN STUDYING THE DARK ENERGY, AND I MIGHT BE ABLE TO GET SOMEONE THROUGH IT. NOT MORE THAN ONE, THOUGH.
BEYOND THAT...
...I'M AFRAID I HAVE TO GO. I ABSORBED ALL THE DARKNESS FROM AERO, AND NEED TO DO RITUAL PURIFICATIONS TO REGAIN MY MYSTIC EQUILIBRIUM.
IN THAT CASE, DOCTOR...
...I WILL TAKE YOUR PLACE.
WELL, ALL RIGHT! WE GOT ANOTHER GAL IN THIS SHINDIG!
GIVE IT UP FOR THE PLATINUM BLONDES!
MAN, I KNEW I SHOULD HAVE ASKED THE PANTHER TO PUT A ROOF ON THIS THING.
THIS MUTANT-RELATED, STORM?
YOUR GUESS IS AS GOOD AS MINE, AT THIS POINT.
BUT I'M HERE AS A REPRESENTATIVE OF KRAKOA AND THE X-MEN--IN CASE WE HAVE INTERESTS THAT NEED TO BE PROTECTED.
GLAD TO HAVE YOU, STORM.
WE CAN SHARE INTEL ON WHAT WE DO KNOW, AND MAKE SURE WE'RE ALL UP TO SPEED.

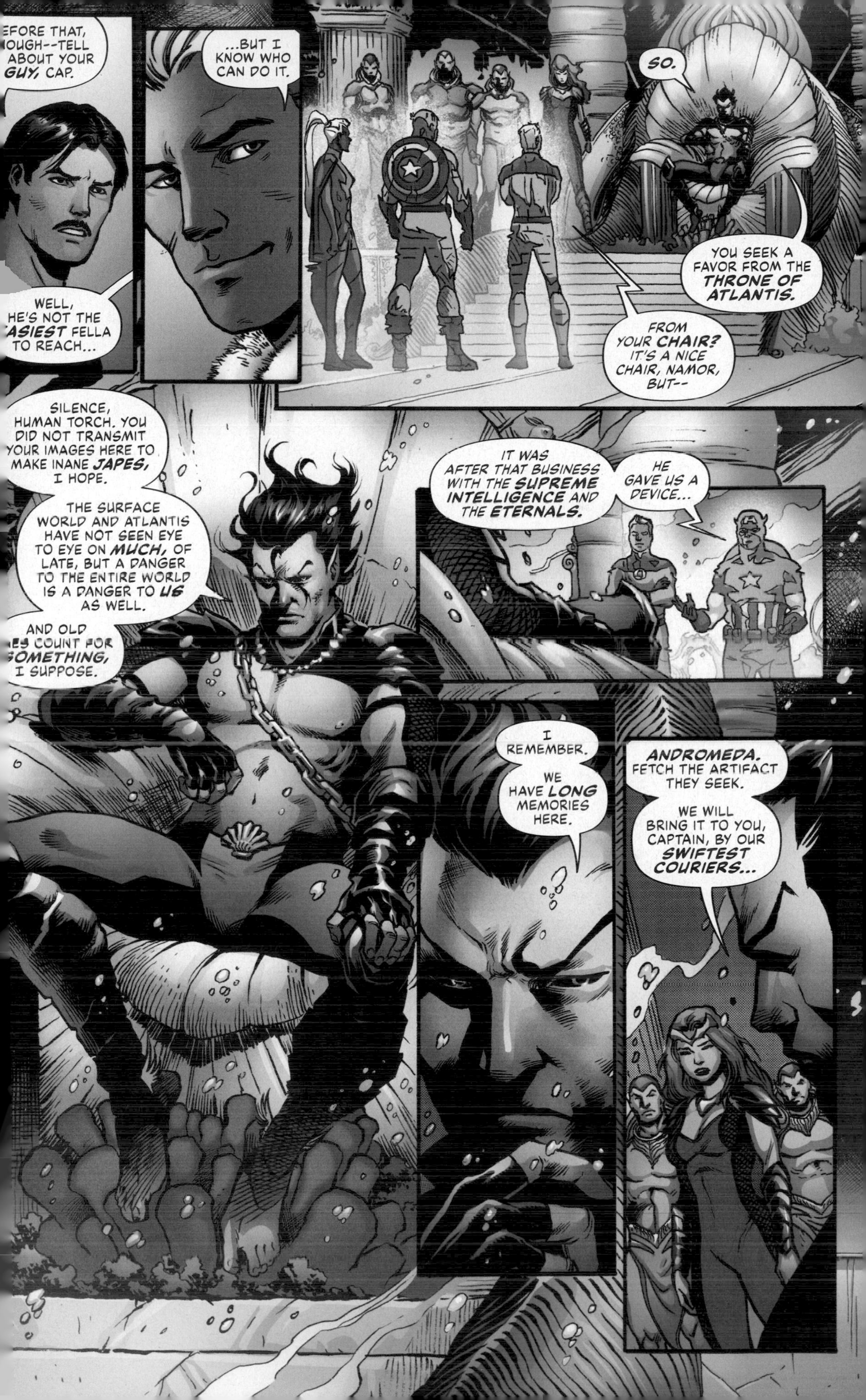
EFORE THAT, HOUGH--TELL ABOUT YOUR GUY, CAP.
WELL, HE'S NOT THE ASIEST FELLA TO REACH...
...BUT I KNOW WHO CAN DO IT.
SO.
YOU SEEK A FAVOR FROM THE THRONE OF ATLANTIS.
FROM YOUR CHAIR? IT'S A NICE CHAIR, NAMOR, BUT--
SILENCE, HUMAN TORCH. YOU DID NOT TRANSMIT YOUR IMAGES HERE TO MAKE INANE JAPES, I HOPE.
THE SURFACE WORLD AND ATLANTIS HAVE NOT SEEN EYE TO EYE ON MUCH, OF LATE, BUT A DANGER TO THE ENTIRE WORLD IS A DANGER TO US AS WELL.
AND OLD ES COUNT FOR SOMETHING, I SUPPOSE.
IT WAS AFTER THAT BUSINESS WITH THE SUPREME INTELLIGENCE AND THE ETERNALS.
HE GAVE US A DEVICE...
I REMEMBER.
WE HAVE LONG MEMORIES HERE.
ANDROMEDA. FETCH THE ARTIFACT THEY SEEK.
WE WILL BRING IT TO YOU, CAPTAIN, BY OUR SWIFTEST COURIERS...

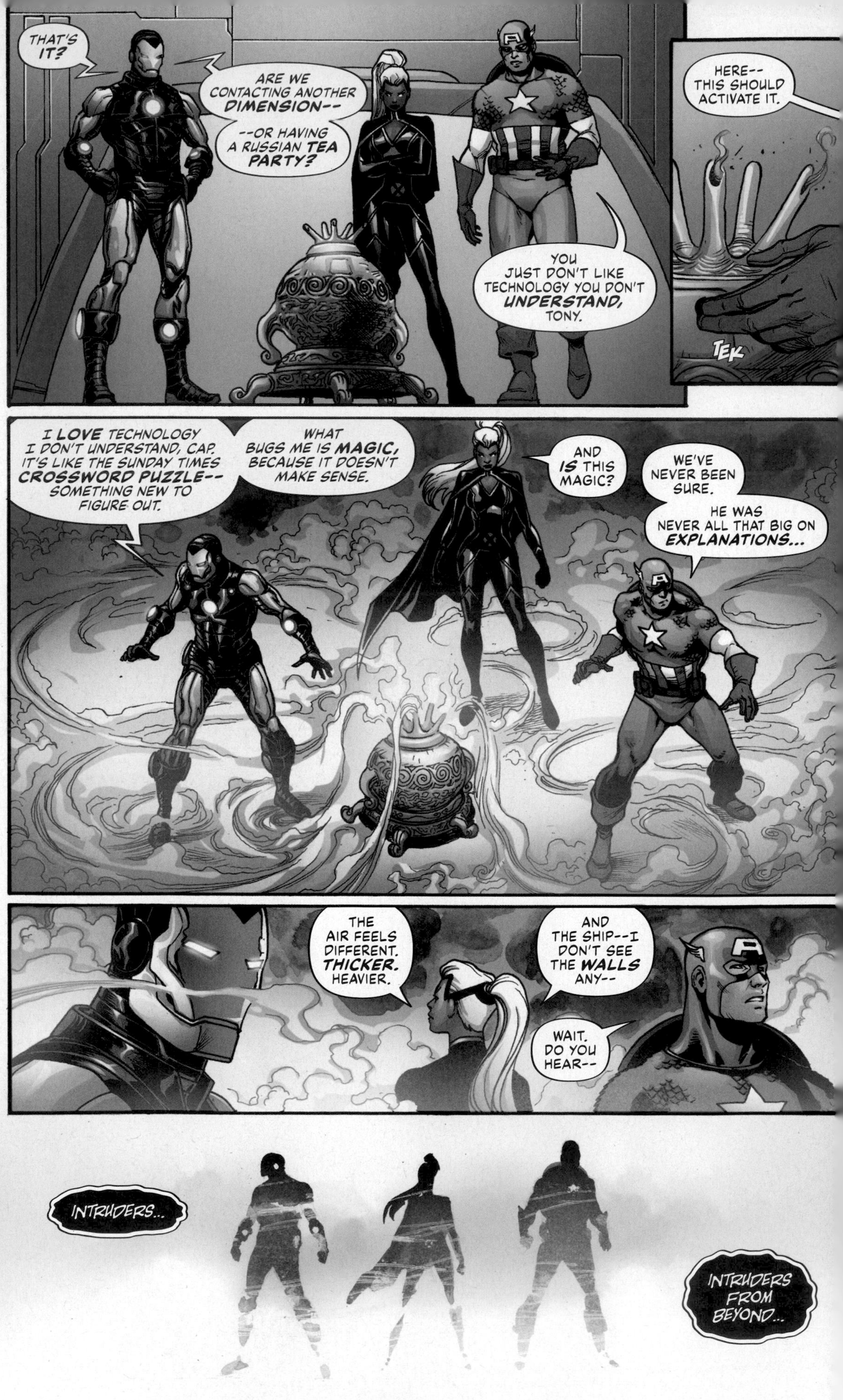
THAT'S IT?
ARE WE CONTACTING ANOTHER DIMENSION--
--OR HAVING A RUSSIAN TEA PARTY?
YOU JUST DON'T LIKE TECHNOLOGY YOU DON'T UNDERSTAND, TONY.
HERE-- THIS SHOULD ACTIVATE IT.
TEK
I LOVE TECHNOLOGY I DON'T UNDERSTAND, CAP. IT'S LIKE THE SUNDAY TIMES CROSSWORD PUZZLE-- SOMETHING NEW TO FIGURE OUT.
WHAT BUGS ME IS MAGIC, BECAUSE IT DOESN'T MAKE SENSE.
AND IS THIS MAGIC?
WE'VE NEVER BEEN SURE.
HE WAS NEVER ALL THAT BIG ON EXPLANATIONS...
THE AIR FEELS DIFFERENT. THICKER. HEAVIER.
AND THE SHIP--I DON'T SEE THE WALLS ANY--
WAIT. DO YOU HEAR--
INTRUDERS...
INTRUDERS FROM BEYOND...

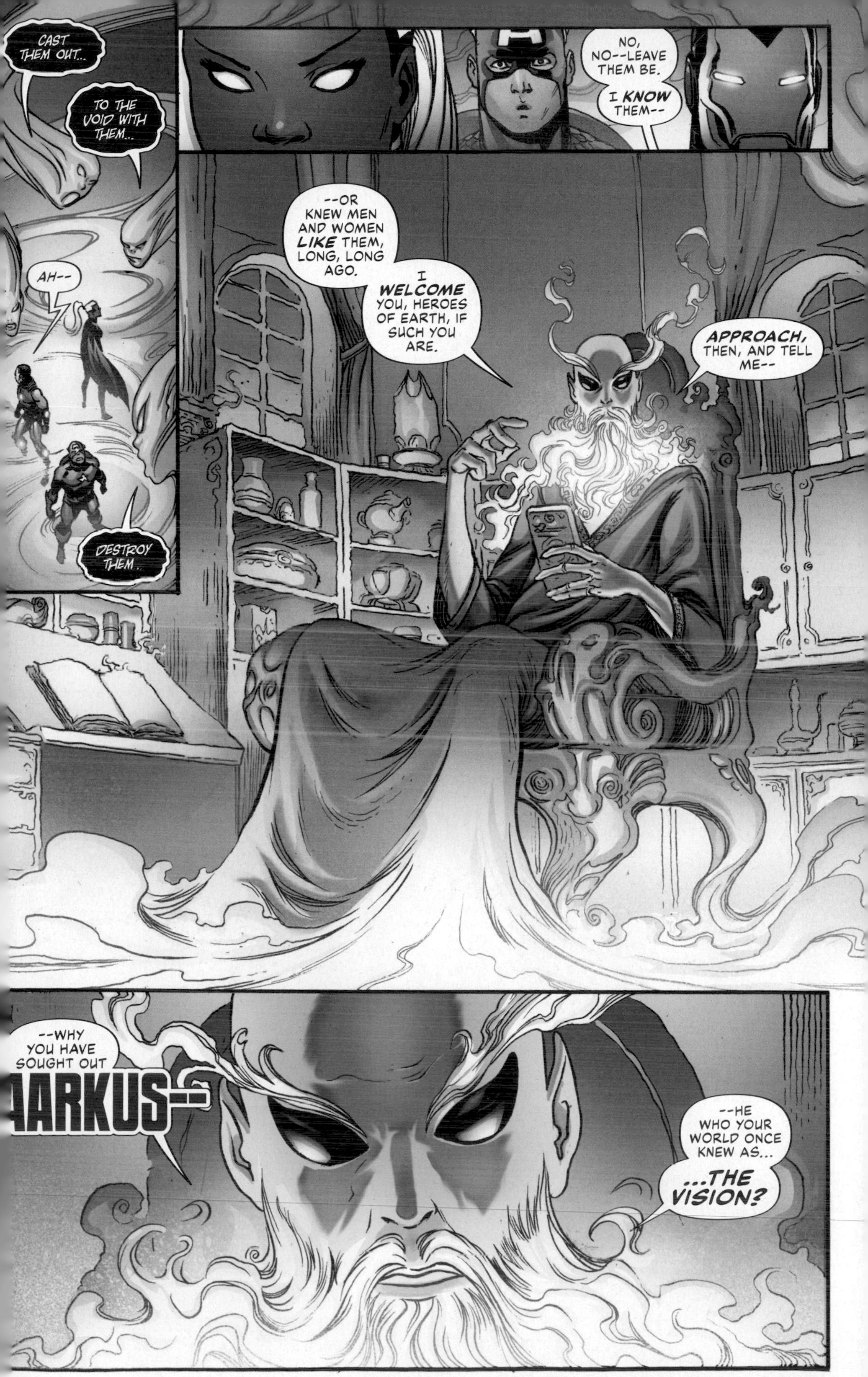
CAST THEM OUT...
TO THE VOID WITH THEM...
AH--
DESTROY THEM...
NO, NO--LEAVE THEM BE.
I KNOW THEM--
--OR KNEW MEN AND WOMEN LIKE THEM, LONG, LONG AGO.
I WELCOME YOU, HEROES OF EARTH, IF SUCH YOU ARE.
APPROACH, THEN, AND TELL ME--
--WHY YOU HAVE SOUGHT OUT
AARKUS--
--HE WHO YOUR WORLD ONCE KNEW AS...
...THE VISION?

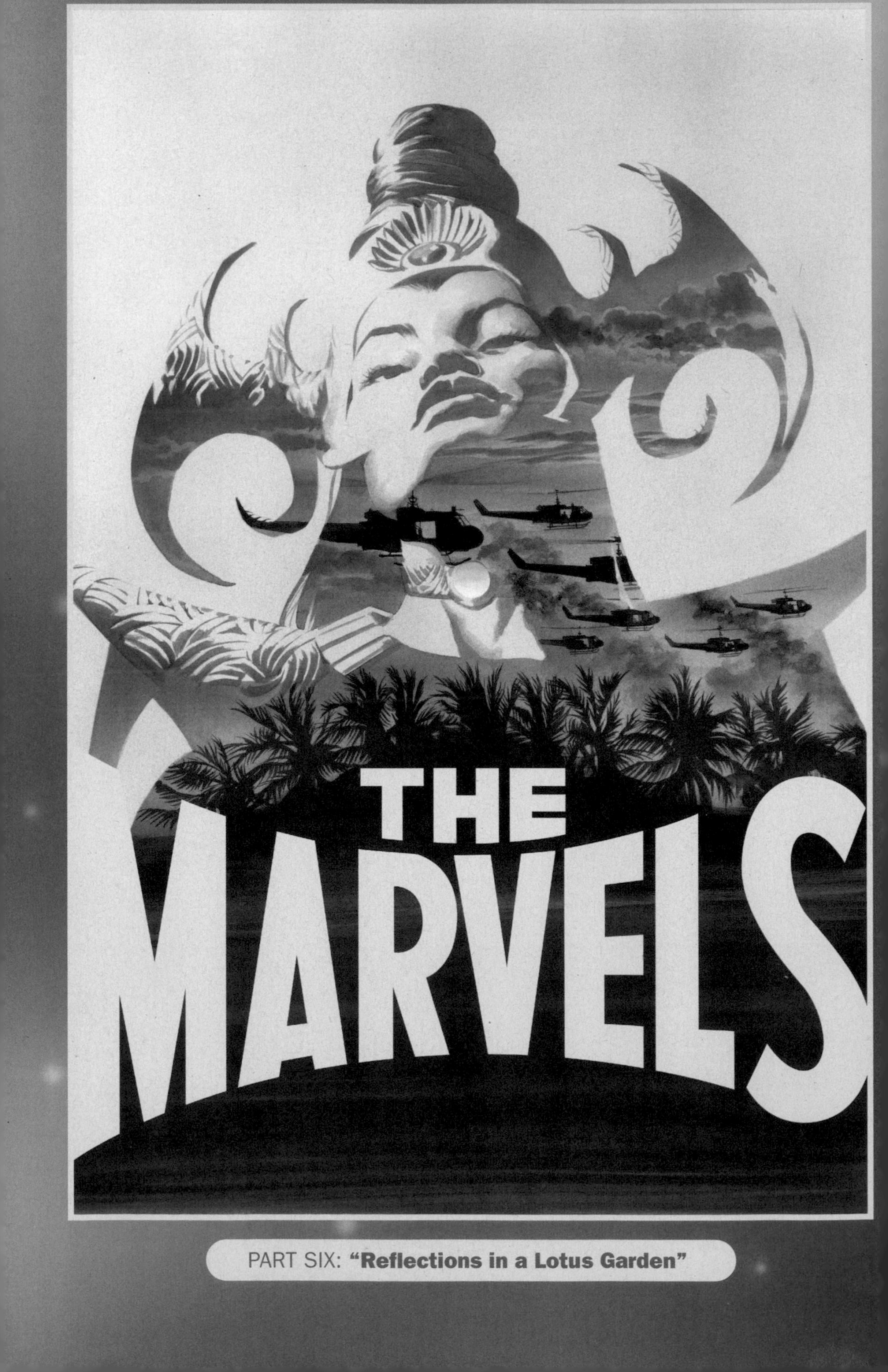
THE
MARVELS

PART SIX: **"Reflections in a Lotus Garden"**

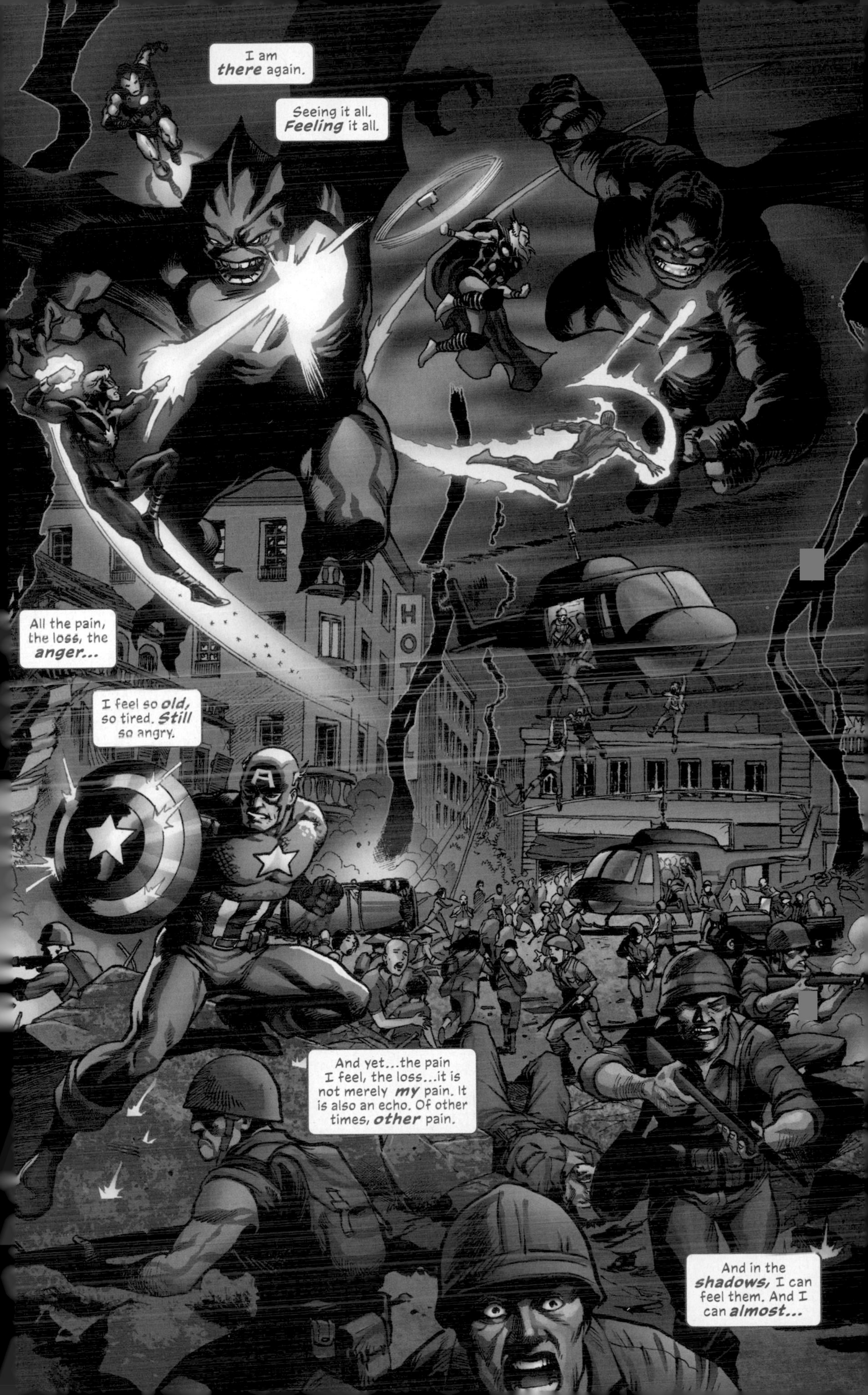
I am *there* again.
Seeing it all. *Feeling* it all.
All the pain, the loss, the *anger...*
I feel so *old*, so tired. *Still* so angry.
HOT
And yet...the pain I feel, the loss...it is not merely *my* pain. It is also an echo. Of other times, *other* pain.
And in the *shadows,* I can feel them. And I can *almost...*

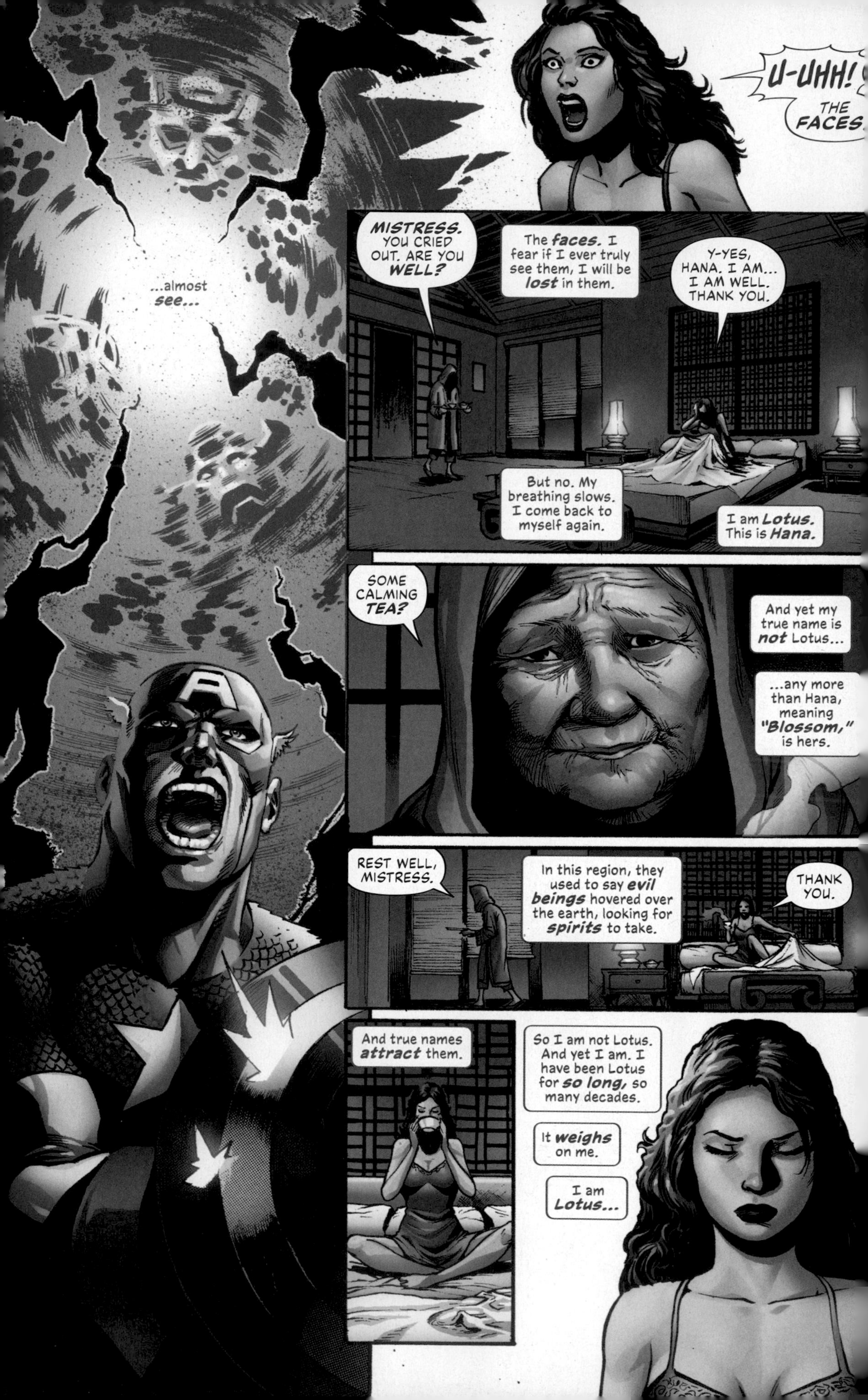

U-UHH!
THE FACES.
...almost see...
MISTRESS. YOU CRIED OUT. ARE YOU WELL?
The faces. I fear if I ever truly see them, I will be lost in them.
Y-YES, HANA. I AM... I AM WELL. THANK YOU.
But no. My breathing slows. I come back to myself again.
I am Lotus. This is Hana.
SOME CALMING TEA?
And yet my true name is not Lotus...
...any more than Hana, meaning "Blossom," is hers.
REST WELL, MISTRESS.
In this region, they used to say evil beings hovered over the earth, looking for spirits to take.
THANK YOU.
And true names attract them.
So I am not Lotus. And yet I am. I have been Lotus for so long, so many decades.
It weighs on me.
I am Lotus...

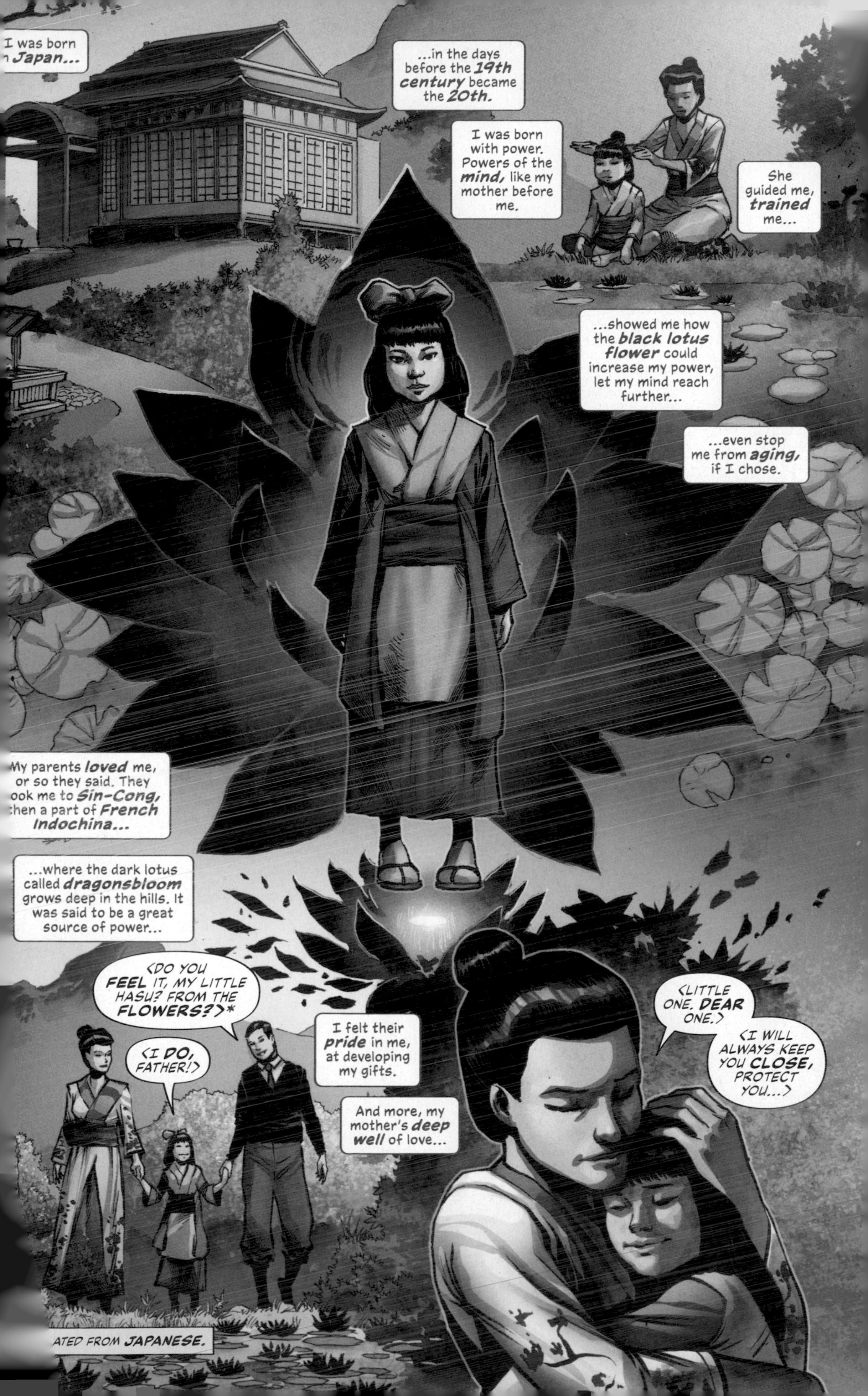

I was born n Japan...
...in the days before the 19th century became the 20th.
I was born with power. Powers of the mind, like my mother before me.
She guided me, trained me...
...showed me how the black lotus flower could increase my power, let my mind reach further...
...even stop me from aging, if I chose.
My parents loved me, or so they said. They ook me to Sin-Cong, then a part of French Indochina...
...where the dark lotus called dragonsbloom grows deep in the hills. It was said to be a great source of power...
<DO YOU FEEL IT, MY LITTLE HASU? FROM THE FLOWERS?>*
<I DO, FATHER!>
I felt their pride in me, at developing my gifts.
And more, my mother's deep well of love...
<LITTLE ONE. DEAR ONE.>
<I WILL ALWAYS KEEP YOU CLOSE, PROTECT YOU...>
ATED FROM JAPANESE.

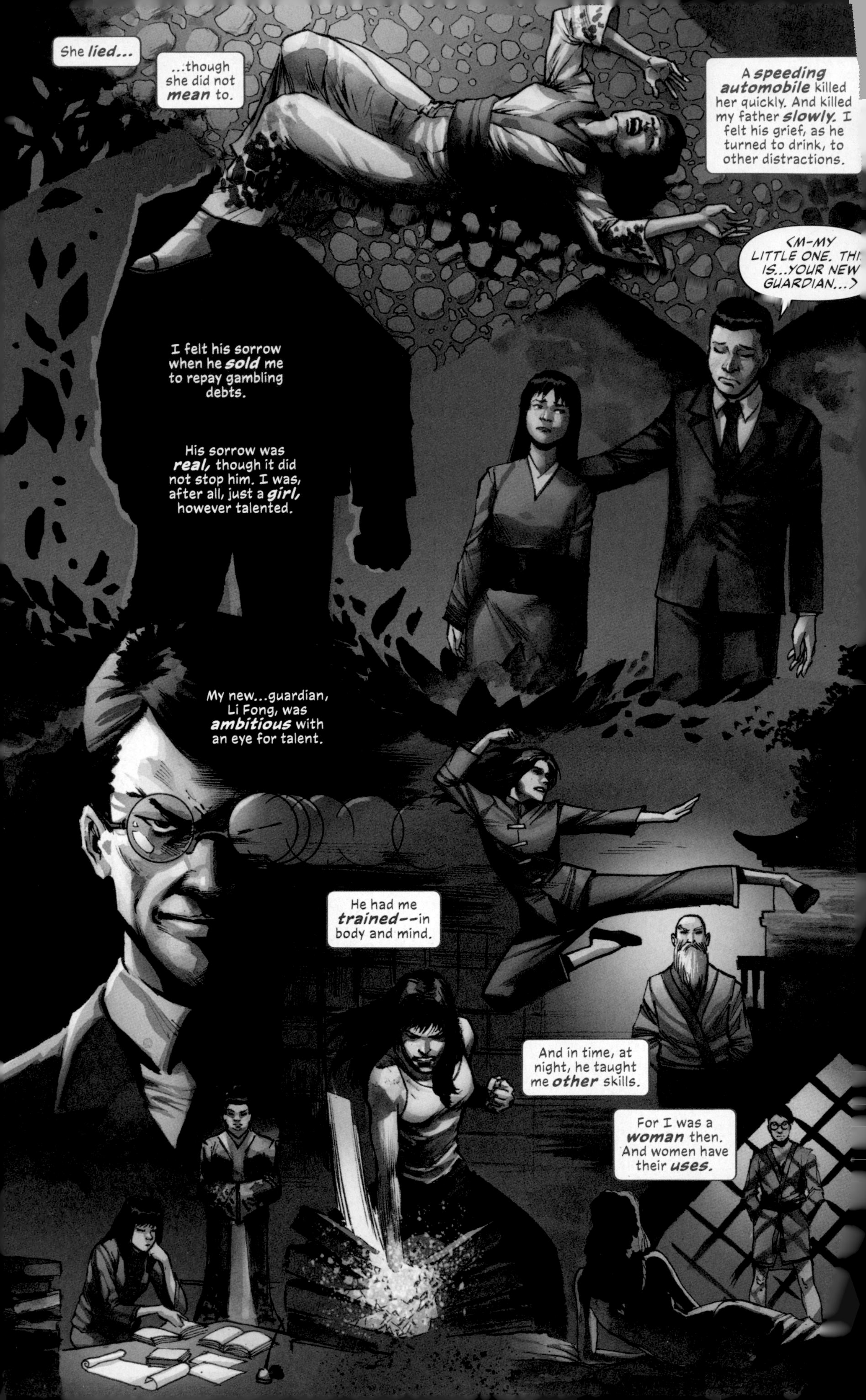
She lied...
...though she did not mean to.
A speeding automobile killed her quickly. And killed my father slowly. I felt his grief, as he turned to drink, to other distractions.
<M-MY LITTLE ONE. THI IS...YOUR NEW GUARDIAN...>
I felt his sorrow when he sold me to repay gambling debts.
His sorrow was real, though it did not stop him. I was, after all, just a girl, however talented.
My new...guardian, Li Fong, was ambitious with an eye for talent.
He had me trained--in body and mind.
And in time, at night, he taught me other skills.
For I was a woman then. And women have their uses.

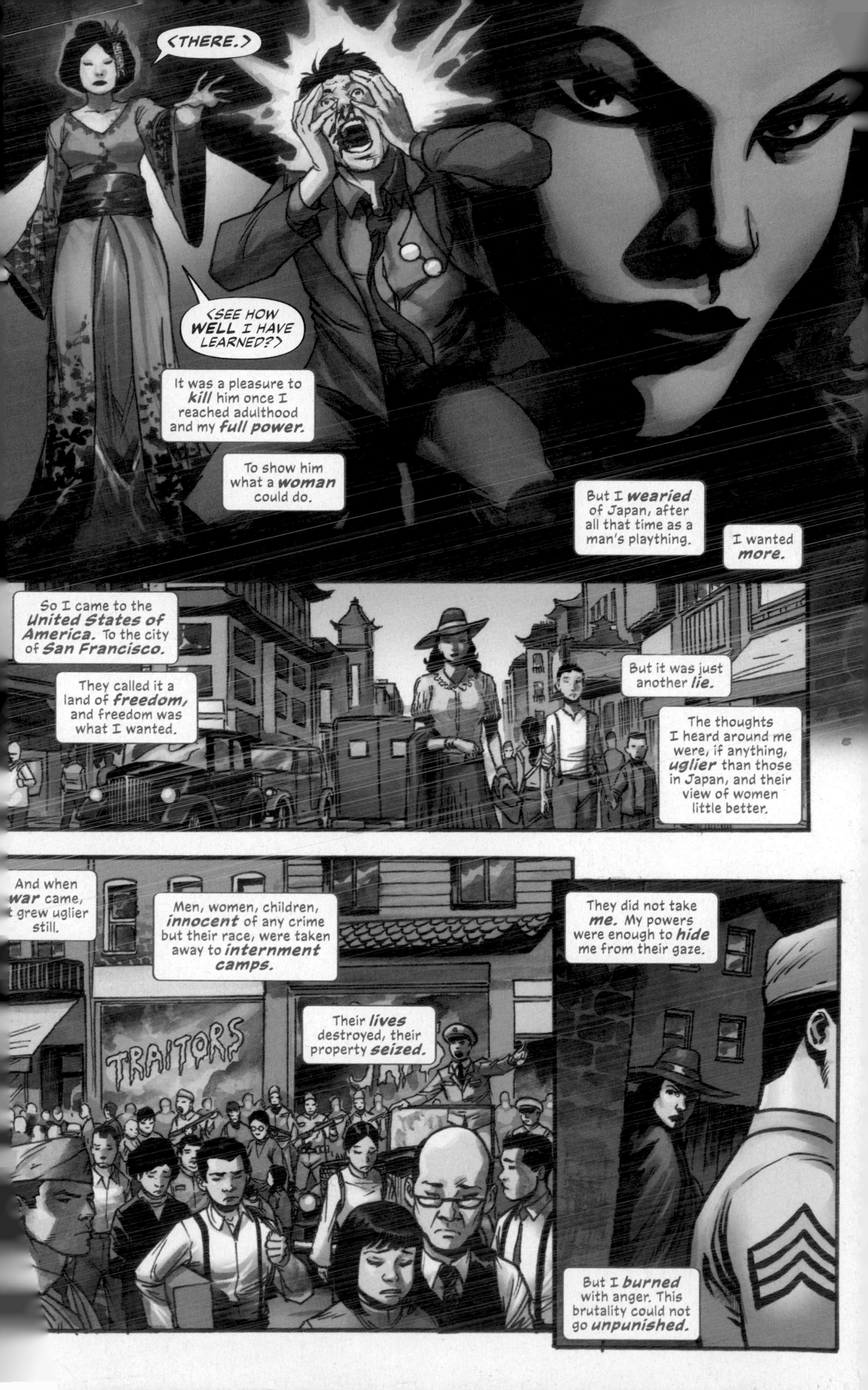
<THERE.>
<SEE HOW WELL I HAVE LEARNED?>
It was a pleasure to kill him once I reached adulthood and my full power.
To show him what a woman could do.
But I wearied of Japan, after all that time as a man's plaything.
I wanted more.
So I came to the United States of America. To the city of San Francisco.
They called it a land of freedom, and freedom was what I wanted.
But it was just another lie.
The thoughts I heard around me were, if anything, uglier than those in Japan, and their view of women little better.
And when war came, t grew uglier still.
Men, women, children, innocent of any crime but their race, were taken away to internment camps.
Their lives destroyed, their property seized.
TRAITORS
They did not take me. My powers were enough to hide me from their gaze.
But I burned with anger. This brutality could not go unpunished.

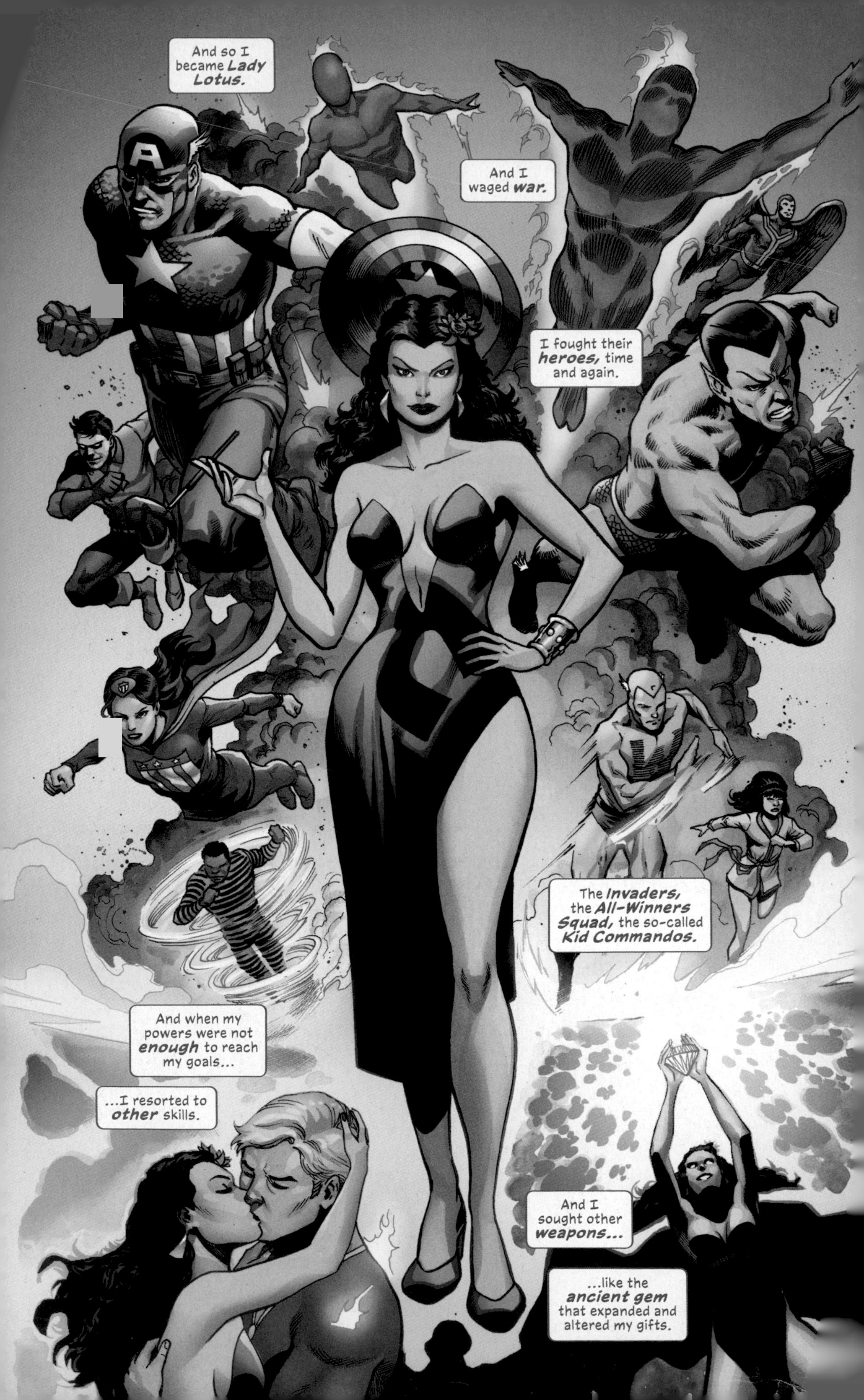

And so I became **Lady Lotus.**
And I waged **war.**
I fought their **heroes,** time and again.
The **Invaders,** the **All-Winners Squad,** the so-called **Kid Commandos.**
And when my powers were not **enough** to reach my goals...
...I resorted to **other** skills.
And I sought other **weapons...**
...like the **ancient gem** that expanded and altered my gifts.

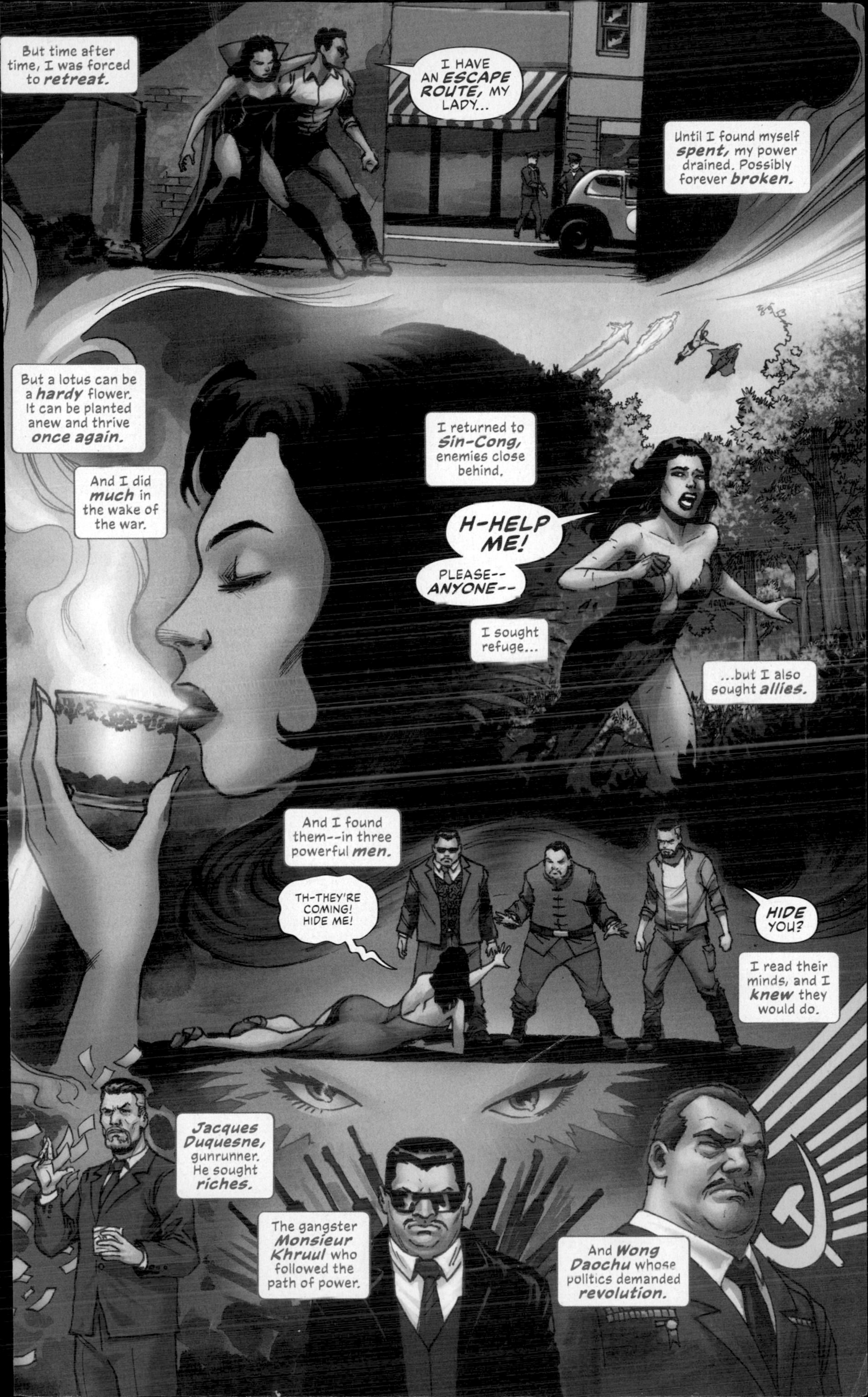
But time after time, I was forced to retreat.
I HAVE AN ESCAPE ROUTE, MY LADY...
Until I found myself spent, my power drained. Possibly forever broken.
But a lotus can be a hardy flower. It can be planted anew and thrive once again.
And I did much in the wake of the war.
I returned to Sin-Cong, enemies close behind.
H-HELP ME!
PLEASE-- ANYONE--
I sought refuge...
...but I also sought allies.
And I found them--in three powerful men.
TH-THEY'RE COMING! HIDE ME!
HIDE YOU?
I read their minds, and I knew they would do.
Jacques Duquesne, gunrunner. He sought riches.
The gangster Monsieur Khruul who followed the path of power.
And Wong Daochu whose politics demanded revolution.

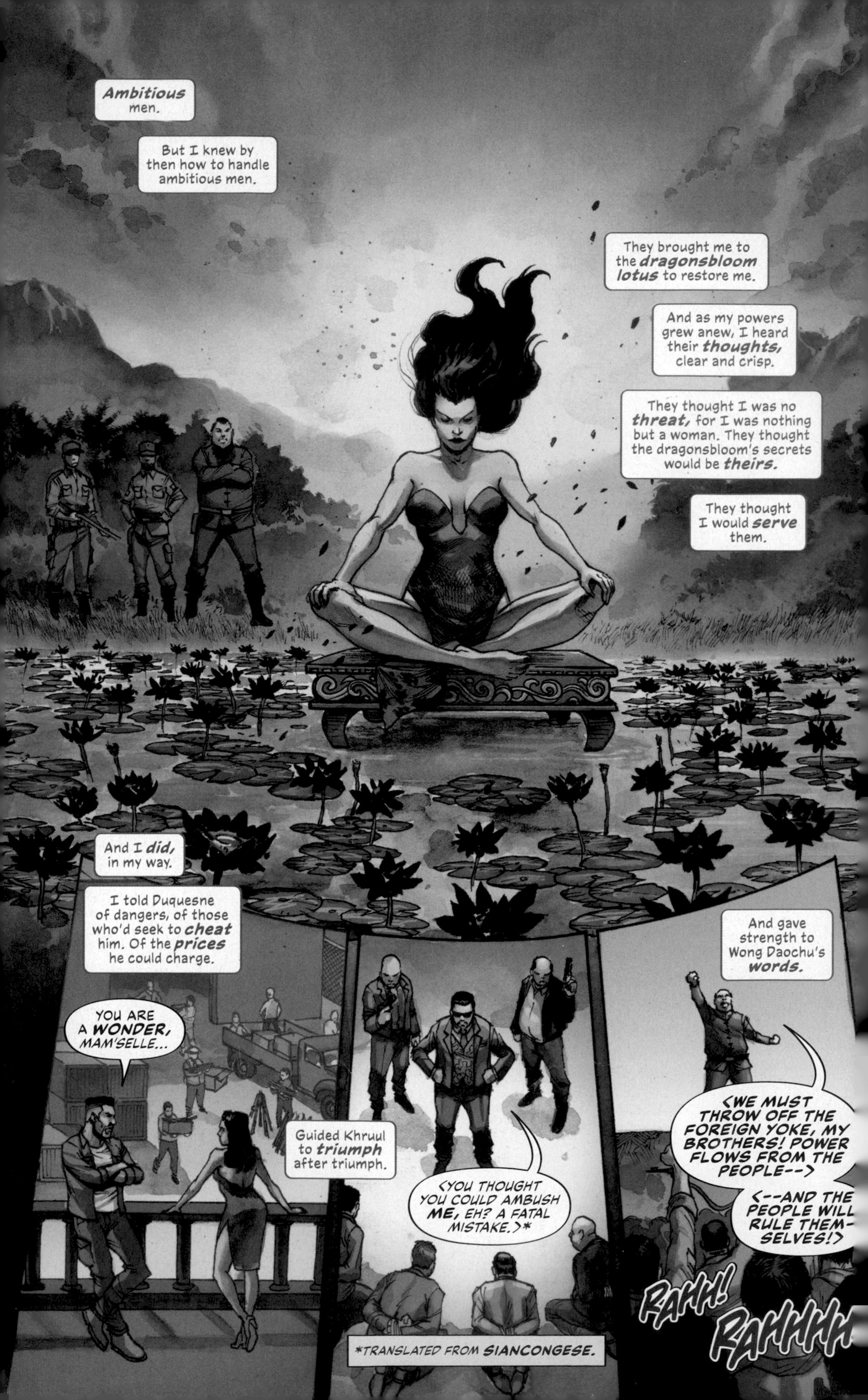
Ambitious men.
But I knew by then how to handle ambitious men.
They brought me to the dragonsbloom lotus to restore me.
And as my powers grew anew, I heard their thoughts, clear and crisp.
They thought I was no threat, for I was nothing but a woman. They thought the dragonsbloom's secrets would be theirs.
They thought I would serve them.
And I did, in my way.
I told Duquesne of dangers, of those who'd seek to cheat him. Of the prices he could charge.
YOU ARE A WONDER, MAM'SELLE...
Guided Khruul to triumph after triumph.
<YOU THOUGHT YOU COULD AMBUSH ME, EH? A FATAL MISTAKE.>*
And gave strength to Wong Daochu's words.
<WE MUST THROW OFF THE FOREIGN YOKE, MY BROTHERS! POWER FLOWS FROM THE PEOPLE-->
<--AND THE PEOPLE WILL RULE THEM-SELVES!>
RAHH!
RAHHHH
*TRANSLATED FROM SIANCONGESE.

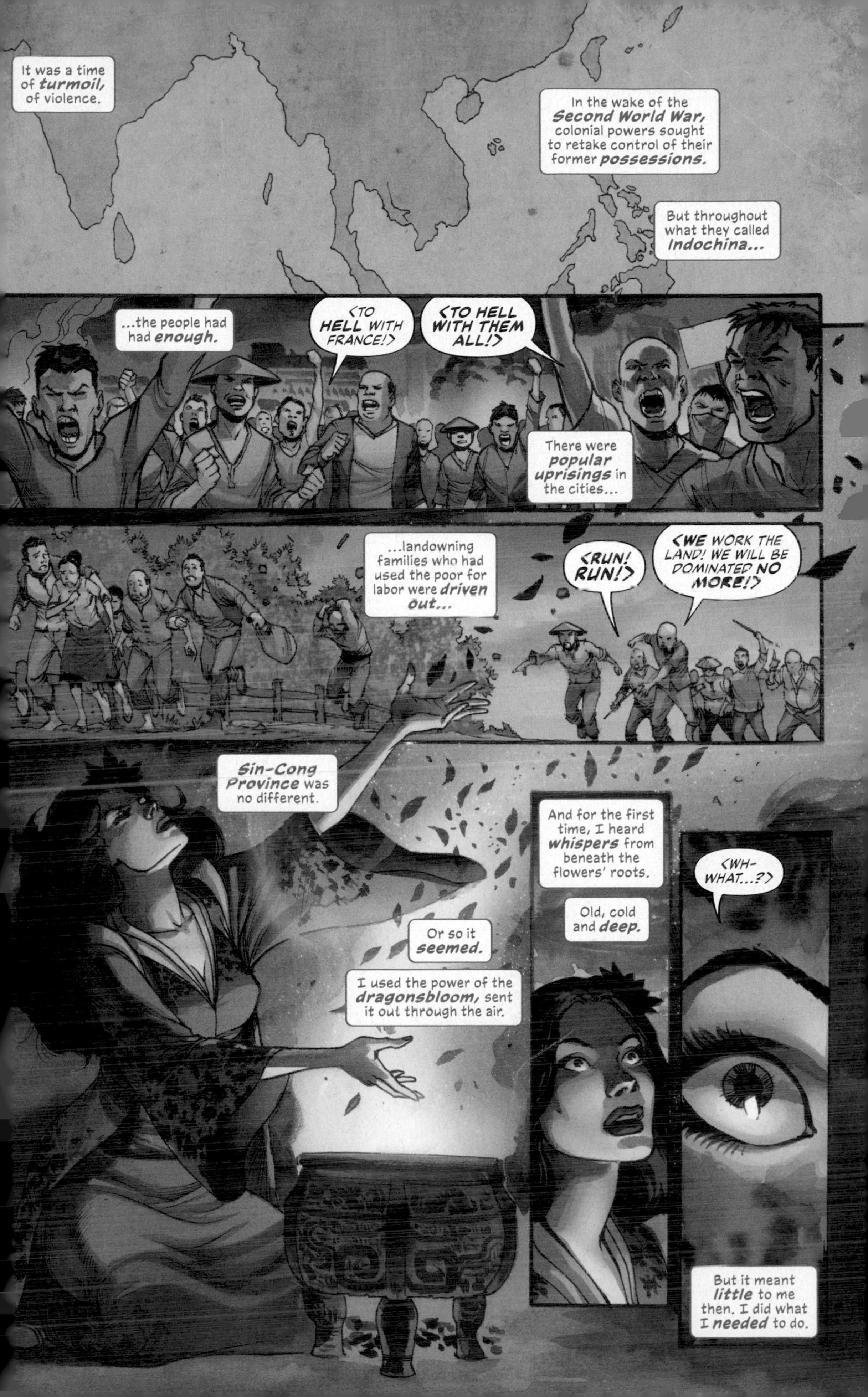
It was a time of turmoil, of violence.
In the wake of the Second World War, colonial powers sought to retake control of their former possessions.
But throughout what they called Indochina...
...the people had had enough.
<TO HELL WITH FRANCE!>
<TO HELL WITH THEM ALL!>
There were popular uprisings in the cities...
...landowning families who had used the poor for labor were driven out...
<RUN! RUN!>
<WE WORK THE LAND! WE WILL BE DOMINATED NO MORE!>
Sin-Cong Province was no different.
Or so it seemed.
I used the power of the dragonsbloom, sent it out through the air.
And for the first time, I heard whispers from beneath the flowers' roots.
Old, cold and deep.
<WH- WHAT...?>
But it meant little to me then. I did what I needed to do.

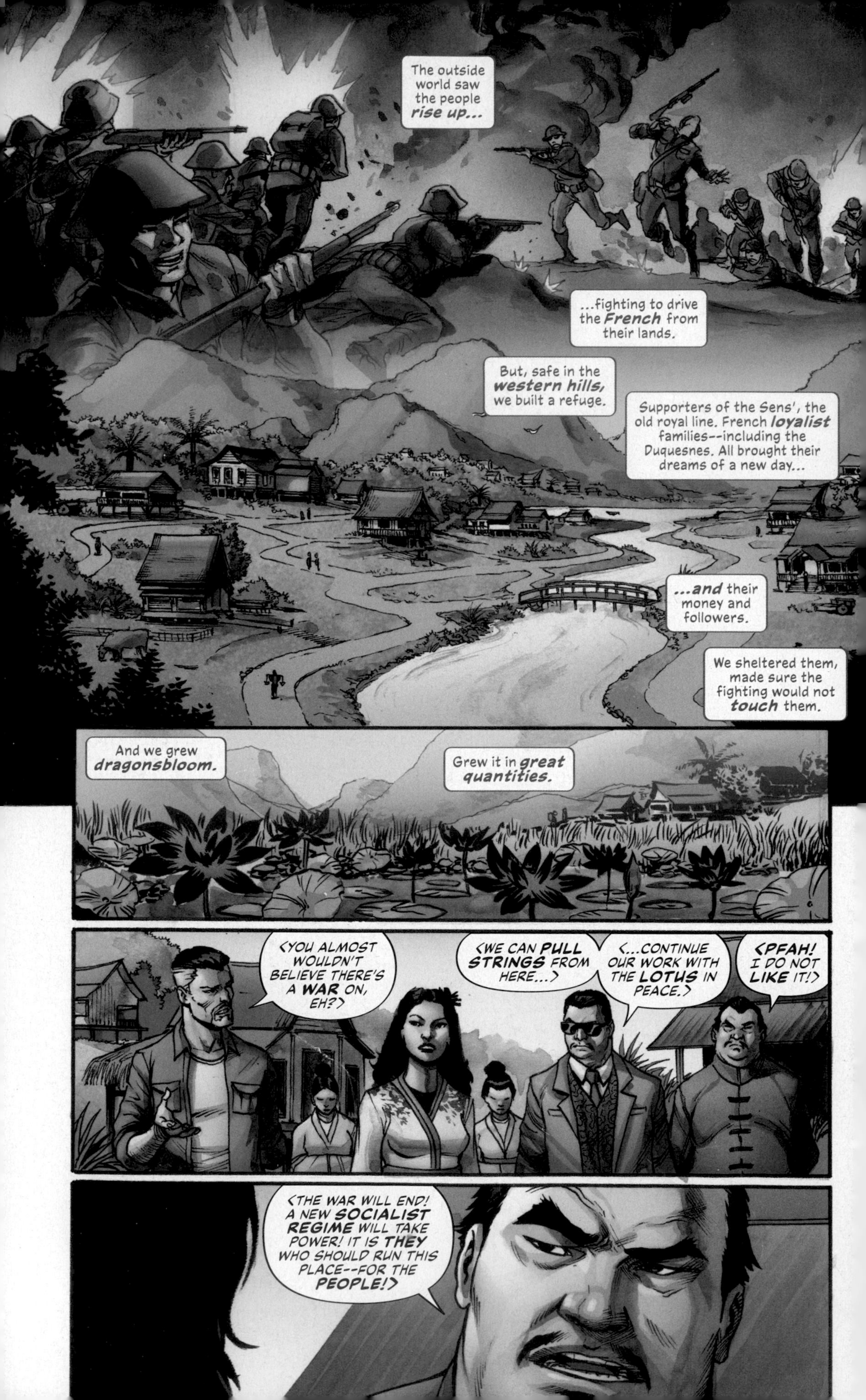

The outside world saw the people *rise up...*
...fighting to drive the *French* from their lands.
But, safe in the *western hills,* we built a refuge.
Supporters of the Sens', the old royal line. French *loyalist* families--including the Duquesnes. All brought their dreams of a new day...
...and their money and followers.
We sheltered them, made sure the fighting would not *touch* them.
And we grew *dragonsbloom.*
Grew it in *great quantities.*
<YOU ALMOST WOULDN'T BELIEVE THERE'S A **WAR** ON, EH?>
<WE CAN **PULL STRINGS** FROM HERE...>
<...CONTINUE OUR WORK WITH THE **LOTUS** IN PEACE.>
<**PFAH!** I DO NOT **LIKE** IT!>
<THE WAR WILL END! A NEW **SOCIALIST REGIME** WILL TAKE POWER! IT IS **THEY** WHO SHOULD RUN THIS PLACE--FOR THE **PEOPLE!**>

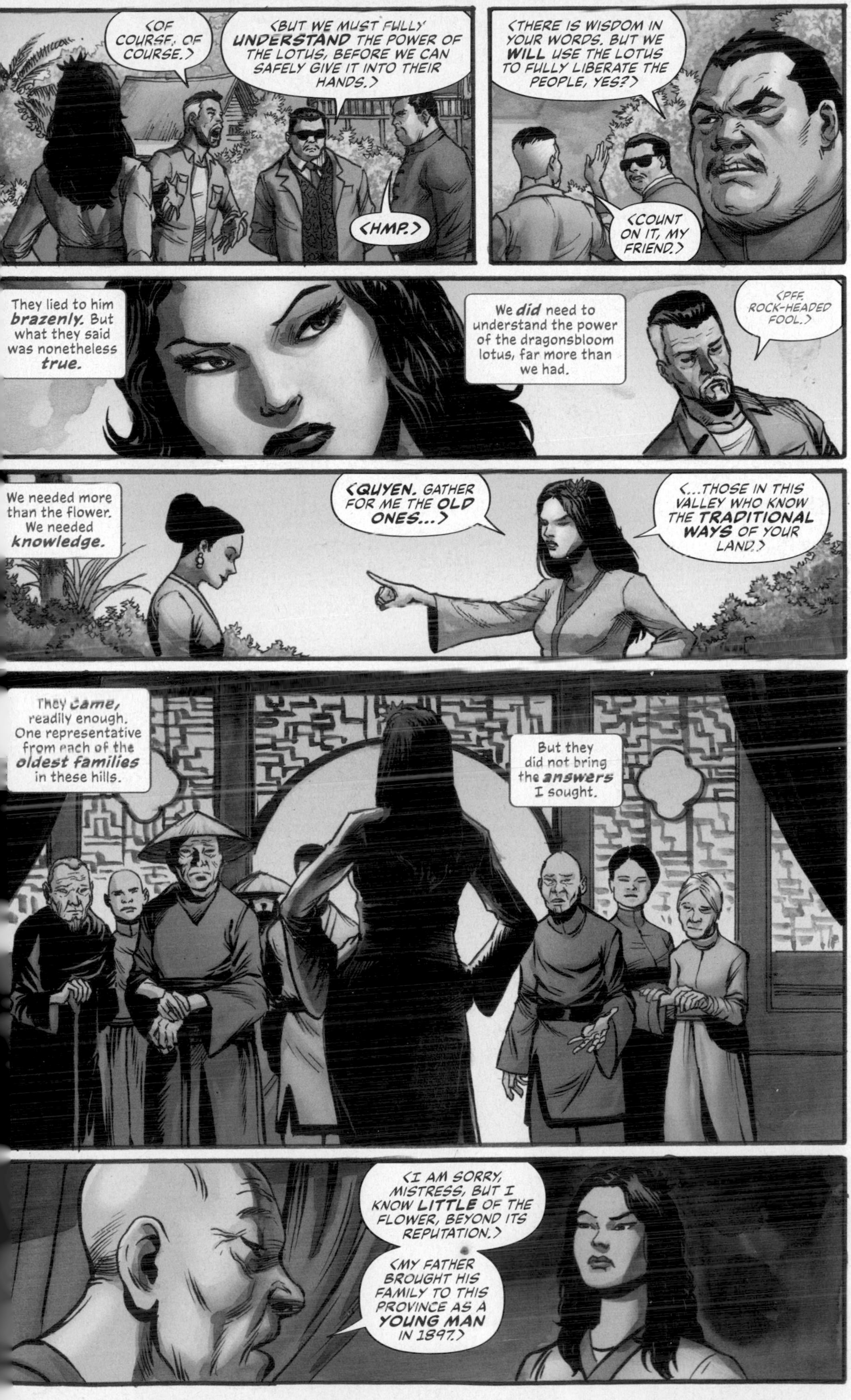
<OF COURSE. OF COURSE.>
<BUT WE MUST FULLY UNDERSTAND THE POWER OF THE LOTUS, BEFORE WE CAN SAFELY GIVE IT INTO THEIR HANDS.>
<HMP.>
<THERE IS WISDOM IN YOUR WORDS. BUT WE WILL USE THE LOTUS TO FULLY LIBERATE THE PEOPLE, YES?>
<COUNT ON IT, MY FRIEND.>
They lied to him brazenly. But what they said was nonetheless true.
We did need to understand the power of the dragonsbloom lotus, far more than we had.
<PFF. ROCK-HEADED FOOL.>
We needed more than the flower. We needed knowledge.
<QUYEN. GATHER FOR ME THE OLD ONES...>
<...THOSE IN THIS VALLEY WHO KNOW THE TRADITIONAL WAYS OF YOUR LAND.>
They came, readily enough. One representative from each of the oldest families in these hills.
But they did not bring the answers I sought.
<I AM SORRY, MISTRESS, BUT I KNOW LITTLE OF THE FLOWER, BEYOND ITS REPUTATION.>
<MY FATHER BROUGHT HIS FAMILY TO THIS PROVINCE AS A YOUNG MAN IN 1897.>

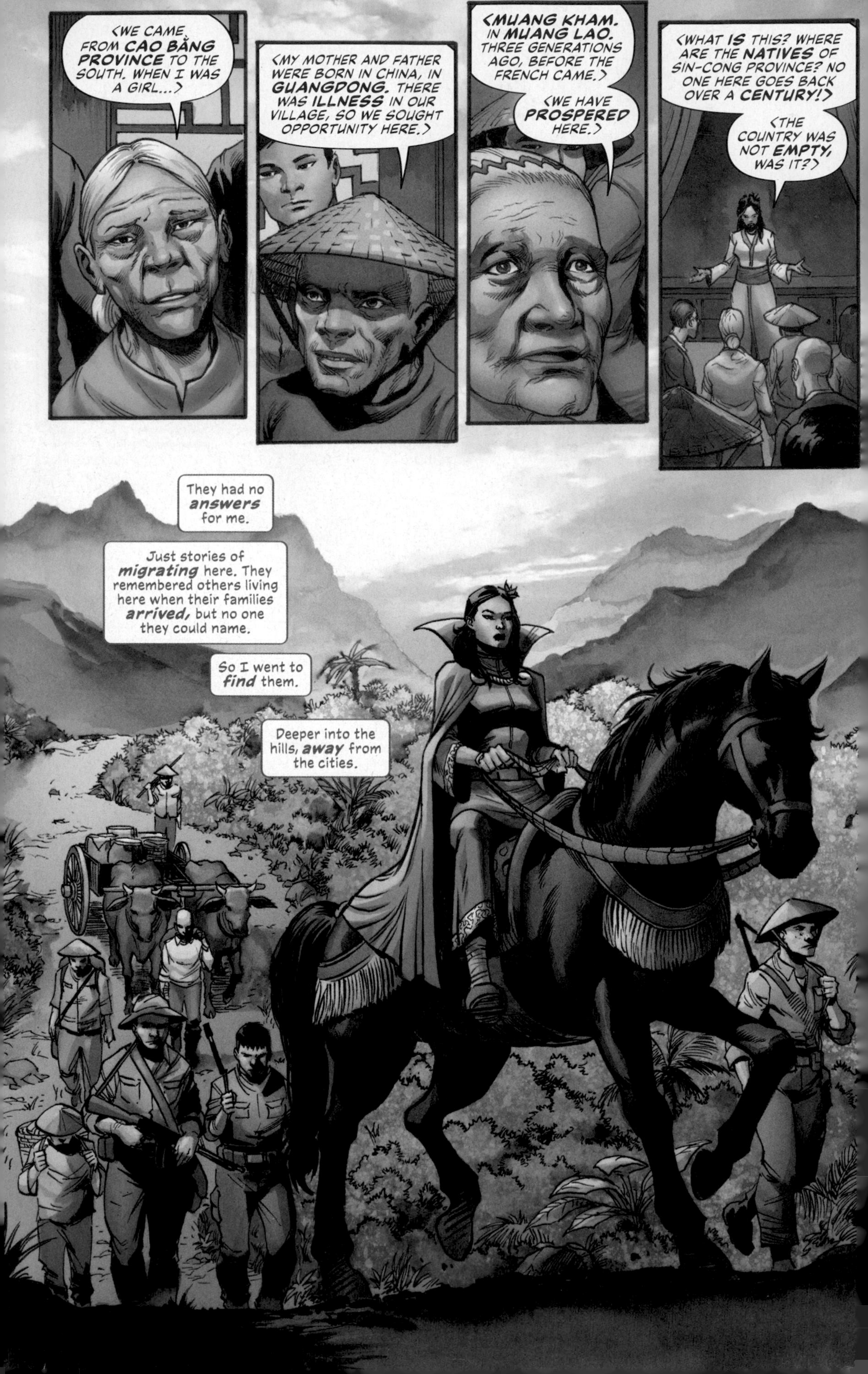

<WE CAME FROM CAO BẰNG PROVINCE TO THE SOUTH. WHEN I WAS A GIRL...>
<MY MOTHER AND FATHER WERE BORN IN CHINA, IN GUANGDONG. THERE WAS ILLNESS IN OUR VILLAGE, SO WE SOUGHT OPPORTUNITY HERE.>
<MUANG KHAM. IN MUANG LAO. THREE GENERATIONS AGO, BEFORE THE FRENCH CAME.>
<WE HAVE PROSPERED HERE.>
<WHAT IS THIS? WHERE ARE THE NATIVES OF SIN-CONG PROVINCE? NO ONE HERE GOES BACK OVER A CENTURY!>
<THE COUNTRY WAS NOT EMPTY, WAS IT?>
They had no answers for me.
Just stories of migrating here. They remembered others living here when their families arrived, but no one they could name.
So I went to find them.
Deeper into the hills, away from the cities.

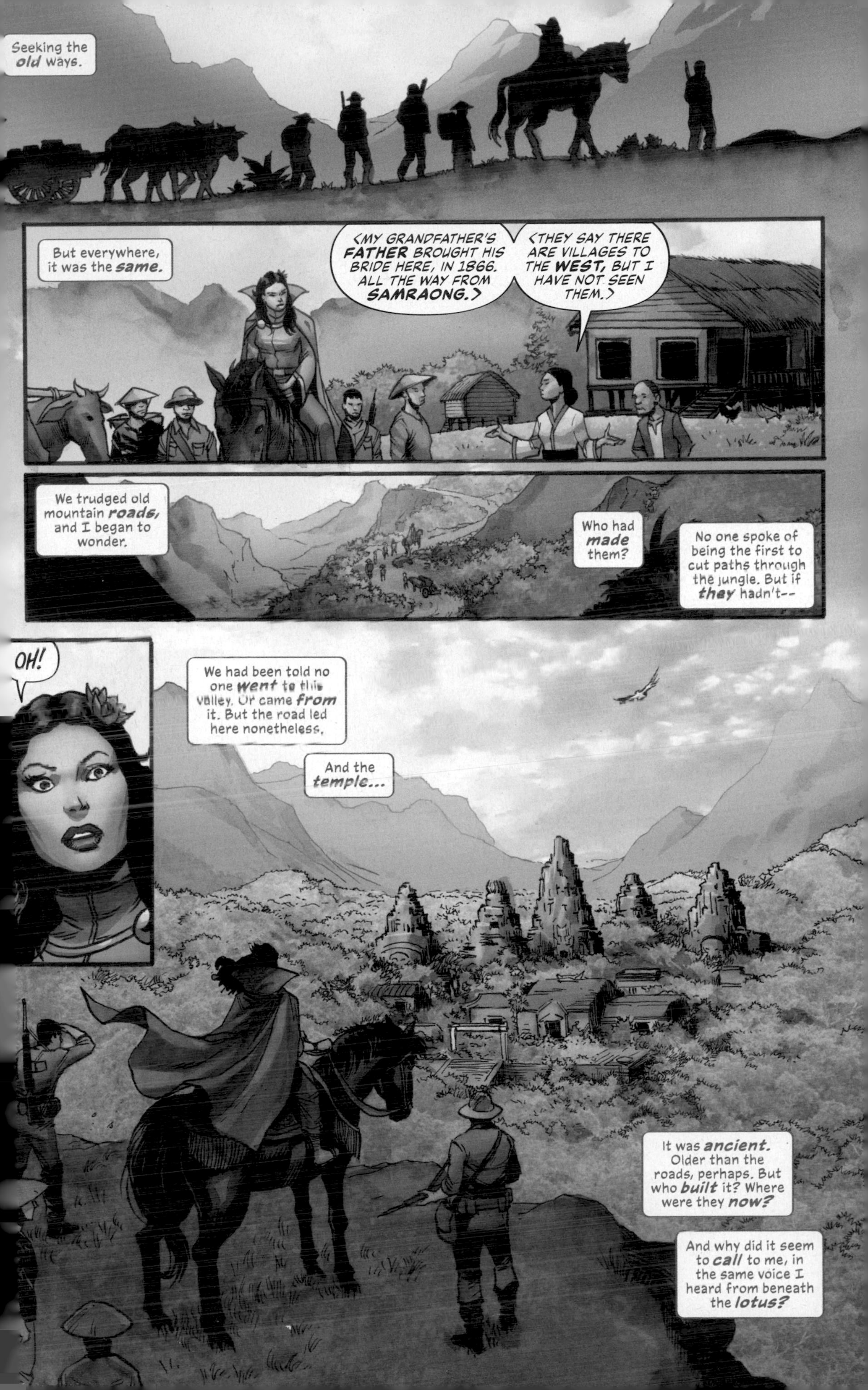
Seeking the *old* ways.
But everywhere, it was the *same.*
<MY GRANDFATHER'S **FATHER** BROUGHT HIS BRIDE HERE, IN 1866. ALL THE WAY FROM **SAMRAONG.**>
<THEY SAY THERE ARE VILLAGES TO THE **WEST,** BUT I HAVE NOT SEEN THEM.>
We trudged old mountain *roads,* and I began to wonder.
Who had *made* them?
No one spoke of being the first to cut paths through the jungle. But if *they* hadn't--
OH!
We had been told no one *went* to this valley. Or came *from* it. But the road led here nonetheless.
And the *temple...*
It was *ancient.* Older than the roads, perhaps. But who *built* it? Where were they *now?*
And why did it seem to *call* to me, in the same voice I heard from beneath the *lotus?*

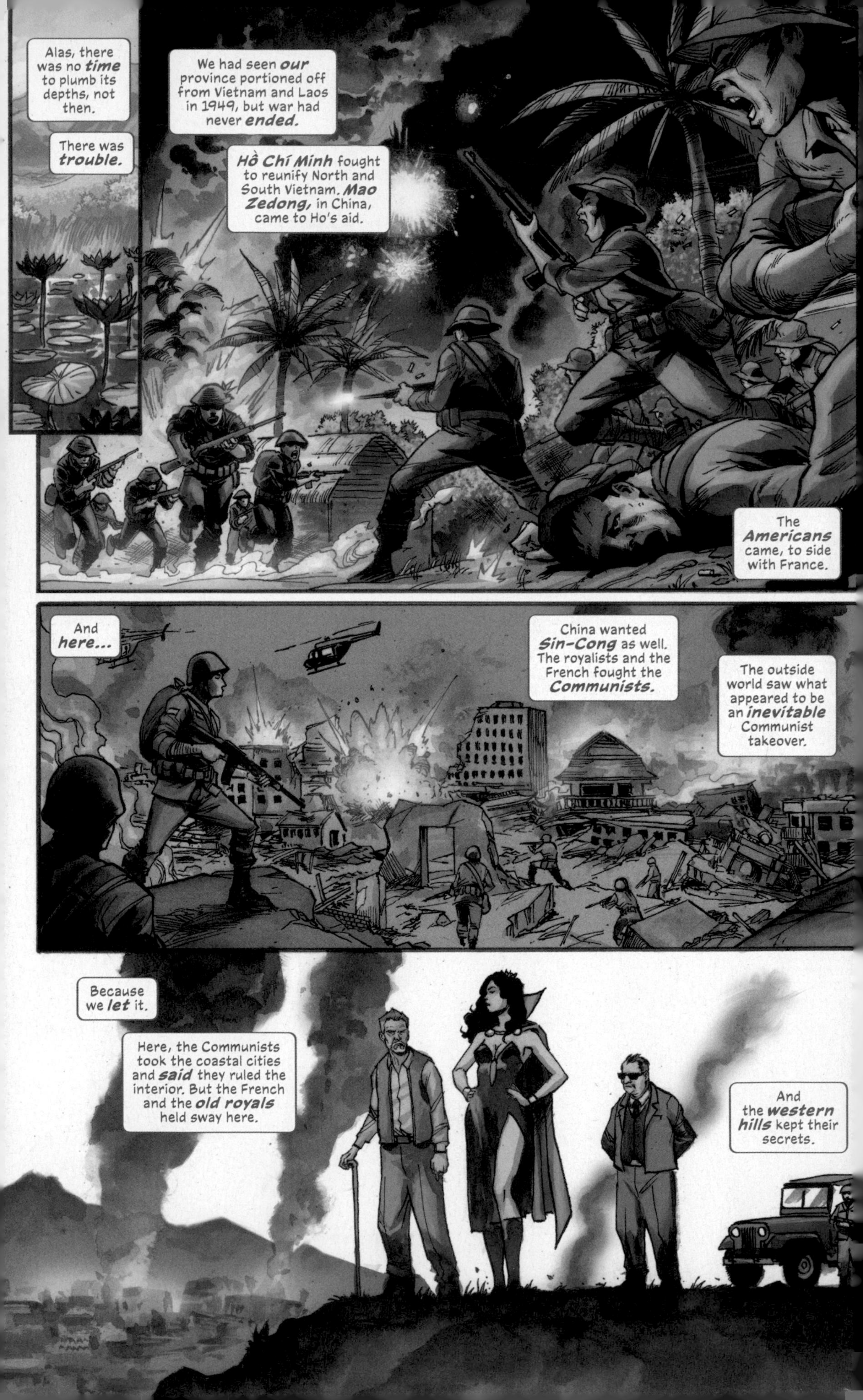

Alas, there was no *time* to plumb its depths, not then.
There was *trouble.*
We had seen *our* province portioned off from Vietnam and Laos in 1949, but war had never *ended.*
Hồ Chí Minh fought to reunify North and South Vietnam. *Mao Zedong,* in China, came to Ho's aid.
The *Americans* came, to side with France.
And *here...*
China wanted *Sin-Cong* as well. The royalists and the French fought the *Communists.*
The outside world saw what appeared to be an *inevitable* Communist takeover.
Because we *let* it.
Here, the Communists took the coastal cities and *said* they ruled the interior. But the French and the *old royals* held sway here.
And the *western hills* kept their secrets.

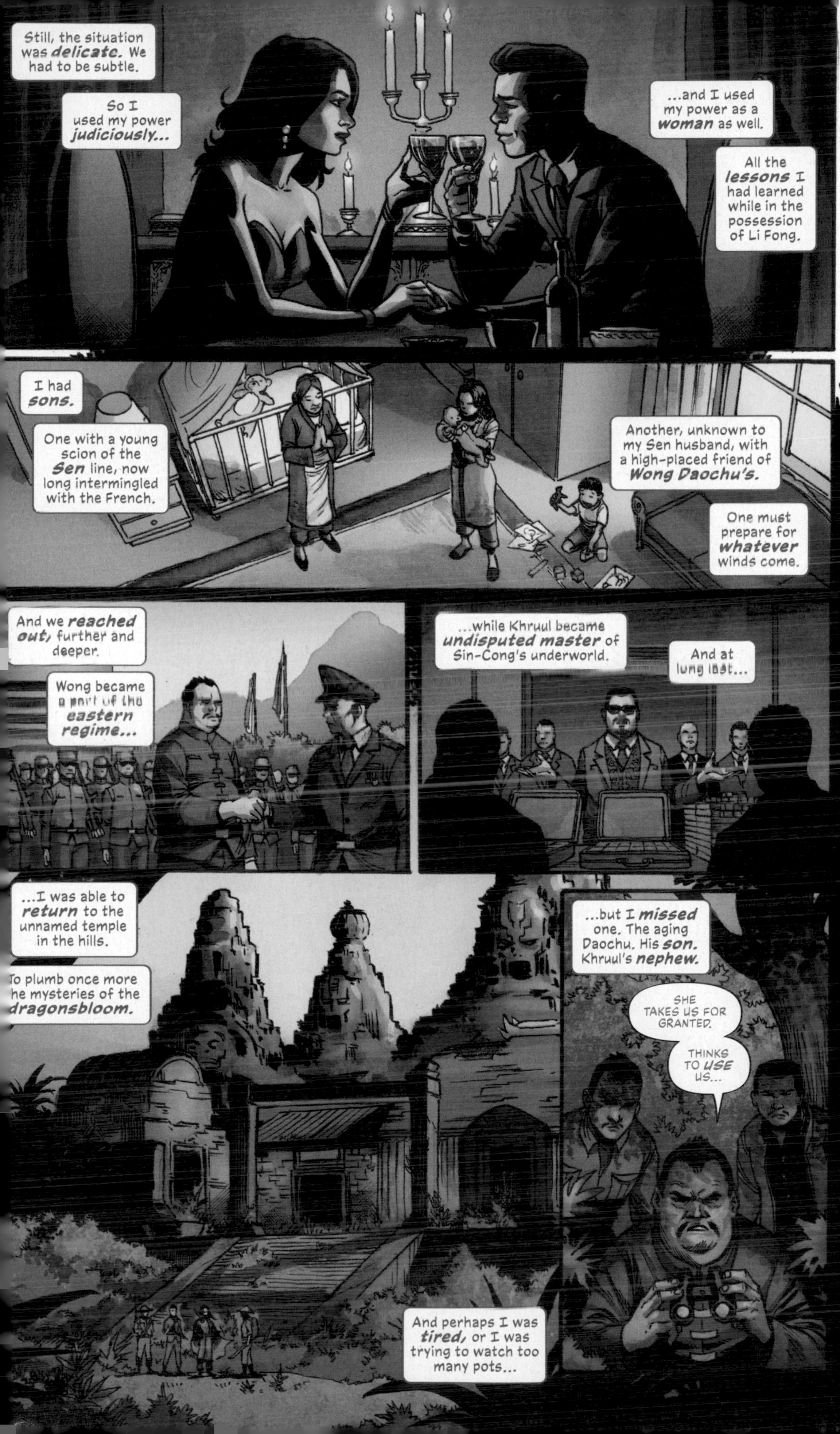
Still, the situation was delicate. We had to be subtle.
So I used my power judiciously...
...and I used my power as a woman as well.
All the lessons I had learned while in the possession of Li Fong.
I had sons.
One with a young scion of the Sen line, now long intermingled with the French.
Another, unknown to my Sen husband, with a high-placed friend of Wong Daochu's.
One must prepare for whatever winds come.
And we reached out, further and deeper.
Wong became a part of the eastern regime...
...while Khruul became undisputed master of Sin-Cong's underworld.
And at long last...
...I was able to return to the unnamed temple in the hills.
To plumb once more the mysteries of the dragonsbloom.
And perhaps I was tired, or I was trying to watch too many pots...
...but I missed one. The aging Daochu. His son. Khruul's nephew.
SHE TAKES US FOR GRANTED.
THINKS TO USE US...

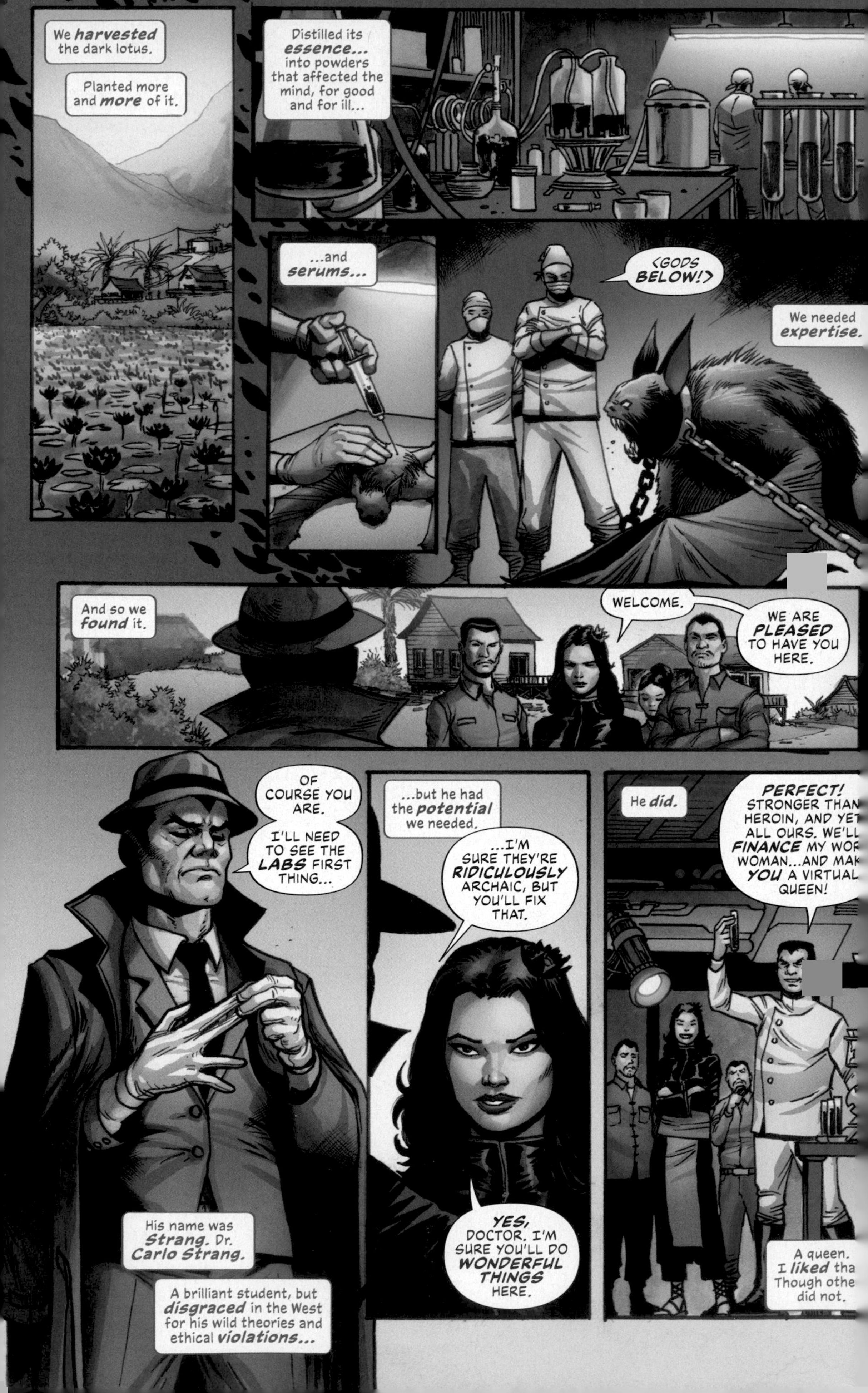
We harvested the dark lotus.
Planted more and more of it.
Distilled its essence... into powders that affected the mind, for good and for ill...
...and serums...
<GODS BELOW!>
We needed expertise.
And so we found it.
WELCOME.
WE ARE PLEASED TO HAVE YOU HERE.
OF COURSE YOU ARE.
I'LL NEED TO SEE THE LABS FIRST THING...
His name was Strang. Dr. Carlo Strang.
A brilliant student, but disgraced in the West for his wild theories and ethical violations...
...but he had the potential we needed.
...I'M SURE THEY'RE RIDICULOUSLY ARCHAIC, BUT YOU'LL FIX THAT.
YES, DOCTOR. I'M SURE YOU'LL DO WONDERFUL THINGS HERE.
He did.
PERFECT! STRONGER THAN HEROIN, AND YET ALL OURS. WE'LL FINANCE MY WOR WOMAN...AND MAK YOU A VIRTUAL QUEEN!
A queen. I liked tha Though othe did not.

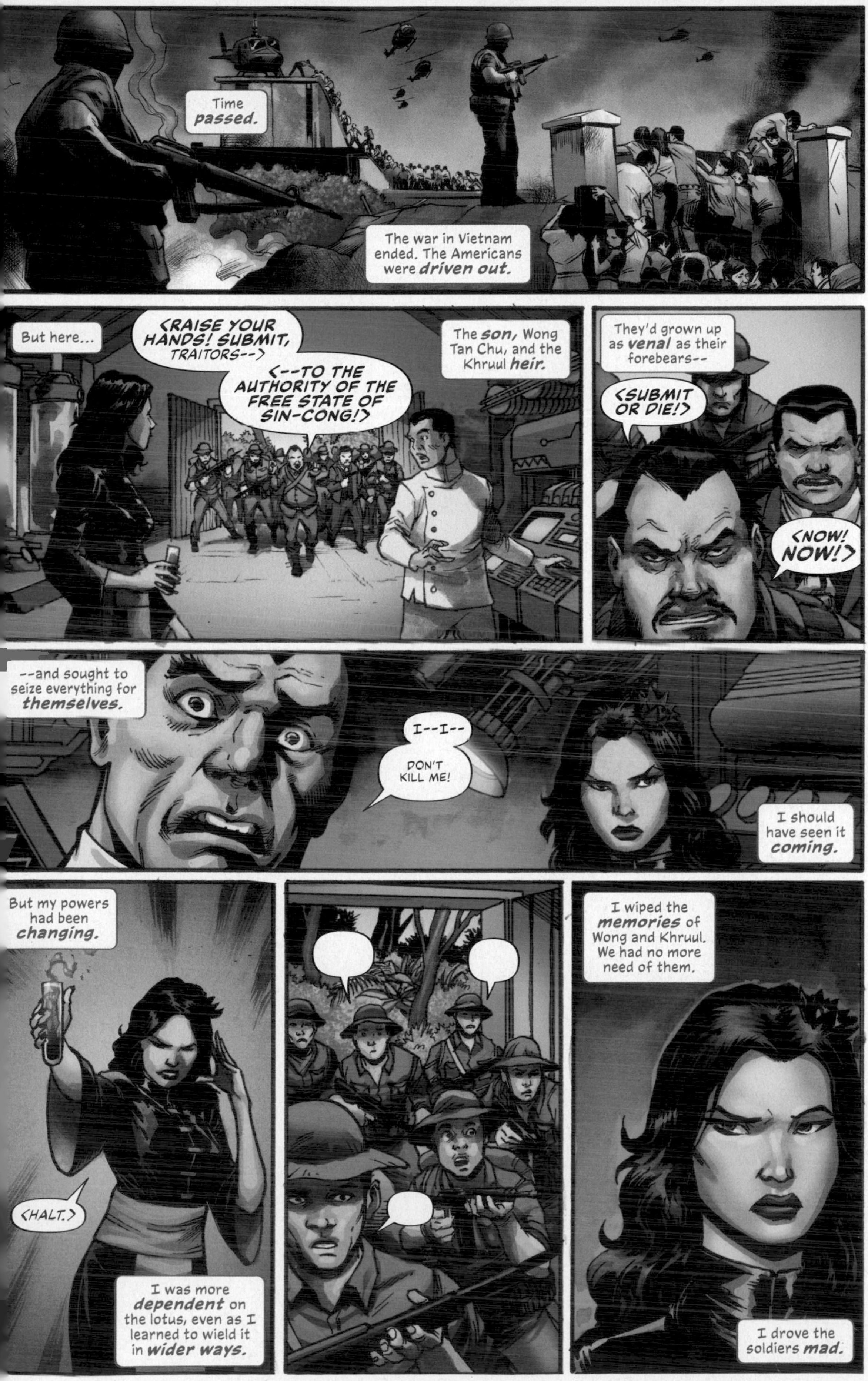

Time passed.
The war in Vietnam ended. The Americans were driven out.
But here...
<RAISE YOUR HANDS! SUBMIT, TRAITORS-->
<--TO THE AUTHORITY OF THE FREE STATE OF SIN-CONG!>
The son, Wong Tan Chu, and the Khruul heir.
They'd grown up as venal as their forebears--
<SUBMIT OR DIE!>
<NOW! NOW!>
--and sought to seize everything for themselves.
I--I--
DON'T KILL ME!
I should have seen it coming.
But my powers had been changing.
<HALT.>
I was more dependent on the lotus, even as I learned to wield it in wider ways.
I wiped the memories of Wong and Khruul. We had no more need of them.
I drove the soldiers mad.

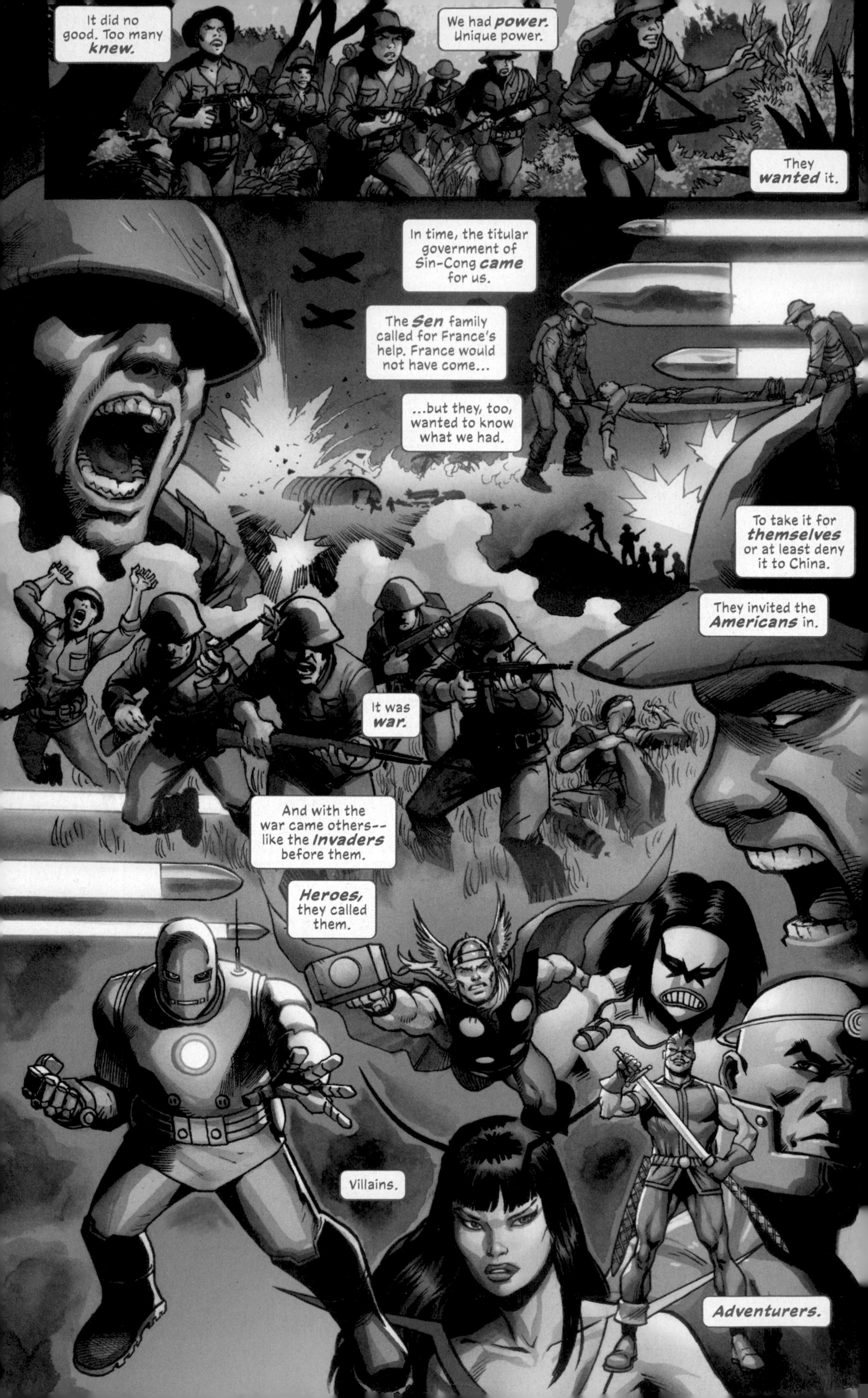
It did no good. Too many knew.
We had power. Unique power.
They wanted it.
In time, the titular government of Sin-Cong came for us.
The Sen family called for France's help. France would not have come...
...but they, too, wanted to know what we had.
To take it for themselves or at least deny it to China.
They invited the Americans in.
It was war.
And with the war came others--like the Invaders before them.
Heroes, they called them.
Villains.
Adventurers.

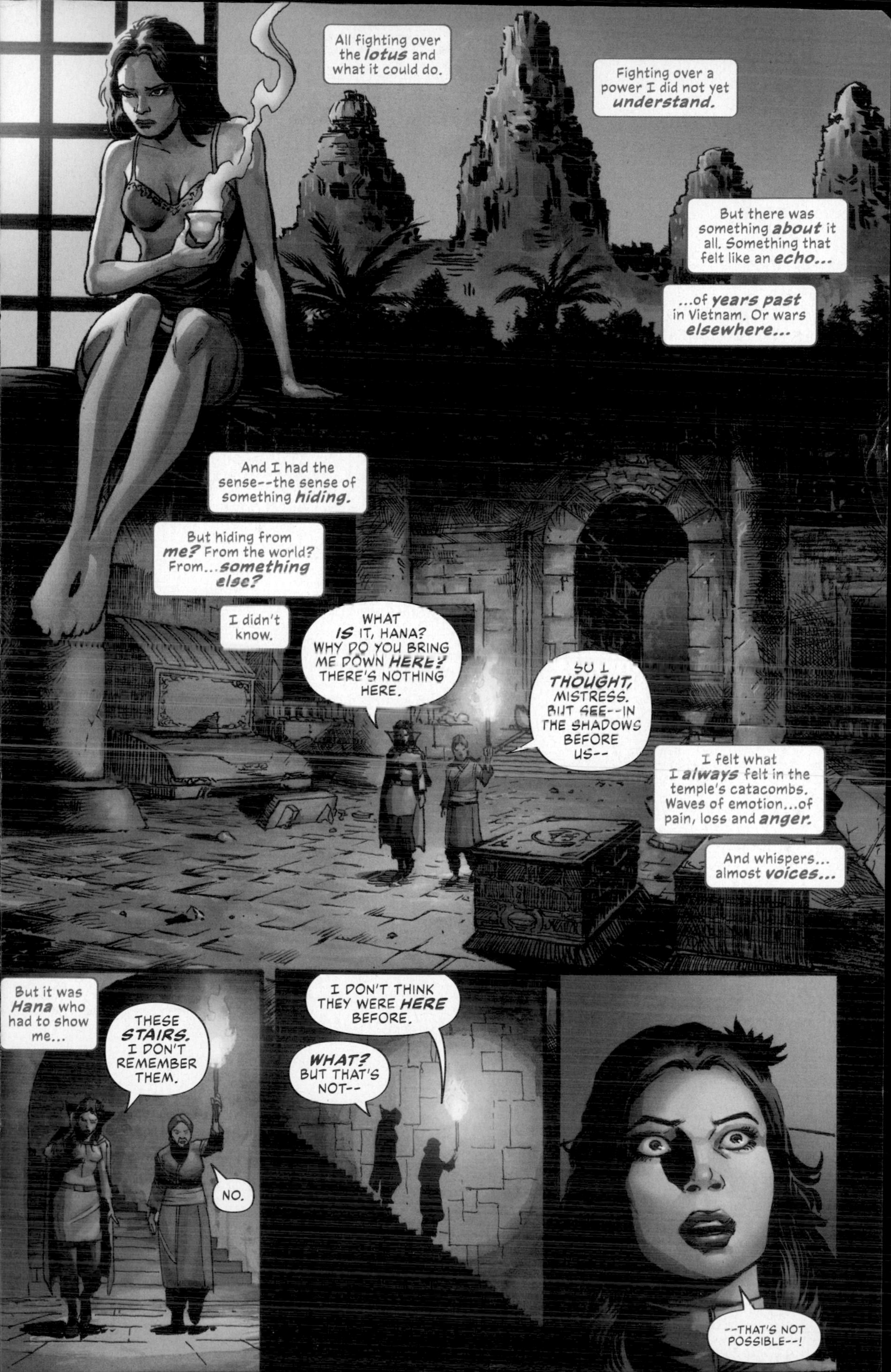

All fighting over the lotus and what it could do.
Fighting over a power I did not yet understand.
But there was something about it all. Something that felt like an echo...
...of years past in Vietnam. Or wars elsewhere...
And I had the sense--the sense of something hiding.
But hiding from me? From the world? From...something else?
I didn't know.
WHAT IS IT, HANA? WHY DO YOU BRING ME DOWN HERE? THERE'S NOTHING HERE.
SO I THOUGHT, MISTRESS. BUT SEE--IN THE SHADOWS BEFORE US--
I felt what I always felt in the temple's catacombs. Waves of emotion...of pain, loss and anger.
And whispers... almost voices...
But it was Hana who had to show me...
THESE STAIRS. I DON'T REMEMBER THEM.
NO.
I DON'T THINK THEY WERE HERE BEFORE.
WHAT? BUT THAT'S NOT--
--THAT'S NOT POSSIBLE--!

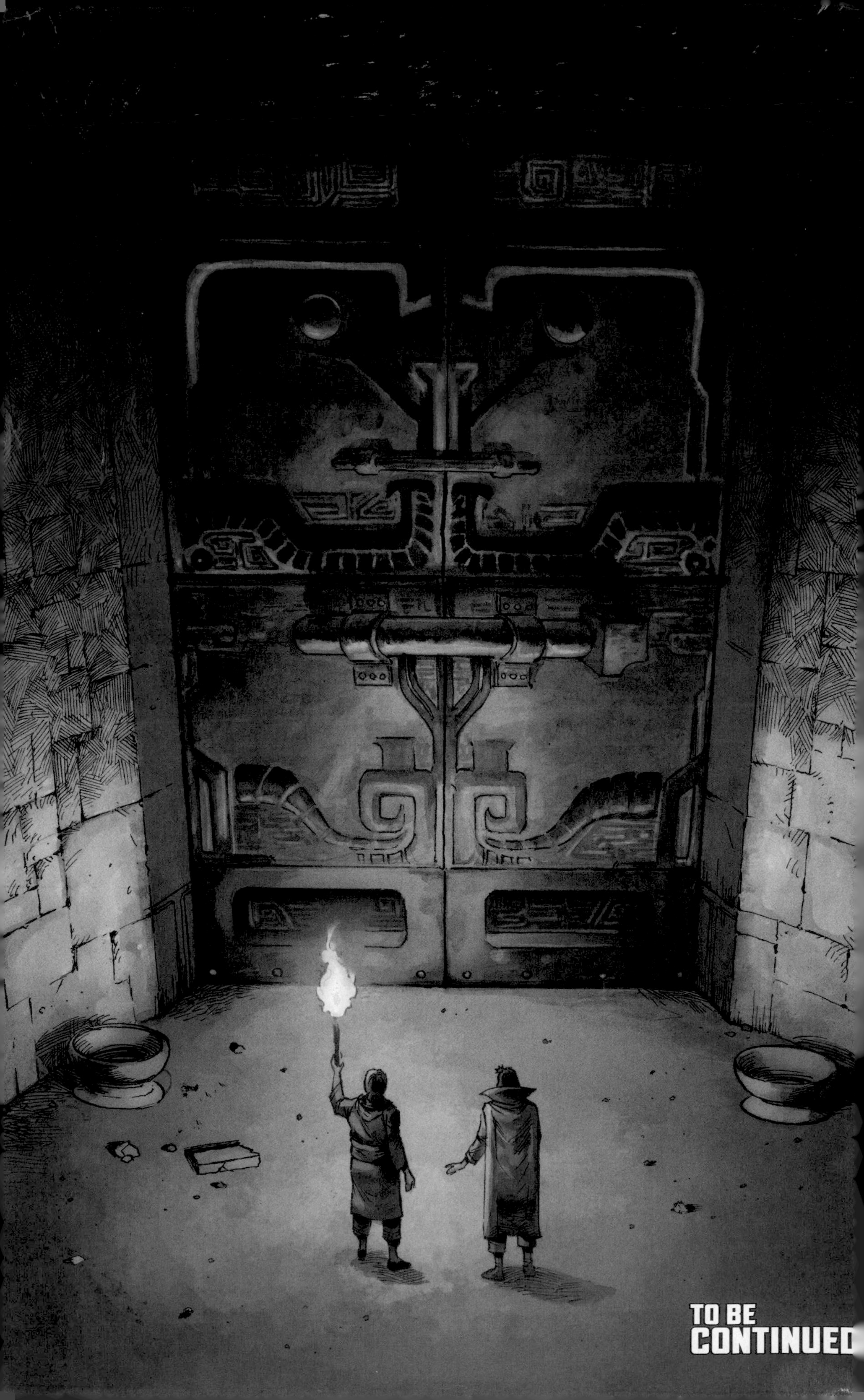
TO BE
CONTINUED

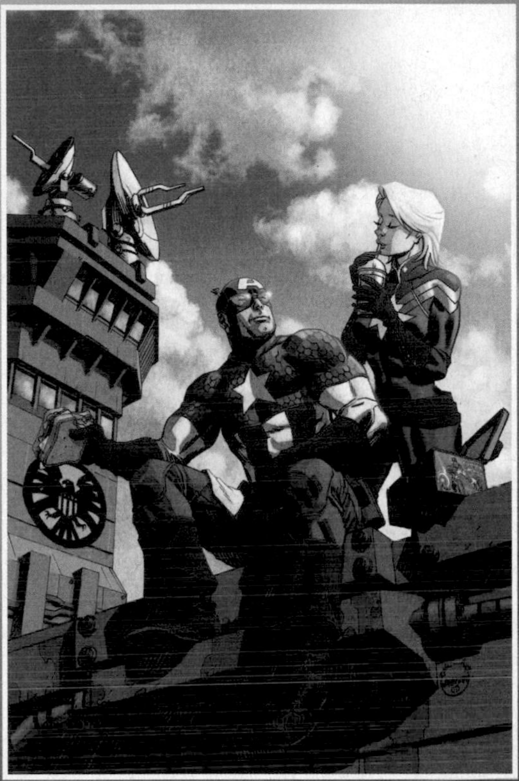

#3 VARIANT BY
DAVE JOHNSON

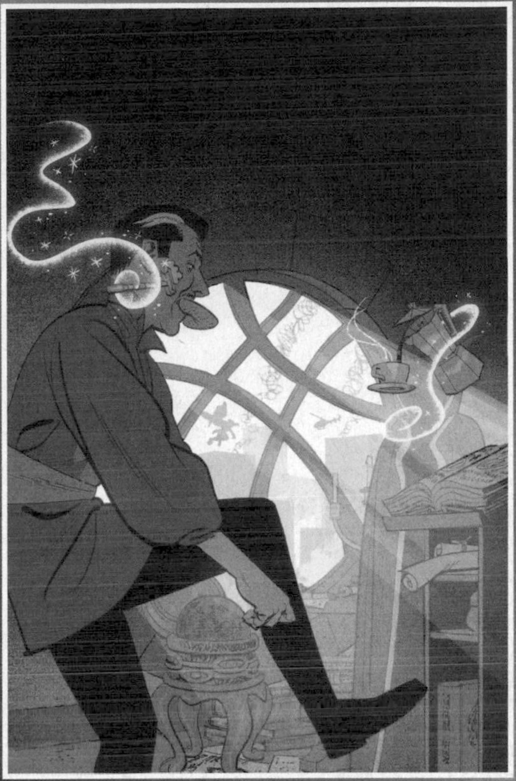

#4 VARIANT BY
GREG SMALLWOOD

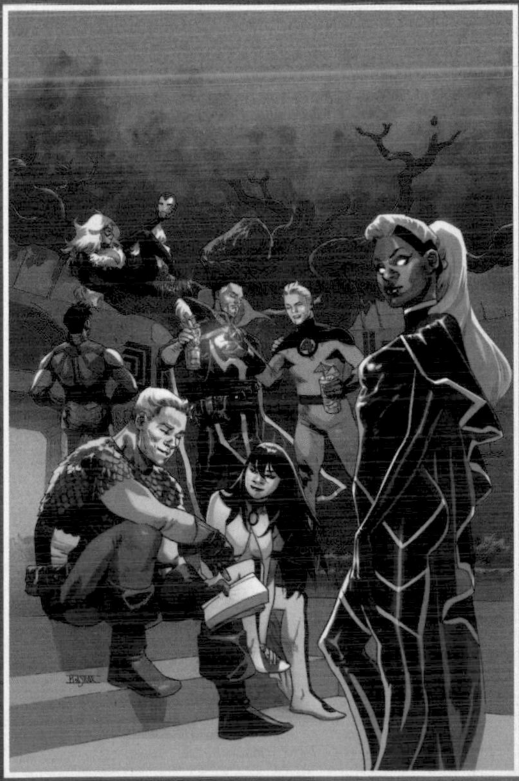

#5 VARIANT BY
MAHMUD ASRAR & **DAVE McCAIG**

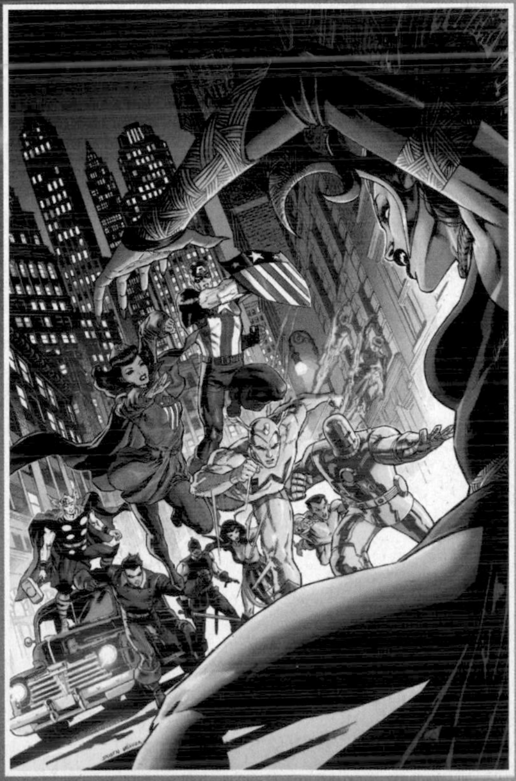

#6 VARIANT BY
DUSTIN WEAVER

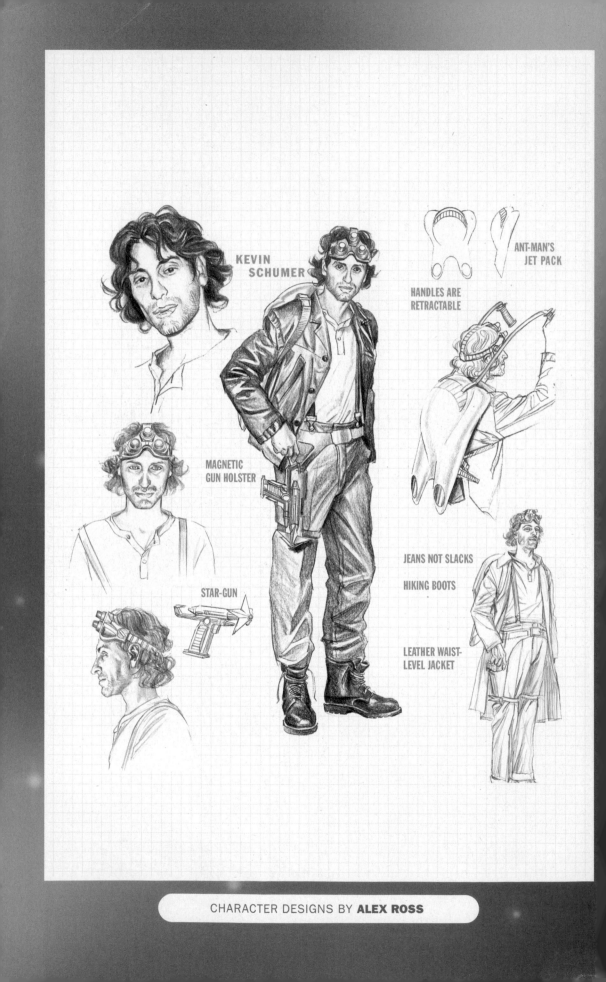

KEVIN
SCHUMER

ANT-MAN'S
JET PACK

HANDLES ARE
RETRACTABLE

MAGNETIC
GUN HOLSTER

JEANS NOT SLACKS

HIKING BOOTS

STAR-GUN

LEATHER WAIST-
LEVEL JACKET

CHARACTER DESIGNS BY **ALEX ROSS**

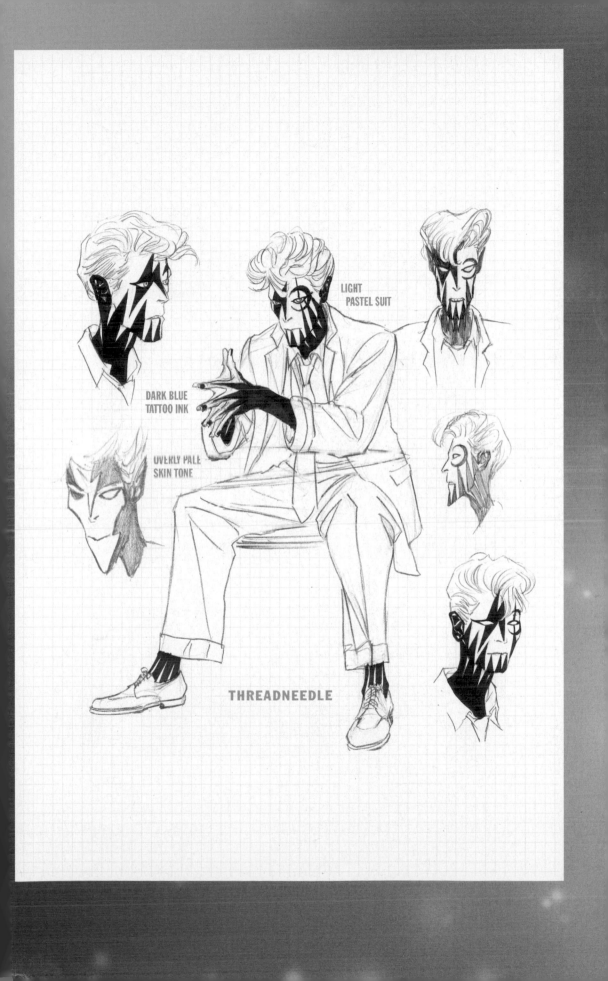

DARK BLUE
TATTOO INK

OVERLY PALE
SKIN TONE

LIGHT
PASTEL SUIT

THREADNEEDLE

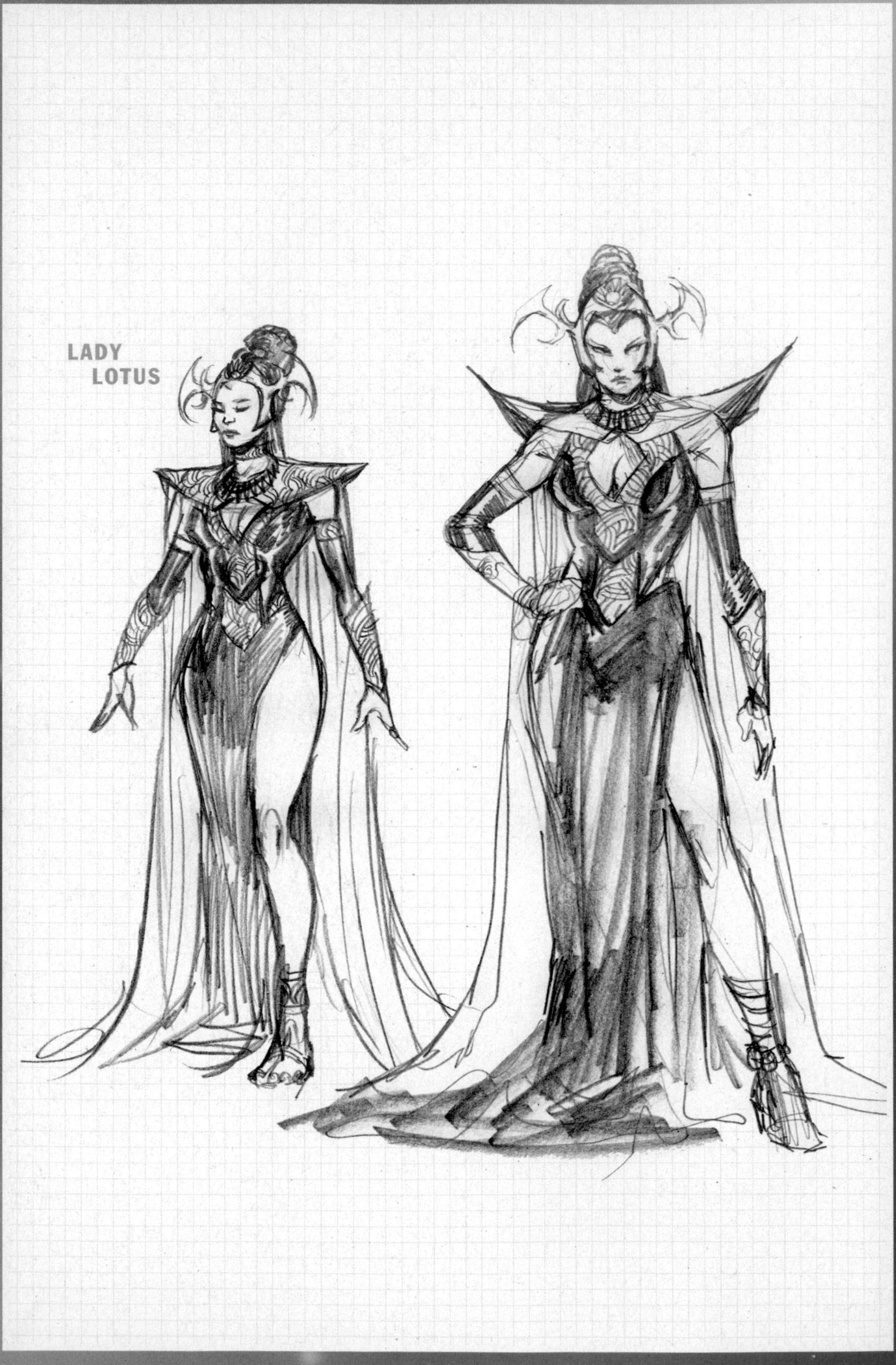
LADY
LOTUS

CHARACTER DESIGNS BY **YILDIRAY CINAR**